Eero Saarinen Jayne Merkel

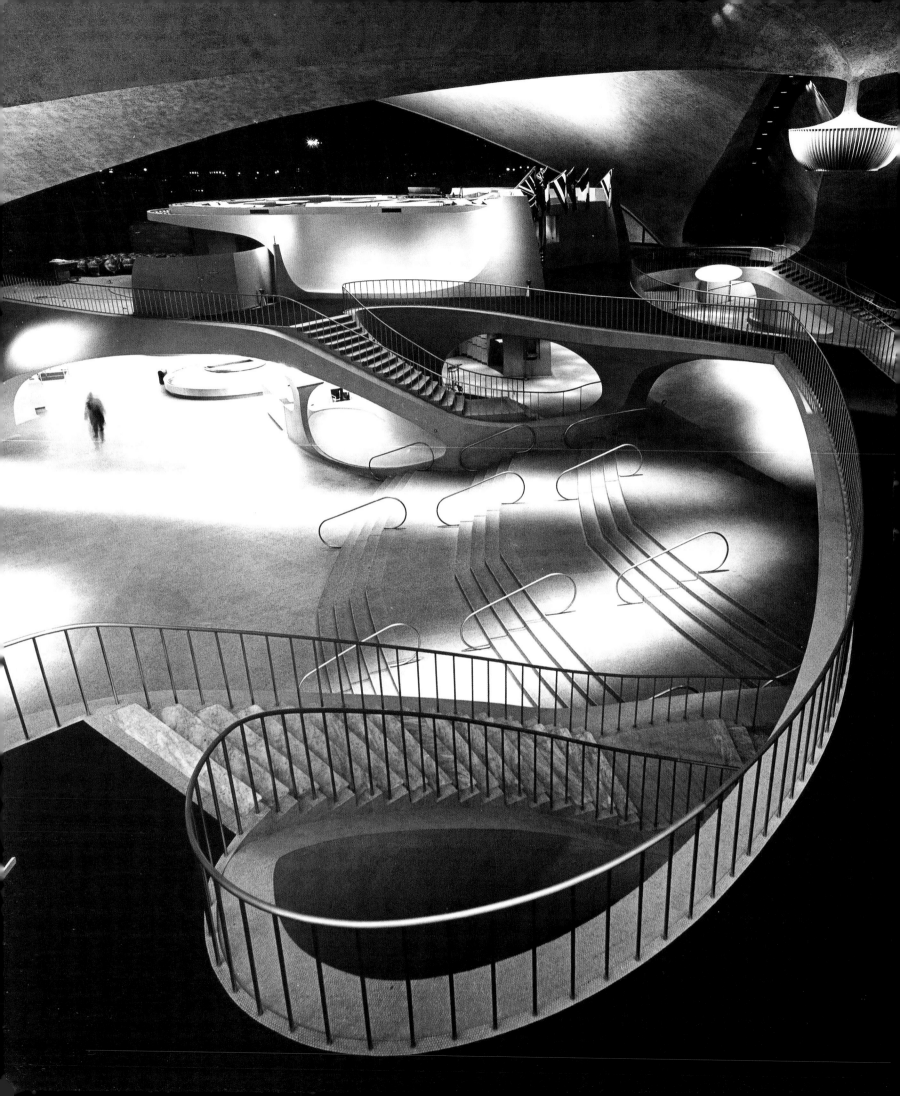

Eero Saarinen Jayne Merkel

Previous page: Trans World Airlines Terminal, Idlewild Airport
(now John F. Kennedy Airport), New York, New York, 1956–62,
view of lobby.

Contents

6   **Introduction**
A Man of His Time

11   **1. Son of Eliel**
Growing Up under the Drafting Table

21   **2. Creating Cranbrook**
The Cranbrook Schools, Institute of Science, and Academy of Art

35   **3. Family Business**
The Education of Eero and the Work of Saarinen and Saarinen

55   **4. Breaking Away**
First Independent Projects and Furniture Designs

69   **5. A Break and a Breakthrough**
The General Motors Technical Center

83   **6. GM Progeny**
Corporate Campuses for IBM, Bell Labs, and Deere & Company

103   **7. College Explosion**
Campuses for the Modern World at Antioch, Drake, and Brandeis

113   **8. The Cutting Edge on Campus**
The MIT Auditorium and Chapel, and the Yale Hockey Rink

133   **9. College Buildings in Context**
Concordia, Chicago, and Morse and Stiles Colleges at Yale

151   **10. Building the Basics in a Small Midwestern Town**
A Bank, a House, and a Church in Columbus, Indiana

163   **11. Big Ambitions in Big Cities Abroad**
American Embassies in London and Oslo

173   **12. Big Ambitions in New York**
The Vivian Beaumont Repertory Theater at Lincoln Center and
the CBS Building

191   **13. Symbolizing Modernity**
The Milwaukee War Memorial and the Saint Louis Gateway Arch

205   **14. Taking Flight**
The Trans World Airlines Terminal and the Athens and Dulles
International Airports

230   **Postscript**
The Legacy

234   **Acknowledgments**

234   **Notes**

247   **Buildings, Projects, and Furniture**

249   **Bibliography**

251   **Index**

255   **Photo Credits**

Opposite: Eero Saarinen (1910–61) at Eero Saarinen and
Associates Office, Bloomfield Hills, Michigan, c. 1955

Few architects at any time have created buildings with the popular
appeal of Eero Saarinen's. For a half century, people have been queuing
up to enter his Saint Louis Gateway Arch, marveling at the sweep of
his TWA Terminal at Kennedy Airport, and trying to copy his churches.
Yet, his buildings embody the spirit of a particular place and time—the
optimism of the American postwar period, when the country was
beginning to play a leading role for the first time, not only as a military
and economic power, but also in art, technology, education, and culture.

A golden boy from childhood, Eero Saarinen was one of the most celebrated architects in America when he died of a brain tumor in 1961;
he was barely in his fifties and working on seminal buildings for some
of the most influential institutions of the day. He had designed headquarters for CBS and John Deere, residential colleges and a hockey rink
at Yale University, an auditorium and the chapel at the Massachusetts
Institute of Technology, the University of Chicago Law School, and the
American embassies in London and Oslo. With the complexes he had
planned for General Motors, IBM, and Bell Laboratories, he had practically invented the suburban office park, and at Dulles Airport he had
encapsulated the experience of modern air travel. He had developed
glass walls to reflect the landscape, exposed self-rusting steel beams,
devised new kinds of cast stone, and used concrete sculpturally to
symbolize the boundless promise of technology. Every move he made
was reported in the magazines; every misstep he took (buildings that
came in over budget, inventions that faltered) was noted by his contemporaries. He had been on the cover of *Time*. He was a part of every
conversation about serious architecture at the time and an influential
juror for major competitions.

Ten years later, his name was rarely mentioned in critical circles. Though
his buildings were still admired by the general public and by most
practicing architects, the attention of the press and in the architecture
schools turned to the more sober and self-consciously rational work of
Louis I. Kahn and then to the Postmodern architects who had lost faith
in the future and were questioning the premises of modern architecture—
decrying its lack of symbolism, and looking to the past for inspiration.
Before this desire to look backward in order to move forward had run
its course in the 1980s, interest in historic architecture emerged in
America. It captivated the man in the street in a way that modern
architecture had never done, and the historic-preservation movement
was born. Soon revival styles appeared, not only in architecture, but
also in film, fashion, music, and automobile and furniture design.

In the 1990s, even Modernism came back into fashion, accompanied by
an enthusiasm for new spatial forms, technological invention, and a

These corporate complexes belonged to a new building type, the suburban office park, which was based on the American college campus and the planned residential subdivision. But GM, Bell Labs, and Deere & Company were completely different from one another; each was tailored to its landscape context and the task at hand, both practically and symbolically—shiny, colored steel for a carmaker, high-tech glass for high-tech labs, rough and rusted steel for a tractor manufacturer.

All of Saarinen's buildings were uniquely designed to meet the peculiarities of their programs. He never had an identifiable style—perhaps one reason interest in his work dissipated soon after his death. He was difficult to classify and difficult to copy, and he wasn't around to create new works that could command attention. Buildings that are out of sight can be out of mind. In the late 1960s and early '70s, architectural interest turned to urban problems, and many of Saarinen's buildings were in suburbs or at universities, not in city centers. Others were inaccessible even to enthusiasts, in corporate compounds behind gates.

This seclusion is ironic for it is so foreign to the spirit of Eero Saarinen's work, which exudes an open enthusiasm and faith in the future—sentiments that were in short supply during the Vietnam War and the riots in the cities that took place at the same time. These traumatic, divisive events, along with the radical changes brought on by the computer revolution, created anxiety when they first appeared and contributed to the desire to retreat into the premodern past, encouraging architects to seek inspiration in familiar classical forms for a while.

blurring of the boundaries between art, architecture, and landscape—all areas Eero Saarinen had pioneered. The architect-designed furniture of the 1950s, including Saarinen's—considered radical in its own time—became stylish and widely popular with people who had not been born when he was alive. This book is an attempt to explain the scope of what Saarinen did, how it was seen at the time, and, to a lesser extent, what his heirs think about it now.

Attitudes toward the art of the past are always colored by those of the present. Eero Saarinen's work is of interest today in part because of his technical innovation, for architects working early in the twenty-first century are also exploring new materials and techniques. For the American embassy in Oslo, Saarinen produced a molded native granite that gave rise to a new local industry. For the Morse and Ezra Stiles Colleges at Yale, he developed a new masonry technique to give the buildings a texture similar to that of their neo-Gothic neighbors, without copying them or exceeding the budget. At the General Motors Technical Center in Warren, Michigan, Saarinen introduced use of the neoprene gasket in the curtain wall—the same kind of rubber lining used to attach windshields in cars. He also gave the GM buildings the shiny finish and bright colors popular in automobile design, covering the short side walls in glazed bricks created specifically for the complex. For Bell Labs in Holmdel, New Jersey, he developed glass that deflects intense sunlight and reflects the surrounding landscape so that the building almost seems to disappear. At the Deere & Company Headquarters in Moline, Illinois, he used self-rusting Cor-Ten steel, for the first time in an architectural design, to express the structural system and to provide gigantic sun screens that project beyond the windows—an aesthetic similar to that of the large-scale farm equipment the company manufactures.

After World War II, when Eero Saarinen's practice blossomed, just the opposite was true. The future looked so bright that many architects scorned old buildings (no doubt one reason the next generation, in reaction, embraced them). Some architecture schools actually stopped teaching architectural history. But Eero Saarinen never forgot the history he had learned at his father's knee. Respect for the architecture of the past was only one of the legacies of his famous father, Finnish architect Eliel Saarinen, who also imparted a solid work ethic, serious ambition, a love of competition, wide-ranging international connections, and a sense of how to attract clients and work with them. Although Eero practiced with his father for fourteen years, he was able to develop a strong voice of his own early on.

Like his father, Eero Saarinen saw architecture as part of a continuous tradition and frequently drew on historical sources for ideas, though his approach was so fresh that the roots were rarely evident. His Morse and Stiles Colleges at Yale and the University of Chicago Law School are among the very few successful modern buildings on historic campuses that are respectful of their surroundings and original at the same time—yet they are completely different from one another. The Yale dormitories are massive and stony, the law school light and crystalline. Both draw inventively on specific qualities in the nearby Collegiate Gothic structures.

At the beginning of the twenty-first century, when the value of historic buildings is taken for granted and Saarinen's buildings, though still fresh, are old enough to qualify for landmark status, they are recognizable as both modern and historic. The TWA Terminal at Kennedy Airport, for example, has difficulty serving the purpose for which it was built today since air travel now requires economies of scale unimaginable when it was designed. The women's dormitories at the University of Chicago were demolished to make way for a larger business school. The American Embassy in Oslo will soon be sold (with preservation restrictions, at least) and replaced because it is vulnerable to attack on its prominent urban site. Others, such as the IBM Research Center in Yorktown, New York, and its Manufacturing Facility in Rochester, Minnesota, have been expanded exponentially by IBM architects and Saarinen's successors; here, as elsewhere, an unusual effort has been made to retain the spirit of the original design.

On the whole, Saarinen's buildings have been extremely well preserved, partly because their guardians appreciate them and have been told that they are significant and partly because he attracted clients with unusual interest in architecture and a commitment to building well. Saarinen was able to encourage his clients' interest and bring them into the design process; many became lifelong friends and architectural aficionados. J. Irwin Miller, who built two houses, two churches, and a bank with Saarinen, went on to create a foundation to encourage architectural innovation in Columbus, Indiana. The Cummins Engine Foundation pays the fees of the prominent architects selected by an independent board to design public buildings. Eero was its first chairman.

William A. Hewitt, who had commissioned the Deere & Company Headquarters when he was the company's chairman—and later became an ambassador—encountered this question on an application for a government post toward the end of his career: "What is the most important thing you have ever done?" As he later explained, "I showed the question to my wife, and she quickly replied, 'There's no doubt. The most important thing you ever did was build that building with Eero.' All considered, I think she is right, because it was an experience in which I became deeply involved, and it greatly enriched my life. But beyond that, it added a new dimension to our business, a heightened style of going, an additional pride in what we were about. In many fundamental ways, it has raised the sights of all the people both in and outside our community who in one way or another are affected by Deere & Company."[1]

Eero Saarinen's buildings managed to do something similar for numerous institutions because he believed that the purpose of architecture was "to shelter and enhance life on earth."[2] That is why he tried not only to fulfill the structures' purposes but also to express their users' highest aspirations. His ambition was enormous—to make architecture as much or more than it had ever been before. "The only architecture which interests me," he said, "is architecture as a fine art. That is what I want to pursue. I hope that some of my buildings will have lasting truths. I admit frankly I would like a place in architectural history. Whether I do or not and how big a niche depends, in the end, on native talent and one cannot ask for more than one has. But one has to work as hard as one can."[3]

Sadly, his faith in talent and hard work was unwarranted, at least in the short run. The place in history that Eero Saarinen earned has not been adequately recorded, delineated, or defined. Much less has been written about him than about many lesser talents. What follows is an attempt to both set the record straight and lay the groundwork for future studies with the story of an extraordinary architect and his surprisingly rich body of work.

Opposite: Gesellius, Lindgren, and Saarinen, Hvitträsk, the Saarinen family home in Kirkkonummi, Finland, 1901–03, north elevation.

As the only son of a famous architect, Eero Saarinen was surrounded by architecture from infancy on. His father, Eliel Saarinen (1873–1950), worked out of a studio in his home, both in his native Finland, where he designed the Finnish National Museum and the Helsinki Railroad Station, and, later, in America, where he designed the first schools and museums at Cranbrook, near Detroit. Eero's nursery in Finland was a crisp, airy, white-paneled room with abstract ornament, frescoes, stenciled decoration, and geometric furniture—all designed for the space—and lots of natural light. The family home overlooking Lake Hvitträsk outside Helsinki was a masterpiece of Arts and Crafts design and a center of intellectual activity, where the Saarinens entertained the composers Gustav Mahler and Jean Sibelius, the art critic Julius Meier-Graefe, the writer Maxim Gorki, the sculptor Carl Milles, and numerous architects and intellectuals from throughout northern Europe. Work, play, and family life were intertwined in a stimulating, glamorous atmosphere.

"I was a very lucky little boy," Eero once told an interviewer. "The whole family would sit at one end of the studio. As a child, I would always draw and I happened to be good at it. Therefore, I got more attention from drawing than anything else. That made me draw more and more.

Later, [Geza] Maróti, a Hungarian sculptor who was a friend of my parents, took me in hand and made me really work at it. I was only praised if what I did was good, not the way children are praised for anything they do."[1]

Eero and his older sister, Pipsan, who became a successful decorator, drew while their father and his associates designed everything from silverware to city plans. Their mother maintained art studios in their homes and made architectural models for her husband, who was also a distinguished teacher, writer, and theorist. The children observed their parents' commitment to breaking new aesthetic ground and saw those efforts rewarded as their father won important commissions and competitions.

High standards, ambition, diligence, talent, beautiful surroundings, a private tutor, international connections, and sisu—a Finnish quality that combines toughness, resilience, and tenacity—were Eero's legacy. Though he was already twelve years old when he first came to America with his family, he considered himself American. He was, however, always grateful for the childhood he had spent in rural Finland.

Juho Saarinen, the Grandfather

Eliel Saarinen had grown up in more modest circumstances. His father, Juho Saarinen, was a clergyman, but one who had also been ambitious.

From left: Eero Saarinen on Eliel Saarinen's shoulders, at Hvitträsk, c. 1912; Loja, Eero, Eliel, and Pipsan Saarinen, c. 1915; Pipsan, Loja, Eliel, Eero, and Juho Saarinen at Hvitträsk, c. 1917.

"He was the son of a tenant farmer, but he decided he wanted to go to school, so he taught himself how to read. Then he found a well-to-do Swedish couple to sponsor him. (In Finland then, you would live at home until you were ten; then you would live with a family near your school)," Eero Saarinen's daughter, Susan Saarinen, explained. "His last name, Johannes, meant 'Eunice's boy,' and he decided at thirteen that he was going to change it to reflect the more modern approach to naming, so he took the name of a prominent Swedish family. That raised a lot of eyebrows, so at fourteen he changed his name again, to Juho Saarinen. That's where our name comes from."[2] (Saarinen is a Finnish name, which must have seemed less pretentious. Made-up last names were very common in Europe at the time, as most people did not originally have surnames at all.)

Juho mastered three languages (Swedish, German, and Russian) in addition to Finnish. "He did so well in school that he became a Lutheran minister and brought up eight children. The Puritan ethic doesn't hold a candle to the Finnish work ethic," Susan said.[3] Eventually Juho became, according to Eliel's biographers, "a real gentleman of the old school,"[4] living abroad and able to give his family educational advantages. He was assigned to a church in Rantasalmi, Finland, where he met his wife, Selma Broms, the daughter of a parish priest. Then they were sent to churches in Liisilä and Spankkova, both in Ingria—an ethnically Finnish region on the Gulf of Finland behind the Russian border—and finally to one in Saint Petersburg. Since Selma was Swedish speaking, they taught their first son, Hannes, to speak Swedish, but they often spoke Finnish

to their second son, Gottlieb Eliel Saarinen, who was born in Rantasalmi in 1873.[5] They were living in Russia when Eliel reached school age, and they sent him back to Finland for his schooling. But it was the time he spent at the Hermitage on visits to his parents that he considered "the most significant part of my training."[6]

Eliel Saarinen, the Father

In 1893, Eliel enrolled concurrently in the Helsinki Polytechnical Institute (now University of Technology) to study architecture, "the choice of a cool mind," and in the Imperial Alexander University (now University of Helsinki) art school to pursue painting, that of "a warm heart." Eventually architecture won out because it presented a greater challenge. "Architecture had gone astray [and] something had to be done about it,"[7] he later explained. "It had gradually become the business of crowding obsolete and meaningless stylistic decoration on the building surface."[8]

Eliel Saarinen was in a hurry to change that. Before he graduated, he had opened an architectural office in Helsinki with two other students, Herman Gesellius and Armas Lindgren.[9] They enjoyed immediate success, winning two prizes and "an unbelievable amount of commissions"[10]—so many that Eliel was unable to accept a traveling scholarship at graduation (though the director of the school gave him the money anyway and he traveled extensively later). Even before he went abroad, however, Eliel and his young partners had begun to work in a manner similar to that of the Arts and Crafts movement in England and of Henry Hobson Richardson in the United States, using original ornament on forms similar to those found in Romanesque architecture, drawing inspiration from nature, and emphasizing the inherent characteristics of the materials they chose.

Like other Finnish artists at that time, they were involved in the National Romantic Movement, trying to develop an indigenous style for their country, which had been ruled by Swedes or Russians during most of its history and remained a duchy of the czarist empire with limited independence. To the Finnish, developing an identity did not preclude absorbing influences from abroad, particularly recent ones.[11] What they wanted to avoid were the classical stucco buildings built by their rulers, and the only interesting indigenous buildings they could find in Finland were rural churches and barns, so those were what they drew on in the beginning. The results often looked more Richardsonian than native, because, like the American architect, they were designing buildings for a modern time (the programs were similar), and they used a lot of granite—a tough local material that was considered similar to the Finnish character.[12]

In 1898 Gesellius, Lindgren, and Saarinen won a competition to design the Finnish Pavilion at the Paris Exposition of 1900. Eliel went to Paris to supervise construction and found most of the exposition buildings too fussy. He was not the only one to relish the simplicity of his firm's design. It got good reviews from the critic Anatole France and won the Diplôme Commémoratif and the Gold Medal.[13] As a result of that success, Eliel began to earn an international reputation. He was offered teaching posts in Europe but declined them as he had numerous buildings to do at home. The firm's offices in Helsinki were so filled with visitors that, the following year, the young architects decided to move their main studios to a residential compound in the country. They went to a heavily forested hill overlooking Lake Hvitträsk, eighteen miles west of the city, where new coastal railroad service made it possible to get to Helsinki, though it was beyond commuting distance.

Eliel moved out to the rural site to oversee the building of the compound, which would be named after the lake. He had recently separated from his first wife, Mathilda Gyldén, whom he married in 1899 and would divorce several years later.[14] She went on to marry his partner Herman Gesellius. Mathilda lived in the Saarinen house on the south side briefly with Eliel, while the Lindgrens occupied the more rustic north wing, and Gesellius, who was still a bachelor, lived in the house across the courtyard.

The large, comfortable houses at Hvitträsk (1901–03), which have steep pitched roofs and chubby towers, are picturesquely sited and asymmetrically arranged around courtyards. The shared studio connected two of the houses and could be entered from outdoors. Though they were made of rugged native materials (log walls, rough stone, stucco, brick vaults, terra-cotta tile roofs, and shingle siding that was added later), their interiors were filled over several years with handmade furniture, lighting fixtures, and ornament that the architects had designed. The complex is now a museum.

In 1903 Gesellius's sister Loja, who had been studying sculpture in Paris, returned to Finland, moved into the house across the courtyard with her brother, and met Eliel. They fell in love and were married the next year, and Loja moved into the Saarinen house. At about the same time, the Lindgrens moved back to Helsinki, so after Mathilda married Gesellius, the Gesseliuses moved into the north wing. They remodeled it and eliminated the rustic touches. Eliel and Loja, meanwhile, embarked on the first of many trips abroad. They traveled throughout Germany, England, and Scotland studying railroad stations, as Eliel was preparing to enter a competition to design a new Helsinki station.

Loja and her brother, who were part German, were the children of a prosperous importer. Since, like many educated Finns, she spoke no Finnish, Swedish became the language of the Saarinen household, though Eero learned to speak Finnish by visiting his cousins. Loja was a spirited and talented, if stern, woman who made sculpture, took photographs, and later in life became a well-known weaver. She was more a companion and colleague of her husband than most women of her time were, and the mother of Eliel's two children. The first, a daughter, Eva-Lisa, nicknamed Pipsan, was born in 1905.

Besides designing villas, churches, office buildings, apartment houses, a paper mill, and banks, the young partners at Gesellius, Lindgren, and Saarinen won a competition to design the Finnish National Museum in 1902. Though that commission provided an opportunity to further explore Finnish vernacular traditions, by that time they had begun to adopt a more self-consciously modern idiom similar to the French and Belgian Art Nouveau, German Jugendstil, and Austrian Secession movements.

By the middle of the first decade of the twentieth century, the partners were ready to design major modern buildings, but also found themselves growing in different directions. Armas Lindgren left the firm (and Hvitträsk) in 1905 to become the head of the architecture school at the Institute of Technology in Helsinki.[15] The year before, Eliel's competition scheme for the new Helsinki Railroad Station (1904–19) had won first prize; however, as a result of criticism from the writer Gustaf Strengell and the architect Sigurd Frosterus (who had submitted a more modern scheme), Eliel revised his design and produced a symmetrical one with a central arch, simplified horizontal masses sheathed in brick and copper, the first large reinforced concrete vaults in Finland, and various planning innovations.[16] Though it features ornamentation based on ancient Finnish myths, the decoration is stylized and intended to reinforce the overall composition. The Helsinki station is one of the first examples of Eliel's concept of "total design"—encompassing everything from door handles to city planning—that became a mainstay of his son's work as well.

Clockwise from top: Herman Gesellius and Pipsan and Eliel
Saarinen in Hvitträsk studio, c. 1912; Hvitträsk living room,
1901–03; Eero and Pipsan's nursery at Hvitträsk, 1901–03.

Gesellius worked with Eliel on the station and other projects for several
years after Lindgren left the practice, but they dissolved their partnership in 1907, and Gesellius opened an office in Helsinki. Herman and
Mathilda Gesellius remained at Hvitträsk, however, in separate quarters
from the Saarinens, until Herman died in 1916, and Mathilda moved to

France. Eventually, Eliel's family took over the entire compound. His
father, Juho, fled Saint Petersburg during the Bolshevik Revolution in
1917 and spent his last years there. After he died in 1920 and they
emigrated to the United States, the Saarinens returned to Hvitträsk every
summer until World War II. Eliel and Loja are buried there.

Eero Is Born as Eliel Branches Out

Eero Saarinen was born at Hvitträsk on his father's birthday, August 20,
in 1910.[17] By that time, Eliel's work was becoming increasingly refined,

symmetrical, and geometric. And he was becoming an internationally known figure who traveled to Europe regularly to see new work and to visit prominent architects such as Peter Behrens and Josef Maria Olbrich.[18] The Helsinki Railroad Station, which was under construction from 1905 to 1919, was widely published. Working on his own, Eliel continued to win competitions, including one in 1908 for the Finnish Houses of Parliament. (His former partners, working together, won second prize.) Eliel's unexecuted scheme, sited on a hill approached by steep steps and flanked by wings, resembled the classical cathedral in the center of Helsinki's Senate Square and the United States Capitol building in Washington, DC. But it was composed of streamlined rectangular forms, as his own first design for an office tower and New York skyscrapers would later be, and it had the first flat roofs Eliel had designed.[19]

Eliel built city halls in Joensuu (1910–14) and Lahti (1911–12), Finland, designed office buildings in Helsinki (1910, 1914, 1917, 1921), a railroad station in Viipuri (1904–13; destroyed in 1941), a school in Lahti (1922–23), and a bank in Tallinn, Estonia (1911–12). Like other Finnish architects before and after World War I, he also worked on city plans, anticipating a period of growth. Although he drew on ideas from Baron Haussmann's plan for Paris, the Saint Petersburg of his youth, Daniel Burnham's City Beautiful plan for Chicago, Camillo Sitte's writings, Tony Garnier's published but unbuilt scheme for the "Cité Industrielle," and Ebenezer Howard's Garden Cities of To-Morrow, he combined and adapted them inventively to the problems at hand, and his artful renderings made his plans seem realizable.

Eliel worked with Helsinki's first official town planner, Bertel Jung, from the time he was appointed in 1907. Four years later, Jung prepared a plan for the city's first municipal central park, with zones for various uses and a system of greenbelts similar to those being built in Vienna and the United States. In 1912–13, Saarinen planned new major north-south and east-west arteries for the growing city center.[20]

In 1910 a group of Finnish industrialists engaged Eliel to plan a new suburb for 170,000 people northwest of the downtown Helsinki peninsula.[21] Five years later, they exhibited Loja's convincing models of Munkkiniemi-Haaga, an "ideal city" with very un-Finnish terraced houses and blocks of flats arranged around courtyards, diagonal axes, parks, and sculpture, as well as freestanding villas. These satellite towns were connected to the city center by an unusually advanced system of trams, railways, and multilaned roads to accommodate increasing traffic. Only the main avenue, the street plan of the southeast area, and a villa suburb on the bay were built.[22] Eliel's plans were progressive but not radical—intended to foster humane development within the social status quo. But though he invested money in the scheme, Eliel always expressed concern about the conflict between land speculation and the public good.

Then in 1915, one of the principal promoters of the Munkkiniemi-Haaga plan—Eliel's friend and client, Julius Tallberg—commissioned him, Jung, and Einar Sjöström to develop a plan for the expansion of the entire city center. The idea was to show how essential facilities could be accommodated so that they would not have to be relocated on the outskirts. With the outbreak of the Finnish Civil War of 1918, the task fell to Saarinen, who produced a thoroughly researched plan for an inner city surrounded by garden city "daughter towns" similar to Munkkiniemi-Haaga, with decent workers' housing located near industry, new harbor facilities, and green spaces to provide healthful light and air. These parts of an integral whole were, as usual, tied together by a sophisticated transportation network. Because of the war, little of the "Pro Helsingfors" (the Swedish name for Helsinki) plan was realized, but its components were debated for decades, and the experience paid off for Eliel in the international arena.

He won first prize in a competition to plan Tallinn, Estonia (1911–13), and second prize in one for Canberra, the new capital of Australia (1911–12). However, as his reputation grew, his practice dwindled because many of his commissions were canceled after the onset of World War I.[23] The Finnish Civil War precipitated additional economic and political crises. Eliel was already earning most of his living from his oil paintings when Tallberg, who had become his principal patron, died in 1921. In July of that year, a fire broke out in the tower at Hvitträsk, and though it expired before destroying the houses and studios, it cast an additional pallor. Eliel continued to design buildings, enter competitions, win them, and publish his work abroad. But the bustling household full of colleagues and assistants had grown quiet.

To America

In 1922 Eliel Saarinen, who had never seen a skyscraper, won second prize (and twenty thousand dollars) in the much-publicized international competition for the Chicago Tribune Tower. His stepped-back tower with vertical detailing received more critical acclaim than did the winning entry by John Mead Howells and Raymond Hood, of New York, who submitted a scheme that was technologically advanced but decorated with lacy Gothic tracery—or than those of Walter Gropius and Adolf Meyer, Ludwig Hilberseimer, Max Taut, and other architects who submitted avant-garde geometric designs.[24] The Chicago architect Louis Sullivan called Saarinen's submission a "masterpiece,"[25] which must have delighted Eliel, since his Helsinki and Viipuri Railroad Stations had been inspired by Adler and Sullivan's Transportation Building, the most innovative structure at the Chicago Columbian Exposition of 1893. Because Saarinen's tower was forward-looking but not too advanced for mainstream taste, it proved to be enormously influential. Even Hood (working this time with André Fouilhoux) adopted its simplified decoration in the Radiator Building in New York the following year.[26]

Clockwise from top left: Gesellius, Lindgren, and Saarinen, Finnish National Museum, Helsinki, 1901–12; Eliel Saarinen, Helsinki Railroad Station, interior; Helsinki Railroad Station, exterior, 1904–19.

The prize gave Saarinen the opportunity to see the type of building (and city) that he had had to imagine when working on his design. He set sail for America in February 1923 with his friend Gustav Strengell, who could speak some English. Eliel must have sensed that he might find work in Chicago, for his family joined him in April and settled in suburban Evanston, Illinois. Curiously, a few months before Eliel had entered the competition, Loja had dreamed that she had found a jewel and returned it to its owner in Chicago.[27]

For Eero, who was twelve, and Pipsan, who was eighteen, their father's decision to come to America was critical. In Finland, Pipsan had been studying at the Atheneum Art School and the University of Helsinki. The move to Evanston cut her off from friends and teachers, so that she was forced to rely on the family's resources, and would find her family difficult to please. Eero, on the other hand, was young enough to develop a life of his own. He had just won his first competition, sponsored by a Swedish newspaper, for illustrating a story with images made out of matchsticks. His grizzly story, which Eliel helped him write, was about a woman who had two suitors but ended up alone because they burned themselves up.[28]

Though he would soon adjust, Eero could not sleep during the first night the family spent in a New York hotel. In the morning, he told his father, "The traffic is all mixed up and wrong. It ought to be changed.[29] When Eero went to school, he was placed in a class with much younger children since he did not speak English. However, within two weeks he had learned enough of the language to enter the fifth grade, and by the next year, when the family had moved to Ann Arbor, Michigan, he was in the eighth grade with students his age, and comfortable enough with his classmates to become art editor of the school newspaper.

Despite the enthusiastic reception Eliel received in America, he was not initially offered any commissions, so on his own initiative he went to work on an ambitious plan for the Chicago lakefront (1923). He saw it as an update of Daniel Burnham's 1909 plan for Chicago, which had influenced some of his own earlier plans. "Upon my arrival in Chicago," he wrote, "I expected to see Grant Park (the heart of Mr. Burnham's plan) and the boulevards finished, or at least in the process of being built. But Grant Park lay untouched, and the monumental boulevard seemed to have been forgotten."[30]

He realized that, fifteen years later, there were new problems to solve, and he wanted to demonstrate how a skyscraper could be used to best advantage in the streetscape. In his Chicago Tribune Tower competition brief, he had criticized the idea of building an isolated tower like the one requested,[31] so his plan for Chicago had one similar to his Chicago Tribune Tower scheme, but it was surrounded by lower buildings with geometric parterres, much like those that would be created at Rockefeller Center almost a decade later. The bold and ambitious plan included a fifty-seven-story hotel with four thousand rooms.[32]

From left: Eliel Saarinen, proposed Finnish Parliament Building, 1908, winning competition scheme; Eliel Saarinen, Town Hall, Lahti, Finland, 1911–12.

The main problem Eliel saw at the time was a steady increase in automobile traffic—twenty-five thousand cars entering the downtown commercial Loop every day, creating traffic jams and destroying the pedestrian environment. His "Project for Lake Front Development of the City of Chicago" was primarily an attempt to solve that problem. A major boulevard along Lake Michigan, intended to relieve traffic congestion, was integrated with formal parks. Partially submerged, it led to a three-level underground parking garage for forty-seven thousand cars.

Eliel undertook the study to learn about the city where he was living and to show what he had to offer potential clients. Promptly published in *The American Architect and Architectural Review* by a neighbor,[33] Eliel soon saw his effort pay off. He was offered a teaching post at the University of Michigan for the next fall. Thirty years would pass before Chicago would have underground parking, and no plan quite like his was ever proposed again, let alone realized.

To celebrate Eliel Saarinen's arrival in Ann Arbor, members of the Michigan Society of Architects and the Detroit Chapter of the American Institute of Architects, concerned about the deteriorated Detroit riverfront, organized a dinner and invited the publisher of the *Detroit News*, George Gough Booth, to be the featured speaker. They hoped to interest Saarinen in developing a plan for it that Booth would finance.[34]

Eliel did draw up a plan with Booth's patronage.[35] It was less extensive but more grandiose than the one he had done for Chicago the year before. Dominated by a great domed structure flanked by colonnades, similar to the central pavilion at the Massachusetts Institute of Technology, it was anchored by another Tribune-like tower. This plan was not executed either. But the encounter changed the course of both the Booths' and the Saarinens' lives. It even had an effect on modern American architectural history.

This page, clockwise from top left: Eliel Saarinen, Greater Helsinki Plan, 1915–18, central section; Eliel Saarinen, Chicago Tribune Tower competition entry, 1922; Eliel Saarinen, Chicago Lakefront Plan, 1923.

Opposite, from top: Eliel Saarinen, Detroit Riverfront Plan, 1924; two views of the Chicago Lakefront Plan, 1923.

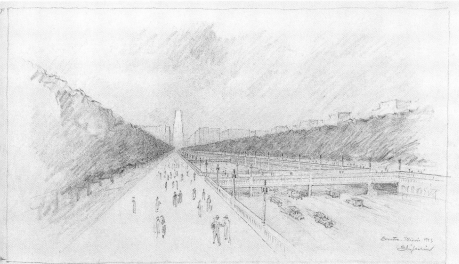

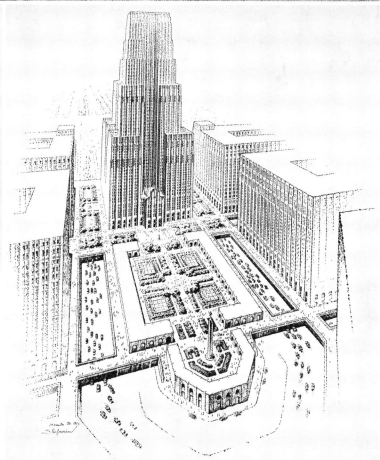

Opposite: Eliel and Eero Saarinen in an architecture studio at
the University of Michigan, Ann Arbor, c. 1924.

Eliel Saarinen was planning to return to Finland with his family perma-
nently at the end of the 1925 school year before George Booth
(1864–1949), impressed by his plan for the Detroit riverfront, asked
him if he might be interested in working on an artists' colony he was
thinking of building on his country estate. Booth's plans were vague, his
taste was conservative, and what he was offering was not exactly
spelled out. But Saarinen did not have a great deal to lose; no significant
commissions were in the offing. He decided to move to suburban
Detroit and began working on plans for the schools, studios, and museums that would become the Cranbrook Educational Community
(1925–42), a unique collection of superbly crafted, inventively decorated
early modern brick buildings in a park setting.[1] He, too, had once
thought of founding a school where architects could hone their skills,
along with artists and craftsmen, because he believed that architecture
encompassed everything from city planning to furniture.[2] And he
believed, "Creative art cannot be taught by others. Each one has to be
his own teacher. But [contact] with the other artists and discussions
with them provide sources for inspiration."[3]

Eliel's decision meant that his children would become Americans instead
of Finns. Both Eero and Pipsan would eventually meet their spouses
and begin their careers at Cranbrook. While his sister remained at home,
working with her parents, Eero entered the ninth grade at Baldwin
High School in Birmingham, Michigan, and he became a popular student
known for his talent. His soap carvings were placed on exhibition and
written up in the local newspaper, where the superintendent of schools
called him "a genius" and the reporter noted that he had already entered
a professional architectural competition, sponsored by the American
Gas Association, to design a house.[4] His father always encouraged him
to take on challenges extraordinary for his age, yet he managed to
have a normal childhood. Eero became so at home in the United States
that even after studying in Paris, going to college in New England, and
spending two years on a traveling fellowship in Europe, he returned to
Michigan to teach and practice with his father. He became an American
citizen in 1940. Though it was not obvious then that this choice would
lead to commissions unavailable anywhere else at the time, one of the
things he had learned from his father was that an ambitious architect
had to go wherever the chance to build serious architecture took him.

For Eliel, that chance came at Cranbrook, but not until he had proved
himself to his client, who was not sure what he wanted when the work
began. A number of utopian communities had been established in the
Midwest in the late nineteenth century but, because of the emphasis
on arts and crafts, Cranbrook as an idea would also resemble artists'
colonies elsewhere, such as William Morris's in Kent, England, which

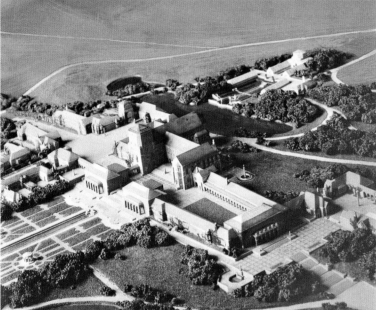

From top: Eliel Saarinen, Arts Building Project for the 1913 Industrial Exhibition, Helsinki, 1910; Eliel Saarinen, Cranbrook School and Academy of Art campus, 1925, model; Eliel Saarinen, Cranbrook School, pencil-on-paper aerial perspective, 1926.

Booth admired,[5] as well as ones that Saarinen knew—at Darmstadt, in Weimar, and the Wiener Werkstätte in Vienna. Hvitträsk, of course, had been something of one, too.

Arts and Crafts communities were often associated with museums and schools of "applied" or "industrial arts." Booth had even started one, the Detroit School of Design, which soon became affiliated with the Detroit Museum of Art.[6] The most famous and progressive school of this type was the Bauhaus in Germany, which was also a kind of artists' colony, but one intended to accommodate industrial technology instead of craft. There was a whole spectrum of models for Booth and Saarinen to draw on, though the idea appealed to the two men for somewhat different reasons, as their experience had been very different before they met.

Booth's ancestors had been coppersmiths in England—in the village of Cranbrook in Kent. George had worked as a designer and a salesman at his father's ornamental ironworks in Windsor, Ontario, and though he had only an eighth-grade education, after building up the business, in 1887, at the age of twenty-three, he met and married Ellen Warren Scripps (1863–1948), the daughter of the founder of the *Evening News* (later the *Detroit News*), and eventually became its publisher.[7]

The Booths employed artisans on their property and contributed to local museums, art schools, and artists' studies abroad. But George was not satisfied with what they produced. He started to imagine a community where artists could study and work in a bucolic setting: his 350-acre estate twenty miles northwest of Detroit, a city that was becoming increasingly industrialized. The idea of living and working in a rural setting also struck a chord with Eliel, who had built Hvitträsk about the same distance from Helsinki.

George and Ellen Booth had purchased their property, surrounded by apple orchards, in 1904 and hired the Detroit architect Albert Kahn, who was known mainly for his modern factories, to build some farm buildings. Three years later, Kahn, who also built traditional mansions, designed their big, dark redbrick Tudor-style house.[8] The landscape gardener H.J. Corfield surrounded it with Italianate terraced gardens, and his successor, O.C. Simonds, planted thousands of pines, maples, and other native trees on the property.[9] In 1912, some rather quaint concrete-block farm buildings with Tudor trim were built to the west of the house by a lesser-known Detroit architect, Marcus Burrowes.

But Bloomfield Hills was becoming a suburb by that time. Commuter rail arrived to link it to Detroit, so the Booths built a waiting room for interurban passengers and set up a trust for an elementary school (which would be called the Brookside School and designed by their son, Henry Scripps Booth).[10] And in 1924, they hired Bertram Grosvenor Goodhue Associates of New York to build Christ Church Cranbrook, a stone Episcopal church in the Gothic style.[11] George Booth specified the English Perpendicular Gothic style and insisted that the church be built in the traditional manner, without steel structural supports. All these buildings were erected across the road from the Booth house and what would become the Cranbrook campus.

By the time Eliel Saarinen arrived, Booth had realized that a working farm would be incompatible with the educational community he envisioned, so he had decided to convert Burrowes's farm buildings into a boys' school. He had even sketched out a plan and hired his son, Henry Booth, and his friend from architecture school J. Robert F. Swanson to implement it in stages while they worked on other buildings for him. They had just graduated from the University of Michigan, where they had studied with Saarinen. Swanson, who spoke some Swedish, had even served as a translator for the Saarinen family while they learned English.[12]

Swanson and young Booth had been working on the school for months when their former professor arrived, but they endorsed Saarinen's idea of building the community all at once instead of in stages and with new buildings instead of renovations. George Booth was initially taken aback when he saw Saarinen's exquisite, detailed rendering of the school, for though it was based on his own sketches, it appeared that it would cost much more than he had planned. But the day before the Saarinens were to leave for Finland, he approved the design and invited Eliel return to Michigan in the fall to develop it.[13]

Cranbrook School

When work on Cranbrook School resumed in the autumn of 1925, the contractor Albert Charles Wermuth, who had built Christ Church, helped Saarinen convince his patron that it would cost more to renovate than to replace the Burrowes buildings. (Much later, Eero and Eliel would design a house for A.C. Wermuth in Fort Wayne, Indiana.)

The Saarinens moved into an old farm building that had housed Italian laborers, and the one next door was fixed up for Swanson and some of the draftsmen. The arrangement was certainly convenient for the handsome young architect and Pipsan Saarinen, who had met in Ann Arbor. They started seeing one another secretly because her parents wanted her to marry someone more successful. But she had her own ideas. The two young people fell in love, decided to elope, and ran off in May to nearby Toledo, Ohio.

As soon as Eliel and Loja realized what had happened, they followed them, but by the time they got there, the lovers had tied the knot. Undeterred, they whisked their daughter off to Finland. Eventually they relented, as she held firm; the family returned in the fall, and Pipsan rejoined her husband. Swanson felt that he had to resign from work at Cranbrook, but he found other architectural commissions, while Eliel and Henry Booth developed the Cranbrook Architectural Office. Pipsan, however, continued to work with her parents. (Later she formed a successful design partnership with Swanson. And much later, he went to work with Eero and Eliel as the business manager of their firm until disagreements with Eero made the relationship untenable and he resigned.[14]) Pipsan's relationship with her parents remained strained; they favored her brother. Loja, who had always worked alongside her husband and had founded her own weaving studios (which did work not only for Cranbrook but for Frank Lloyd Wright and the young Charles Eames), curiously reprimanded her daughter for taking her own career seriously.[15] What Eero drew from this is not clear. But he did marry privileged, accomplished, and talented women.

Building Cranbrook School began according to Eliel's plan in 1926.[16] Though most of the Tudor farm buildings were demolished, they set the tone for the small-scale campus, and the architect managed to turn the blacksmith shop into a library, some stables and barns into classrooms, and the silo into an observatory. The new buildings, in dark red brick, with double-pitched roofs and tall, thin leaded-glass windows, are organized around a series of courtyards, on the footprints of their predecessors.

Traces of the old farm are not immediately apparent, but Cranbrook School is more traditional and, curiously, more Scandinavian in feel than the architects' recent projects had been. It has extensive decorative brickwork and sculptural ornament, mostly by Eliel's friend Geza Maróti, who was one of the first artists to work at Cranbrook.[17] Though their details are original, the buildings recall the Red House that Philip Webb had designed for William Morris in 1859 and the Lahti Town Hall that Eliel built in 1912, as well as the terrace houses grouped around courts that he had envisioned for Munkkiniemi-Haaga. Cranbrook School also recalls farm courtyards common in Finland and, of course, the quadrangles on many American campuses.

What the boys' school is not like is the grand, formal design for an "Arts Building" at the Helsinki Industrial Exhibition of 1913 that Eliel had drawn up in 1910. Elements of this scheme turned up in the master plan for Cranbrook that Eliel prepared as soon as he arrived in 1925, but instead of buildings dominating the landscape, in Michigan the rolling wooded lay of the land played a greater role.

The most impressive things about the Cranbrook School are the ways
the buildings are physically made, integrated with the landscape, and
related to one another. Though the school was built to accommodate
three hundred boys, it is almost domestic in scale because it is composed of small buildings facing one another in intimate clusters.[18]

The entire Saarinen family was involved in the design. Loja created a
model of Eliel's plan. Pipsan decorated ceilings and trusses. Eero, who was
fifteen when the project began, designed the school seal, decorative
metalwork, carved stone imps that peer down from the walls, and the
decorative tiles of boys playing sports on the fireplace in the hall by
the auditorium. Eliel outfitted the refectory-like dining hall with chairs
and tables, silverware, dishes, and glassware, providing a perfect
example of the "total design" he advocated.

George Booth walked by the dining hall one day after the foundations
had been poured and, sensing that the proportions of the hall were
not right, insisted that the problem be rectified, despite the cost. His
commitment to detail made it easier for Eliel to concede to his demands.
And his tendency to keep trying to get it right taught Eero a lesson
he never forgot. As a mature architect, he would continue to fine-tune
designs even after construction had begun.

Cranbrook Academy of Art: Beginnings

Although the Academy was to be the centerpiece of the community,
its first buildings are plainer than those at the boys' school but have the
same gabled roofs, dormers, decorative brickwork, and tall, leaded-
glass windows. They were built in 1925–26, before Booth's concept
for the Cranbrook Academy of Art was fully formed, because the
architects needed a place to work while they were designing the boys'
school. The Cranbrook Architectural Office soon became a small firm,
headed by Eliel and staffed largely by young Michigan graduates.[19] And
Eero, as a high school boy, often worked alongside them.

Instead of placing the Architectural Office in the landscape, Saarinen
located it on Lone Pine Road, on the corner of Academy Way, a new
street leading into the Cranbrook compound. During the next two
years, crafts studios were built next door—in the same red brick, with
large windows facing a garden and overhanging slate roofs—for the
artists who came from around the world to work on the decoration
for the buildings and, eventually, to teach at Cranbrook.

With the Cranbrook dream becoming a reality, Eliel Saarinen started
designing a house for his family there when he returned from Finland
in the fall of 1928. And though Pipsan was married and Eero was ready
to leave home, the design once more was a family affair. Eliel designed
the house itself and most of the furniture, which was built in the wood-
working shops of the Academy's new Arts and Crafts Center by the
new resident cabinetmaker, Tor Berglund, from Stockholm. Loja designed
the gardens, draperies, rugs, and upholstery fabrics, which were made
in the commercial weaving studios she had established there. Eero
designed the master bedroom, which, with its spare streamlined geometric furniture, painted gray-green to match the walls, and series of
mirrored doors, is the most avant-grade room of the house. And it would
have seemed even more so if ruffled bedspreads had not been added.
Although the Saarinen House (1928–30) was altered over the years when
later directors of the Academy lived there, it was restored in the mid-
1990s and is now a house museum open to the public (like Hvitträsk).

The rest of the furnishings are, like much of Eliel's architecture, original
in design but traditional in materials and craftsmanship—quite unlike the
industrial-looking furniture being produced at the Bauhaus but similar
to that in the interiors at the Exposition Internationale des Arts Décoratifs
et Industriels Modernes of 1925 in Paris, which the Saarinens (and
Booths) had attended. Like much of Eliel's work, the house looks less
radical to twenty-first-century eyes than it did to the author of an article
in *House Beautiful* three years after it was completed (and a year after
the Museum of Modern Art's influential "International Style" exhibition).
Henry Macomber described it as "a modernism completely controlled
by good taste" and noted "the doors between rooms have been dispensed with, the entrances are finished in maple stained gray, and
there is no mantelshelf."[20]

The exquisite octagonal dining room has a gold-leafed domed ceiling
over an inlaid circular dining table and fourteen fir chairs with fluted
backs outlined in black.[21] The walls are covered in rectangular fir panels,
with corner niches painted red (a Pipsan touch); the rug, mural, and
light fixture are parts of the ensemble.

The sparsely furnished living room, used mostly for receptions, has side chairs made by Berglund of rare woods and a rigid couch covered by a rya rug in the Finnish manner. A simple rectangular fireplace sheathed with gray and rust tiles from the local Pewabic Pottery was never used because Loja did not want smoke to dirty the bricks. Her predilections so irked Frank Lloyd Wright, who often came to visit, that he once kicked the perfectly stacked, unused logs that she kept on the andirons, growling, "That's what I think of your damned symmetry!" Eliel came to her rescue with, "You are always Frank, but you are not always Wright."[22]

The same fanatical attention to detail prevailed in the "book room" alcove, where all the Saarinens' many volumes were rebound in russet and gold leather to match the color scheme. Eliel and Loja spent most of their time there. They breakfasted in another alcove off the master bedroom upstairs, and entertained guests and students in an alcove between the living room and the barrel-vaulted, forty-seven-foot-long studio. The studio was the real heart of the house, with three drafting tables overlooking an enclosed garden and an officelike alcove at the other end.

What is most remarkable is that the Saarinen House is located not in a landscape but right on Academy Way, across the street from the studios.

A low brick wall, broken only by the brick staircase leading to the front door, runs along the sidewalk edging a small flat front yard. The lot is rather constricted, especially for a place like Bloomfield Hills, where houses occupy large plots of land. The house even abuts the one next door, which was built for Eliel's friend, Swedish sculptor Carl Milles and his family. Later residences and dormitories, built directly to the north, maintained the street line, like the houses in progressive English and American town plans of the time and like those in Eliel's own designs for relatively dense European-style neighborhoods.

Clearly, Eliel saw the Academy as a close-knit community where artists would live and work and teach and exchange ideas, the way he did with his partners in the early days at Hvitträsk. And that is the way Cranbrook functioned in the early days with students devising a project to design and the artists (and architects) in residence advising them informally. This was the environment Eero Saarinen returned to after college.

When they began planning the community, George Booth's taste was quite conservative, but when he saw the house that Saarinen had built, he immediately invited him to design the girls' school, even though he had already asked his son, Henry, to develop a scheme for it.[23] Since it was Ellen Booth who had championed the idea of a girls' school, she participated actively in the planning with her husband, Eliel, and Loja. And the four of them saw to it that the school for two hundred girls, which offered "finishing" as well as college preparation, had numerous facilities for the arts.

Kingswood School for Girls

Eliel Saarinen's approach to the design of the Kingswood School (1929–31), which he worked on in his new home studio, was very different from those at the Cranbrook School and the Academy. To take advantage of the views, light, and topography of the site's rolling lakeside terrain, he spread the buildings out along an east-west spine, with a wing of classrooms extending north around a courtyard and dormitory rooms stretching south toward the water. The long, low Kingswood School buildings, attached to one another by spacious porches and colonnades, look more modern and unusual than those at the Cranbrook School, designed only a few years earlier. The Kingswood buildings bear some resemblance to Frank Lloyd Wright's Prairie Houses (c. 1897–1917), with their horizontal thrust, overhanging eaves, and geometric decoration inspired by natural forms. The detailing clearly derives from the Saarinen House, too.

Kingswood School also seems more American than the boys' school and the family house because it is so frankly scaled to the automobile. Its entrance is at the end of a long driveway off verdant Cranbrook Road.[24] Eliel was clearly adapting to his new home, and he had learned

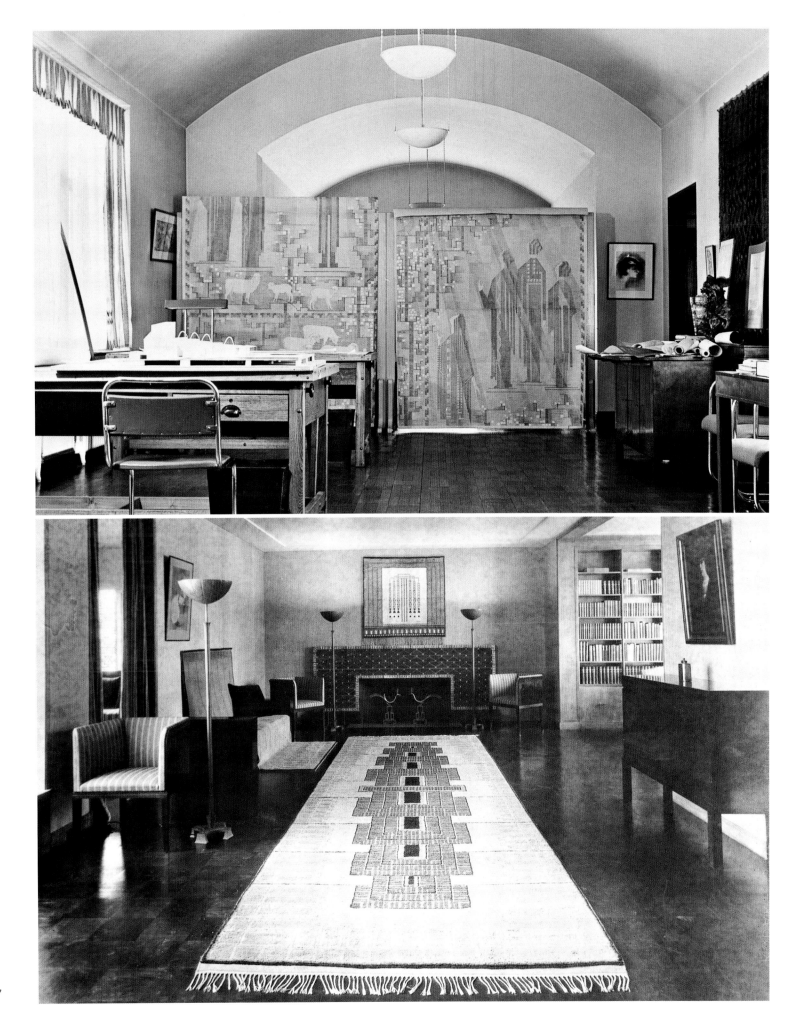

a great deal from building the boys' school. The classrooms and dormitory quarters, sparse at Cranbrook School, are well planned and artfully decorated at Kingswood. The auditorium is big enough to use for dances and accessible from both dormitories and classrooms. The dining room is as spectacular as the one at Cranbrook School but brighter and furnished with round tables to encourage conversation. Eero designed the rounded birch chairs with vermilion trim.

Eliel's painterly sensibility is evident in the landscape-derived palette of the exterior: earth tones in the variegated brick walls and Mankato stone columns, the blue-green of the lake echoed in horizontal strips of brick, painted window frames, and the standing-seam copper roofs, which were quickly weathered with urine the workers collected for the purpose and applied.[25]

Inside, landscape tones again predominate. The color scheme for each dormitory room was chosen to harmonize with its specific view.[26] Rooms throughout the school are connected by generous, light-filled corridors—like the hallways and public spaces with walls of glass that Eero would later use in his college buildings and laboratories. Those at Kingswood are filled with leaded glass in abstract patterns that he designed with his father.

In the two-story auditorium, dark-stained oak floors and wainscot are set off by light gray walls, and the ceilings are decorated, by Pipsan, with silver leaf, which is echoed in the warm gray velour stage curtain's silver Fabrikoid ornament. Light from three rows of patterned windows is augmented by silvery light fixtures suspended from within a grid of domes to produce indirect lighting—another device Eero would later use.

The Kingswood School was in the vanguard in 1931 when the buildings were completed. The birch side chairs that Eero designed for the dining room and library (and that are used throughout the school) anticipate similar ones that Alvar Aalto would create for the Viipuri Library two years later.[27] The open rectangles on the chairs' curved backs and under their seats are edged in deep pink paint to match the geometric patterns in the woven upholstery on their solid birch seats. Though they already show the sculptural sensibility of the young man, who was not yet twenty years old when the project began, they relate to the overall scheme. The tubular-steel chairs Eero designed for the auditorium, however, which were covered with green upholstery, belong to a dif-

ferent aesthetic entirely—the machine-made one, emphasizing the use of industrial materials, that was in vogue at the Bauhaus. They resemble the canonical chairs that Marcel Breuer and Mies van der Rohe had created only a year or two earlier and were refining at the time.[28] Even before he left for art school and college, Eero Saarinen was embracing an aesthetic that was distinct from his father's and being rewarded for doing so. George Booth gave him reproduction rights to the furniture, which he never gave to Eliel for anything he designed in his long career at Cranbrook.[29]

The Cranbrook Institute of Science

Kingswood, which most historians rightly consider Eliel Saarinen's masterpiece, turned out to be impossible to equal. The Depression diminished Booth's fortune, but he didn't stop building. Even before the girls' school was completed, he started planning the Cranbrook Institute of Science (1931–37)[30] and put up a temporary concrete-block structure to replace an observatory in the tower at Cranbrook School that had never functioned properly.[31] The temporary structure was built during the summer of 1930 on Sunset Hill, an elevated plain in the middle of the estate, a site that Henry Booth had chosen for Kingswood but that Eliel had rejected.

Though the temporary Institute was already in place when he started on the permanent one, Eliel wanted to build nearer the edge of the campus so that access would be easier and the center of the estate could remain as landscape. But Booth insisted, so the new building became essentially an addition to the temporary structure. Saarinen's Institute of Science building is hard to see today, as there have been various alterations, including an impressive addition by Steven Holl, of 1992–95, which enclosed a courtyard on the north. The original block had wings projecting north and south at right angles. Glass-brick ribbon windows, connected by bands of concrete, accentuated its horizontality, as did flat, overhanging roofs. A semicircular parking lot surrounded the east end, and an elliptical reflecting pool with sculptures by Carl Milles led to a flat-roofed entrance porch on the south.

The yellowish brickwork is similar to that at Kingswood—a slight departure from Eliel's tendency to make each building at Cranbrook slightly lighter than the last. Each building was successively plainer and more modern, too. By the late '30s, International Style Modernism was well established in influential critical and academic circles in America, and Eliel Saarinen was well aware of the trend. He always talked about wanting to create an architecture for his own time, as his son would. And though the Institute of Science does not look particularly modern now (especially when compared with work being done in Europe at the time), it was considered so in its day.

Clockwise from top left: Saarinen House, bathroom; dining room; master bedroom. All the rooms were conceived by Eliel except the bedroom, which was designed by Eero.

Architectural Forum praised Eliel's direction: "When the first buildings at Cranbrook Academy were completed, they attracted countrywide attention for the refreshing manner in which they met the problem of educational buildings. Omitting any consideration of the masterly handling of the large-scale plan, Cranbrook was of immediate importance because it demonstrated beyond the possibility of refutation that Collegiate Gothic was neither the ultimate, nor even a particularly good, expression for U.S. academic architecture. In the buildings that followed there was no repetition, but a steady development toward simpler forms, with new materials used wherever they seemed suitable."[32]

This statement represents a point of view that the editors of *Architectural Forum* and other publications were promoting at the time, but it does not really describe Eliel Saarinen's contribution. (And it makes the then-common mistake of judging a building by whether it conforms to a trend rather than on its merits. Today most people find Collegiate Gothic campuses a good deal more appealing than modern ones.) Eliel Saarinen never experimented with industrial materials or exposed raw concrete. He was not the technical innovator that Eero would become. Eliel's work was forward-looking but not avant-garde. He was at his best (as at Kingswood) when he was using ornament and handicraft in his buildings. Still, at the Institute of Science, as always, he provided an appropriate expression for the purpose, which the limited budget of only $238,000 encouraged.[33] The interiors were even more functional-

looking than the outside—an extreme departure from Kingswood, though some of the light fixtures and motifs devised for that school were used again at the Institute of Science. Exhibit areas were not particularly flexible, though they were ample and well lit.

Cranbrook Academy of Art: Late Work

Though artists continued to arrive at Cranbrook throughout the late 1920s and early '30s, the Academy of Art did not admit its first official students until 1932. Saarinen and Booth had always agreed that the students should work independently, directed by the resident faculty, but they found that some of the students who arrived were unprepared to do so. Remedial courses had to be created. Also, with Booth's resources depleted, the institution needed to attract students who could pay tuition (only architects received scholarships). "To save the Academy as the Depression deepened, Saarinen and Raseman," a Detroit architect brought in to serve as executive secretary, "redefined the school as a post-graduate institution with departments of architecture, sculpture, and painting."[34] For a while there were still no formal classes, school terms, or formal critiques, but eventually courses were established for all students. Then came a system of credits, and finally, in 1943, degrees were conferred—just in time to benefit from the GI Bill, introduced the next year. Eventually, the school awarded a BFA. as well. But what made it a magical place were the people Eliel Saarinen, who became its director and was called president, was able to attract there as resident artists, visiting speakers (such as Frank Lloyd Wright, Le Corbusier, Alvar Aalto, Lewis Mumford, and Ely Jacques Kahn),[35] and students—and the physical setting he had created.[36]

That setting embodied the evolution of Eliel Saarinen's work over almost two decades, though the Academy studios and dormitories built between 1931 and 1933 are more traditional in style than other buildings of the time, because they were intended to create gradual transitions between the early Academy buildings and the late ones.

The Cranbrook Academy Museum of Art and Library (1938–42) are very restrained and geometric inside and out, but probably not because Eero had returned to Cranbrook, as some critics have supposed. Eliel Saarinen's movement toward abstract forms had continued while his son was in college and traveling between 1930 and 1936, in keeping with the trend at the time. Eliel's last buildings at Cranbrook are extremely flat and linear, and Eero's sensibility was muscular and sculpturesque.

Before he designed them, Eliel visited museums throughout Europe and North America, as he had toured railroad stations before entering the Helsinki Railroad Station competition years earlier. Though the author of the first monograph on his work, Albert Christ-Janer, says he learned more from looking at lighting, ventilation, and air-conditioning in industrial buildings,[37] there is nothing of the industrial aesthetic in the design, which he began in 1938 and completed in 1942, just in time, for the United States had entered World War II, and not much civilian building would take place for some time.

After the war, American architecture changed significantly, partly because of the influence of a new group of European architects who had come to the United States[38] and partly because of new technology and new types of commissions. Eliel Saarinen's work changed too, though more slowly, as he practiced with Eero. But he always remained a man of his time, and that was the first half of the twentieth century.

The Cranbrook Academy of Art Museum of Art and Library are classic prewar buildings though they are assertively rectangular, with flat roofs and windows set in grids. The walls are made of beautiful brickwork with an almost golden glow. A monumental colonnade, with abstract patterns on its floors and ceilings and magnificent sculptured copper doors, rises above the blocks on each side, connecting the library and the museum to one another and forming a backdrop to the outdoor spaces on either side.[39] Though this "Propylaeum" is adjacent to the studios at the end of Academy Way, instead of maintaining the street line, the library and museum buildings run perpendicular to the street, where they frame gardens with something of the formality of Eliel's first plan for Cranbrook.[40] The severity is relieved, to some extent, by the Triton Pool on the south and the Orpheus Fountain on the north, both by Carl Milles, who designed lively figurative sculptures for a series of picturesque gardens and fountains throughout the campus.[41] This is another lesson that Eero never forgot—"the interplay of architecture and

This page, from left: Eliel Saarinen and Frank Lloyd Wright at Cranbrook Academy of Art, April 1935; Le Corbusier and Eliel Saarinen at Cranbrook Academy of Art, November 1935.

Opposite, from top: Eliel Saarinen, Cranbrook Academy of Art Museum and Library, 1938–42; Eliel Saarinen, Cranbrook Academy of Art Studios, 1931–32, behind steps to peristyle and Triton Fountain by Carl Milles.

sculpture"— though he would choose different kinds of artworks and landscape designs for his more abstract, mid-twentieth-century buildings.

Despite the severity of Eliel's museum and library facades, they are more classical than modern, recalling both Karl G. Langhans's Brandenburg Gate in Berlin (1789–93) and Josef Hoffmann's preliminary sketch for the Austrian pavilion at the Exposition Internationale des Arts Décoratifs et Industriels Modernes in Paris (1925).[42] The towering central arcade is not only a commanding presence; it also disguises the fact that the library is rectangular, while the museum has a T-shaped plan.

At the museum, detailing had to create the effects because the architect had learned the importance of providing flexibility. Movable white marble pedestals echo the white marble floor plates, curved up on the ends to meet the wall. There are galleries of different sizes, shapes,

and light conditions. And though the detailing is very restrained, there is always the sense of a human hand, as in the magnificent labyrinth-patterned copper doors leading into the art galleries from the portico. Eliel Saarinen clearly intended these buildings to be Cranbrook's crowning glory. In many ways they were his as well—the first classicizing design he was able to build, since the Finnish Parliament and Memorial Hall for the City of Detroit remained only plans. In a few years, he would be designing very practical wartime housing and then working alongside his son, whose impulse was to break out of classical (and all other kinds of) molds.

Opposite: Eero (holding pipe) and Eliel Saarinen with
Cranbrook architecture students on the steps of the new
Cranbrook Academy of Art Museum and Library peristyle,
May 1941.

Much has been made of the inestimable influence on Eero Saarinen of his famous father. After all, Eliel was the head of the family and a great teacher, and his son worked with him for the first fourteen years of his twenty-four-year career. But when Eero left home, at nineteen, he went not to architecture school but to art school in Paris, as his mother had done in her youth.[1] Because he came from a family that thought it was important to be modern,[2] Eero enrolled at the Académie de la Grande Chaumière (1929–30), where Alberto Giacometti and Alexander Calder had studied, instead of at the Académie Colarossi, where his mother had gone, or the famous École des Beaux-Arts, which most Americans attended in Paris.

Eliel had entered art school at about the same age, but he had enrolled concurrently as an architecture student. His interest was in painting, whereas Eero gravitated toward sculpture, as his mother had. Like Eliel, however, Eero never abandoned the thought of architecture. He had told a newspaper reporter several years earlier that he just assumed he would become an architect,[3] and after his foray in Paris, he came back to America and went to the School of Architecture at Yale University in New Haven, Connecticut, in the fall of 1931.

Ironically, Yale, like other American architecture schools at the time, had not yet embraced the modern movement that Eero had been exposed to all his life. Yale adhered to a traditional curriculum, based on that at the École des Beaux-Arts in Paris, which encouraged the use of historic prototypes to solve modern problems. Eliel Saarinen did not use them in his own teaching, which involved a more personalized approach, but he must have felt that the time-honored method would impose discipline on his son. And Eliel had never abandoned a respect for architectural history the way some early modern architects, such as Walter Gropius, did.

Exposure to a rigorous traditional approach did not dampen Eero's enthusiasm for architecture or for Modernist experimentation, though his tendency to abstract forms was sometimes criticized at college reviews. His scheme for a police station, which had an asymmetrical plan similar to that of the Kingswood School and even bolder geometric elevations, was deemed "diagrammatically good," but one juror observed that it left "something to be desired in its indication of detail study."[4] On another jury, a critic said his design for an American Academy in Florence "lacks finish and character."[5] Still, it received a second medal, and Eero managed to complete the four-year architecture program in three years, winning so many prizes that he received one for winning the most prizes. He was even awarded the prestigious Charles O. Matcham Traveling Fellowship. Clearly, some experimentation was tolerated—and rewarded.

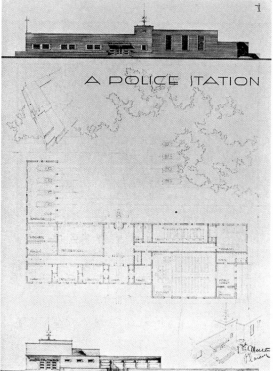

From left: Eero Saarinen, student project for a Memorial Tunnel entrance, c. 1930; student project for a police station, c. 1930.

Some of his student work demonstrated remarkable precocity, even for someone who had had a head start. A Memorial Tunnel entrance, which received the Spiering Prize, maintained the rough-hewn form of the mountain by "scooping out" a tall chunk of "rock in a semicircle at the tunnel entrance and cutting back huge steps" on both sides to produce an approach that jurors called "monumental though primitive in character and as enduring as the mountain itself."[6] Nothing like anything his father had ever done, it resembled earthworks that sculptors would create in the 1960s and 1970s, while serving a functional purpose. And though it was forward-looking, it would have played into the Beaux-Arts romantic fascination with ruins.

Although he was an intense competitor, Eero Saarinen was a popular student at Yale. His classmates nicknamed him "Second Medal Saarinen," because when he didn't win the first prize, he managed to win the second. And for years afterward, they invited him to join them on projects, in ventures, and in their clubs. For instance, Worthen Paxton invited him to join the group at the office of Norman Bel Geddes; he joined the Office of Strategic Services during World War II along with numerous Yale graduates. He was invited to join the Cosmos Club in Washington, which also counts a number of Yale alumni among its members. His ability to be one of the boys while excelling professionally proved especially important later. He had a rare talent for communicating with clients and made devoted patrons out of some of them. Still, he did arouse some jealousy. His talent, advantages, and success—even the fact

that people liked him—engendered detractors who delighted in calling attention to his every misstep.

As soon as he graduated in 1934, he entered a competition open to all Finnish architects for the Helsinki Central Post Office and Telegraph, to be located next to his father's Helsinki Station. His flat-roofed, spare, geometric scheme was both modernist and contextual. The facade, featuring a grid of punched windows and vertical slits, reflected the interior structural frame, and a setback at one corner accommodated a bend in the street—a gesture of which Eliel would have approved. The scheme won third prize and was published in *Arkkitehti* magazine with the other winners.[7]

The same year, he left for a two-year trip through Europe and the Middle East. Traveling with the sculptor Carl Milles and various young American friends, he went to see ancient buildings in Egypt, Greece, Syria, Palestine, and Italy, where he also visited Renaissance sites as well as buildings by Giuseppe Terragni. In Germany he saw the work of the avant-garde and was particularly impressed by that of Mies van der Rohe and Erich Mendelsohn. In France it was Le Corbusier who fascinated him; in Sweden, Gunnar Asplund; and in Finland, Alvar Aalto.

Eero worked for a while in Helsinki on the renovation of the Swedish Theater, which his father had been commissioned to remodel but had turned over to his old friend Jarl Eklund when he left for America. Eliel had kept working on the project and even sent Eklund some new drawings,[8] but Eero did many more, including some rather traditional ones, before settling on an International Style addition to the classical building that had been built in 1860 and renovated after a fire in 1867.

While he was at Eklund's office, he also designed a mixed-use Forum (c. 1935) with shops and other facilities for the middle of Helsinki that had a flat roof, curved end, and smooth facade reminiscent of the work of Mendelsohn, but it was never built.

In Finland, modern architecture arrived without the polemics that accompanied it in Germany, where it was intended to sweep away the past. Aalto attributed the smoother transition in his country to Eliel Saarinen, who had helped bridge the gap between the past and the future.[9] Eliel tried to make new buildings fit sensitively into the existing context, something that Eero, almost alone among his contemporaries, also tried to do. His 1936 addition to the Swedish Theater, which features smooth white walls without ornament, conforms to the scale of the street and reinforces the street line with storefronts.

Eero also had an unusual (for a Modernist) respect for precedents. During the summer of 1935 at Hvittträsk, he spent hours teaching the history of architecture to a young girl his parents had befriended at Cranbrook. Florence Schust (called "Shu") was an orphan who had enrolled at Kingswood instead of an eastern boarding school, because she found the buildings so beautiful. "When I came," she explained years later, "I walked into the art department expecting to be asked to do some kind of a little still life. But the teacher, Rachel DeWolfe Raseman, unbeknownst to me, was the first lady graduate in architecture from Cornell. She said, 'What would you like to do?' And I said, 'I'd like to design a house.' I didn't even know I was saying it practically. But I did, and she was thrilled of course to have somebody interested in her interest."[10] Word got around Cranbrook about the talented girl who was inclined toward architecture, so Eliel went to see what she was doing, got to know her, and invited her to his Cranbrook home. Eero had left for college, so the Saarinens practically adopted her and took her with them to Finland during the summers. She became a lifelong friend of Eero's and a collaborator on some of his most important projects after she married Hans Knoll and helped found the Knoll International furniture company. (In those years, she was known as Florence—or Shu—Knoll. After Hans died, she married Harry Hood Bassett, a prominent banker, and became Florence Schust Knoll Bassett) At one point Eero was in love with her.[11] But in 1935, when he was spending time in Finland on his traveling fellowship, Shu was more like a little sister, and what Eero thought his little sister needed to know about was the history of architecture. Like his father, he never saw any conflict between being a man of his time and a connoisseur of the architecture of the past.

Eero at Cranbrook
Shu was back at Cranbrook in 1936 when Eero returned to Bloomfield Hills after his travels, went into practice with his father, and began teaching at the Cranbrook Academy of Art. She was only one of a remarkably talented group of young people who had come to study and work there. (She later left to study architecture at the Architectural Association in London, Columbia University, and with Mies at the Illinois Institute of Technology).[12] The sculptor and designer Harry Bertoia was at Cranbrook, as were the designers Charles and Ray Eames, Benjamin Baldwin, and Eero's sister, Pipsan. The architects Ralph Rapson and Harry Weese were around, as was Lily Swann, a beautiful young sculptor from New York who had come to study with Carl Milles.

"It was a very vibrant and exciting and dynamic time. We did whatever we liked. There was no fixed curriculum," Rapson recalls.[13] Eliel and Eero's office was in the Cranbrook studios, and even though Rapson was engaged in a study project of his own, he was more interested in the real work being done in the next room. Cranbrook functioned on the apprenticeship model that Booth and Saarinen had envisioned.

"The minute I arrived, I was so enthralled with the whole idea that I just made myself part of the Saarinen office," Rapson said. "My studio was opposite Eliel's. I worked a great, great deal on many of the Saarinen projects, just sitting with Pappy—we called Eliel Pappy—and helping him. It was quite interesting to me that Eero and his father were so completely different and yet so similar in many ways. Eliel was very quiet, very reserved, very dapper, whereas Eero was, if anything, just a bit sloppy. His work habits were much different, too.

"I admired Pappy because he seemed to know exactly what he wanted to design," Rapson added. "It was almost like unrolling a sheet of paper. He could start at the top and just draw. He didn't make many preliminary studies, and Eero just went on endlessly with sketches. We never quite seemed to arrive at a given design. We'd go on through hundreds and hundreds of options. Eero always had to have somebody working with him, and it just so happened that during my years there, I was the one that did that. We would work hours and hours, late into the evening, even though we didn't have deadlines. At some point, I'd say, 'Eero, I'm quitting. I've got to go to bed,' and he would quit. But he always seemed to want someone to sound out, to talk to, to experience, and have this banter back and forth. Of course, a lot of my ideas were never realized. He did respect one of my abilities—that I was able to draw fast. I remember Eero once getting exasperated with me and saying, 'Gosh, you can make anything look good, whether it's good or bad design.' But we had great times together."

At Cranbrook Eero found contemporaries who shared his interests and became his most important lifelong friends. And because students worked in various visual arts, the boundaries between art and architecture blurred.

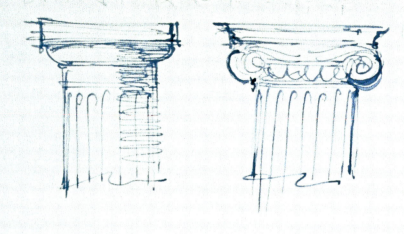  

EARLY CHRISTIAN

CONSTANTINE 324

GUILOCHE

BYZANTINE

SICALY *
RAVENNA . . *
ITAL.

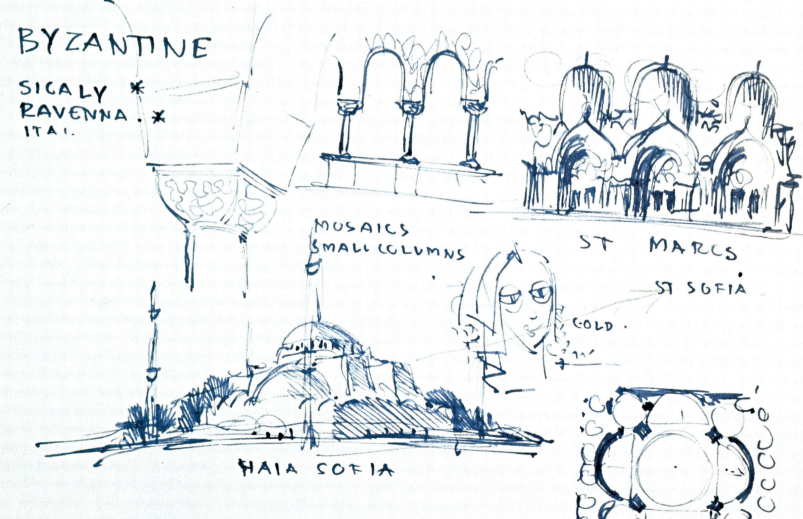

MOSAICS
SMALL COLUMNS

ST MARCS

ST SOFIA

GOLD.

HAIA SOFIA

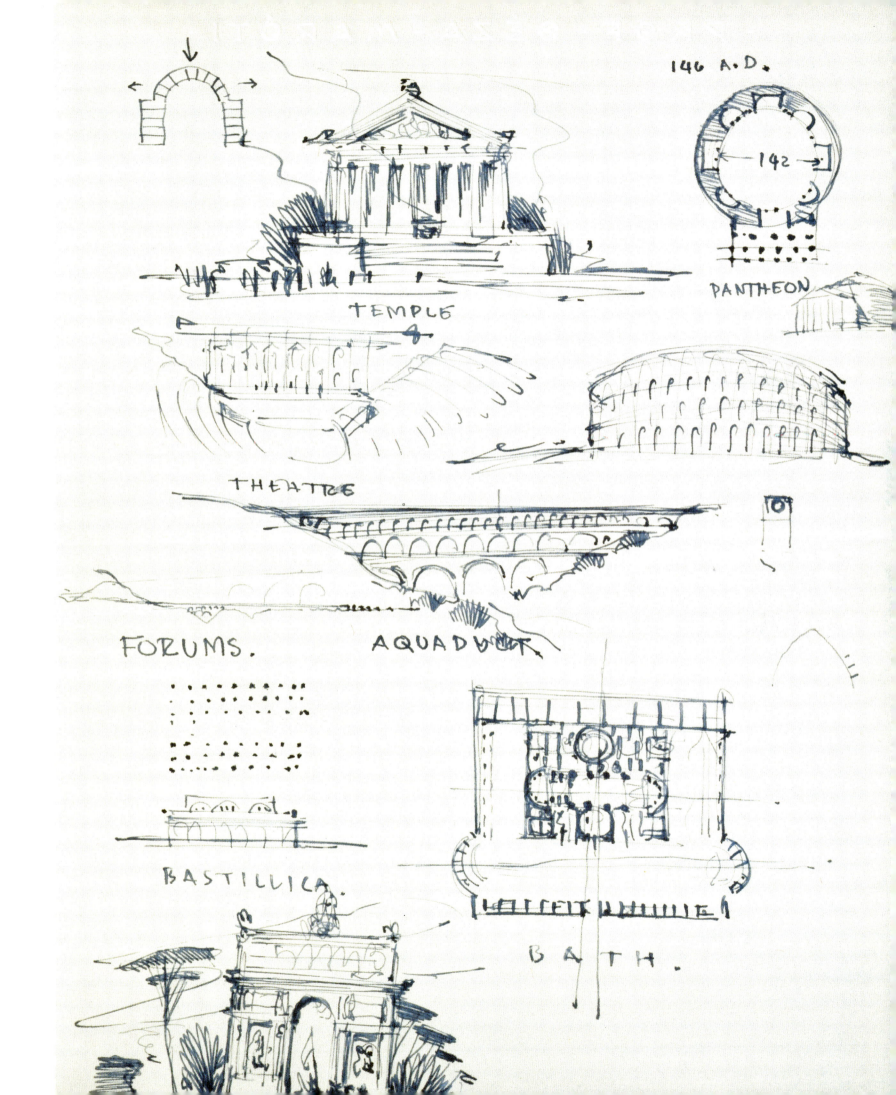

146 A.D.

142

PANTHEON

TEMPLE

THEATRE

AQUADUCT

FORUMS.

BASTILLICA.

BATH.

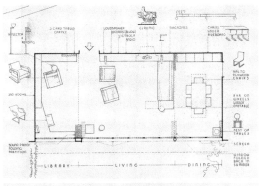

BUFFET SUPPER

DINNER FOR TEN

5 HOUSE TYPES, ONE & TWO STORY, ONE TO THREE BEDROOMS

ELIEL & EERO SAARINEN, ARCHITECTS   **J. ROBERT F. SWANSON, ASSOCIATE**

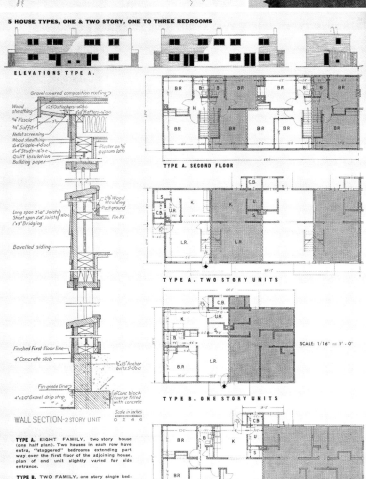

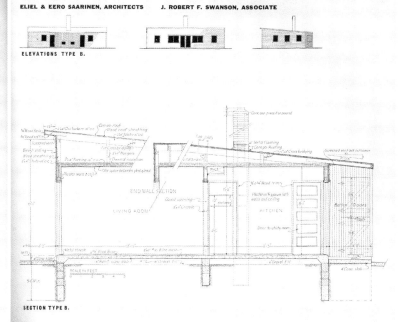

TYPE A. EIGHT FAMILY, two story house (one half plan). Two houses in each row have extra, "staggered" bedrooms extending part way over the first floor of the adjoining house. Plan of end unit slightly varied for side entrance.

TYPE B. TWO FAMILY, one story single bedroom plan. Note coal bin, utility room and storage closet, necessary features in basementless houses of this type.

TYPE C. TWO FAMILY, one story, three bedroom house. Core of plan, near party wall, is identical with that of the one-bedroom unit.

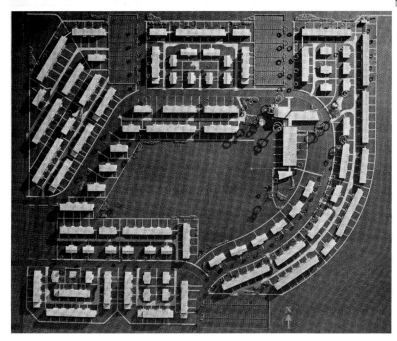

This page, clockwise from top left: Eero Saarinen, "A Combined Living-Dining Room-Study Designed for The Architectural Forum," 1937, published in *Architectural Forum*, October 1937; Saarinen, Swanson, and Saarinen, Defense Housing for Kramer Homes, Center Line, Michigan, 1941–42, as published in *Architectural Forum*, October 1941.

Pages 38–39: Drawings Eero Saarinen made to teach Florence Schust (Knoll Bassett) architectural history at Hvitträsk, 1935.

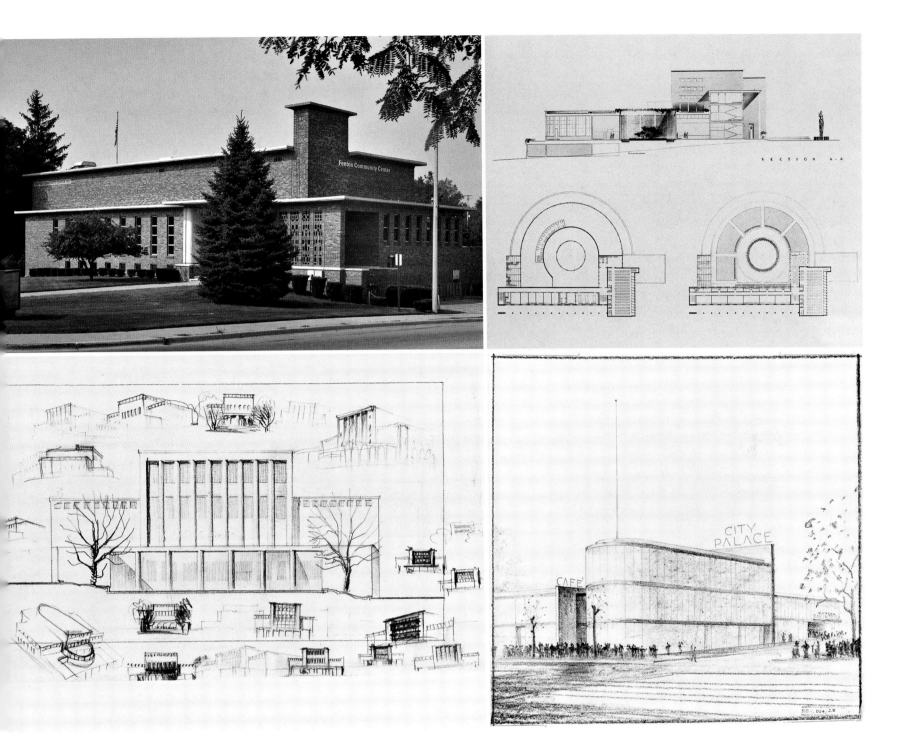

Clockwise from top left: Saarinen and Saarinen, Community Center, Fenton, Michigan, 1937–38; Saarinen and Saarinen with Ralph Rapson and other Cranbrook students, Goucher College campus plan and library competition scheme, 1938 (placed second); Eero Saarinen, sketch for the Forum, a mixed-use commercial project proposed for central Helsinki, c. 1935, pencil and charcoal on tracing paper; Eero Saarinen, sketches for renovation of the Swedish Theater being designed with Jarl Ecklund, Helsinki, 1936.

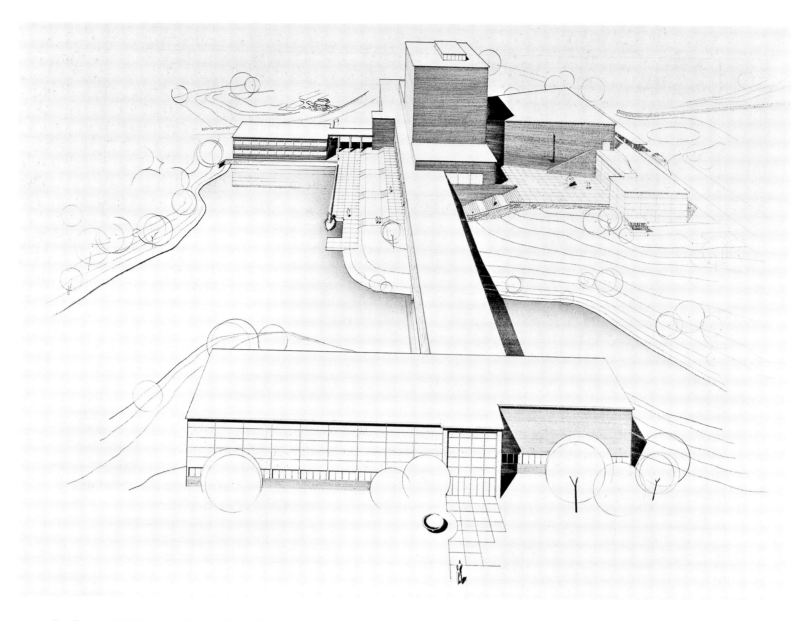

Eero Saarinen, Ralph Rapson, and Frederic James, Festival
Theater for the College of William and Mary, 1939, First Prize
winning competition scheme.

Florence (Shu) Knoll Bassett recalls how Eero's sculptural sensibility led the sculptor Lily Swann to a breakthrough in her work. "Lily had a piece of stone, and she was kind of trying to chip out a bear or something. Eero saw what she was doing and said, 'This is what you ought to do!' He took some clay, and pounded it down flat, and then he started to mold it into forms, animals or whatever, and she had a whole new career."[14] That tutelage led to Lily becoming Eero's first wife in 1939.

Eero's most fertile relationship at Cranbrook was with Charles Eames, who became his closest friend and a frequent collaborator, but he entered competitions with Rapson and other people, too.

The first project Eero worked on in Michigan was a city plan for the Flint Institute of Research and Planning (1937) in Flint, under Edmund N. Bacon, who later became an influential planner for the city of Philadelphia and the author of a landmark book, *Design of Cities*.[15] Bacon had come to Cranbrook to study with Eliel after working in Shanghai, "the only place in the world where there were architectural jobs in the early 1930s." He thinks he was accepted on the strength of a letter about his "awareness of the architecture [in Shanghai], not as discrete objects but as a sensation over time."[16] Certainly, that is how Eliel saw cities. Bacon (who was the son of the publisher of Eliel's book *The City*[17] and is also the father of the actor Kevin Bacon) remembers "life at Cranbrook as eight times more intensive in every sense of sensory response as anything I've ever experienced before or since." He says, "Eliel didn't teach us—he led us. He would take a smooth marble table and pour a drop of water on it. Then he would tap his thumb down on it, which would make little drops go out from it . . . . [and] say that this is the way the city should develop."[18]

In 1937, Eero was asked to design a cultural center for Flint as part of Bacon's master plan. Always one to try everything, he produced two schemes. One was similar to the work of his father; the other was more

From top: Saarinen and Saarinen, Tanglewood "Shed" for the Berkshire Music Festival, Lenox, Massachusetts, 1938; Eero Saarinen (with pipe), Ralph Rapson, and Frederic James working on the Festival Theater competition for the College of William and Mary, February 1939.

streamlined and Art Moderne. Clearly, he was trying to decide which direction to take—or what would be acceptable now that he was back in his father's domain.

A project he did on his own the same year, "A Combined Living-Dining Room-Study, Designed for The Architectural Forum," was considerably more radical.[19] It was squarely in the International Style, both formally and conceptually. Consisting of a simple rectangle with a glass wall facing a garden, it was similar to a house he would design for his mother after his father died in 1950 and to the Ash Street House Philip Johnson would build for himself in 1942 when he was in architecture school at Harvard. Although Eero's project was described in the magazine as "part of a small house or an apartment with a roof terrace," it was shown with a flat roof and hints of vegetation outside. The flexible interior spaces

had built-in bookcases, cabinets, and furniture by Alvar Aalto. The little pavilion prefigured Eero's interests in modular elements and thin-wall construction, which he later explored on a massive scale at the General Motors Technical Center.

Also in 1937, Eero and his father designed their first building outside Cranbrook. The Community House (1937–38) in Fenton, Michigan, resembled Eero's Helsinki Post Office project of three years earlier with its flat roofs, plain walls, and asymmetrical organization, but it was a bit more formal, like Eliel's work.[20] At around the same time, they designed a flat-roofed academic building, Nikander Hall, which steps down a hillside at little Finlandia University (formerly Suomi College), a Finnish-language school in Hancock, Michigan.[21]

That spring Worthen Paxton, a Yale classmate who admired Eero's talent, invited him to work with him and other young architects in the New York office of the industrial designer Norman Bel Geddes on General Motors' Futurama Pavilion for the 1939 World's Fair. During the two months he spent there, working around the clock, Eero was exposed to the kind of imagery that industrial designers like Bel Geddes were using and the ways they presented their ideas graphically. After he left, a streamlined look—gently curved forms with linear accents that suggest a sense of speed—would resurface occasionally in his work for several years.

While he was in New York in the spring of 1938, Eero entered a competition on his own for an art center for Wheaton College in Norton, Massachusetts, and managed to place fifth even though there were 243 submissions and some of the best-known architects in the country had entered. The critic Talbot Hamlin praised the "unforced loveliness of proportion, direct use of materials, and simple detail"[22] of Eero's design, which had a pinwheel plan similar to Kingswood's but with more abstract, geometric elevations.[23] His success marked an important first step toward making a name for himself independently of his father.

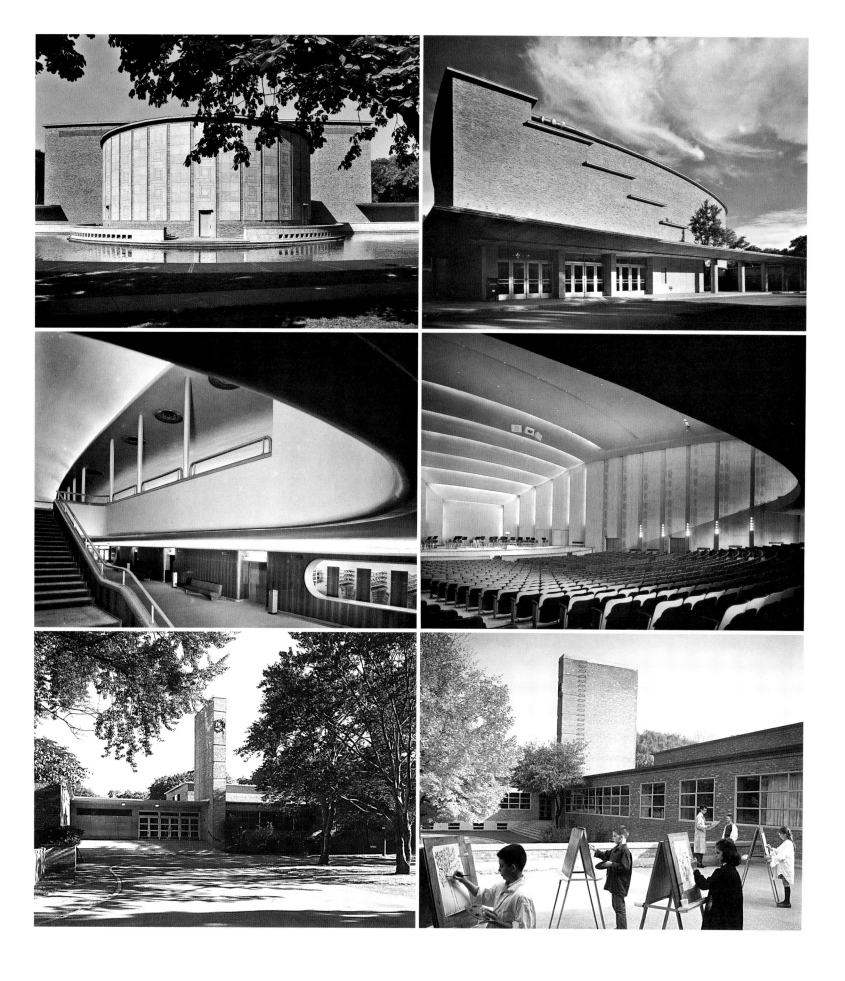

The competition, which had been sponsored by the Museum of Modern Art and *Architectural Forum* magazine, was the first American competition expressly for a modern academic building. It coincided with the arrival of Walter Gropius, Mies van der Rohe, and other prominent European modern architects in America and the simultaneous adoption of modern curricula in the architecture schools at Harvard (where Gropius went to teach) and Columbia. A professor of art, Esther Seaver, seems to have been the catalyst for the competition. She enlisted support from various authorities, secured permission from the college president, the trustees, Museum of Modern Art director Alfred Barr, and the influential Time publication, *Architectural Forum*. Professor Seaver also served on the jury, along with Walter Curt Behrendt, John Wellborn Root, TVA engineer Roland Wank, Stanley McCandless of the Yale Drama School, MoMA curator of architecture John McAndrew, Edward Durell Stone, and George Nelson from *Architectural Forum*. Although the competition was open to anyone, four architects were invited to enter and paid four hundred dollars each to do so: Gropius, William Lescaze, Richard Neutra, and the lesser-known Detroit school architects Maynard Lyndon and Eberle Smith. None of them won (victory went to a pair of young Americans, Richard M. Bennett and Caleb Hornbostel, who, like Saarinen, was the son of a prominent architect and working for Bel Geddes). Gropius and his Bauhaus colleague Marcel Breuer received the second prize. Lyndon and Smith won one of the three fifth prizes, as did Percival Goodman and twenty-eight-year-old Eero. Neutra received honorable mention, as did George Howe, Gordon Bunshaft (with his collaborator Robert A. Green), G. Holmes Perkins and Frances W. Hartwell, the only woman among the winners.

When he returned to Bloomfield Hills in the summer of 1938, Eero entered an invited competition for a campus plan and college library for Goucher College in Baltimore with his father, Ralph Rapson, and other young architects from Cranbrook. The architects invited to compete ranged from traditionalists like McKim, Mead & White and Ralph Adams Cram to the newly arrived European Modernists. It attracted only thirty-five entries. The jury for this new campus, which was eventually built, did not have a Modernist bias.[24] For that reason, Gropius withdrew and urged the other Modernists, except the Saarinens, to do so, too (only George Howe actually did). The jurors honored the faculty's request for informal, functional buildings that respected the landscape, with no concern for style. Each of the four winners took a different approach.[25] The Saarinens' scheme, which won second prize, was

composed of low, T-shaped buildings forming an elongated central courtyard and respecting the existing terrain. It was anchored by a rather massive library that had a semicircular reading room with glass walls and rows of little punched square windows similar to those that became popular in the Postmodern period of the 1980s (when Eliel's work was much admired again). Still, it was lighter and more in line with the International Style than the first-place winner by Moore and Hutchins, which resembled Frank Lloyd Wright's Prairie Houses, but it was more traditional than the schemes submitted by Harrison and Fouilhoux, Lescaze, and Neutra, all of which failed to win.

The next year, Eero won first prize in an important competition for a theater and fine arts building at the College of William and Mary in Williamsburg, Virginia. He was not even planning to enter until he saw sketches that Rapson and Frederic James, a set designer at Cranbrook, were making for it. Suddenly, he changed his mind and asked if he could join them—demonstrating his abilities as a talent scout and skillful collaborator. The scheme they submitted in late 1938 is more like the one Saarinen created for Wheaton on his own than like the one they had worked on together with Eliel for Goucher. It engages a lake and the terrain more emphatically, and it has more expressive volumes, like those of the Wheaton winner by Bennett and Hornbostel—more evidence that Eero knew a good idea when he saw it. The crisp, light-filled volumes of Saarinen, Rapson, and James's Williamsburg Festival Theater and Fine Arts Building were never built, but they helped make a name for Eero (and Rapson) when the winning designs were exhibited at the 1939 New York World's Fair, the Museum of Modern Art, and ten other institutions.[26] The competition was published in the *New Yorker* and *Time*.[27] And even though, as at Wheaton, the deck was stacked in favor of Modernists because of the makeup of the jury, the victory was significant since there were more than 122 entries, many from such well-known architects as Philip L. Goodwin and Edward Durell Stone (architects of the Museum of Modern Art, who came in second), Richard Neutra and Hugh Stubbins (who both won honorable mentions), Gropius and Breuer, Harrison and Fouilhoux, and Keck and Keck (none of whom placed).[28]

The William and Mary building (sometimes also called the National Theater) was to have been built where the first theater in America had been located and managed by the American National Theater and Academy, a short-lived institution chartered by an act of Congress in 1935 to reinvigorate the legitimate theater, which had been devastated by the Depression. Its president and founder was A. Conger Goodyear, who was also president of the Museum of Modern Art at the time, and its advisory board was composed of "a veritable Who's Who in American Theater."[29] The dean of the Harvard Graduate School of Design, Joseph Hudnut, wrote the program for the competition, and the professional adviser was Kenneth Stowell, the editor of *House Beautiful* and, later, of *Architectural Record*, so it provided some very useful contacts.

Saarinen and Saarinen

Although none of the competitions led to commissions, they were all covered in the magazines.[30] Keeping the Saarinen name before the public and meeting influential people—along with Eliel's considerable achievement at Cranbrook (which was widely published too)—eventually paid off.

Eliel had been friends with the composers Gustav Mahler and Jean Sibelius in Finland, and he became acquainted with the Russian-born conductor of the Boston Symphony Orchestra, Serge Koussevitzky, who invited him to develop a master plan for the orchestra's new summer home at the Berkshire Symphonic Festival, Tanglewood, in Lenox, Massachusetts, in 1937. The next year Eliel designed a fan-shaped, clear-span, board-and-batten pavilion to seat six thousand with a low, flat roof and an open-ended rear wall so that as many as twelve thousand more listeners on the lawn could become part of the audience. But when he heard the size of the budget, he told the trustees that all they could build was a shed, so the building came to be known as the "Tanglewood Shed" (now officially called the Koussevitzky Shed). Because Eliel refused to compromise on its design, it was actually constructed by another architect, Joseph Franz, with a forest of thin steel columns in the interior; but the overall feeling of the rustic wood structure with a dirt floor and basic benches was what he intended and what still gives Tanglewood its unique character.[31]

Around the same time (1938), Koussevitzky recommended Eliel to a group in Buffalo that wanted to build a new music center. They had even hired a local firm, Kidd & Kidd, but had begun to have second thoughts about the firm's rather old-fashioned work. Soon the group brought in the newly formed firm of Saarinen and Saarinen to produce a more modern scheme for the Kleinhans Music Hall, though Kidd and Kidd remained involved as local architects. Charles Eames and Ralph Rapson joined the team, which produced a building with three up-to-date, acoustically impressive halls of three sizes. One is just a tiny rehearsal hall; the larger two are shaped specifically to accommodate sound and are wrapped in a curved yellow brick shell. The exterior has patterned brickwork and a reflecting pool, like Eliel's buildings at Cranbrook, but the big curved shapes, which express interior volumes, are more modern, sculptural, and typical of Eero. (Eliel was fond of noting the similarity to a violin, which takes its shape from its purpose.) The influence of Normal Bel Geddes is apparent in the streamlined lobby between the two largest halls, on two levels. It has wood-paneled walls with curved cutouts for concessions, built-in benches supported on Plexiglas horizontal planes that appear to float, and cove lighting

concealed behind glass tubelike elements. The building, completed in 1940, does not have a clearly defined front entrance; the doors are wedged between the two fan-shaped halls, and it is hard to grasp the form of the building as a whole from any one point of view. But Koussevitzky called it "the dream of a lifetime—perfect and complete." The violinist Jascha Heifetz described it as "a joy to play in," and the singer Baron Josef von Trapp said, "Never have we given a performance in such a perfectly equipped and masterfully constructed hall."[32] The interior of its stepped-down, wedge-shaped symphony hall was echoed in many of the auditoriums Eero later designed for academic and corporate buildings, including Kresge Auditorium at MIT and the auditoriums at IBM's Yorktown Research Center, Bell Labs, and Deere & Company.

At about the same time, the Chicago firm of Perkins, Wheeler & Will invited the Saarinens to work on an elementary school in the northern suburb of Winnetka, Illinois. The progressive superintendent of schools, Carleton W. Washburne, wanted the new Crow Island School (1939–40) to provide a modern environment suitable for his learn-by-doing educational philosophy, based on the teachings of John Dewey. If the one-story, flat-roofed, asymmetrically planned school does not look unusual today, it is only because it was so influential that its type became the norm.

"Eliel and Eero Saarinen and Perkins, Wheeler & Will, working with a highly creative school administration, designed this building almost as if none had ever been designed before," *Architectural Forum* wrote. "In 1955, Crow Island appears, if anything, more significant than it did 15 years ago [when it opened]."[33] Unlike a traditional, symmetrical, two- or three-story school with a gabled roof and colonnaded entrance intended to function as a neighborhood landmark, the Crow Island School was designed to blend in with nearby houses. Its S-shaped plan that spreads out over a corner site affords each classroom its own outdoor space, visible through oversize windows. The plan and form are modern, but the handmade quality of the brickwork and detailing, created in the studios at Cranbrook, keeps the school from looking industrial the way too many of the schools that arose in its wake do. It even has a menagerie of little ceramic animals by Eero's wife, Lily, crawling all over it. The school was (and is) so highly regarded that Perkins & Will is still considered a major designer of schools today.

In 1939, Saarinen, Swanson, and Saarinen, with Eero in charge, won a federally sponsored competition for a gallery of art to be affiliated with the Smithsonian Institution on the Washington Mall. (Actually, there were three federal competitions held in Eero's lifetime, and he won them all.[34]) The Smithsonian competition had drawn entries from four hundred of the most prominent architects of the time. In winning, the firm showed that "the monumental tradition of Washington can be given

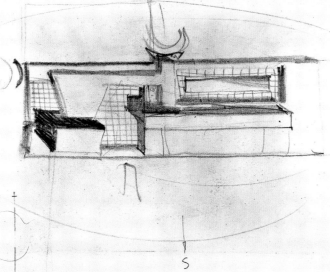

From top: Eero Saarinen, Eliel Saarinen, and J. Robert F. Swanson with model of Smithsonian Art Gallery competition scheme, November 1939; Smithsonian Art Gallery competition scheme, aerial sketch of plan.

appropriate expression and new vitality, within the framework of modern architecture," as *Architectural Forum* proclaimed.[35] It wasn't just talent or experience that led to the prize. The team, which included Charles Eames and Ralph Rapson, made an extraordinary effort. "First Eero thought out the whole thing carefully," Eames recalled, "and then told us the first thing to do would be to make a hundred studies of each element that went into the building. We would then pick the best, and never let our standards fall below that. Then we would make a hundred studies of the combinations of each element. Then we would make a hundred studies of the combinations of combinations. When the whole thing was finished, Eero was almost in tears, because it was so simple. And then, of course, we won the competition."[36]

The Smithsonian design was delicately composed of long, low, thin-walled, rectangular blocks. There was a vertical accent, some applied decoration, and a reflecting pool—all signs that Eliel was very much involved, though in the design's geometric simplicity and boldness, he went farther toward abstraction than he had ever gone before. The project, which was to be a center of contemporary American art, was never built, first because of the onset of World War II and then because Congress repeatedly refused to fund it. But in architectural circles, it was considered a victory for Modernism in America. Actually, the victory

had been pretty much assured by the requirements that entries maintain "a strict adherence to function" and provide "maximum flexibility in the organization of space," and by the jury, which included architects Walter Gropius, George Howe, and John H. Holabird; Harvard dean Joseph Hudnut, a strong advocate of Modernism, was the professional adviser.[37] The competition polarized the architectural profession. Traditionalists saw it as a sign that their values were being undermined by a new establishment. Modernists saw the lack of financial support for the project as evidence of the philistinism of official Washington.[38]

In fact, resistance to modern architecture was not confined to the Capitol (or to the capital). The Saarinens' stark modern design for Hall Auditorium (a building that also had a small theater and an inn) at Oberlin College in Ohio (1941) was not built because faculty members at the otherwise progressive school felt that it was too much of a departure from the Romanesque Revival buildings by Cass Gilbert on their campus.[39]

Ecclesiastical architecture is usually the last bastion of change because people have strong emotional attachments to their churches and do not want to see them altered. But in the little city of Columbus, Indiana, the Saarinens were invited to design a church in 1939 for an ecumenical, nondenominational New Testament Christian congregation, largely because of one woman on the building committee, Nettie Irwin Sweeney Miller, whose family had donated the land. The pristine Tabernacle Church of Christ, built 1940–42, now called the First Christian Church, makes it possible to see what the Smithsonian Art Gallery (and perhaps the Oberlin hall) might have looked like.[40] It, too, is composed of rectangular blocks with strong vertical accents (here in the form of a freestanding, rectangular, 160-foot-tall bell tower) juxtaposed with boxy shapes and long horizontal blocks. But the delicate yellow brickwork, subtle decorative accents, and sensitive siting make it seem much more Scandinavian than International Style. And the way that its classroom wings—which have bands of windows and are raised on pilotis—nestle into the site, below the ground but following the street line around the block, makes it a good neighbor in an old residential area very near the main street. The interior of the 144-foot-long sanctuary, which seats eight hundred but still feels intimate, has whitewashed brick walls, an asymmetrical plan with columns along one side and tall, thin white glass windows along the other. All these elements lead to a single, spare, stainless-steel cross slightly off to one side above the altar, and a porous wooden altar screen much like one Alvar Aalto later installed in the Kaufman conference rooms for the Finnish Cultural Center at the United Nations in New York counters the symmetry further. But what makes it quietly spiritual is its considerable height (forty-five feet) and the way natural light bathes the interior in a celestial glow. All seems silent, even when music is playing. The church's very chasteness may be the reason the congregation embraced it even though it was one of the first modern churches in America.[41]

Visiting the site in Columbus with his father while the church was under way, Eero met the son of the head of the church's building committee, J. Irwin Miller, who had been at Yale just before he was. While Miller's mother and Eero's father met to discuss the building, which sits cattycorner from the Millers' home, the two "youngsters" became good friends. Miller later asked Eero to design two houses, the family bank, and his own church, which had broken away from the original Tabernacle Church of Christ congregation. All four of the Saarinen buildings in Columbus are superb examples of their types.[42]

The Tabernacle Church of Christ commission led to inquiries from other congregations. In 1946, Saarinen, Saarinen, and Associates was invited to design Christ Church, the main Episcopal church in downtown Cincinnati, less than one hundred miles from Columbus. The scheme was published in *Architectural Forum* in December 1949, though the church was not built; however, a modern one strongly influenced by the design was later constructed by local architects. The next year, in

Minneapolis, where Eliel had designed an octagonal, skylit Christian Science Church in 1925 that was never built, the firm was asked to design a church with Hills, Gilbertson and Hayes Architects, that was executed between 1948 and 1949. Christ Church Lutheran resembles the building in Columbus, with its blocky forms, separate bell tower, brick interior walls (unpainted here), asymmetrical interior focused on the altar, and subtle lighting. It has the same serenity and stark Scandinavian elegance.[43] The year it was completed, Saarinen, Swanson, and Saarinen published three versions of a project for the First Baptist Church in Flint, Michigan, with a similar character. One had a coffin-shaped plan with the Sunday-school classrooms located below the sanctuary.[44]

The client for another of Eero's houses (he designed very few) was the contractor who had built the Tabernacle Church of Christ, A.C. Wermuth. Although it was Eliel who had worked with him over the years, the house in Fort Wayne, Indiana, by Saarinen and Saarinen owes as much to the son as to the father (as well as a good deal to Frank Lloyd Wright). The A.C. Wermuth Residence (1941–42) spreads out over the land on a hilly site to maximize views through picture windows. Rooms flow into one another, and fieldstone walls connect interior and exterior spaces. Materials typical of the area, such as stone and clapboard (which Gropius and Breuer also used in their American houses), are combined with modern ones, such as reinforced concrete and large modular sheets of glass.

During World War II, Saarinen, Swanson, and Saarinen designed a number of master plans and workers' housing for defense plants. The Defense Housing for Kramer Homes in Center Line, Michigan (1941–42), resembled some of the town plans that Eliel had done in Finland during World War I. Vehicles were restricted to an elliptical loop around a central open space with a school, a park, and playgrounds, while short streets led to parking lots in the surrounding neighborhoods. Groups of attached one- and two-story houses faced walkways with service drives in the back. The 477 flat- or gable-roofed houses were arranged in staggered rows and set either at right angles, on diagonals, or in semicircles around the open center. The efficient one- to three-bedroom units were built for an average of $3,075.[45] Since they had to be erected quickly and cheaply, Eero was able to experiment with prefabrication and modular construction.

The firm also designed dormitories for three thousand workers at a bomber plant intended to become part of a planned community of six thousand families in Willow Run, Michigan, southwest of Detroit (1942–43). Both plans were extensively published.[46] Although the more ambitious plan for Willow Run was never realized, *Architectural Forum* ran an eighteen-page article on it "because it accepts in a realistic and economical manner the existence of the automobile and establishes

the level on which planners, builders, realtors, and investors will have to compete in the postwar period." The article noted the "separation of pedestrian and automobile traffic" and observed that the commercial area "would have presented an appearance vastly different from and superior to the usual congested shopping street." Though the plan went through various revisions and the number of neighborhoods was reduced from five to three, its essential features, such as a surrounding greenbelt and "schools which provided a social as well as architectural center," were preserved. The authors concluded that "the town of Willow Run is the most workable and most human guide to the integrated community produced to date."[47]

When Eero joined Donald McLaughlin and other Yale classmates in Washington, DC, as a civilian consultant to the Office of Strategic Services (OSS)—the precedessor of the CIA—in 1943, he opened a small branch of the Saarinen office there to do work for the National Capital Housing Authority. The office's Lincoln Heights Housing Center (c. 1943–44) has long, low, gabled housing blocks integrated with the land. It offered Eero a chance to investigate new technologies with such young architects as John Harkness and Norman Fletcher, who had been students of Walter Gropius at Harvard and went on to found the Architects Collaborative with him in Cambridge, Massachusetts, after the war.

At the OSS, (an organization that competed with Hitler's propaganda machine), where Dan Kiley, Oliver Lundquist, and some of Eero's other friends were also working, he designed a curve-walled War Room for the White House, put together a booklet on *Army Personnel Control, Troop Basis and Accounting System*,[48] with sans serif type, swaths of primary color, and numerous diagrams and flowcharts, prefiguring the graphic representation that became stylish after World War II, and became a Department Chief in charge of all Agency's visual communication. [49]

Crisis at Cranbrook

The war work, the war itself, and internal politics at Cranbrook also changed the way Eliel Saarinen practiced architecture and paved the way for the very different kind of practice Eero would inherit. At the end of 1941, George Booth suddenly demanded that Eliel move his office off campus and fired Eero. During Christmas week, Booth sent Eliel a type-written letter:

4. Breaking Away: First Independent Projects and Furniture Designs

Few sons or daughters of famous artists grow up to equal their parents' achievements. For that matter, very few major architects are able to groom anyone the way that Eliel Saarinen did his son—and not only his son, though Eero was his most successful pupil. Frank Lloyd Wright, who modeled his Taliesin workshop partly on Cranbrook,[1] never produced a student who achieved the recognition Eero Saarinen did. That was partly because Eliel was a generous teacher, whereas Wright, with his larger-than-life personality and talent, dominated his students, who became unpaid (or paying) employees in his practice. Cranbrook, of course, differed from Taliesin in other important ways. It offered a variety of visual arts, and even though Eliel designed Cranbrook and attracted most of the artists and students, he served at the behest of his patron. Still, the school did provide the kind of mutually stimulating environment that both he and Booth had intended.

One of the first students at Cranbrook, Carl Feiss, described what made it work: "Eliel was constantly wandering in and out [of the studios]. . . . He never gave what, in common architecture school parlance, would be called a 'crit.'" . . . His genius as a teacher was to make it appear that he believed that we knew as much about architecture as he did. . . .

Since we knew that that was nonsense, we did everything we could to prove that it wasn't nonsense. The result was that we all worked harder and learned more in our few years at Cranbrook than ever before (or probably after)."[2]

Eero, of course, had been exposed to this technique all his life, but at Cranbrook he was also surrounded by interesting and energetic young people who were now under its spell. And as they branched out, they provided a foil to the powerful, if subtle, influence of his father as well as sounding boards for his own ideas. The students there had many different kinds of talents and the desire to test them. And they were encouraged to bridge the usual professional boundaries, as Eliel always had. Harry Bertoia became a sculptor and a designer; Florence (Shu) Knoll Bassett worked as an interior architect and furniture designer while she built the Knoll International design program; and Charles Eames went on to design everything from books to stage sets.

Eames (1907–78) had practiced architecture in Saint Louis for almost a decade working in traditional styles until a commission for a house in 1936 presented an opportunity to explore a more modern idiom. What he chose to do resembled the buildings at Cranbrook, complete with draperies by Loja.[3] Thus, it is not surprising that he decided to come to Cranbrook to study with Eliel in 1938. When he arrived he branched out into furniture design and began to experiment with other media.

He was appointed instructor of design the next year and joined the Saarinen office part-time. His first marriage (to Catherine Woermann) ended.[4] He began thinking differently about architecture. "It wasn't until I started to work for Eliel Saarinen, and with Eero, that I had any conception of what 'concept' was," Eames admitted.[5] He also met Ray Kaiser, a painter who had studied with Hans Hofmann. She became his second wife in 1941 and his partner as radical all-purpose designers.

"Charlie," as Eero called him, began to share Eero's fascination with new technology, prefabrication, and modular construction, all of which the younger Saarinen saw as necessary for the fast-changing modern world. Eero provided some of the impetus for Charlie's experimentation, and Charlie stimulated him in return. The designer Niels Diffrient—who came to Cranbrook to study painting after World War II, switched to architecture, and then worked for Eero in the early 1950s—remembers Eero as "very somber and solid," except when "Charlie was around, he was more bubbly. The two of them would just pass ideas, like sparring."[6]

In 1939 Eero and Eames created a lightweight tensile structure for an exhibition of faculty work at Cranbrook, an architectonic installation that daringly suspended long wooden planes to divide the space with surfaces for the display of superimposed images.[7] It was Eero and Charles's first collaboration and a harbinger of Charles and Ray Eames's influential installations of the 1940s and 1950s.[8]

Their efforts earned national recognition in 1940 when their team—which included Cranbrook colleagues Ray Kaiser Eames, Don Albinson, and Harry Bertoia—won two first prizes in a competition for "Organic Design in Home Furnishings," sponsored by the Museum of Modern Art. One prize was for a homey wooden version of the modular metal cabinets Marcel Breuer had created at the Bauhaus. The other was for double-curved chairs similar to Alvar Aalto's bent plywood ones, but softer and more sculpturesque, with the wiggly forms of Surrealist art and an imminent Abstract Expressionism. The plywood-shell chairs were covered with foam-rubber padding and upholstered with fabric designed by Marli Ehrman, which won first prize in the woven-fabric category. Both

the chairs and storage units had a lightness that made them suitable for a modern house. The easy-to-pack-and-ship chests, domesticated with Honduras mahogany veneer and simple cubic indentations that functioned as pulls, came in various sizes and configurations based on an eighteen-inch module. They were equipped with interchangeable shelves, drawers, and doors, and they could be set directly on the floor or raised on thirteen-inch legs, which made it easier to clean under them or to place them against a wall with baseboards. The system carried the principle of standardization farther than had any others produced in the United States before. The chairs were actually manufactured by the Haskelite Corporation and the Heywood-Wakefield Company, with a few subtle changes, such as wooden legs instead of aluminum ones. But because of the onset of World War II, they were never mass-produced and marketed.[9] Still, they influenced furniture that both Eero and the Eameses, separately, would later create for the market.

Eero also designed whole buildings for mass production. In 1940, the United States Gypsum Company hired him to devise new uses for their products, and he and Ralph Rapson came up with what they called a Demountable Space, intended to serve as a community center. The building, which looked assertively experimental, could be reconfigured or expanded in modular units. Its tensile roof hung from a central mast similar to that on Buckminster Fuller's Dymaxion House (1927–30); pipes for plumbing and heating were contained in prefabricated cores.

The next year, Eero arrived at another idea for manufactured housing. The Unfolding House (c. 1942) was to be made of modular trailer units that could be shipped to a site and arranged in various combinations. Its shimmering, gently curved metallic roof could unroll to spread over additional space when it was needed.[10] Its prestressed metal skin prefigured the use of a similar surface on the Saint Louis Gateway Arch (1947–65).[11]

Like his father, Eero was fascinated by the way buildings were made. But instead of taking an Arts and Crafts approach, using traditional materials and producing beautifully crafted objects, he wanted to explore new technology, structural forms, mass production, and industrial processes, the way Le Corbusier and the architects at the Bauhaus had talked about doing—not only to produce housing and furniture inexpensively on a large scale, but to create a radically new kind of architecture. These were concerns that his father and brother-in-law did not share but that some of his young Cranbrook colleagues did.

The opportunity to break out of traditional ways of doing things is what persuaded Eero's old friend Florence (Shu) Schust to quit her day job as an architect in the office of Wallace Harrison[12] soon after she started moonlighting for Hans Knoll. The German-born son of a family of furniture manufacturers, Knoll had started a new company and hired her to create showrooms to help customers see how modern furniture would look in domestic settings. Modern design had begun to catch on in Germany before the war, but the leading architects from the Bauhaus had come to America as the Third Reich gained power, so Knoll expected Modernism to take root in the United States. Little did he know that he would happen on such a direct connection to some of its best talents. Soon after he met Shu, she started working with him full-time, fell in love with him, and married him in 1946. (Eero had advised her not to, because he was afraid, rightly, that the dashing young European would remain too much of a ladies' man.)

Almost immediately Shu and Eero started developing a chair that evolved out of the one he had designed with Charles Eames for the MoMA show. "He was like a brother," Knoll Bassett recalls, "and since . . . we talked a lot, one thing led to another in the development of his furniture. His first piece was laminated wood because we weren't able to get other materials. It was the only laminated chair he did." The Grasshopper Chair (1943), with its bent wood arms "was a perfectly nice chair, but it wasn't one of the great successes."[13]

Shu's business and Eero's career as a furniture designer developed in tandem. "The beginnings were very tough," she says. "Not only was it difficult to get contemporary work, but it was extremely difficult to get the furniture produced once we had the client. Everything was difficult. Fabrics were difficult. Even the glues were inferior. The only material available at the time was wood. Everything was on a wartime basis. We had to use lots of ingenuity to get anything produced at all."

The Grasshopper Chair led to Eero's experiments with molded fiberglass furniture. "His plan was to do a whole series of fiberglass chairs," Knoll Bassett remembers. "I said, 'Why not take the bull by the horns and do the big one first?' and that's what happened. Eero developed the Womb Chair [1946–48]. This was at my specific request because I was sick and tired of structured chairs which held you in one position. I said I wanted a chair which was like a basket full of pillows, something I could curl up in. Eero designed the chair and did the prototype . . . He worked with the molds himself."

He even helped her find a New Jersey shipbuilder working in fiberglass whom they persuaded to create some models. "He was very skeptical," Knoll Bassett remembers. "I guess because we were so young and so enthusiastic and because we just begged him so much, he finally gave in and worked with us. We had lots of problems and failures before we finally got a chair that would work."[14]

This page, from left: Eero Saarinen, Pedestal Table for Knoll International, 1955–57; Eero Saarinen, Number 71 Armchair for Knoll International, c. 1950, aluminum with black painted and chrome finish, steel, wood, and leather upholstery.

Opposite: Sketches for Pedestal Chair, c. 1955; model in Pedestal Chair, c. 1957.

Diffrient, who was working for Eero as a model maker when the chairs were designed, explained, "He came at a solution by process of elimination. . . . You got what you got by throwing away everything that wasn't as good—but you tried everything. I had thought it was going to be a simple job of doing a chair with him for a month or two, but it was a year's effort."

Diffrient was impressed by Eero's effect on the Knolls. "One day Hans and Shu Knoll turned up. Hans with a camel's hair coat draped over his shoulder, his blond Aryan good looks and tan in the middle of winter, sauntering in. It was the first time I had ever seen people who exuded such a sense of the world." But Shu was part of the family. "What I didn't appreciate was that Eero had an inside track with Knoll. Whatever he produced is what they did."[15]

Eero, Shu, and Charles Eames all absorbed Eliel's sense of the whole. "Perhaps the most important thing I learned from my father," Eero said, "was that in any design problem one should seek the solution in terms of the next largest thing. If the problem is an ashtray, then the way it relates to the table will influence its design. If the problem is a chair, then its solution must be found in the way it relates to the room."[16]

Eero's swooping Pedestal Chairs (with a circular base that narrows into one slim leg and then spreads out again to form a seat) take the form

they do because "the undercarriage of chairs and tables in a typical interior makes an ugly, confusing, unrestful world. I wanted to clear up the slum of legs. I wanted to make the chair all one thing again."[17] The white plastic Pedestal Chairs (sometimes called Tulip Chairs) were to consist of one piece, but in order to make them sturdy enough, the legs had to be made of aluminum with a matching fused plastic finish. Even more handsome, perhaps, than the chairs are the tables designed to complement them, which came in various sizes and heights with ceramo marble tops. The whole group, which dates from the mid-1950s, was made by Knoll.[18]

Furniture gave Eero Saarinen opportunities to experiment with new materials, structural techniques, and manufacturing, all of which he was investigating in the first architectural projects he did on his own or with friends while he was in practice with his father in the 1940s. In 1943, with Oliver Lundquist, he designed the PAC (Pre-Assembled Component) system for Arts & Architecture magazine's Designs for Postwar Living housing competition. That small but lively publication sponsored a whole series of events during and after World War II to help solve, in imaginative ways, the housing crisis that was anticipated when the troops came home. This one was underwritten by twenty-three manufacturers of building materials. Their flat-roofed, glass-walled housing units, composed of packaged service cores that could be variously combined and configured, won first prize.

The architects explained their rationale: "The economic and social demands for postwar housing must be met by extensive utilization of our assembly-line potential. The PAC method exploits the assembly-line integration of all internal fixtures within hulls 3 x 9 meters. The biological and mechanical functions of the home—sleeping, dressing, bathing, cooking, washing, heating and cooling—are standardized and

RELAXATION

ONE QUARTER FULL SIZE

SIDE CHAIR

ONE QUARTER FULL SIZE

CONVERSATION

ONE QUARTER FULL SIZE

SOFA UNIT

ONE QUARTER FULL SIZE

This page: Eero Saarinen, Womb Chair for Knoll
International, 1946–48.

Opposite: Charles Eames and Eero Saarinen, chairs designed
for the "Organic Design in Home Furnishings" exhibition at
the Museum of Modern Art, 1940.

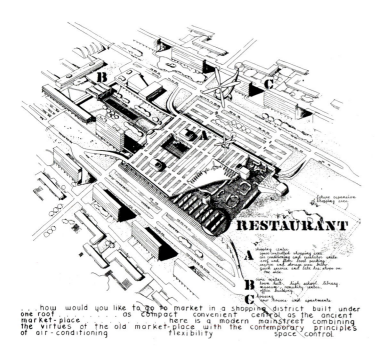

...how would you like to go to market in a shopping district built under one roof ... as compact convenient central as the ancient market-place ... here is a modern mainstreet combining the virtues of the old market-place with the contemporary principles of air-conditioning flexibility space control.

This page, from left: Saarinen, Swanson, and Saarinen, shopping center project, 1944; Serving Suzy restaurant, which was to be located in the shopping center.

Opposite: Eero Saarinen, Unfolding House project, 1942.

incorporated into PAC's 'A' and 'B.' 'A' contains kitchen utility, bath and a single bedroom; 'B', double and single bedrooms and bath. PACs can be used in a variety of combinations: 'A,' 'AB' and 'ABB.' By attaching these units to the living space (which can form a single house or row housing, motels or even a tent) a maximum adaptability is achieved. Because the PAC's can be standardized for a wide variety of climates and income groups, it is estimated that PAC can answer 80 percent of post-war housing demands. The social functions of the home are allowed a greater individuality by virtue of the standardization. . . . Prefabrication methods are adaptable to the living space but local whims may govern."[19]

The next year, Saarinen, Swanson, and Saarinen published designs for a restaurant and gift shop of the same character, sponsored by Pittsburgh Plate Glass and intended for a hypothetical shopping center. Rendered by Eero in the crisp linear style he used in his own submissions, the drawings are accompanied by the statement (stenciled like a cut-out, handwritten, or printed in all lowercase letters): "How would you like to go to market in a shopping district built under one roof as compact, convenient, central as the ancient market-place. Here is a modern main street combining the virtues of the old market-place with the contemporary principles of air-conditioning, flexibility, space control."[20] The idea, which Eero first proposed for the Forum in Helsinki around 1935, does not sound very enticing to anyone who has been to a modern shopping mall, but it was a visionary concept at the time, and it is shown with its roof pulled away, in the midst of a Corbusian new town complete with two-level roadways, long, narrow housing blocks, and a heliport. As the architects explained, the under-one-roof shopping center

"was entirely enclosed, with parking areas both on the roof and at ground level."[21]

The Serving Suzy restaurant (1944), however, still seems fresh, with its oversize lettering, wide-open spaces, and columns slicing through roof planes. The idea was that "the cafeteria comes to the customer rather than vice versa." A big wheeled serving cart, akin to the mobile lounges Eero designed later for Dulles Airport (1958–63), was intended to "simplify the service and let each customer actually see the food he is ordering and have it served, while avoiding the necessity of standing in line as in a cafeteria. Another advantage derived from the Serving Suzy is that customers come in and sit down at available places without encountering the common cafeteria difficulty of finding oneself all equipped with a loaded tray and no place to put it."[22]

For the same imagined shopping center, the architects envisioned a gift shop (1944) with multiple levels separated by ramps, where different types of merchandise would be displayed. There was even a revolving turntable where craftsmen could be seen at work. The front and rear walls were to be made entirely of glass, inviting views through the whole shop from one entrance to the other. Display tables with free-form shapes, gridded lightweight hung ceilings, and stocky columns gave the shop a perky, updated Corbusian air very different from the solid, sober rectangles the firm was producing at the time for projects such as the Veterans Memorial Building in Lapeer, Michigan (1946).[23]

In 1945 Eero created designs with Charles and Ray Eames for the Museum of Modern Art exhibition "Integrated Building: Planning Kitchen, Bathroom And Storage Space," which also included projects by Brooks Cavin, Huson Jackson, George Nelson, and Henry Wright.

The most exciting and best-known schemes Eero worked on at the time, however, were the two houses he designed with Charles Eames for *Arts & Architecture*'s Case Study House program,[24] which was initiated by the same visionary editor, John Entenza, who had sponsored the PAC system competition in 1943. Entenza had purchased *California Arts & Architecture* in 1938. Two years later, he changed its name (eliminating the "California"), brought in Herbert Matter (who had been at Cranbrook) and Alvin Lustig to redesign it, turned away from the eclectic array of projects the magazine had been publishing, and focused the editorial program on experimental modern design. Using his own inheritance to underwrite it, he continued to edit *Arts & Architecture* for the next thirty-seven years.[25]

Various institutions tried to encourage creative thinking to help meet anticipated postwar housing needs. The Museum of Modern Art in New York held fourteen exhibitions on houses between 1933 and 1955, some with full-scale mock-ups in the sculpture garden. *Arts & Architecture* not only sought designs for thirty-six experimental houses over a twenty-one-year period (1945–1966) but also published them, built them, found owners for them, and opened most of them to the public.

The majority of the houses were in or around Los Angeles and designed by some of the most talented up-and-coming architects of the time (Richard Neutra, Eero Saarinen and Charles Eames, William Wurster and Theodore Bernardi, Craig Ellwood, Pierre Koenig, Ralph Rapson, and Raphael Soriano). And although innovations in technology and mass production actually occurred more on the East Coast and in rather traditional-looking houses (principally in the Levittown communities on Long Island and in Pennsylvania), adventurous modern houses were more popular in southern and northern California, where Eichler Homes produced similar experimental dwellings. But the influence of the Case

Study House program was by no means confined to the West Coast or to *Arts & Architecture*'s readership. The houses were published in other magazines, partly because they were so outstanding and partly because Entenza's assistant, Susan Jones, who spoke three languages, made a point of keeping in touch with editors around the world, at a time when an international perspective was far less common than it is today.

The two Case Study Houses that Eero Saarinen and Charles Eames designed together in 1945—Numbers 8 and 9 (all the houses were numbered)—were intended for adjacent sites on a five-acre plot of land in Pacific Palisades that Entenza had purchased for the program. (Case Study Houses Number 18 by Rodney Walker and Number 20 by Richard Neutra, both of 1947–48, are also located on that parcel.) And though Numbers 8 and 9, which overlook the Pacific Ocean, are within shouting distance of one another, they were designed to provide privacy for the two owners in a natural-looking landscape.

The two Saarinen and Eames houses are effectively foils for one another. Number 9, which was designed for Entenza himself and built in 1949, is a compact, square, rearrangeable one-story retreat for a bachelor and planned to accommodate parties. It is set directly on the ground. Number 8, intended for Charles and Ray Eames, was designed to be what we would call today a "live-work space." Its long, narrow, open-walled, steel-framed box straddled the space between a pair of slender steel columns and high ground on the sloping site.[26] Although they were the first steel-framed buildings in the Case Study House series, the structure was hidden behind walls in the Entenza house but prominently exposed in the one built for the Eameses. Entenza's was built largely as designed and published, but Charles and Ray Eames altered theirs substantially during construction in 1948, enclosing the open lower level, changing the orientation so that only one end faces the sea, and connecting what had been a freestanding workshop and photo lab to the other end. Having "fallen in love with the meadow," they moved the house to the edge of the site, the way Eliel Saarinen had done with the buildings at Cranbrook. And instead of treating the walls as neutral containers, they filled the frame with panels of different colors, textures, and translucencies.[27]

It was this house that was shown as Number 8, rather than Saarinen and Eames's original design, when the Case Study House program later became the subject of an exhibition and a book-length catalog, even though the original design had been published in *Arts & Architecture* in 1945 and again in 1950 (after the house was built) and appears in literature distributed at the house today.[28] The Eames House, as it is called now, remains much as it appeared when the owners built it and when they died many years later. It is now owned and occupied by their successor firm, the Eames Office.

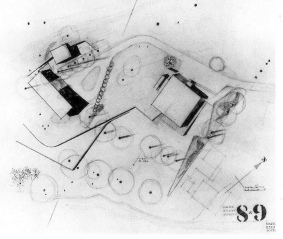

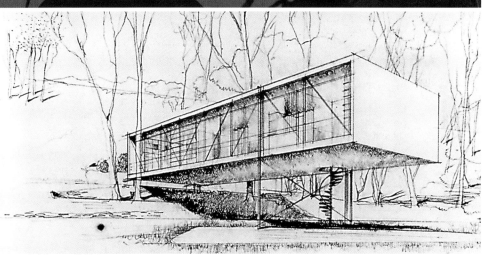

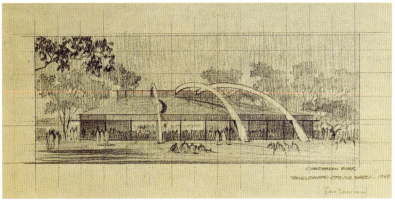

After John Entenza moved out of Number 9, it eventually fell into such disrepair, its view obscured by vegetation, that when the current owners purchased the site to build a new house in 1994, they did not know it had ever held any architectural significance. They were about to demolish it when they learned of its history, and though they went ahead with plans to erect a larger contemporary house in its front yard, they completely restored the Entenza House as an outbuilding.

Now behind the gate of the newer house, it faces the street unprepossessingly. Between a big garage and a wall with a couple of small bedroom windows, the narrow entryway leads into a big, multilevel open space with a curved, built-in couch and a view of the ocean. The entire south-facing wall is glass, and an overhanging roof shelters the terrace, which is continuous with the main living space and the meadow beyond.

Because the architects followed Entenza's directive to experiment with modern industrial materials, the house has a thin quality. Its exterior and interior walls are made of ferroboard, tack-welded to the structural frame. Inside, the walls are finished with plaster, and partitions are made of gypsum board. The color scheme is black, white, and gray, with some browns and tans and an occasional bright accent, such as a red window frame in the kitchen, selected by Ray Eames.[29]

The house occupies a perfect 54-by-54-foot square; but because the space is unevenly divided, its regular shape is not apparent. Service rooms on the north are closed off with fixed walls, while the public spaces on the south open into one another with movable partitions. Progression through the house, which moves from the entrance on the north to the ocean-view terrace, is subtly directed by the arrangement of walls and columns, ceiling panels that run north-south like the path, and several steps that lead downward toward the light and outdoors. The unexposed support system is rather complex: four thirty-one-foot-long structural bays pinwheel around an eight-foot cube in the center. The interior experience could have been even more dynamic: While the house was being designed, Saarinen sent Eames a sketch that suggested more dramatic biomorphic shapes, accented with contrasts in levels and surfaces, but these ideas were not adopted.[30]

art of opera," which he believed had become ossified and provincial in America. The hall's series of parabolic, graduated, laminated wood bowstring trusses, strengthened by tensile rods, not only provided clear-span acoustically shaped roofs for the hall but also looked modern enough to serve as the "laboratory" he wanted. Both halls were what reporters at the time called "severely functional," and, like Eliel's earlier Koussevitzky Shed at the other end of the Tanglewood grounds, they both "opened out onto the lawns permitting out-of-doors audiences far larger than the seating capacity. Several smaller studios, little more than primitive cabins, were also added to the school's facilities" during the summer of 1941. (Although the opera house is still in use, a snow-storm in 1958 destroyed the bowstring trusses, which were replaced with steel ones and a girder designed by a local architect.[31]

In 1949, the year before Eliel died, Saarinen, Saarinen, and Associates was asked to design a tent for the Goethe Bicentennial Convocation and Music Festival, in an Aspen, Colorado, cow pasture. This, too, can be attributed to Eero, who was actively involved with the summer institute at Aspen and who relished the challenges that such a project involved. He designed a flameproof tent to accommodate an audience of two hundred and the entire Minneapolis Symphony Orchestra for only fifty-five thousand dollars (fifteen thousand dollars for the tent and the rest for site work, lighting, and the twenty-three-by-one-hundred-foot building that housed dressing rooms, lavatories, and storage space for the tent during the winter).

Site work involved scooping out an eight-foot-deep well in order to provide clear sight lines to the orchestra, then piling the earth up to four feet around the rim to extend the seating area and create a barrier against outside sounds. On the advice of acousticians Bolt and Beranek, the architects built a pleated plywood band shell on the stage that sloped up to thirty feet, suspended from a network of standard pipe scaffolding. Five floodlights on top of the four main masts lit the interior through the canvas at night without generating heat inside. They made the tent, which echoed the shape of nearby mountains, glow from the outside.

In the Aspen Music Tent, Eero combined his musical heritage, interest in structure, and sculptural sensibility with simple, time-honored materials. With this and other contemporaneous projects, Eero was able to establish himself as a pioneering architect in his own right before he was forty years old—and while his father was still alive.

The differences between Case Study Houses 8 and 9 (and between Saarinen's and Eames's ideas for Number 9) pinpoint the differences between the two collaborators. To Charles Eames, everything, even architecture, was design—the visual effect was preeminent. That is why he and Ray could go on to design books and posters, create stage sets, take photographs, and direct films, as well as continue to design furniture, outdoor spaces, and the occasional building.

To Saarinen, everything, even furniture, was architecture—spatial, sculptural, structural, functional, adaptable, and related to everything around it. He continued to work on projects of increasingly larger scale—whole college-campus plans and five enormous suburban corporate complexes where he was able to develop his interests in industrial materials and processes, modular design, and the relationship between architecture, landscape, and modern life.

Having worked independently may have made it easier for Eero to take the lead on occasional projects, such as the outdoor theaters, designed by the family firm toward the end of his father's life. All were innovative modern structures in rural settings made with traditional materials and a rustic feel.

The first, built in 1941, consisted of a 1,200-seat opera house and a 400-seat chamber music hall at Tanglewood. Although the larger one was often called a "Theater-Concert Hall," it was built primarily for opera because the conductor, Serge Koussevitzky, wanted to "re-create the

Opposite: General Motors Technical Center, Warren, Michigan,
1948–56, water tower and lake with styling dome in distance.

An extraordinary opportunity arrived just as Eero Saarinen was coming into his own as a designer, receiving recognition, and figuring
out how modern technology could create a new kind of architecture.
Initially, however, the project came not to him but to his father, because
of the relatively traditional work he had done in the past.

General Motors was becoming the biggest corporation in America, first
by consolidating and acquiring other companies and then by emphasizing
research and styling to surpass the success of the Ford Motor Company,
which had had a head start in mass production. The officers had named
as their chief of design the flamboyant Hollywood designer Harley Earl,
who gave GM cars their distinctly American look. And they had decided
to consolidate their research and design divisions separately from manufacturing and management, on their own suburban campus. The idea
of having a separate campus for research came from Charles Kettering,
a brilliant inventor who had helped GM introduce starters, efficient fuels,
and practical diesel engines. The GM chairman, Alfred P. Sloan Jr., liked
the idea of consolidating various operations outside Detroit but still
within half an hour of the headquarters, which were also beyond the
city center. Like most American corporate leaders, GM officers were
thinking in terms of plain industrial buildings, especially since they had

a remote location in mind, but Earl managed to convince Sloan that
the architecture should reflect the sense of style and quality of engineering that they were trying to produce. That required a visit to
the nearby Ethyl Corporation laboratories that had been designed by
Albert Kahn, the architect of the GM Corporate Headquarters in Detroit
and of George Booth's mansion at Cranbrook. The Ethyl labs were
anything but startling—more like a modern school than a factory—but
they did have Art Moderne trim and a prominent central entrance that
gave the building a certain dignity. It was enough to convince the
managers, who had worried that handsome buildings might distract
employees, that good ones could actually be stimulating. Convinced
that if they were going to do it, they ought to do it right, they then
talked to prominent architects and people at architectural schools and
found that one name, Eliel Saarinen, came up more often than any
other. He got the job.[1]

It turned out to be quite a commission: a hundred-million-dollar project
with sixty million dollars for the buildings alone, twenty-five of them
edging three sides of a gigantic rectangular lake on a 320-acre campus
that took eight years (1948–56) to design and build. Because the buildings were both technologically and stylistically pioneering, the entire
time the center was under construction, major articles on its architecture
appeared in magazines around the world; when it opened, the company's executives were joined at the ceremonies by President Sukarno

This page, from top: Grouped around the scale model in July 1945 for the newly announced General Motors Technical Center are (left to right) C.F. Kettering (vice president in charge of research), C.K. Wilson (president), C.L. McCuen (vice president in charge of engineering), B.D. Kunkle (vice president), Eero and Eliel Saarinen and J. Robert P. Swanson (Saarinen, Saarinen, and Swanson), Alfred P. Sloan Jr. (chairman), Harley J. Earl (vice president of the styling section), and N.J. Davidson (executive engineer); Bird's eye sketch of the General Motors Technical Center with tall building in lake, 1949, sketch by Glen Paulsen for cover of *Architectural Forum*; Ludwig Mies van der Rohe, Illinois Institute of Technology, Chicago, Illinois, 1939–56, photomontage of preliminary master plan, 1941.

Opposite: Saarinen and Saarinen, proposed General Motors Technical Center, Warren, Michigan, 1945, drawings by Hugh Ferriss.

Indonesia and various high-ranking military officers. Even the president of the United States, Dwight D. Eisenhower, sent a speech to be read in absentia.[2] The influence that the GM Tech Center had on contemporary architecture was enormous.

The commission arrived in December of 1944, even before World War II had ended, but as soon as preliminary plans were prepared (and approved), the then-twenty-million-dollar project (the budget and program grew over time) was put on hold while shortages in building materials subsided and the company prepared for peacetime production.

It was just as well, for the initial scheme, though certainly impressive, was rather outmoded by the time it was done. It was not "another Cranbrook," as Eero once described what the clients had wanted, but it did resemble the General Motors Pavilion that Albert Kahn and Norman Bel Geddes had created for the 1939 World's Fair, where Eero had worked on the Futurama Building with Bel Geddes.[3] Eero, however, had moved on to light, modular construction and geometric forms. In the first GM scheme (1945), clusters of long, low, gently curved buildings are positioned around an almost oval lake, surrounded by a test track. In dramatic aerial perspectives by popular illustrator Hugh Ferriss, the tracks look like the Art Moderne streamlines on some of the buildings that also have sweeping, curved roofs or deep canopies. Other buildings resemble International Style blocks, like those in Saarinen, Swanson, and Saarinen's Smithsonian Art Gallery scheme but lacking their clarity. It was as though Eliel Saarinen and Robert Swanson, who were primarily responsible for the initial design—Eero was still in Washington, though he contributed some drawings—were trying to design the new complex in a version of Eero's style.[4] Although Eero's work, by then, was more direct, there is something romantically futuristic and slightly unreal about the scheme as shown in Ferriss's dramatically lit renderings. They look like movie sets, and it is not clear how the five groups of buildings in the complex would relate to one another. Nevertheless, the idea of this gigantic research complex captivated the press. The alluring drawings

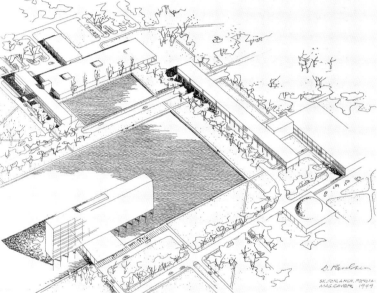

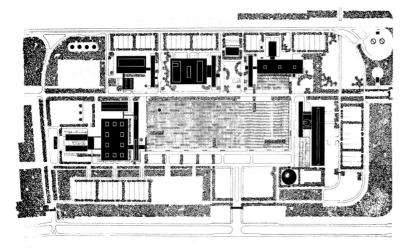

This page: General Motors Technical Center, c. 1948, plan.

Opposite: General Motors Technical Center, 1948–56, aerial view.

of the preliminary design were published in *Architectural Forum*, *Architectural Record*, *Pencil Points*, and *Architect and Engineer* in 1945.[5]

Three years passed before the clients were ready to build and, when they were, the 1945 design turned out to be over budget. By that time, Eero and Eliel had done campus plans for Antioch (1945) and Stephens (1947) colleges, and Drake (1947) university. Robert Swanson had left the firm. Eero had won the competition for the Saint Louis Arch (1947–65). Eliel had won the AIA Gold Medal in 1947 (before Frank Lloyd Wright, Walter Gropius, or Mies van der Rohe) and, at seventy-four, was getting ready to pass the leadership of the firm on to his son, though he would remain involved on a day-to-day basis until he died two years later, and Eero would always consider his advice.

When work on the GM Tech Center resumed in September 1948, Eero was fully in charge. The first thing he did was simplify the scheme. Although he drew, as his father had, on the pioneering Detroit factory buildings of Albert Kahn, he was now more impressed than ever by Mies van der Rohe. He studied the new campus that Mies was building on Chicago's South Side for the Illinois Institute of Technology (IIT) after leaving the Bauhaus, moving to America, and becoming IIT's director of architecture. Eero even went to see him and often asked his advice as the GM project progressed. Mies's exquisitely proportioned disposition of rectangular buildings on a flat, forty-acre site bears a superficial resemblance to what Eero would create in a much larger setting in Michigan, but there are more differences than similarities. All of Mies's buildings are essentially boxes with steel structural frames made visible on their facades. In fact, the exposed steel I-beam "columns" and horizontal beams, contrasted with buff brick or glass infill, are the only ornamentation. With these boxes alone Mies created a subtle composition

of solids and voids. The spaces between the buildings were almost as important as the structures themselves in turning six city blocks in the middle of a dense, decaying slum into a pristine oasis with crisp new buildings spread out over two superblocks. The campus was not even surrounded by fences at first, though American campuses are often gated, especially in urban areas. The school is distinguished by the predominance of space and abstract form. Even the landscaping is sparse. It is an architect's dream, but for the average citizen, it is entirely too subtle, with little incident, color, or relief from the rectangular buildings and the spaces between them.

The GM Tech Center also has long horizontal blocks spread out around a central opening on flat midwestern land, but the resemblance to the IIT buildings almost ends there. The gigantic GM campus is in the middle of a nine-hundred-acre plot, surrounded by land that was still being developed when it was built (and is sprawling even today).

"The Center was, of course, designed at automobile scale," as Eero explained, "and the changing vistas were conceived to be seen as one drove around the project."[6] But there is one dominant organizing element—a man-made rectangular lake, 1,780 feet long and 560 feet wide. It covers twenty-two acres, more than half the size of the whole IIT campus. Some of the buildings around it are very long, though none rises more than three stories, and they are based on a much smaller (five-foot) module than Mies's twenty-four-foot one. Also, the emphasis in the Tech Center building is on the curtain wall instead of on the structural frame, which is dominant at IIT. Because of the glass or porcelain enamel skins on the long walls, the GM buildings shine, and their short ends are covered with colorful glazed bricks that help distinguish one division from another, in bright red, dark red, dark blue, light blue, tangerine, orange, intense yellow, and gray. There is variety within the complex because functional elements like the numerous exhaust stacks on the two Dynamometer buildings are emphasized through color (bright blue paint) and exaggeration (the stacks are quite tall).

Eero even gave the center the character of an automobile. "General Motors is a metal-working industry; a precision industry; a mass-production industry," he said. "Thus, the design is based on steel—the metal of the automobile. Like the automobile itself, the buildings are essentially put together, as on an assembly line, out of mass-produced units. And, down to the smallest detail, we tried to give the architecture the precise, well-made look which is a proud characteristic of industrial America."

An earlier scheme featured a ten-story administration building that Saarinen believed "gave the project a strong, vertical focal point. When

that building was dropped from the program, we sought vertical focal points in other ways. Where the administration building would have been, we put the great fountain, a 115-foot-wide, 50-foot-high wall of moving water. Then, instead of hiding the water tower, we designed it to be a proud 132-foot-high, stainless-steel-clad spherical shape and set it in the pool as a vertical accent in the whole composition. The water ballet with its playing jets, by Alexander Calder, is another visual accent."

Like his father, he used water, landscaping, and art to enhance the composition, only here the art is more modern and the verticals are emphatically functional. Besides the dancing Calder fountain, there is a huge abstract sculpture, *Bird in Flight*, by Antoine Pevsner, and a thirty-six-foot-long shimmering screen between the restaurant entrance and dining area, made by Eero's friend from Cranbrook, Harry Bertoia. The hemispherical Styling Dome, where cars could be displayed, has a reflective stainless-steel skin and thus provides another accent. The built area is surrounded by thirteen thousand trees, and beyond them is a fence with a gate house, so that the complex, quite unlike at IIT, is impenetrable. No one can enter without permission.

The other main difference is that while Mies's buildings outwardly symbolize modern technology (they wear their structural systems on

their sleeves, so to speak), the Tech Center actually is high-tech for its time. "One of the things we are proudest of," Eero said, "is that working together with General Motors, we developed many 'firsts.' I think that this is part of the architect's responsibility."

"We had previously used a baked enamel-finished panel on the Pharmacy Building at Drake University, which may well have been the very first instance of the now so familiar metal curtain wall. But General Motors represents the first significant installation of laminated panels and the first use anywhere of a uniquely thin [2 1/2-inch-thick] porcelain-faced sandwich panel which is a complete prefabricated wall for both exterior and interior. For the project we also developed the brilliantly colored glazed brick. The ceilings in the drafting rooms are the first developed completely luminous ceilings using special modular plastic pans. Perhaps the greatest gift to the building industry is the development of the neoprene gasket weather seal [similar to those used in windshields], which holds fixed glass and porcelain enamel metal panels to their aluminum frames. It is truly windproof and waterproof and is capable of allowing the glass or panels to be 'zipped' whenever a building's use changes. All of these developments have become part of the building industry and a common part of the language of modern architecture."

The light pans in the ceiling grid could be shaded with diffusers or covered for different lighting effects. The air-conditioning system was also incorporated into the ceiling grid of the office spaces, as were the electrical outlets, which alternated with sprinkler heads. And the ceiling grid itself was coordinated with the structural grid, the sprinkler nodes, and the air-conditioning so that it could provide anchor posts for the movable partition system, insuring that the partitions would be aligned with the grid.[7] It was the completely controlled environment that became the norm for American corporate office space and is being reevaluated in the early twenty-first century, when natural light and fresh air from operable windows are valued again, partly because they save energy.

Eero Saarinen and his associates worked closely with the scientists and engineers at the Technical Center on these innovations. One of the things they learned was the way the automobile industry used large-scale models, mock-ups, and test assemblies in the design process. The architects used these same techniques at GM to test sections of the curtain wall and other parts of the buildings at full scale and went on to make that kind of testing part of their office practice.

Eero's Office

Something like the scientific method of trial and error—with many, many trials—was very much a part of Eero Saarinen's office procedure. Just as he would make countless drawings for every aspect of a competition design, he had his associates work on dozens of studies for every detail of every building.

Robert Venturi worked in Saarinen's office from 1951 until the middle of 1953, when the GM Tech Center was being designed. "I worked on one of the buildings just to the left of the restaurant. By that time the vocabulary had been established, a kind of Miesian vocabulary. The one place where there was some variation among the buildings was in the entrance pavilions, so that was the main thing I did," Venturi remembers. "The way you worked with him, was he sat down (after he gave you an assignment) and then he didn't see you for maybe two or three weeks. You were to come up with options, which is not a bad way of working. I came up with a number of ideas which were pretty good, but he didn't seem to like any of those, particularly, which is all right."[8]

At the time, Venturi objected to the fact that "each of Eero's buildings was different. When I left, he very nicely called me into his office and asked if I had anything to say about how the office worked. I was rather frank and said that the fact that he did not have a singular approach, I took that as a sign of weakness. Well, now I don't necessarily agree with that idea. I think Saarinen was heading where we were in questioning the tenets of Modernism, but he wasn't saying that so I feel that his kind of questions weren't as useful as ours."

Saarinen may not have been questioning the tenets of the Modern Movement so much as carrying them to a logical extreme. Venturi points out that "there were approximately forty people in the office then, and everybody was a productive architect, except Joe Lacy (the manager), one bookkeeper, one secretary, and a chauffeur who did errands. Compare that to today," he stresses, "when half the people would be doing marketing or public relations or something. It tells you something about America in general."

Those forty people were involved solely in the design of the buildings. Like many famous architects (and like Eliel), they did not make construction documents (working drawings) for GM, though they did make them later for other projects. In the early 1950s, they were done for Saarinen's office by Smith, Hinchman & Grylls, a Detroit architectural and engineering firm where Minoru Yamasaki was chief of design. Yamasaki, who became one of the best-known architects in the world, eventually left that firm but stayed in Detroit to practice on his own and remained a close friend of Saarinen's.

The architects in Saarinen's office worked extraordinarily long hours, especially for the 1950s, when most people worked from nine to five. Kevin Roche, who as chief of design coordinated the efforts of all the designers—and later, with John Dinkeloo, inherited the practice when Saarinen died—said they would work eight to twelve hours a day, "every day of the year, no holidays." What impressed Roche most was Saarinen's "extraordinary dedication. He was able to focus on a problem with great intensity. He could draw a scheme faster than anyone could think about it and then throw it away and go on. He would come up with hundreds and hundreds of possibilities in order to arrive at something. He never stopped working even when the project was in working drawings, or when it was under construction; he constantly tried to improve it"[9]

The day Gunnar Birkerts came to talk to Saarinen about a job, he waited until three o'clock in the morning before he was interviewed.[10] Birkerts had grown up in Latvia and been educated in Germany. The architects in Saarinen's office had come from all over the world. Venturi, Dinkeloo, Paul Kennon, and Charles Bassett were Americans; Roche was from Ireland; Cesar Pelli was from Argentina; Anthony Lumsden was English but had been educated in Australia; and Olav Hammarström was from Finland and had come to the United States to work with Alvar Aalto on the Baker House dormitories at MIT. All these people

This page: General Motors Technical Center, enclosed
pedestrian bridge.

Opposite: General Motors Technical Center, Administration
Building staircase and lobby with furniture designed by
Eero Saarinen and Florence (Shu) Knoll Bassett.

went on to have successful careers. After GM was published, architects
flocked from Japan and other countries—and in greater numbers. 11

While the GM project was under way, the firm left the old school
building into which Eliel had moved his office when he was forced to
leave Cranbrook, purchased a small plot of land in Bloomfield Hills,
and built a modest version of the laboratories Eero was designing for
GM. It was a two-story, "brick-ended, wood and glass" building adorned
with "some of the simplest detailing anyone is likely ever to find in an
architect-designed structure," as *Architectural Forum* said at the time.

"Drafting-room windows by-pass beams, [and] reach to the ceiling, which
is also the bottom of the roof planking and hence within 4 inches of the
roof top. This creates a wonderfully thin roof line. Conduit for fluorescent
lights is exposed along the ceiling but the combination is efficiently
sophisticated: the wood beams mask the fluorescents from glaring by
putting blinders on them. The building is oriented with its long axis east
and west, putting most of the glass north. These simple wood connections would be enough to scare the nails off of most journeymen carpenters. [Alex Gow was the brave contractor.] The beams are joined to the
columns merely by notching plus lag-screws through into the end grain,
and although this is the kind of technique visible in some of our oldest,
strongest barns, you don't see it much in today's office buildings."12

The office space was constructed for twelve dollars per square foot,
which was very little even then. Although most architects of his generation built houses for themselves but rented office space in existing

This page: Eero Saarinen and Kevin Roche using GM technology to design TWA models at the Eero Saarinen and
Associates office, 1957.

Opposite: General Motors Technical Center studio with ceiling
grid containing diffusers for different lighting effects, electrical
outlets, air-conditioning ducts, and sprinkler heads.

buildings, Saarinen, who virtually lived at the office, did just the opposite.
He lived—or rather his wife and children lived—in a big brick Victorian
house in Bloomfield Hills that he had modernized. The office space he
created was simply functional, but it demonstrated what his work was
about—innovation integrally tied to the art of building. It was different
from Eliel's home studio in Finland, where Eero had "grown up under a
drafting table," as he put it, or Cranbrook, where he had begun his
career. Time and circumstances had dealt him a very different hand
(greater opportunities but also more intense demands), and he played
it zealously.

The Clients

Eero Saarinen's new office not only looked a little like the facilities he
was building for GM; it functioned like them. Most of the activities at
the Tech Center—research, process development, engineering, and
styling—also involved trial and error. When the complex was dedicated
in 1956, Charles Kettering, the GM inventor whose idea it had been to
create a research center (isolated from management and manufacturing),
said, "We now have a place where we can make an infinite number of
practice shots; the only time we don't want to fail is the last time we
try."[13] Kettering was a prolific industrial designer from Dayton, Ohio,
who had invented the electric cash register, a battery ignition system for
automobiles, a generator to bring electricity to farms, synthetic high-
octane gasoline for airplanes, and, during World War I, an unmanned
bomber. After he joined General Motors in the early 1920s, he developed
better automobile finishes, antiknock gasoline, more efficient fuels, and
improved diesel engines as well as a mechanical heart and a device for
sterilizing blood plasma.[14] But his main contribution to medical science
was through his philanthropy to the Kettering Laboratories at the
University of Dayton and to the Memorial Sloan-Kettering Hospital in
New York, which he endowed along with GM's former chairman,
Alfred P. Sloan Jr.

Another force in the company at the time was Harley Earl, the tall, dapper
automobile designer from Hollywood who put tail fins and chromium
strips on cars, invented the wraparound windshield, and introduced
two-tone paint jobs during his tenure (1927–59). He was the one who
had fought for ambitious architecture at the GM Tech Center, and he
was the company's secret weapon, because his innovations appealed
to the pleasure principle and therefore increased sales. His family had

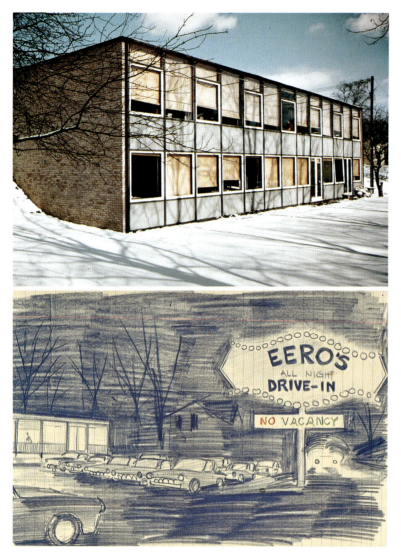

made limited-edition automobiles for silent-movie stars before he was lured to Detroit by the president of Cadillac. His rather outrageous, completely American sensibility set him apart from sedate Eastern Establishment tastemakers, such as Saarinen's client at IBM, the designer Eliot Noyes, who promoted a considerably more restrained aesthetic.[15] In some ways, Earl's cars resembled Eero Saarinen's boldest buildings, except that their decorative flourishes were superficial—a quality that offended Eero so much that he special-ordered his own Oldsmobile without any chrome.

What appealed to Eero was the company's potential for technical innovation and the fact that its mass-production apparatus could be put in the service of architecture in the way early Modernist architects had imagined it would. And he made GM's function explicit in the Tech Center architecture with its slick metal skins and bright colors.

The scale, however—understandably geared to the automobile—makes the place too big to grasp and negotiate on foot. The architects made some attempt to create spaces to walk around and to individualize some of the twenty-five enormous buildings in the complex where five thousand scientists, engineers, designers, technicians, and assistants

worked. There is a central restaurant (in addition to cafeterias in various buildings) with a human-scaled plaza overlooking the lake, but in general the Tech Center is overwhelming. Buildings are three thousand feet long, and although the five-foot module proved practical for office and laboratory arrangements, it was too small to read at a distance and therefore does not order the whole.

"Each of the staff organizations prides itself on its own individuality and range of activities. Each wanted its own personality," Saarinen explained. "We tried to answer this desire architecturally in the main lobby of each of the five groups. In four of them, the visual climax to the lobby is the main staircase. These staircases are deliberately made into ornamental elements, like large-scale technological sculptures."[16]

For help on the interiors, Eero turned to his old friend Florence (Shu) Knoll Bassett, who designed a number of tables and other furnishings to complement the elegant, squarish lounge chairs he had designed for the lobbies. Even though the furnishings were made with modern materials, they were treated with such delicacy and detailed with such refinement that the interiors, at least the lobby spaces, possessed an elegance never before seen in modern American corporate architecture. These spaces may look familiar today, but they were radical when they were built. And the magazines certainly noticed.

At least eighteen articles had been published on the architecture of the GM Tech Center by the time it was completed. *Architectural Forum* covered it five times: nine pages in 1949, thirteen in 1951, one each in 1953 and 1954, and eight in 1956, when it also garnered eight-page spreads in *Art in America*, *Architectural Record*, and *L'Architecture d'aujourd'hui* and six pages in *Life*. It showed up in *Interiors*, *Architecture and Building News*, and *Werk*. *Art in America* called it the "greatest architectural phenomenon of our time."[17] *Architectural Forum* said, "They don't look like buildings as we know them; the result looks more like an exalted industrial product,"[18] and later the magazine called it "an Industrial Versailles."[19] At a time when color printing was expensive and technically difficult, the very colorful GM Tech Center was depicted in full-color spreads repeatedly, so it looked even more dramatic on the page. And with its shimmering stainless-steel dome and water tower, massive lake, and dancing fountains, it was extremely photogenic, more exciting in pictures than in person because of the huge scale.

The General Motors Tech Center was eight years in the making, and when it was dedicated on 16 May 1956, GM was at the top of the business world—the biggest, richest, and most powerful company in America. Technical and design innovations that took place at the center, along with clever marketing, helped GM surpass its competitors. On 31 December 1955, it became the first American corporation to make more than a billion dollars in one year.

It was a high point in the history of the company and its hometown, before foreign automakers started making inroads in the American market and the urban riots of the 1960s showed the downside of suburbanization. Detroit, in particular, suffered. But in 2002, General Motors moved out of its semisuburban headquarters and into the Renaissance Center, an enormous mixed-use complex built in 1976 in an unsuccessful attempt to bring downtown Detroit back to life. And since GM arrived, the complex, at least, has thrived. The company is also enlarging the Tech Center, not quite according to Saarinen's plan (a six-story office building built in 2002 changes the horizontal emphasis), but on land he had designated for expansion. The original complex served the company well for half a century, and its success changed the architect's life and career.

This page: IBM Rochester, courtyard.

Opposite, from top: IBM Rochester, curtain-wall facades;
wall panels.

use so that the land around it would remain open. Over time, however, commercial activity developed north of the city near IBM, and eventually the company decided to sell off some of the original 397 acres. As a result, the complex is no longer as protected or isolated as it was in the 1950s.[22]

The High-Tech Corporate Laboratories
Another building that Saarinen was asked to design for IBM before the Rochester plant was even finished, however, still looks very much the way it did when it was built, even though it is located in Westchester County, New York, where land is very valuable, and it has been expanded twice. Planning for the Thomas J. Watson Research Center in Yorktown, New York (1956–61), near Mount Kisco, began in 1957, coinciding with preparations for the enormous Bell Telephone Laboratories in Holmdel, New Jersey (1957–62), near the coastline in northern Monmouth County. Since the requirements for the two projects were similar, the

Saarinen office decided to work on them simultaneously—with the permission of both clients. The buildings they produced look very different, inside and out, despite the fact that both have reflective glass skins and similar arrangements of laboratories inside.

As always, Saarinen's architects conducted an extraordinary amount of research before they designed the work spaces, and so did their clients.[23] The Bell building committee, working with a plant engineer and executive assistants at the company's existing laboratories, developed a set of criteria: maximal flexibility everywhere, adaptable laboratories, centrally located common facilities such as the cafeteria, minimal foot traffic past offices and laboratories, central air-conditioning, short walks from parking lots to buildings, roadways free of pedestrians or outside traffic, and low construction and operating costs.

At both Bell Labs and IBM Watson, scientists' private enclosed offices open onto short interior corridors across from their laboratories. The short corridors lead to much longer, glass-walled passages for general circulation along outer walls, which look out onto the landscape or, in some cases at Bell Labs, overlook skylit atriums. All offices and labs are

which have, unavoidably, grown up on the roof. The building's convex, dark glass facade either looks like a black void or reflects the landscape, depending on light conditions, and the crescent shape hides the parking lot in the rear. The short end walls are faced with rough stone, some of it hewn from the site. "From the main access drive, sweeping across the north front, the building appears as a three-story structure." From the parking lot, it looks like one story. "One walks on a bridge over a Japanese garden designed by Sasaki, Walker & Associates and enters on the third floor. If one comes in from the garden below, one sees a two-story building and enters on the second floor," Saarinen explained.[28] (Although it contains three usable floors, because zoning in the area permitted only a two-story building, the first level is considered a "terrace.") The structure, which hugs the hilltop, was, as usual, only one of several schemes that the architect considered. One design consisted of a sort of stepped pyramid, but the more unobtrusive alternative was selected both for functional reasons and because it kept the hillside intact.

The Watson building, which cannot be seen from the road, comes into view at the end of a long winding drive, its almost-black glass seeming to rise out of a heavy stone base. The entrance is sheltered by a large cantilevered concrete canopy, flanked by long, raking fieldstone walls. At each end, jagged, abstract, silvery-gold nine-foot sculptures, by Seymour Lipton, seem to soar outward. They were intended to symbolize "the scientist's search into the unknown," according to the architect, who commissioned works of contemporary art for his buildings whenever he could.[29]

Inside, the rough stone of the landscape covers walls in the light-filled, two-story lobby, in the 270-seat wedge-shaped auditorium, and on the inside of the corridors that lead to offices and laboratories. The long corridor in the rear, which faces the garden, has alternating bands of glass and stone.

The architect was as concerned with the "character" of the place as his clients were with preserving the atmosphere of the neighborhood: "It has always seemed to me that scientists in the research field are like university professors—tweedy, pipe-smoking men. We wanted to provide them with a relaxed, 'tweedy,' outdoor environment as a deliberate contrast to the efficient precise laboratories and offices."[30]

In arguing for character of this kind, Saarinen came close to making an argument for the "meaning" that Postmodernists have claimed modern

placed back to back, with closets and storage between the offices and four-foot-wide utility cores between the labs (serving two labs at once), because research showed that utility ducts take up a significant amount of room when laboratories are separated by hallways. The arrangement also makes it possible to combine or subdivide offices and laboratories. At IBM, as at Bell Labs, "the cross corridors, on which the laboratories and offices are located, are only about 120 feet long," Saarinen explained, so the scientists can interact casually.[24] Watson's outer, general-circulation corridors run continuously along either side of the 1,090-foot-long building, but because the building curves, "no stretch of the peripheral corridor ever looks more than 80 to 100 feet long."[25] Bell Labs was initially only 700 feet long, but because it is rectangular, the facade looked longer from the outside even before it was extended.

IBM's Thomas J. Watson Research Laboratories are nestled into 240 rugged, wooded acres, because the owners wanted to preserve the rural character of the landscape. "The building was curved in a crescent, following the configuration of the hill. It is planned so that this curve can embrace the hill even further by extending the crescent in future expansion," the architect explained at the time.[26] And, indeed, after the original eighteen bays (numbers 12–30) were built, ten more were added to one end in 1980 (aisles 31–40). Seven more were added to the other end in 1984 (aisles 1–6).[27] The crescent shape not only masked the expansion; it permitted asymmetrical additions imperceptibly. The most noticeable change is a forest of antennae of various kinds,

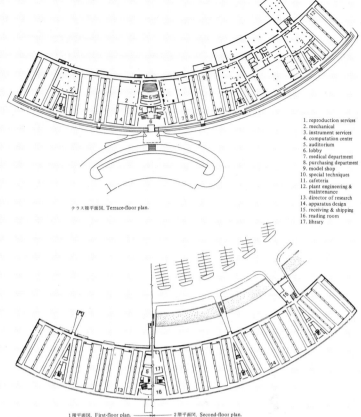

テラス階平面図. Terrace-floor plan.

1. reproduction services
2. mechanical
3. instrument services
4. computation center
5. auditorium
6. lobby
7. medical department
8. purchasing department
9. model shop
10. special techniques
11. cafeteria
12. plant engineering & maintenance
13. director of research
14. apparatus design
15. receiving & shipping
16. reading room
17. library

1階平面図. First-floor plan. — 2階平面図. Second-floor plan.

architecture lacked. Venturi was probably right. Saarinen was trying to do—and often achieved—what the Postmodernists who caused his work to go out of style were striving for. But because it looked modern and was made of modern materials, they rejected it out of hand, along with the much more abstract glass-and-steel boxes he was breaking away from.

The Bell Labs building is a box, but Saarinen (and Anthony J. Lumsden, who was project architect) made it almost visually disappear under some light conditions via a fully mirrored facade that reflects the pond in front and the gentle, man-made landscape around it. Much larger than the IBM site, Bell's 460-acre plot, located an hour south of New York City near the Jersey Shore, is only slightly rolling and more like a farm than like a forest, so there was no way to hide the six-story, 715,000-gross-square-foot building among hillocks and tall trees. The soil on the coastal alluvial plain would not even support the building; it had to be built on piles.

The company had chosen the site almost thirty years earlier because it was free of the man-made static noise at its more developed research locations. At the beginning, the small Holmdel labs were used for research on short-wave radio.[31] After the building opened, the emphasis switched to international television transmission via Telstar, microwave transmissions, and radio astronomy. The Bell planners also liked the fact that housing was less expensive around Holmdel than in northern New Jersey, nearer Manhattan. The area is still sparsely settled.

The enormous and flat mirrored facade—1,186 feet long and 74 feet high—is very visible from the main public road. It was slightly shorter when the building opened in 1962: 700 feet long and only 135 feet deep (as opposed to 350 feet now). As elsewhere, expansion was supposed to occur in a more aesthetically satisfying way, to the rear instead of at the sides. But whereas two more blocks of laboratories identical to the first were added in the back between 1964 and 1966, along with a cruciform garden court, further additions made to the east and west in 1982 changed the original scale and proportions. As big as it is, the building would have been even more massive if the service spaces and shared facilities were not located underground, beneath a concrete podium that supports the five upper floors.[32]

The impression that the gigantic mirror makes from a distance is softened somewhat by an oval, six-acre man-made lake, well-maintained landscaping, and ever-changing patterns of natural light and clouds that wash across the surface. (Original smaller ponds on each side were replaced in 1982 by a larger one in the rear with an island, bridge, and nature walk.) Water is supplied by three deep wells. A striking, white, cup-shaped 127-foot water tower on three heavy legs holds three hundred thousand gallons worth of reserves and provides a vertical accent that resembles a radar antenna. The big lake contains six million gallons of water for firefighting and absorbs evaporation from air-conditioning. And an oval "ring road" surrounds the building and its parking lots, separating pedestrians from vehicles and various streams of traffic.

This page: IBM Watson, facade with additions.

Opposite, from top: IBM Watson, entrance; rear courtyard with Japanese garden by Sasaki, Walker & Associates, approach from parking lot.

The sense of spaciousness and light gives way, however, even on a sunny day, in the five-story reception area, where folds in the skylight, bush-hammered exposed concrete walls, and green and gray fabrics create a subdued, almost eerie atmosphere. It is an immense place—elegant in its detailing but rather somber. Even though the original blocks were divided by the atrium (and the additions by a garden court), these five-story open spaces overwhelm the senses. They seem frighteningly quiet and empty. Perhaps in 1998, when there were 4,700 people working there, the place filled up, but in 1962, when most of the original 2,600 employees were tucked away in private offices and laboratories off semiprivate corridors, the excitement that the institution's discoveries generated was probably confined to the laboratory benches themselves, where there is plenty of the bright fluorescent lighting the clients requested.[33]

The critic Anthony Vidler found the place lifeless even in its heyday. He observed in *Architectural Design* several years after the Bell Labs building opened, "All that could give life is placed beneath its floor, in the com- munal basement," where the auditorium and original computer room as well as mechanical and service spaces are "without daylight." However, he admired the fact that "the expensive materials and impeccable technology of American business architecture is brought to a pitch of refinement here."[34] Walter McQuade had observed in *Architectural Forum* that "this gleaming scientific instrument is not only symbolic of modern science, but symbolic also of yielding architecture to science"— though he, too, called it "formidable." He added that the clients con- sidered it "an economical triumph in both first cost and upkeep."[35]

The mirrored glass that was developed especially for the building is a low-brightness reflective glass that deflects 70 percent of the sun's heat while admitting 25 percent of its light. The skin (all ten thousand square feet of it) is laminated with a thin film of aluminum bonded between the panes to protect the metal from the weather. Saarinen had already investigated the reflective properties of glass at General Motors. He had found them disturbing on MIT's Kresge Auditorium (1952–55) because they masked its shape and structure, but he used reflections to enliven the facade at IBM Rochester and exploited them in Yorktown. At Bell Labs "We wanted to keep the continuous outside glass walls free of all window shading," he explained in 1959. "We have all along wanted to encourage the manufacture of translucent wall materials that would act as a continuous transparent window from the inside

Clockwise from top: Bell Telephone Laboratories, Holmdel, New Jersey, 1957–62, rear facade with original reflective glass and vertical circulation core; lobby; interior work space.

but would, on the exterior, be a reflecting surface against the fierce heat of the sun. Steps in this direction have been taken by the manufacturers of tinted glass, but now, we believe that the development of this new material will represent a major breakthrough."[36]

Mirrored glass became the material of choice for commercial buildings in the 1970s. It is still enormously popular, especially in developing countries and warm climates. There are some horrific examples made of it—buildings with little character and no visible means of support, curtain-wall buildings that are anti-Miesian in their lack of concern with expressing structure. But mirrored glass does one thing it was supposed to do: reduce heat gain and the need for window shades. Thus, it is relatively environmentally friendly, though less so than the natural light, operable windows, and exterior shading devices of many recent buildings. From a technological standpoint, the development of mirrored glass for Bell Labs was a breakthrough, but not one that was achieved in time for the opening. "As in the development of many new products, manufacturing difficulties were encountered in the perfection of this new glass. Rather than hold up building construction," the clients decided "to use gray glass on the front and side facades. The reflective, mirrored glass, in spite of some irregularities in appearance, was installed on the rear facade."[37] The reflective glass worked so well that eventually all four facades were sheathed with it, requiring five thousand three-by-six-foot panes. Part of Saarinen's genius was the ability to persuade clients to go along with experiments of this kind, despite the cost and risks involved.

With the help of his gifted partner, John Dinkeloo, who was in charge of production and technical developments, Saarinen was one of the great technological innovators, a talent valued in many disciplines in his time but not fully appreciated in architecture, where structural innovation, structural purity, and structural expression were considered more important than development of materials, expression of function, or a concern with site.

Deere & Company

For another corporate campus of a very different kind, Saarinen and Dinkeloo developed architectural uses for another material—a self-rusting steel known as Cor-Ten—to express the character of the client's business. John Deere was a manufacturer of farm equipment in Moline, Illinois, one of four small cities clustered on the banks of the Mississippi River in the middle of the midwestern farm belt. The founder of the eponymous, family-run company had moved there from New England four generations earlier, in 1843. He settled in Moline to produce a plow he had invented that was strong enough to till the rich, sticky midwestern soil, and his heirs had gone on to develop engine-driven tractors. Just before the building program for the new headquarters began in 1955,

the company had started making construction equipment and garden tractors for the suburban market, so, like Saarinen's other clients, Deere & Company was a very modern organization, though its work was earthier and more rugged. The site, which the architect helped select, was generous, exuberant, and dramatic. At Deere, he also had an extraordinary client.

William A. Hewitt, the chairman of the company, was married to John Deere's great-great-granddaughter. "He led the way, and his board supported him, as did his wife," recalls David Powrie, project architect for the building. "It was remarkable. That was the period when corporate pride meant something."[38] In 1937 the company had hired a well-known industrial designer, Henry Dreyfuss, to "help make our farm equipment aesthetically pleasing as well as safe, comfortable, and easy to operate," but it had never employed an outside architect. Hewitt set out to find "the best architect we could persuade to design our new headquarters."[39] He subscribed to architecture magazines. He talked to Bob McNamara, his "friend from Berkeley days," who "had just finished an administration building for his staff at the Ford Motor Company, and he sent me a big box of architects' prospectuses he had collected." (Robert McNamara, then president of Ford, later became secretary of defense under presidents Kennedy and Johnson.) Hewitt asked Dreyfuss for advice and was told: "If you want to work with an architect's architect, put Saarinen on your list." He did. And he visited numerous buildings by the architects on the list, including the General Motors Technical Center. "Afterwards," he said, "I went by to meet the architect, and talked with him in his wooden office building. Then and there, I decided Eero Saarinen was the man for the job."

Saarinen went out to Moline and helped Hewitt scout four hilly, wooded sites in a truck with a thirty-five-foot telescoping tower that they borrowed from a utility company. The site Saarinen chose consisted of four farms totaling 720 acres. A year later, when the company had acquired the land (for six hundred dollars per acre), he came back and selected a site at the highest point, with long views east and south. His first sketches show a reinforced-concrete structure suggestive of the raw strength of the huge tractors that the company made.

"It was to be an inverted pyramid with a central courtyard. There were a lot of them in those days. That was something that was in the air," Powrie remembers. "It was very monumental, and Bill Hewitt thought it was too much identified with power." Also, it did not have the theater, cafeteria, or expansion plan that he had requested.

"When I asked him how he was going to handle those," Hewitt said, "Eero didn't exactly answer me. He just puffed his pipe. Then we exchanged a few pleasantries and he went back to Bloomfield Hills."

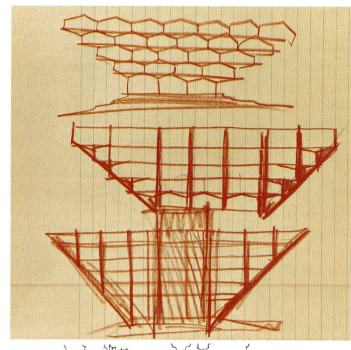

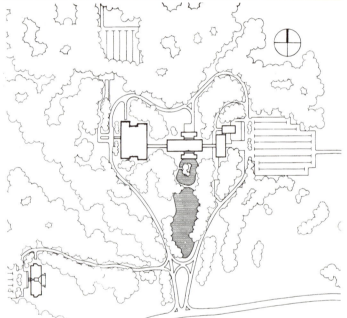

When they had first decided to work together, Hewitt had told him, "I'm not going to breathe down your neck." Saarinen had replied, "Well, Bill, maybe you should breathe down my neck." Clearly, he meant it, for three weeks after the cool reception to the first scheme, the architect invited Hewitt and his colleagues to the office in Michigan. "There he showed us a model, complete with land contours, trees, shrubs, and a pond. It was for a steel building down in a little valley, straddling a ravine, with everything accessible under cover, plus an expansion plan. It was essentially what was built."

"It was characteristic of Eero to just switch everything around 180 degrees." Powrie said. "Instead of [on] a hilltop, he put it in a valley, and instead of concrete, John Dinkeloo found a steel that would work. I remember his coming into the office with a fistful of samples of steel—from US Steel or one of those companies—with a beautiful brown patina."

Dinkeloo had considered more common corrosion-resistant materials, such as stainless steel and aluminum, and rejected them as too costly. Neither would have had the visible strength and immediate impact of the material that he chose, a corrosion-resistant steel alloy that had been developed in 1933 for the railroads. It does not have to be painted because it oxidizes in a few years, creating a dense, protective, almost-black coating that then stops rusting.[40] The dark patina gave the steel the quality that Hewitt was looking for when he suggested that an iron building might best represent "the special character of Deere & Company."[41] Certainly, it suggested old pieces of farm equipment in the fields and, at the same time, a new kind of industrial building, both refined and appropriate. Cor-Ten had never been used architecturally before. Dinkeloo and Saarinen figured out a way to make it impart a completely new kind of rugged intensity.

They set up a test patch at the site so they could study how the material would weather. "Some of our engineers were a little alarmed," the chairman confessed, "thinking, 'We've been warning farmers against rust for 120 years, and now Hewitt wants to build a big rusty building—and make us work in it.'"

Because the building did not stand near any others, the steel frame did not require concrete or asbestos coating to meet the fire and safety codes for buildings in urban areas. The glass facade that provided views of the landscape was covered with deep, slotted, rectangular Cor-Ten sunscreens that protect the glass-walled structure, give it a three-dimensional character, and still provide views out, without the need for blinds. The bridges that link sections and lead to the entrance have the same refined industrial aesthetic. Once the unpainted steel weathered, it almost matched the surrounding oak trees, which had been carefully preserved. "Every tree that was anywhere near the building or the road was tagged and evaluated. The composition derived from the trees; the trees partly designed the layout," Powrie explains. And because it is eight stories tall, the 350,000-square-foot building for a thousand employees does not take up as much land as do most suburban office buildings, and the workers are closer to nature.

After the best existing landscape elements had been preserved, Sasaki & Walker of Boston created a magnificent landscape plan for the entire site, with weeping willows, duck-filled ponds, and hills and valleys intended to offer the best possible views of and from the building.

As Saarinen explained, "The complex is approached from the valley below. We planned the roads carefully, keeping in mind how the buildings would be seen as one drove along the man-made lakes to the parking lot east of the complex." The site looks more like a verdant park than an office building as you enter the magnificent landscaped grounds, which have a vaguely Japanese feel. It is not immediately apparent that the building is made of steel. Its almost-black exterior supports and sunscreens resemble the dark wood beams of an ancient Asian temple. But as you come closer, its ruggedly elegant texture is perceptible and unlike that of any other building, except, perhaps, those that have been influenced by it.

The entrance, on the east side, leads to an exhibition hall, where the company's enormous products are displayed. The shiny green tractors in that 210-foot-long, 35-foot-tall space are surrounded by a 100-foot-long collaged mural that Saarinen's friend Alexander Girard created with two thousand items he found in the Deere & Company archives. "A glass-enclosed flying bridge stretches from this building to the fourth-floor level of the administration building," the architect explained. "In the future, a similar bridge will reach to the west building. Like the exhibition hall, it will be on the high slopes of the ravine."[42]

The executive floor is reached by going down from the main entrance. Even farther down, on the lowest level, the executive dining room is situated slightly below the terrace that goes around the lake, so the lake water is at window level. The handsome cafeteria is down there, too, as is an art gallery with Grant Wood paintings and a spectacular 384-seat auditorium.

This page: Deere & Company Headquarters, bridge from entrance and exhibition hall to executive offices.

Opposite: Deere & Company Headquarters, facade detail with sunscreens and exposed structural supports.

"Quite simply, this is one of the most delightful small theaters to be found in the entire gamut of contemporary architecture," wrote the critic John Jacobus, who had not always been impressed by Saarinen's work. "Since the 'actors' in this theater are often tractors and other self-propelled machines . . . the stage with its revolving floor is backed by huge glazed doors which give out on a brick-walled compound which can be used for 'live' demonstration of the machinery. Architecturally, the theater possesses one splendidly whimsical conceit, which is also deceptively sensible: three tiers of balconies designed 'in reverse' the highest of the three is thrust out further forward than the others, the lowest tier being the furthest to the rear. The result is a gain in intimacy on the part of the 'skied' spectators."[43]

Although it is one of the greatest works of American architecture, the Deere & Company headquarters is not among Eero Saarinen's best-known buildings today, probably because it is located in an area few people visit. The public is welcome on the grounds in a way it is not at GM, but you have to know it is there. When the building opened in 1964, however, it was considered the architect's most unqualified success.[44] It won a First Honor Award from the American Institute of Architects the next year[45] and the AIA's 25-Year Award almost as soon as it was eligible, as half a dozen of Eero Saarinen's buildings already had.[46] (In fact, Eero and Eliel Saarinen together won more AIA awards than any other architects.) The building was also the subject of a (generally flattering) anthropological study on how people use space.[47]

The *Architectural Forum* critic Walter McQuade, who had always admired Saarinen, commented on the very clean office plans, which look contemporary even today. Banks of floor-to-ceiling filing cabinets separate private offices on the long outer walls from the spacious

From top: Deere & Company Headquarters, office interior; cafeteria; auditorium.

secretarial areas—an efficient minimalist approach that Saarinen used in numerous buildings.[48]

McQuade also noted, "Cor-Ten was used for all it is worth" and explained how the rusting process works. Cor-Ten "in effect bakes itself into a tight, dense protective exterior coating which has the richness in finish of an old Etruscan coin." He explained why the curtain wall is almost invisible and yet efficient: "At the plane of the windows the structural members are aligned to form openings without any added framing materials."[49] A perfected version of the neoprene gasket developed at GM takes care of thermal expansion. The protected lower floors are fitted with clear glass; on the five upper floors, reflective glass bounces off 52.3 percent of heat from sun and 62 percent of light.

The success of the Deere & Company building is much more than a matter of technical achievement, however, as McQuade observed: "It is of surpassing elegance. There is a depth of feeling in Deere which makes it much less transitory than most modern architecture. Its fineness and quality probably surpasses anything by Saarinen completed to date; and this applies to the siting too."[50]

He, of course, was right. At Deere & Company, Saarinen managed to create a completely new kind of glass-walled building—one that was truly sculptural without using curved elements—and to tie it to the landscape in a way few buildings had ever been before, or have been since. Even his most severe critics pronounced this building a remarkable achievement. In explaining why, John Jacobus articulated the reservations he had once had about the architect: "Eero Saarinen was a singular architect during a decade of Modernist conformity. The urge that drove him to make every design a new start, a new beginning in which accumulated gains of personal experience could only be used in peripheral or incidental ways exacted a terrible toll in terms of bogus monuments and pretentious structural soliloquies. Yet in spite of everything, of the naive commemorative arch, the flawed yet striking airport termini, and the earnest, bombastic embassies, we sensed that he was driving at some certain thing just beyond the threshold of his as well as of our own awareness. I think it is likely that the future will cherish his work, even the botched jobs, because he was willing to plunge into the unknown. . . . While it would be an exaggeration to claim that the John Deere & Company Administrative Centre . . . would have inaugurated a new phase in his work (since, in effect, every one of his buildings represented a new style or category), we do encounter there a really different tone, a profundity in his work. At last we have from his pen a total and organic design."[51]

What impressed Jacobus most was that the architect "ceased here to be concerned about obvious and naive effects of a picturesque nature in order to concentrate upon some guttier issue. Saarinen found his way back to the very tradition in which his first success, General Motors, was nurtured; a tradition compounded of Mies, of the myriad uneven designs of the Albert Kahn staff, and of a particular American pictorial vision of a metallic industrialized building style set in an ordered, uncluttered landscape—the vision of Sheeler, Demuth and Hopper." He was trying to place Eero Saarinen in a larger cultural context. What mattered to Jacobus was "that at John Deere, Saarinen has rescued this design idiom of crisp details and sharp linear contours from further debasement at the hands of fashionable decorators. John Deere, by its constructive clarity, its boxlike forms and its stress on right-angle intersections, turned its back upon the immaturities of Dulles and TWA with their sagging shell vaults and the inconclusiveness of IBM, Yorktown, where rough masonry and random forms compete in futile contrast with the sleek curve of the glass wall."

Jacobus observed that "at Moline he contrived a more genuinely architectural solution to the problem of relating the building to its environment. Instead of concentrating upon one single image, he concerned himself with the integration of the building to its setting through the imaginative handling of space and circulation." He recognized that the sunshades enliven the mass of the building while giving character and protection to the office spaces inside. "The outer structure sheltering the glass wall serves to integrate rather than isolate the working spaces from the landscape."

"I know of no other modern glass-walled office building that so dramatically establishes and maintains this important relationship under so many contradictory conditions of light and weather," Jacobus wrote. "Certainly not since Le Corbusier's Marseilles Unité has the concept of a facade in depth been handled so satisfactorily. Not even the Japanese have managed to come up with anything so satisfactory in terms of the visual penetration of exterior and interior."

Although he called John Deere a "total work of art," Jacobus predicted that "it seems unlikely that there will be any significant legacy in others outside of Saarinen's entourage. Saarinen was pre-eminently a client's architect (Mies and Louis Kahn, for purposes of comparison, are architects' architects), and he worked best when and where the client was around not to interfere but to stimulate and provide."

Hewitt certainly did that for Saarinen. There have never been many clients like him. It is interesting that Jacobus identified Saarinen as a "client's architect." The term aptly describes Eero Saarinen. He possessed an unusual ability to learn from his clients, to teach them, and to create

dynamic, mutually satisfying relationships with them. It is an ability that is essential to producing architecture of quality but one that tends to be undervalued in architectural circles.

Jacobus was not the only critic to come to value Saarinen more after the architect's death than he had during his lifetime. Despite his extraordinary achievements, Saarinen was frequently criticized. He was often envied. His importance was downplayed in academic circles. Still, he managed to be involved with a number of the most significant social, cultural, and technological trends of his time during his brief career. His contribution to the development of the suburban corporate campus was only one of them.

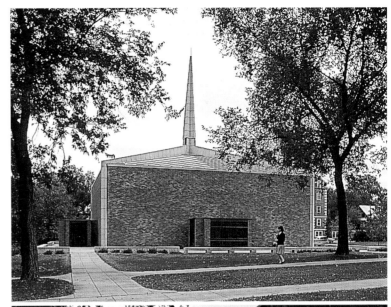

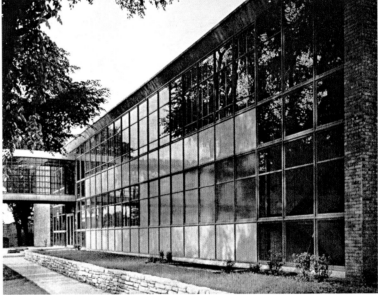

From top: Eero Saarinen, Stephens College Chapel, Columbia, Missouri, 1953–56; Saarinen and Saarinen, Drake University, Pharmacy Building, 1945–50.

more exciting when he met a like-minded architect of extraordinary talent—Matthew Nowicki (pronounced "Novitsky")—and began an unusually close friendship and working relationship with him, similar to the one he enjoyed with Charles Eames. Nowicki agreed to work with him on the Brandeis project, and their hand-in-hand collaboration was among the most fertile of the architects' careers.

Nowicki was the mentor of a young Polish architect, Mark T. Jaroszewicz, who had recently come to work for Saarinen. Jaroszewicz had escaped from Poland after Hitler's invasion, joined the Polish army in France, and been eventually "pushed by the Germans to the Swiss border," where he was disarmed and imprisoned but ultimately, like other captured college students, was allowed to complete his studies (at the Swiss Federal Institute of Technology). He had emigrated to the United States in 1945.

Nowicki, who had encouraged Jaroszewicz to become an architect, was already practicing when the war began and had designed the prize-winning Polish Pavilion at the New York World's Fair of 1939. During the war, Nowicki joined the Polish underground army, became an aide-de-camp to the commander in chief, and participated in the tragic Warsaw Uprising of 1944. Throughout the occupation, he had led a team of architects that developed plans for the rebuilding of Warsaw after the war—plans that were never realized. When the war ended, he was appointed cultural attaché to the Polish consulate in Chicago and defected to the United States. He had worked with Wallace Harrison and the international team that designed the United Nations Headquarters in New York and had been named head of the School of Architecture at North Carolina State University.

Jaroszewicz, who joined Saarinen's office soon after the Brandeis commission arrived in 1949, later explained, "Matthew came to visit us shortly afterward. I introduced the two of them, and it was a joy to see the instantaneous rapport and friendship between these two brilliant men."[19] Saarinen was working rather frantically on the sketches for the Brandeis brochure on a tight deadline. Nowicki, like Saarinen, loved to draw. "His infectious enthusiasm was matched only by the incredible speed with which he transformed the most complex ideas into brilliant architectural reality."[20] The two men, who were the same age and shared a vision of what architecture could be, came up with a series of lively, sculpturesque schemes for the Brandeis buildings in a matter of months.

Saarinen used Nowicki's vibrant sketches to describe the proposed buildings throughout the brochure (and saw to it that he was separately

compensated for them). He also included some very detailed perspective renderings by J. Henderson (Jay) Barr, an architect in his office who had worked on the Saint Louis Arch competition, and he inserted a cross section of the laboratory plan that the firm had developed for Drake University to show exactly how the proposed ideas might take form. The whole ambitious scheme was published in November 1949 in a brochure titled *Foundation for Learning—Planning the Campus of Brandeis University*. A larger, second edition was printed in the spring of 1951, and the scheme was republished in an article Saarinen wrote for *The American School and University* in 1951–1952.[21]

Nowicki's sketches show flat-roofed rectangular academic buildings and dormitories with brick walls and generous windows similar to the ones Saarinen had built at other colleges, but the walls in these sketches exhibit more texture and depth, some curved elements on their entrances, and deep balconies on their ends. There are entire sculpturesque structures—an auditorium with a domed roof perched on columns, a perforated bell tower, and a vaguely hexagonal chapel

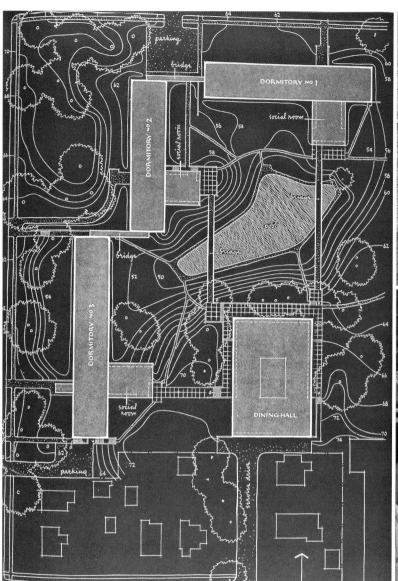

Clockwise from left: Drake University expansion plan; dormitories; bridge with dining hall in background.

with solid, curved brick walls and a circular altar, intended to serve all three major American faiths. These buildings pulsate. They are filled with the energy that Saarinen had invested in his organic furniture and the little grotesques he designed for the Cranbrook School as a boy. They have the playful spirit of the Serving Suzy restaurant (1944) and the structural boldness of the Saint Louis Arch. Clearly, Nowicki, who was also interested in expressive form and saw architecture as a humanizing art, helped Saarinen break out of the International Style straitjacket that never quite provided an outlet for his sculptural impulses. Saarinen was not intimidated by Nowicki's genius but, rather, liberated by it—just in time.

"A very few months after the project's completion," Jaroszewicz recalled, "Eero came to my drafting board, and I noticed his hands shaking as he lit his pipe. I looked up and saw two great tears running down this self-controlled Nordic man's face. He said, 'Mark, I have tragic news.

Matthew was killed in an airline crash yesterday.' Matthew was returning from a stint as consultant to the planning of Chandigarh, India (a job later taken over by Le Corbusier), when his airliner crashed outside Alexandria in Egypt. Among the many eulogies printed in *Architectural Forum*, Eero's struck me as one of the most meaningful. He said, 'What Matthew's death left undone, will take a generation of architects to accomplish.'"[22]

Eero Saarinen did realize some of the ideas that he and Matthew Nowicki had devised for Brandeis, but not at that school. The spirit of his master plan was followed at Brandeis, with the academic center asymmetrically arranged on the sloping crest of the hill, three right-angled clusters of dormitories surrounding it on lower ground, and a chapel set off in a grove by a pond. But whereas the university announced in 1950 that the master plan had been adopted and that the proposed buildings would be constructed over the next ten years at a cost of $22,715,000,[23] the only buildings Saarinen realized at Brandeis were the dormitories in the Ridgewood and Hamilton quadrangles, where he did not even have full architectural control.[24] Despite its ambitions,

108

Brandeis had difficulty accommodating its growing programs while still amassing an endowment, so it reverted to the earlier practice of piece-meal construction by friends and donors even after the master plan had been approved.

The Ridgewood Quadrangle was not a part of the original master plan. It was built in early 1950 to house faculty and married students on the edge of the campus, where it would not interfere with the development of the plan. It qualified for financing because the units could later be sold to independent buyers. Its five blocks of two-story row houses were composed of rectangular units of brick and glass arranged around irregular quadrangles. However, the choice of colors and materials was left to a local architect, Archie Riskin, who made the working drawings and supervised construction.

Collaborating with another local firm, Richmond and Goldberg, Saarinen prepared the construction specifications for the women's dormitories in Hamilton Quadrangle, which were part of the original plan but were moved slightly so that the dormitories could surround an existing pond and accommodate a student center. The first rooms were ready in January 1952, but the student center took two more years to complete; the other units were not finished for a number of years and were completed by Archie Riskin.

Saarinen's Brandeis master plan also changed subtly over time as a result of the architects' research. While working on plans for the proposed nonsectarian chapel, Saarinen associate Wilhelm von Moltke was told by a representative of the Boston Archdiocese that "the Roman Catholic Church would not consecrate a Chapel which is being used by any other church,"[25] so Eero revised the scheme with the revolving altars. In the 1951 edition of the *Foundations for Learning* brochure, a circular greenhouse was added to the science complex. The three small build-ings designed to house the fine arts were combined into a single larger one that contained a museum. The athletic area was further developed. And the women's dormitory complex was rearranged around a pond, with a student center and fewer rooms. The Ridgewood Quadrangle was also included in the 1951 brochure, though it was not part of the original plan and is not shown in the overall master-plan rendering.

Saarinen's work for Brandeis was completed in July 1952 with the sub-mission of a detailed model of the master plan. The model showed how fully the buildings would be integrated into the hilly terrain, with the main academic complexes surrounding an open space near the top of a hill and stepped down into a series of courts. One of the men's residence halls was eliminated, the Ridgewood Quadrangle and the athletic center were incorporated, and there was a new pattern of roads. The original design for a chapel with a rotating altar—which had

been substituted for a later one with separate areas for each faith to accommodate Catholic demands—was reinstated, as there was no longer any hope that the ambitious buildings he had imagined with Matthew Nowicki would be built.[26] But the peculiar castle left over from the medical school was preserved, even though its conversion to dormitories had proved unsuccessful. Von Moltke later explained that "the castle was part of the past, like a romantic historical remnant. In a way, it was like the rocks, it belonged to the terrain."[27] Even on a completely new campus, Saarinen maintained a respect for the past, at least partly because it contained vertical and sculptural interest.

Despite a similar outcome, Saarinen's relationship with Brandeis did not end as well as the one with Antioch. There was a dispute about fees because the architect had failed to inform the university that his original estimate for the master plan had been too low. Also, the Hamilton dormitories were not completed on time, though it is not clear that Saarinen was responsible for the delays. Then there was the theater that was to be built for a music festival during the first commencement exercises in June 1952. Since Saarinen had worked on the Tanglewood Shed (1938), designed the Tanglewood Opera House (1941) and the Aspen Music Tent (1949), and proposed an amphitheater in the Brandeis master plan, he would have been the logical choice for all the alter-natives being considered by the university (a shed, a tent, an amphithe-ater). But Dr. Sachar awarded the commission to Max Abramovitz, his student from the University of Illinois, who was now practicing archi-tecture in New York with Wallace Harrison. During the 1952 commence-ment ceremonies, the site of the University Chapel was consecrated in the location where it had been proposed in Saarinen's master plan, but that commission went to Harrison & Abramovitz too.

Soon after that commencement, when the Saarinen master plan was completed, the Office of University Planning was dissolved, and Dr. Berkowitz was relieved of responsibility for the physical development of the campus.

The following January, after a donor for the chapel had been found, Harrison & Abramovitz's design was unveiled, and instead of being a nonsectarian chapel, it was solely for Jewish worship. The university's decision to build a purely Jewish chapel may have been motivated by the donor's desire, but Brandeis students saw the change in plan as a violation of the nondenominational principles on which the university had been founded. They resented the fact that they had not been consulted and protested vehemently in the school newspaper.[28]

Dr. Sachar argued that Brandeis was simply following the tradition of most nonsectarian schools. Chapels are usually built, he said, "through the interests of the denominational group which provides the main

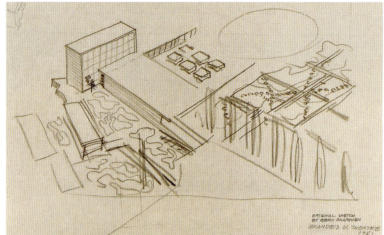

This page, from top: Eero Saarinen, Brandeis University, Waltham, Massachusetts, conceptual sketch of Brandeis University Theater, 1951; Eero Saarinen and Matthew Nowicki, Brandeis Union with bell tower, 1949, sketch by Matthew Nowicki; Brandeis University campus plan, aerial overall.

Opposite: Eero Saarinen and Matthew Nowicki, Brandeis University Chapel, sketch by Matthew Nowicki, 1949.

support for the college" but are open to all students.[29] At Brandeis, however, an interfaith chapel had special significance. In the 1950s, most Jews valued the nonsectarian ideal because their ancestors had suffered from sectarianism throughout history. As a result of the protests, the next June Harrison & Abramovitz submitted an alternative scheme with facilities for the other two faiths included. But the students considered them unacceptable because they were unequal. Finally, in October, university officials decided to build three separate chapels.

Saarinen played no part in any of this, but the difficulties that Dr. Sachar experienced with the students did not incline him to bring Saarinen back. In 1955, he named Harrison & Abramovitz university architect, and the firm developed a new master plan very similar to Saarinen's. The buildings they constructed are competent and generally follow the direction of Saarinen's earlier schemes, but they do not have the lively spirit of those he designed with Nowicki. Occasional commissions went to other architects—usually very good ones from Boston, such as Hugh Stubbins; Benjamin Thompson; Shepley, Bulfinch, Richardson; and Sasaki Dawson, DeMay)—but Saarinen's firm was not invited to work at Brandeis again.

Adding insult to injury, in 1972, the university's Poses Institute of Fine Arts held an exhibition, "Brandeis Under Construction," at the school's Rose Art Museum. The catalog said very little about the Ridgewood Quadrangle (except that it comprised "the first group of buildings to be completed here by Eero Saarinen, in 1950") or about the Hamilton dormitories, which had been renamed the Sherman Student Center and Shapiro Hall. But it declared, "The master plan by Eero Saarinen (in conjunction with Matthew Nowicki) that was published by the University in 1950 was a tentative sketch for the future. . . . The plan is characteristic of those published by Saarinen in the late forties and early fifties. The buildings lie at right angles in the manner of Mies van der Rohe's influential grid plan for the Illinois Institute of Technology." It mentioned a central plaza with a campanile, a circular auditorium, "International-Style" facades of brick and glass, and a centralized academic area with residential units on the periphery.

As if to justify the fact that the university had severed relations with Saarinen and hired Harrison & Abramovitz, the catalog said: "Saarinen's plan showed limited possibilities for expansion of the central quad and

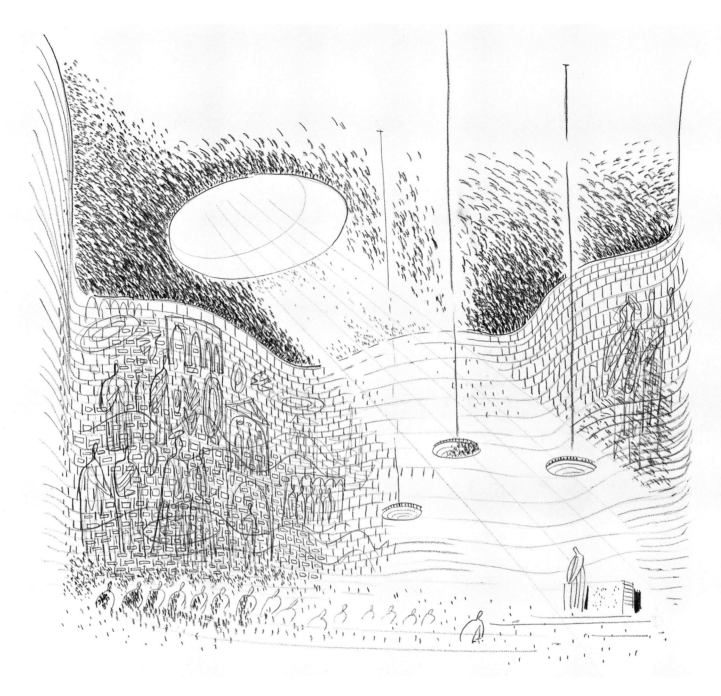

suggested a large financial investment in a relatively short time. The plan seemed to take little regard of the existing hilly terrain, apparently wishfully flattening it to an International-Style ideal, and it nearly ignored the existing Middlesex buildings." This was simply not true, as the plan clearly shows. The catalog even argued that the "custom-made construction and difficult mechanical systems" in Saarinen's buildings "did not help his standing with the university."[30]

Not everyone at Brandeis promoted this view. Later student papers by William Lebovich and Jada Kayer set the record straight and carefully documented the early planning for the new university.[31]

From the standpoint of architectural history, Brandeis's decision not to go ahead with the Saarinen and Nowicki schemes seems tragically misguided. But Brandeis was not Cranbrook. Architecture was not critical to its purpose, and Eero Saarinen had no interest in building anything other than architecture of the highest level.

The loss of the Brandeis commission must have been devastating following Nowicki's death, but Saarinen was not one to dwell on missed opportunities. Before long, he was offered a chance to develop some of their ideas in an even more visible location only a few miles away.

Opposite: Massachusetts Institute of Technology Kresge
Chapel, Cambridge, Massachusetts, 1950–55, interior with
sculptural screen by Harry Bertoia over altar.

Before his relationship with Brandeis ended, Saarinen was invited to
meet with officials at the Massachusetts Institute of Technology (MIT)
about a commission to design an auditorium and a nondenominational
chapel, buildings that would afford him a chance to develop the ideas
he had proposed at Brandeis. Both the Kresge Auditorium and the MIT
Chapel (1950–55) would attract as much attention as the General Motors
Technical Center (1948–56)—and considerably more debate; however,
it would be another year before these projects got under way.[1]

MIT was an ideal place for Saarinen to build. The campus was in a
prominent location, facing the Charles River and Boston's historic Back
Bay. It was a prestigious, technologically sophisticated institution that had
grown from a local engineering school into an internationally acclaimed
university dedicated to "educating the whole man" in the humanities
as well as in science; architecture that aspired to art was consistent with
its program. Under president James R. Killian Jr. (in office 1948–59), MIT
had undertaken an especially enlightened building program, initiated by
Killian's predecessor during World War II, Karl Taylor Compton (in office
1930–48). Unlike their counterparts at most universities, the architects and
planners on the MIT faculty were actively involved in planning facilities,
developing programs, and hiring architects. And there was a tradition of
experimental building. Even the grand Neoclassical domed quadrangle,
designed by Welles Bosworth in 1913, had been made of unit construction, with changeable interior partitions and expandable corridors.[2] In
recent years, the school had commissioned several pioneering buildings.
The Radiation Laboratory was built during World War II from plans by
faculty members L.B. Anderson and H.L Beckwith. The Metals Processing
Laboratory was designed by Perry, Shaw and Hepburn around 1946.
Faculty architect Robert Kennedy built modular "temporaries" for students,
and a faculty team made up of Kennedy, Bill Brown, Vernon DeMars,
Carl Koch, and Ralph Rapson had built the Eastgate faculty housing (now
called 100 Memorial Drive), inspired by Le Corbusier's Marseilles Unité.
In 1947, President Compton and the dean of the School of Architecture
and Planning, William Wurster, had brought the Saarinens' family friend
and compatriot Alvar Aalto from Finland to build the magnificent brick
serpentine Baker House dormitory, which curves in and out along the
Charles and forms a sawtooth pattern on the campus side. It was Wurster
who suggested hiring Eero to design the auditorium and chapel, though
it was his successor, dean Pietro Belluschi, who was in office (1950–65)
when the project began and who had to defend the controversial
buildings when members of the administration questioned them.
Belluschi told them, "Creative masterpieces do not come easily or by
timid approach, and even abstract ideals do change. Architecture,
being a crystallization of ideas, needs to go through the same vitalizing

113

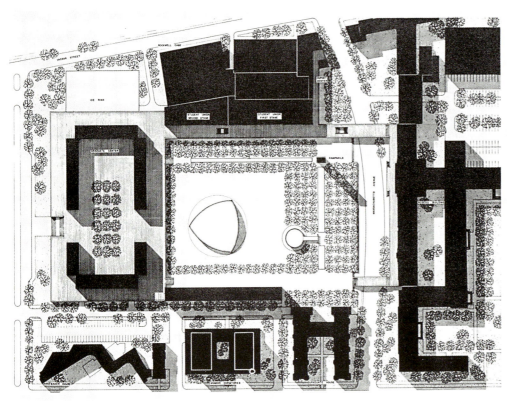

This page, from left: MIT campus plan with Kresge Auditorium and MIT Chapel on plaza; Kresge Auditorium seen from MIT Chapel.

Opposite: Kresge Auditorium and MIT Chapel, aerial.

experimentation which we're ready to advocate for the world of science and engineering. The alternative is sterility."[3]

It helped that ambitious, experimental architecture had become an MIT tradition before Saarinen arrived. There were still anxious moments, but the school gave him license—even encouragement—to break new technical and aesthetic ground with the auditorium and the chapel. Both buildings derived from the Brandeis designs, the chapel most directly.

Like the one he had designed with Nowicki, the MIT Chapel is brick-walled inside and out and lit by an oculus in the ceiling. The wavy walls of the earlier scheme reappeared on its interior, but the outside is a thirty-foot-tall cylindrical drum, a more classical and traditional form than the two had originally imagined. Saarinen invited his old friend from Cranbrook, Harry Bertoia, to design the fluttering metal screen that refracts the light from above the altar, and asked the sculptor Theodore Roszak to create a lacy aluminum bell tower and spire for the top of the flat roof. Instead of an underground entrance like the one in the Brandeis scheme, a glass-walled corridor leads into the sanctuary, separating it from the outside world. The brick outer walls are supported on brick arches that rise out of a shallow twelve-foot-wide moat, lit from below to create reflections and a mystical secondary light source inside. With this device, Saarinen and his partners—Bruce Adams worked

closely with him on this design—were able to create a sense of quiet isolation on a busy urban site (whereas the Brandeis Chapel was to have achieved its isolation by physical separation and a natural setting). Unfortunately, the entry sequence is handled less gracefully than the other parts of the building, as Saarinen later acknowledged.

The interior of the chapel itself, however, has a powerful spiritual quality not associated with any particular religion but common to all. That type of universality made particularly good sense at MIT, where there were students from forty-six countries by the late 1940s.[4] Embraced by the encircling walls and mesmerized by the flickering light, one speaks in a whisper or falls silent, sensing a higher power—or at least a higher purpose. The chapel, with its textured brick walls, similar to those on Aalto's nearby Baker House dormitories, accommodates 130 chairs. It was used for chamber-music concerts, meditation, and Protestant, Catholic, and Jewish religious services when it opened. When Saarinen died, his memorial service was held there.

The auditorium is as bold and lively as the chapel is peaceful and restrained. Instead of the shallow dome plopped atop slanted columns that was proposed for Brandeis, the structure consists of a single cut-away section—one-eighth of a sphere—of thin-shelled concrete resting on its own three pendentive-like points, with its abutments buried in the ground so that the dome seems to rise weightlessly. It is, in fact, exceedingly light, proportionally thinner than an eggshell. At its apex it is only 3 1/2 inches thick; even the base swells to only eighteen inches. It is also very economical in materials and cost (the original estimate was about one hundred thousand dollars), yet it covers half an acre,

spans 160 feet, rises 50 feet, and seats 1,238 in the main hall, with 250 musicians in the orchestra pit or people on the stage and 75 more in the choir loft. An underground theater fifteen feet below grade holds an audience of two hundred.[5] On the lower level, there are also offices, a coat-check room, rehearsal spaces, a sheet-music library, a green room, dressing rooms, an instrument room, a freight elevator, an emergency generator, and two huge air-conditioning units (unusual for the time) that were also used to make ice for a skating rink on the adjacent plaza.

It was not only a radically new kind of auditorium; it represented a new direction in Saarinen's career. His technical innovations at the corporate campuses were largely confined to materials, but here the breakthrough was in structure. Even before it opened, the auditorium caused quite a stir. As "the first large shell structure of a sophisticated architectural character to be completed in the US," it was widely published and vigorously debated.[6] As soon as the MIT projects were announced, *Architectural Forum* (January 1953) devoted a seven-page spread to them, with sequences of drawings showing how the designs had evolved, but without mentioning Nowicki.[7]

The article recognized that the MIT buildings were going to be controversial: "Eero Saarinen and his associates have given MIT something more than a very handsome auditorium and a strange, haunting chapel. They have challenged current thinking and started some basic rethinking about architecture and building." They "represent an overhaul of Louis Sullivan's credo that 'form follows function.' Unlike the typical modern auditorium [such as the Kleinhans Music Hall] with its form directly derived from sight lines and acoustical requirements, Saarinen's assumes a universal shape."[8]

The architect said he chose a dome because "that shape is a recurrent motif of the existing MIT campus; it gives expression to the idea of sheltering a large space—a single room—where many people can congregate; provides an interior where the audience and the stage can be in intimate relation to each other; is the strongest and most economical way of covering an area with concrete."[9] It also provided a completely unobstructed, column-free interior, was dramatic in appearance, and looked extraordinarily modern. However, the auditorium is directional (all the seats face the stage), while the dome is not, though the vaguely triangular arrangment of the interior space fits within the triangular section established by the three pendentives.

As he had done at GM, Saarinen used the client's resources to solve architectural problems. His associate architects were professors Lawrence B. Anderson and Herbert L. Beckwith, of Anderson & Beckwith. Professor Richard H. Bolt's firm, Bolt, Beranek & Newman—the most celebrated acousticians of the time—designed floating clouds hung from the dome to compensate for the concave shape and curved rear wall (which would have compromised the quality of the sound). Most concert halls have plaster ceilings far below the roof that are contoured to enhance acoustics and contain lighting and ventilating shafts. At MIT, Saarinen wanted the curved structure to be visible, so the clouds had to contain the lights and ducts, too, without obscuring the view of the inside of the dome.

The underside is painted a skylike blue-gray, which can be seen behind and between the white clouds. The outside of the dome is covered with an eight-inch-thick coating composed of a felt membrane, two inches

This page, from top: Kresge Auditorium; model. of MIT buildings.

Opposite: MIT Chapel, exterior.

of glass wool, an asphaltic fabric, two inches of cinder concrete, and an acrylic plastic mixed with fiberglass, beach sand, and other materials for weatherproofing and sound insulation. An article in the June 1955 issue of MIT's *Technology Review* explains how the dome was built: "The construction of the concrete shell represents a new and interesting development in architecture. The crown of the dome was formed by building an inner structure of concentric rings, supported by lightweight metal scaffolding. One- by six-inch planking was then bent over sleepers to complete the formwork. The steel reinforcing was placed above this. At the corners where the concrete is thicker and where the slope of the dome is acute, additional forms were placed above the reinforcing.

116

The concrete was poured in three operations at separate times, beginning at the three abutments and working up toward the peak of the dome. An 18-inch upturned edge stiffens the shell and directs rain water to drains at the three abutments. Affixed to the upturned edge are a group of equally spaced exterior lights whose black housing has the form of truncated cones."

"As an important event, perhaps even a pivotal one, in US architecture today the MIT dome deserves thorough study,"[10] another *Forum* article exclaimed. And when it was completed, the magazine invited comments from three internationally respected architectural critics. Bruno Zevi, the editor of *L'Architettura*, said, "Italian architects were puzzled when I published Eero Saarinen's Auditorium." One of the architects of the Rome Railway Station, Eugenio Montuori, said, "You've done it now! We were

already confused between the functionalist and the organic approaches in architecture, between the Le Corbusier and the Wright trends. And here comes Saarinen preaching total irrationalism. You've published it, and the mess is completed." The celebrated engineer Pier Luigi Nervi told Zevi he hated the Kresge Auditorium dome: "I could demonstrate that structural thought and common sense have been allied in all ages. Today structural ideas are invaded by extravagance, and they are deprived of all justification. I really wonder why you published this auditorium in your magazine."[11]

Zevi himself thought: "The idea of a universally valid 'form,' separate from function and from technical requirements is the old classical, or better Neoclassical idea." He saw the chapel as "an evasion of the rational and organic approaches to architecture" and predicted it would be "spiritually

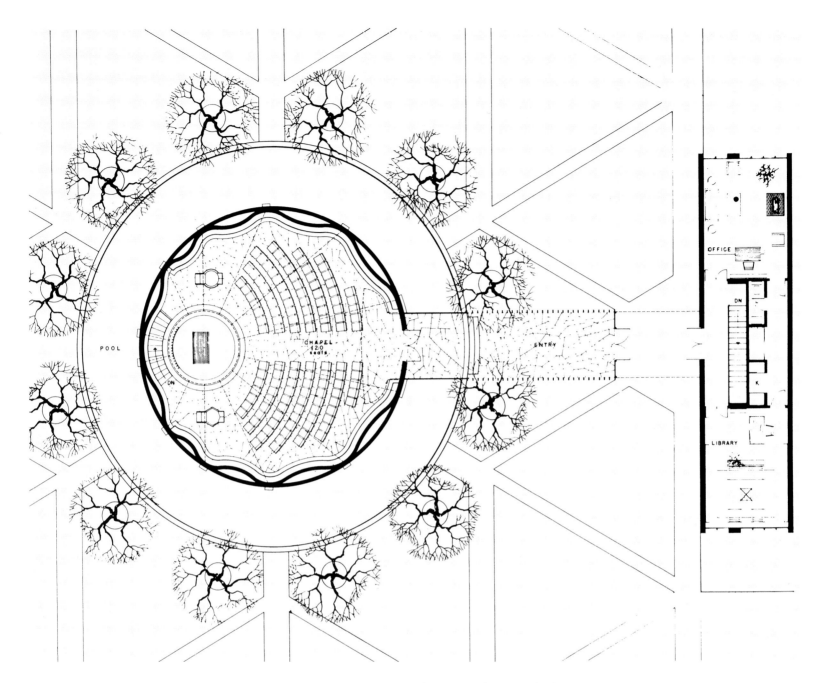

This page: MIT Chapel, plan.

Opposite: MIT Chapel, view into interior from entryway with
sculptural screen by Harry Bertoia.

unsuitable and cultural misleading, as are all 'bright ideas.'" But he said
he would publish it when it was completed because, "I believe, as I have
often written, that Eero Saarinen is one of the outstanding architects
of his generation. To my mind, the mistakes of great architects are
always significant. Saarinen will emerge from the present impasse."

J.M. Richards, the British architectural historian, who admitted that he
had not visited the buildings, told *Architectural Forum*, "The purity of
structural conception shown in the MIT buildings is greatly to be admired,
but purity destroys scale, and how to bring the scale of a building under
control without inhibiting the free and inspiring use of modern technical
possibilities is one of the esthetic problems that modern architecture

has yet to solve. . . . Each of these buildings is founded on one simple
idea, but the two ideas are totally different in kind. The auditorium
exploits the new industrial technology to create its architectural effect; the
chapel uses accepted means . . . to create something preconceived simply
as form. Both ideas are valid; but it interests me to see them employed
simultaneously and so convincingly as part of the same project."

Sigfried Giedion's response was more obtuse. He compared the buildings to Le Corbusier's Ronchamp and said, "This work that brings to
expression the secret boldness that dwells within our times had not to
wait to find recognition."

Like the GM Technical Center, the MIT buildings appeared in the popular
press and the American and European journals because they were "new."
Time covered the auditorium in June 1953 and the chapel in December
1955; they were discussed in *L'Architettura* in Italy, *Construction mod-*

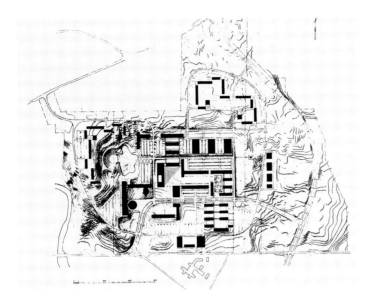

This page: University of Michigan, Ann Arbor, Michigan, North Campus master plan, 1951–53.

Opposite: University of Michigan, Ann Arbor, Michigan, sketch of aerial view showing "forum" on central courtyard.

not be held; therefore we retreated to the woods. We were given the commission to design the Music School. Roughly at the same time, several other buildings were given out for design around the Music School, so we had to retreat . . . , with no hope of any coordinating with the surrounding buildings. At that time we resigned from being consultant for the North Campus."[26]

The university was growing quickly but with limited resources, and the trustees built whatever they could fund instead of investing in a coherent collection of colleges. They cast their net indiscriminately instead of finding the best possible architect for each job or group of buildings, and the primary consultant had no power to coordinate or control what was designed. Instead of the pedestrian environment the master plan had envisioned, the North Campus became the "suburb" *Architectural Forum* had predicted, while the main campus developed an increasingly lively mix of shops, restaurants, bookstores, and cafés on its edges. The contrast remains quite stunning.

Saarinen did not give up without a fight. A few years later, when he heard that some of the regents were unhappy with what had been built, he requested an audience with them and delivered a full lecture on campus planning that later became an article in *Architectural Record*.[27] He placed the problems at Michigan in the larger context of American college building design, attributed the difficulties to architects as well as to administrators, and almost begged to be brought back—but only with control over architect selection, coordination of design, and overall planning. He even mentioned the need to fund buildings in a single year so that a design could be developed properly. Of course, nothing changed.

At Yale, which was private and therefore less subject to outside political pressures, growth occurred more incrementally, and the quality of the architecture was a major concern. Although the university was founded in 1701 and grew throughout the eighteenth and nineteenth centuries, the character of the campus was established much later, between 1917 and the 1930s, according to a plan by James Gamble Rogers for a series of Gothic Revival quadrangles inspired by Oxford and Cambridge universities in England. Like earlier Yale buildings, the quadrangles follow the town grid, maintaining the street line, so the campus is dense and an integral part of the city fabric. Together, the Rogers buildings, which were under construction when Saarinen was a student at Yale, create one of the finest—and certainly one of the most urbane—campuses in America.

Most of the buildings were inspired by medieval prototypes, though some, perhaps in deference to Connecticut Hall of 1750–53, are vaguely Georgian (historic styles were still part of the architecture-school curriculum when they were being built); the campus buildings seem older today than they actually are, a phenomenon most people would consider a virtue. But after World War II, the Yale curriculum, like those at other American schools, was modernized. Architectural historians and critics were judging buildings as much by how modern they were as by anything else. The particular emphasis at the Yale School of Architecture then was on architecture as a fine art, encouraging the cross-fertilization among all the fine arts, as at the Bauhaus and Cranbrook. In the 1950s, when building resumed, the university was committed to modern architecture of the highest quality, not only in the classroom, but in its building program. Under president A. Whitney Griswold, the school commissioned buildings from many of the most highly regarded architects of the day.[28]

The (Ultimate) Hockey Rink
The opportunity to design the new David S. Ingalls Hockey Rink at Yale (1956–59) came just as the General Motors Technical Center and MIT buildings were winding down, so Saarinen could devote his full energies to it. A building type with few serious precedents was ideally suited to his interests and talents. He had learned a great deal about lightweight concrete structures working on the Kresge Auditorium, and he had taken on a new associate with experience in bold construction. David Powrie was a young Canadian architect who had recently returned to Toronto after working for Eduardo Alfonso Reidy and Oscar Niemeyer in Brazil, where concrete construction was arguably more advanced than anywhere else in the world. Saarinen had heard about him from one of Powrie's former professors, who was working with him on Irwin Miller's vacation house in Canada, and he simply called him up at the Toronto office where he was working and asked him to join the unusually talented staff that Saarinen had assembled from all over the world.

Work on the hockey rink began the way every project did, with dogged research. Most hockey rinks are very simple buildings with no architectural pretensions—almost sheds—but Saarinen took nothing for granted. He sent Powrie on a trip to see other college hockey rinks and learn all he could about what worked and what did not; what coaches, players, and university administrators considered ideal; what was completely unacceptable; and all manner of technical considerations such as how to cool the ice, ventilate the space, and provide good views from the stands. When Powrie returned with a list of all the buildings he had seen, noting their structural systems, the size of the rinks, the number of seats, whether they were heated, and so forth, Saarinen wrote him a note addressed to "Bannister Fletcher Powrie," referring to the famous architectural historian who had classified and categorized all the famous buildings in the world.[29]

Always conscious of history, Saarinen wanted to do more than simply solve the practical problems. His growing interest in structural concrete led him to consider the various curved forms that architects were experimenting with at the time, especially cable-hung structures like the ones Matthew Nowicki had used in the Livestock Judging Pavilion in Raleigh. He also wanted, as usual, to come up with a form that seemed particularly appropriate for this purpose—something playful with a big, vigorous sweep like those of hockey players gliding along the ice.[30] He hired Fred Severud, the inventive engineer who had worked with him on the Saint Louis Arch (1947–65) and had helped Nowicki and Deitrick design the livestock pavilion.

Saarinen sketched until he arrived at a form specifically suitable for hockey—raw and rugged but also graceful. The Livestock Judging Pavilion featured two great interlocking parabolic arches supporting a huge suspended catenary roof; it was geometric, symmetrical, and designed to maximize structural forces as economically as possible. Saarinen's rink is organic, irregular, and rather complicated, by contrast. The arches that swoop down and then up—or out—probably appealed to Severud because he liked a challenge and because he was interested in deriving structural principles from nature. He had even written on the subject.[31]

Together they devised a huge, wide parabolic arch for a central spine held in place by a grid of cables running both parallel and perpendicular to it, and hung it in a saddle shape to form a tensioned web. "The cables, which were suspended in catenary curves from the central arch, stretch down to their anchorage in the exterior walls on each side," Eero explained. These semicircular concrete walls slope outward slightly, "both in order to increase structural efficiency and to enhance the visual expression of the stress flows."[32] (Anthony J. Lumsden, who worked in Saarinen's office at the time, also played a role in the design.)

At the ends, the central arch swoops up to support a forty-foot canopy over the entrances (at least it did until the rear was closed to accommodate concessions and the women's locker rooms after Yale College began admitting undergraduate women in 1969). The arch is visible—dominant even—both inside and out, so it visually ties the inside and outside together, setting up the experience of the interior from a distance.

From the outside, the hockey rink resembles a gigantic, humped, slithering beast or, some say, an overturned Viking ship. From the inside, it sweeps you up in a skating movement. Here, perhaps more than anywhere else, Eero Saarinen operated as a sculptor as well as an architect; he created three-dimensional forms that not only were vaguely representational but, like the surrealistic shapes they resemble, also reflected subconscious experience.

He even joked about it. At one point when the rink was under construction, he was asked to explain it. "The David S. Ingalls Skating Rink is deliberately not an ordinary building," he said. "When it is finished, it will probably have many names, because people like to find names for extraordinary buildings. It may be called 'the Roller Coaster,' or 'the Pregnant Whale,' or 'the Turtle,' or 'the giant boat upside-down.'" (In fact, it came to be called the "Yale Whale.") "What intrigues me most, however, is to imagine archeologists 5,000 years from now digging in New Haven and first coming across the prehistoric bones in The Peabody Museum, and then not so far away from there finding this huge, dinosaur-like skeleton. What kind of history will they reconstruct about what formidable creatures Yale men were in the mid-twentieth century!"[33]

Because it is not just an ordinary building, it was not easy to realize. When the Yale corporation first decided to build a new hockey rink in the 1950s, the administration, which was committed to ambitious architecture, conflicted with the Hockey Committee, which simply wanted to put up a functional skating facility. Some of its members soon warmed to the idea of more than a tin can, but others never did. The head of the fund-raising committee resigned midstream, and all along the way, Saarinen, Yale president A. Whitney Griswold, and even members of the art history department had to defend the idea of creating a work of original architecture.

At the beginning, Saarinen was forced to fight for an adequate budget, since the initial allocation of six hundred thousand dollars was based on the cost of a plain wood-and-masonite shed with a steel bent roof that Harvard had recently built. As with previous projects, he concluded that if the client wanted such an uninspired building, he wasn't the architect for it. Even a shed like that, he advised, would cost more then, as costs were rising by about 5 percent a year. Still, when the increased seven hundred thousand dollar budget proved inadequate, there was

The University of Michigan School of Music,
1952–56.

pressure to fire the architect—foiled by President Griswold and the head of university facilities at the time, Norman Buck, who argued that costs rose because of infighting in the Hockey Committee, engineering mistakes, and the underground water table found on the site.[34]

The site had been chosen by a university building committee with the idea of extending the campus north into what was largely a residential area. Since the site was located in a place that would soon be part of the main campus instead of in the remote athletic-center area, it made sense to build a rink with character. But it had so much character that it was controversial, not only because it was ambitious architecture, but because it was architecture of a kind nobody had ever seen before.

When the donor's wife, Louise Ingalls, saw the model, she did not like it one bit. Again, president Griswold had to rally the forces. This time he did it by writing a long, self-deprecating letter to David and Louise Ingalls, explaining that he, too, originally had a negative reaction to the model when he first saw it—until he realized that he was looking at it from a point of view from which no one, except someone in a helicopter, would ever see it. He pointed out that Eero Saarinen was "by far the most distinguished architect Yale has graduated" and that "for all his interest in modern architecture, he has shown the most lively appreciation of traditional forms already here."[35]

He also invited four esteemed Yale art historians—all Yale graduates— to come see the model and write a letter of support, and he enclosed it with his own. The faculty letter was signed by the medievalist Sumner McK. Crosby, George Heard Hamilton (who was both a professor and curator of modern art at the Yale Art Gallery), Renaissance-art historian Charles Seymour Jr., and architectural historian Vincent Scully. They wrote to thank Griswold for "succeeding in drawing out from a man who stands at the top level of the country's architects what looks to be the best and most exciting design he has made." They went on, floridly, to say it possessed "the essential principles of the Gothic construction," "the grandeur and unity of Roman architecture," "delicacy recalling Oriental qualities," and "the character and integrity" of the principles of modern architecture.[36]

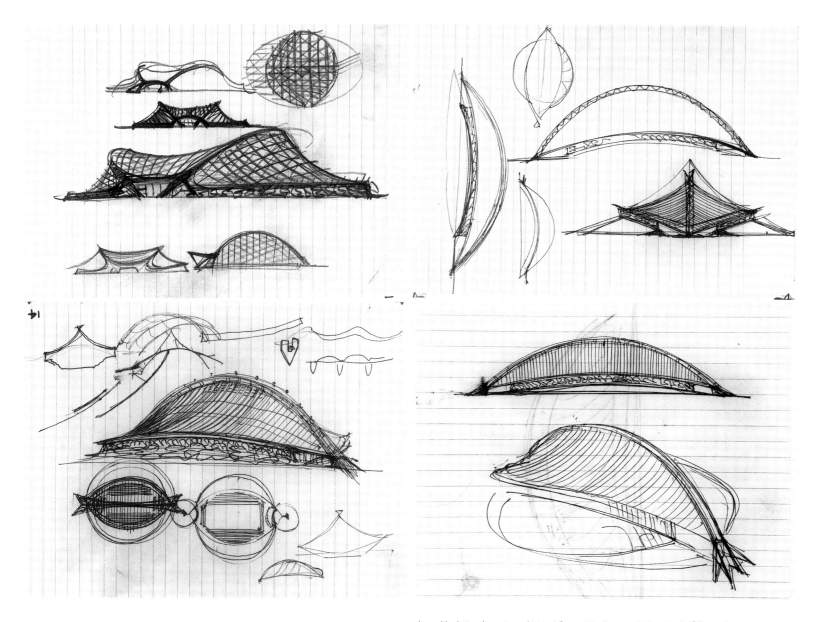

This page: David S. Ingalls Hockey Rink, Yale University, 1956–59, sketches by Eero Saarinen.

Opposite, from top: Ingalls Hockey Rink, section and perspective; plan.

After the letters were sent, Eero made a special trip to Connecticut to see Mrs. Ingalls before traveling to Australia to judge the Sydney Opera House competition, where he would sway the jury in favor of Jørn Utzon, putting Sydney on the world architecture map. In his absence the campaign to save the hockey rink succeeded, and after the building was finished, the Ingallses were delighted.

Saarinen was too. "I believe it is the best building we have done," he said when it was completed.[37] The hockey players admired it. Saarinen loved the fact that one of them said it made him feel "Go, go, go!" The rink certainly received a lot of critical attention in the press. Articles in *Sports Illustrated, Harper's, Life, Criterion, Engineering News Record, Civil Engineering*, as well as, of course, the architecture magazines *Architectural Forum, Architectural Record, Architectural Review, L'Architecture d'au-* *jourd'hui, Baukunst und Werkform, Zodiac*, and *Casabella*.[38] But it was not considered an unqualified success.

Walter McQuade, a fan of Saarinen's, called it "one of the most surprising new buildings in the world" and pronounced it "Saarinen's most successful attempt to mix visual flavor into the recipe of modern architecture." He noted, "This new arena also has precision and delicacy. Functionally the rink is superb. . . . Sight lines will seldom be blocked. . . . Suspended fluorescent lamps throw 60 foot-candles of illumination on the ice— virtually the same kind of shadowless light under which the game of hockey evolved outdoors." Yet, McQuade pointed out, "Saarinen has been accused by some displeased members of his profession of having shaped a gigantic piece of whimsy, a tour de force." As McQuade reports, their objections included: "The location of one of the bases of the enormous arch smack in the middle of the principal bank of doors has been called clumsy. The steel strands which tie the upper arch to the exterior walls are accused of looking like an insecure afterthought to the engineering. The suspended lighting fixtures give the impression of being a false, hung ceiling [and] the heating and ventilating equipment

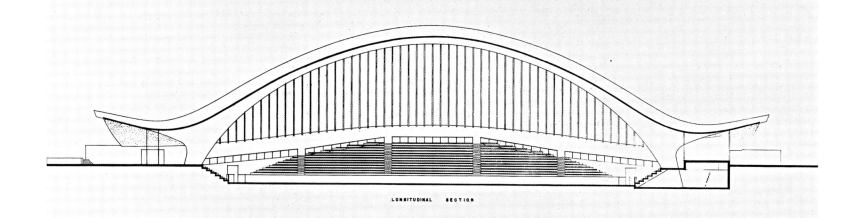

LONGITUDINAL SECTION

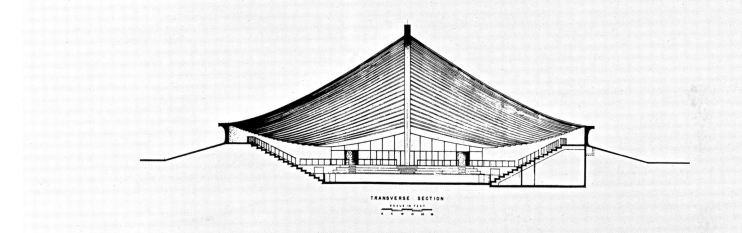

TRANSVERSE SECTION

SCALE IN FEET

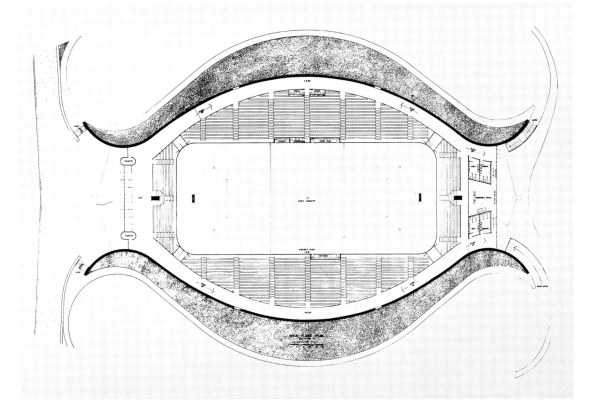

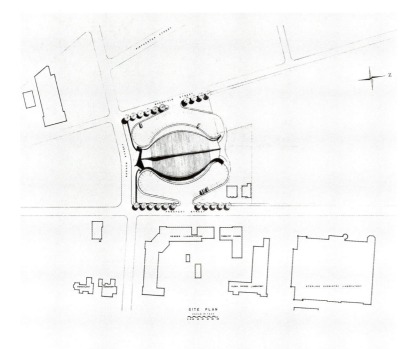

SITE PLAN

dropped into the four rounded corners of the rink is ugly and awkward." He acknowledged that the last point was valid, but he said that the other criticisms "really ask for another building." He admitted that it came in over budget—at close to $1.4 million—but said, "like other venturesome clients Yale got a great deal more in the Ingalls rink than it expected . . . a building it can be proud of . . . whose vigor is particularly appropriate to its formal purpose."[39]

Allan Temko also had some objections: "Three bracing cables run from the arch to the base of the monument to guarantee stability under uneven loads of wind or snow. These independent wires, like Renaissance tie-rods, weaken the entire structural impact because of their thin linear value. Other exterior shortcomings are the bulbous ventilating monitors, the sullen black of the neoprene waterproofing." That neoprene sheath, however, kept the roof from leaking for fifty years—a lesson Saarinen learned the hard way at MIT. But, since the hockey rink roof was not insulated, moisture does condense inside it sometimes, creating a cloud effect.

"But," Temko concluded, "as one is drawn—pulled—through the compressed, hovering entrance, the interior enlarges suddenly in a high, bending volume, which the muscular arch negotiates in a 228-foot bound, with the wooden roof lightly flying above the white sheet of ice. The use of wood is questionable but the space lives, as Saarinen intended, and perhaps justifies the superenergizing of structure, even in so small an arena, which seats only 3,000 in intimate stands and could have been vaulted by much simpler methods. For without question this space is literally one of the most stirring in American architecture."[40]

Yale officials went out on a limb for the David S. Ingalls Hockey Rink. It was one thing to make an extraordinary effort to build a distinguished art gallery but quite another to make such an investment in an athletic facility. What Yale commissioned amounted to so much more than a hockey rink that it was used for concerts, other public events, and even for Yale graduation ceremonies until the student body became too large. The building is a living testament to the importance of architecture as an art and to the university's willingness to take risks to achieve it. Yale's support gave Saarinen the chance to explore the expressionistic, sculpturesque direction he had fought for in Sydney and would develop further in airport-terminal design, foreshadowing similar impulses in the work of Frank Gehry and other architects in the late twentieth and early twenty-first centuries. But it was by no means the only direction he pursued, as his next building complex at Yale clearly shows.

This page: Ingalls Hockey Rink, exterior with guy wires and visible vents. Sculpture on prow by Oliver Andrews.

Opposite, from top: Ingalls Hockey Rink, site plan with neighboring buildings on Prospect and Sachem streets; interior of ice rink.

Pages 128–29: Ingalls Hockey Rink, entrance.

Opposite: Eero Saarinen with cardboard model and drawings
of Morse and Stiles colleges at Yale University, c. 1959.

The David S. Ingalls Hockey Rink became so popular at Yale that it is not surprising that Eero Saarinen was invited to design the first new residential colleges to be built on that campus since the 1920s. But anyone who happened on his Morse and Stiles colleges would have trouble believing they were designed by the same person as the rink. They look more like byways in an Italian hill town. The difference makes sense only in the context of some of Saarinen's other college buildings, his concerns about what was happening on American campuses, and the way he approached every project.

In the early years of his career, Saarinen adapted ideas from some of his college buildings to use in others—the dormitories at Brandeis (1949–50) and Drake (1945–55) resemble those at Antioch (1944–48), while the MIT Chapel and Auditorium (1950–55) were inspired by schemes for Brandeis—but his first concern, always, was to produce the most appropriate design for the job, based on the kind of building that was needed, the institution, and the physical setting. Saarinen's tendency to design for the specific needs of a project became more pronounced over time.

Concordia Senior College in Fort Wayne, Indiana (1953–58), selected Saarinen's firm from a pool of eighteen architects considered to design a completely new campus for a new kind of college, a two-year school intended to prepare college juniors and seniors for graduate study at a Lutheran seminary. Concordia, built by the Missouri Synod (a governing body) of the Lutheran Church, later became a graduate-level seminary and is now called Concordia Theological Seminary.

Saarinen was not conventionally religious—like many intellectuals and creative people in his time, he sought answers to his problems through psychoanalysis—but his grandfather had been a Lutheran minister. He understood the culture of the church and could work productively with the building committee to find the right form for the buildings. "We all felt," he explained, "that they should not be inward-turning and removed like medieval monasteries, but have a tranquil atmosphere of at least partial self-sufficiency."[1]

He could have created that atmosphere in many ways, as he was not only designing the campus from the ground up but also selecting the site. He and Glen Paulsen, a valued associate who had recently returned to the firm, proposed "a village of the North European type. A chapel is in the center, placed on the highest spot, with the other buildings grouped around this central and all important symbol."[2]

The "village" resembles a small Scandinavian town. Although the buildings, which have pitched roofs, are clearly modern—built with steel frames and minimal detail—the approach is representational rather than abstract. The scheme represents a departure from the long, low rectangles of the International Style that Saarinen had used almost exclusively a few years earlier.

Why take such a radically different approach than the one employed at Brandeis? The Brandeis site was very dramatic—hilly, forested, and rocky—so the three-dimensional character could come from the landscape itself. In Fort Wayne, the terrain is comparatively flat. Some of the land, near the road, was wooded, but the sparse old trees in the middle of the proposed location for the buildings were not worth saving, so the structures had to provide the visual interest. And a "village-like cluster with the varied lines of pitched roof" would create "an expressive silhouette," Saarinen explained.

That was only one reason, however. In the four years since he had been offered the Brandeis commission, Saarinen had seen what happened when clusters of long, low rectangular buildings were strewn across the land. "Horizontally emphasized buildings closely related remind me of express trains running rampant against each other," he wrote in an article on campus planning a few years later.[3] He had become disillusioned with other excesses of modern architecture too. In a memo written to Paulsen when the project was beginning, he said, "I think all this God damn modern architecture has too much glass."[4] He still considered himself a Modernist (though what he meant by this was a man conscious of his time), but he was already seeing the limitations of the particular brand of Miesian International Style Modernism that had taken hold in America.

The notes he wrote to his staff testify to his intimate involvement with every aspect of the design, the clients, and the problem at hand. One thing he asked Paulsen to do was submit a hundred questions to the building committee because the clients had not specified what types of classrooms they wanted, how big they should be, or what equipment teachers would need. In some cases, Saarinen thought, the things they had requested needed to be reconsidered. The program, he confided to Paulsen, was "skimpy."

"I picture this as a very closely knit group of buildings," he wrote in his memo. "We talked about whether circulation should be interior or exterior, which is really the difference between a high school and a university, and I am sure it should be exterior. That is the only way to make the outdoors count. For classrooms, they only indicate twenty, and they don't specify definite size. We know that today teaching has come to be done mainly in lecture halls and seminars. I believe less is taught in standard classrooms than before. If we can ask some pertinent questions about that, it will challenge them to really work out their teaching policy."[5]

(One of the things the Saarinen office provided was real help on exactly what to build.)

In another note to his colleagues Dave Geery and Joe Lacy, who helped with site selection, he characterized all the people he had met from the building committee, and suggested how each could be helpful. He brought up all kinds of factors they needed to consider, including the possibility of connecting with city sewers and water if the site was beyond the city limits. He tried to cover every detail.[6]

In the end Concordia acquired a 191-acre site five miles from downtown Fort Wayne. The Saint Joseph River framed the eastern edge. At a slight ridge in the middle of the site, next to a meadow where the architects created a large man-made lake, they located the predominant chapel. All the buildings have pitched roofs, but the roof on the chapel is steeper (with a 23.5-degree pitch from the vertical) than those on the rest of the buildings (which have a 23.5-degree pitch from the horizontal). Pitched roofs were not unpopular at the time. A-frame vacation houses featured steep ones; Carl Koch's mass-produced Techbuilt chalets had low ones; and triangular, high-gabled churches were being built in various parts of the United States. *Architectural Forum* published three of them, plus a prefab version, in the same issue with Saarinen's plans for Concordia Senior College.[7] In Scandinavia, modern architects had never abandoned traditional shapes and materials the way some had done in Germany and America; Saarinen, who traveled to Finland almost every year, retained the influence.

Still, some architects in this country found it shocking that he was using pitched roofs and openly admitting they were intended to evoke a European village. But he was designing to satisfy his clients and himself. The pitched roofs solved the problem of the flat, characterless landscape, pleased members of the committee who had worried that he was "pretty far out," and still managed to win a *Progressive Architecture* Design Award. The roof scheme gave the new small religious college unique character and enabled the chapel, on which Paulsen played a major role, to become the centerpiece of the entire composition. It dominates the campus gently, offering an experience inside that is potent, soothing, and inspirational. The handling of natural light, which enters mysteriously from under the eaves, gives it an otherworldly atmosphere, while the natural materials of brick and wood bring that sense of the spiritual down to earth.

No one would mistake the Concordia campus for anything other than modern. It has an abstract rigor and consistency. All the roof ridges run east-west. The few buildings that are placed east-west instead of north-south have little rows of sawtooth roofs running east-west as well. The same structural system of a five-foot-four-inch module with

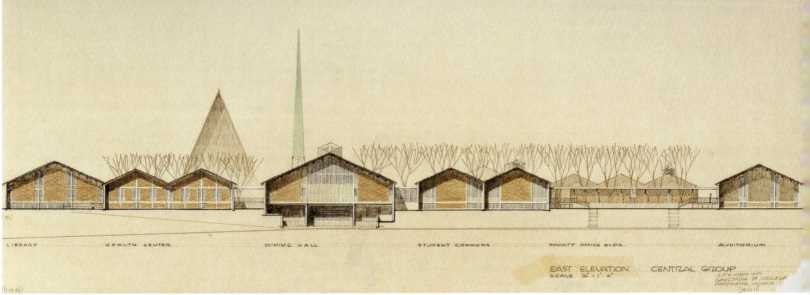

LIBRARY HEALTH CENTER DINING HALL STUDENT COMMONS FACULTY OFFICE BLDG. AUDITORIUM

EAST ELEVATION · CENTRAL GROUP
SCALE ⅛" = 1' 0"

From top: Concordia Senior College (now Concordia
Theological Seminary), Fort Wayne, Indiana, 1953–58, chapel
with academic buildings; elevation of dormitory buildings.

This page, clockwise from top left: Concordia Senior College Chapel, under construction, c. 1957; sketch of plan, c. 1954; lounge in dormitory; model.

Opposite: Concordia Senior College Chapel, interior.

simple, straightforward details is used throughout the campus. "A system of grilled walls [open-patterned brickwork] was devised to control sunlight and reduce the amount of glass on external walls," Saarinen explained.

"After trying precast concrete, terra cotta and wood, we decided on brick. But because of the sloped gable ends, it seemed desirable to have brick that did not require clipping to meet the incline of the roof. The obvious answer was a diamond-shaped brick which could serve for both solid and grilled walls and give some additional textural interest to the gable ends. [But] a diamond-shaped brick was not available on the market, so it was necessary for us to do research in the whole problem of determining the exact size, the number of special shapes needed to meet every condition, its color, and the method of constructing grilles.

This took the cooperation of a brick manufacturer, our structural engineers, a building contractor [A.C. Wermuth, who had built Cranbrook and commissioned a house from the Saarinens], and a consultant from the Masonry Institute in Washington, D.C."[8] So even though the buildings look traditional, new materials were developed for them, as they had been at GM, IBM, Bell Labs, and Deere & Company.

The diamond-shaped bricks were not easy to secure, but they make all the difference. They give the buildings, despite their plainness, the sense of craftsmanship evident in Eliel Saarinen's work and in Scandinavian architecture at the middle of the twentieth century. Eero wanted to use a gray brick and whitewash it so that the buildings with black roofs and white walls would stand out dramatically against the blues and greens of the landscape, but the building committee chose a more traditional pinkish buff brick. Similarly, knowing that the school wanted to commission works of liturgical art to convey a religious message and to expose the students to the arts, he proposed "large black-and-white photo-murals of various kinds. Some of them might be giant size, dramatic enlargements of something like a Dürer or a Schongauer print.

136

Others might be a montage. The important thing is that these murals be designed by the best possible artist in the field," and he mentioned a recent exhibition of photographic art at the Museum of Modern Art[9] (though he did not name it, he was probably referring to "The Family of Man," which Edward Steichen organized in 1955). In the end the committee chose, as Saarinen suspected it would, mostly semiabstract murals and reliefs by midwestern artists who specialized in liturgical art, instead of the more avant-garde artists he was accustomed to working with. The committee did commission some works from members of the Cranbrook community, such as weavings for the chapel and cast-bronze shields of the apostles and the evangelists for the classroom buildings, and ordered handsome communion ware from Georg Jensen.[10]

On matters that did not involve personal taste or ecclesiastical tradition, the committee followed Saarinen's advice more completely. They had intended to house 450 students in three large dormitories for 150 students each, but ultimately they agreed to build clusters of house-size buildings with rooms for 36 students and generous, inviting, multilevel common rooms similar to those at Drake University. The numerous small dwellings, arranged in three separate groups, create a village of the campus and inspire the kind of close-knit community the founders were striving for.

The college, which opened in 1958, took a year longer to build than originally planned. It cost $7,150,000, a good deal more than the original budget of $4,200,000 but a bargain for twenty-five well-made new buildings with landscaping by Dan Kiley.

Women's Dorms

The growing number of female students enrolling in American colleges in the 1950s triggered numerous new dormitories because at that time women were not only housed separately from male college students but also treated differently—pampered, protected, and restricted. Women had to be in their rooms at night earlier than men, their premises were monitored by attendants at the entrances, and they practiced regular fire drills, while their male counterparts did not. The three women's dormitories that the Saarinen firm designed all possessed that sense of sanctuary. Frankly modern in style, they were nevertheless characterized by attempts to relate to their respective campus contexts, which were different in each case.

The Emma Hartman Noyes House (1954–58) at Vassar College, in Poughkeepsie, New York, were built as part of a plan for a corner of the bucolic campus called the Circle, where young women traditionally strolled with visiting suitors. (Vassar, founded in 1861 as a women's college, became coeducational in 1969.) The four-story dormitory curves around one-quarter of the circle, reinforcing existing paths and allowing

for expansion. Plans called for a second structure of the same size to be built later; the two buildings would enclose fully half of the circle. The circular theme is carried on inside; a gigantic round conversation pit (which students call "the passion pit") fills a central space on the first floor, and wide, rounded arches divide the dining room into sections.[11] "The basic structure of the double-loaded corridor scheme carries through and is expressed with considerable skill and taste," *Architectural Record* said. "The ceilings, structure, walls, hangings, table tops, and pedestal furniture are white; the carpeting is beige; the conversation pit is upholstered in soft shades of mauve, orange, and brown." The bricks on the outside were "carefully selected to be harmonious" with other campus buildings and "laid in black mortar to avoid a harsh, 'just-built' look."[12] Angular aluminum bay windows relate to the vaguely medieval-looking brick buildings in the main residential quadrangle. The first floor also contains two ground-floor apartments for house fellows and their families. Upstairs, the 34-foot-wide upper floors have fifty-one double rooms along the 150-foot curving, bay-windowed front and fifty-four single rooms in the back. Oval canopies cover the entrances.

If the interior seems more playful than the exterior, the contrast is less jarring than that at Hill Hall, the women's dormitories built three years later at the coeducational University of Pennsylvania (1957–60). Here, behind severe, blocky brick outer walls punctuated by an alternating pattern of deep-set vertical and horizontal windows and a gate, a festive, light-filled, white-walled, five-story-high courtyard opens up the middle of the space and gives the place what *Architectural Forum* called an "Arabian Nights fantasy" complete with balconies and shutters.[13] The artist Dan Graham, whose own work is inspired by architecture and who has a lively comic vision, sees it as a humorous take on a brothel theme.[14] There was a certain atmosphere of "look but don't touch" in women's dormitories at the time. Men were allowed to visit women's rooms on only one day every year; doors had to stay open, and students had to keep one foot on the floor. Chastity was to be preserved at all costs in the 1950s, when many young women came to college more to find husbands than to prepare for careers. The Penn dorm seems almost to parody that practice. Saarinen was, after all, a man who genuinely liked women and probably viewed the phenomenon sympathetically, though he preferred accomplished women as companions. He once joked that the reason some windows at Penn are vertical and others horizontal was that "Some girls do, some don't."[15] At any rate, the atmosphere at Vassar and Penn is very different from the feeling suggested in the earnest modern lounges at Antioch, Brandeis, and Drake. The Vassar and Penn dormitories are spirited and rather luxurious.

This page: Hill Hall women's dormitories, University of
Pennsylvania, Philadelphia, 1957–60.

Opposite: Hill Hall, interior.

While they are clearly not the buildings that the architect lavished his
attention on most (the firm was overwhelmed with commissions at the
time), they are intelligently planned and intended to appeal to students.
The Vassar dorm cost $1.4 million (for 256 students); the one at Penn,
where four L-shaped buildings surround the court, cost $4 million (for
656 women). The inward turn of the building in Philadelphia derives at
least partly from its inner-city location, where the use of brick on the
largely stone campus relates the complex to Cope and Stewardson's
neo-Jacobean residential quad and to Frank Furness's quirky but powerful library.

The women's dormitories at the University of Chicago (1955–58) were
considerably more sober, in keeping with the character of that school.
Four-story dormitory blocks surround three sides of an open courtyard;

and a freestanding, cruciform dining commons almost fills the fourth.
The dining hall has a glass-walled first floor and a heavy, overhanging,
limestone-sheathed second story that is reminiscent of Saarinen's
University of Michigan School of Music in elevation and of the Milwaukee
War Memorial in plan. The concrete-framed dormitory blocks, like those
at Brandeis and Drake, have vertical bands of glass and masonry, in
this case shot-sawn limestone ashlar in deference to the Gothic Revival
context that Saarinen admired.

"Wandering in the University of Chicago today," he wrote in his 1960
article on campus planning, "one is amazed at the beauty achieved by
space surrounded by buildings all in one discipline and made out of a
uniform material; where each building is being considerate of the next,
and each building—through its common material—is aging in the same
way. One is now far enough removed from the fight against eclecticism
to admire the vision of the time. . . . On a small court . . . built between
1894 and 1900, three different architects—Henry I. Cobb; Shepley, Rutan
& Coolidge; and Charles Klauder—built the four different sides. . . . Imagine
what would have happened if three or four equally eminent architects

140

of our day were asked to do the four sides of a square! (As a mater of fact, we are sweating it out on Lincoln Center and it is a problem.)"[16]

Saarinen realized that the unity was not solely a matter of style: "We must look further to see how the total master plan was achieved. At Chicago, Henry I. Cobb made the master plan not a two-dimensional one but a three-dimensional one, and set the pattern of the Gothic. This plan was respected. The strong-minded, architecturally enlightened members of the Board of Trustees insisted that the plan be carried out substantially as conceived."[17]

Although the Chicago women's dormitories, which were razed in 2001, over the objections of preservationists, to make room for an addition to the business school, did not represent a particularly inspired response to the context, the buildings Saarinen designed for the University of Chicago Law School (1956–60) certainly did. The six-story law-school library is a thoroughly modern, glass-walled, concrete-framed structure with large dramatic spaces as well as cozy crannies. The dark glass facade is pleated, which gives the roofline a jagged edge. The facade glistens

in the sun over its mirror image in a reflecting pool beside the wide green medium strip that divides the south side of the campus from the rest, where it is visible in the distance as well as across the street. In the crystalline law library, Saarinen featured additional Gothic elements he had not found among those he admired at Chicago—the lightly framed, glass-filled walls of High Gothic cathedrals and the delicate pinnacles that give them pointy rooflines. He translated them into a modern design vocabulary that gives library carrels views of the outside world; at night, the walls project a colorful, glowing image of scholars at work. The library, with its dramatic, double-height second-floor reading room, is the centerpiece of a four-building complex that was intended to mediate between an existing stone dormitory for law students on the west, with its steep-pitched roofs, prominent gables, and interior courtyards, and a rather bland modern Bar Association building two blocks east. A two-story administration building, set behind a plaza, connects the library with the residence hall. A long, low, lacy classroom wing edges the pool on the east side and leads to a circular structure, facing the street behind, where a 475-seat auditorium and mock court-rooms are housed. One courtroom seats 190 students and is equipped

This page: Women's Dormitory and Dining Hall, University of Chicago, Chicago, Illinois, 1955–58.

Opposite, from top: University of Chicago Law School, 1955–60; law school with mock-courts building.

for occasional use by the Illinois Supreme Court and other actual courts. That plain, stone-walled rotunda was intended to relate to the Bar Association Center on the next block.[18]

The University of Chicago Law School design is contextual but not actually figurative. It relates to nearby buildings without imitating them. Saarinen used a modern gesture—the pleated curtain wall—as a nod to the nearby buildings. At that time, he still felt compelled to add the phrase "false stage scenery of a bygone era, it is true" to his otherwise flattering description of the Chicago campus. However, *Architectural Forum* praised his design when it was announced in 1956, comparing it enthusiastically to Minoru Yamasaki's Conference Building for Wayne State University, despite calling the existing Chicago campus "pseudo Gothic." But the author clearly delighted in the return to the use of imagery: "Saarinen's great pleated facade gives a soaring Gothic quality to a law library. Both men serve up the richer visual fare found in older architecture but missing in sleek, hard 'modern': a play of sunlight and shadow on depths and angles, and a patterned movement of lines

against the ground and sky."[19] Clearly, the time was almost right for the return to some kind of representation, but people were not quite ready to say so.

By the time the building was completed and published in *Architectural Record* four years later, Saarinen, at least, was calling the dormitories next door "neo-Gothic," but by then both his approach to a Collegiate Gothic context and the nature of the discussion had begun to change.[20]

Morse and Stiles Colleges

The catalyst for the change in Eero's approach was a commission to design the Morse and Ezra Stiles colleges at Yale (1958–62), two new residential communities of 250 students each. They were to be built on a very irregular site on the northwest edge of the campus, between straight diagonal Broadway and curving Tower Parkway and between the soaring Hall of Graduate Studies and the huge Payne Whitney Gymnasium, both built in 1932 in the neo-Gothic style.

Although in many circles (including those Saarinen had grown up in, to say nothing of the Bauhaus) it would have been considered scandalous to build colleges in the "neo-Gothic" and "neo-Georgian" styles in the late 1920s and early 1930s, at Yale—as at most American institutions—historical styles were still the norm. The major works of International

Style modern architecture in Europe (such as Walter Gropius's Bauhaus at Dessau, Le Corbusier's Villa Savoye, and Mies van der Rohe's Barcelona Pavilion) had already been completed by 1930, but American skyscrapers were still being decorated with motifs from the past. At Colonial Williamsburg in Virginia, authentic buildings found on the site were being remodeled or replaced with cleaned-up versions of the "Colonial" past.

The illusion of historical authenticity was useful when Yale's residential colleges were being built to re-create the atmosphere of the small, intimate college it had been in the eighteenth and nineteenth centuries. As with the Harvard "houses," built at the same time in the neo-Georgian style, the idea was to bring together the entire college community because over time rich and poor students had come to live in different places. Each "house" or "college" had rooms for undergraduates with dining rooms, libraries, recreational facilities, and apartments for masters and their wives, in a system modeled on Oxford and Cambridge universities. The Yale colleges, designed by James Gamble Rogers to accommodate about five hundred students each, even looked like the colleges at the British universities, only on smaller, tighter blocks. (Like their British counterparts, the buildings were designed in various styles; most recall medieval buildings, though some are "Georgian" or feature Georgian Colonial elements.) The residential colleges had been put into service in 1933 as Saarinen was about to graduate from Yale, but in time for him to know them.

Saarinen agreed to design the two new colleges, even though the site was "in shadow, irregular, and odd." He began his research by interviewing students. Finding that they liked the old colleges, with their stone walls, cloistered courtyards, and wood-paneled interiors, he decided that the architecture of the new ones "must keep them from looking like poor cousins in comparison to the existing colleges, which have all the luxuries that were possible in the earlier periods when building costs were one-third what they are today and the budget allotment per student exactly what it is today." And he realized that this could not be done "within the general vocabulary of modern architecture."

Students' comments convinced him that the rooms should be "as random as those in an old inn rather than as standardized as those in a modern motel. Instead of building a system and fitting everyone into it, we should try to start with the idea of diversity—of many different rooms, rooms in towers, rooms of varying shapes and sizes and kinds, with various window and study arrangements." The university's decision to

have mostly single rooms reinforced his inclination to emphasize "the individual and his scholarly life." He wanted to make them "of our time, but also timeless."

"We became convinced we would have to create a new vocabulary," he explained, referring to an effort that involved a variety of associates, especially Cesar Pelli, who worked closely with him on the colleges. They made the buildings polygonal to provide different types of student rooms, to fit into the irregular site, and to vary the spatial experiences in the courts.

The architects "conceived of these colleges as early, monastic masonry citadels—buildings whose masonry walls would be dominant and whose interiors of stone, oak, and plaster would carry out the spirit of strength and simplicity."[21] But the budget did not afford them the stone the older colleges had been made of. Saarinen always liked a technical challenge, so they invented a new modern kind of masonry. It was a poured concrete with three-to-eight-inch chunks of stone suspended in it to provide strength and texture—the feeling of the neo-Gothic but in a frankly modern medium. John Dinkeloo found a small concrete company in Cleveland that repaired dams to help them develop the new rubble-filled concrete. The Prepakt Concrete Company used an intrusion wall technique that pumped concrete into the formwork around the rubble and added an expanding agent to keep it from contracting when it dried.[22] After the concrete set, the surface was washed with water under a hundred pounds of pressure to remove some of the mortar on the surface and expose the rubble. The rough stones suspended in the

144

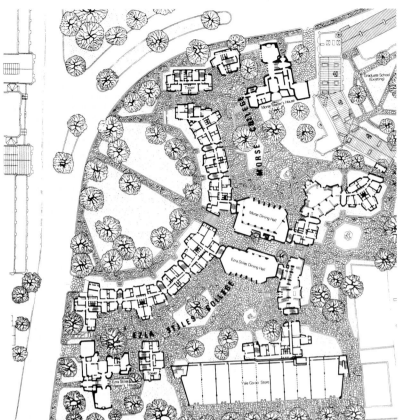

concrete of the tall, tan, polygonal walls wrapping around courtyards recalled Italian hill towns—an image that Saarinen liked and had tried briefly to re-create for the IBM Laboratories at Yorktown (1957–61).

By 1960, Saarinen was willing to say that he was trying to approximate the neo-Gothic, but he felt it necessary to do so in a modern way. Other architects of his generation were beginning to acknowledge a similar interest in the architecture of the past. Louis Kahn, for example, who also loved Italian hill towns, made numerous drawings of them and inserted abstract references to them in his Richards Medical Laboratories at the University of Pennsylvania (1957–65).

At the very end of the 1950s, interest in historic architecture was so widespread among architects who taught at Yale that the architectural historian and theorist Sybil Moholy-Nagy assembled an issue of the Yale architecture journal *Perspecta* devoted to "The Future of the Past." It featured articles by and interviews with five of the most prominent architects of the time—Saarinen, Philip Johnson, Louis Kahn, Paul Rudolph, and John Johansen—all of whom openly acknowledged interest in historic sources, though most of the critics invited to discuss these architects' work did not touch on the topic directly. The critics, however, did make it clear that they were disillusioned with the aspect of modern architecture that had made historic architecture taboo.

In writing about the problem, Peter Collins brought up the then-common term "form-givers," pointing out that it suggests "that to be a good architect one must be some kind of pioneer and confuse modernity

(which is a chronological classification) with beauty." He noted that Frank Lloyd Wright, who was an acknowledged "form-giver," admired Edwin Lutyens, who was considered a hopeless conservative, and that "the four volumes of Lutyens' works were constantly referred to during discussions with students at Taliesin West."[23]

"The contribution of the Bauhaus seems, in retrospect, to have largely confused the issue," Colin St. John Wilson wrote, because Gropius assumed that if modern architecture rejected the past, somehow a new architecture, capable of being mass-produced and therefore creating a brave new material world, would emerge.[24] It did not.

James Gowan pointed out, "Mies does not change. He is still wedded to the machine-age millennium, solving each problem with the most elegant of glass and steel boxes. . . . In America, the Miesian techniques and materials have remained the same and are now charged, not with the impetus of the future, but with the nostalgia of the past."[25] (The glass-and-steel architecture intended to be mass-produced never was, in other words.)

Unlike the puritanical first generation of modernists, Moholy-Nagy explained, "the continuity-starved architects, raised on the lean diet of functionalist supremacy, have displayed a craving for architectural history and theory in their mature years that would have shocked their elders. The top designers of International Architecture, as it developed in the 1950s, have in some gratifying instances discovered a harmonic triad of contemporaneousness, projection into the future, and responsibility

toward the past."[26] The one she discussed first and most enthusiastically was Saarinen, to whom she attributed a visceral sense of beginning again, akin to that of the Romanesque builders. He had, of course, grown up with a respect for historic buildings, even though his father was trying to create a new architecture for the modern world, and he had studied at Yale under a Beaux-Arts curriculum, like that offered at Penn when Kahn studied there. And although Johnson and Rudolph had studied under Gropius at Harvard, both had done so after working in architecture for some time and developing their own ideas.

Strong proscriptions against the influence of historic architecture, representation, symbolism—anything but abstract form, function, and structure—continued to exist in the architectural profession at the time. Still, Rudolph was quoted in *Perspecta* as saying, "The site and symbolism of the particular building set the course."[27] Johnson said, "I cannot but be classically inspired. I can no longer build glass boxes—the pleasant glass box for all uses."[28] Louis Kahn ended a discussion of a project in design saying, "It's very Gothic, isn't it? Does that bother you? I like it myself."[29]

Saarinen, who wrote and lectured far less often than the others (most of his written statements were made to explain projects to clients), gave the most complete explanation of his philosophy in that issue of *Perspecta*. His contribution was based on a lecture he had recently delivered while receiving an award at Dickinson College. "The three great principles of modern architecture," he said, are "functional integrity, honest awareness of structure, and awareness of our time. [But] tools alone do not make architecture. There must be leadership." The "three great men" of architecture, he said, were "Frank Lloyd Wright, Le Corbusier, and Mies van der Rohe." (He did not mention his father or Gropius, as many people would have done then.) Wright's influence "comes from another era; his forms do also. He will influence the world of architecture more through his principles. Le Corbusier, the genius, is the one who has given world architecture the most forms." Mies brought "discipline." Saarinen called him "the culmination of the Bauhaus style." He also said that the situation at the time was not what "the founders of the modern movement had dreamed about sixty years ago. The style that has developed is far too one-sided. Many interesting things have not been explored. The vocabulary of modern architecture is being greatly expanded. Also, architecture has returned to a more personal art. We respect each other's talent but we seldom agree on solutions. You should hear the terrible things we say about each other's architecture." He explained that over the years he had come to the conclusion that there were three other fundamental principles: "the expression of the building, the concern

with total environment" (Eliel's idea that you must always design to the next larger thing), and "carrying a concept to its absolute conclusion."[30]

These statements explain why Saarinen went to such lengths to create a modern equivalent of the neo-Gothic colleges; why simple modern dormitories would not do, nor would mere references to nearby eclectic buildings; why some of the walkways really feel like backstreets in Italian hill towns; and why at Yale there is an elaborate (if not always completely successful) program of sculptures by Constantino Nivola.

Morse and Stiles colleges contained significant functional innovations, such as a single ground-level kitchen that the two dining halls shared, with passageways bridging the kitchen and leading to a curved open space in front of the gym on Tower Boulevard, where another college could be built, if necessary. Instead of the big common rooms of the older colleges, they featured snack bars called "butteries," rooms for billiards and table tennis, and seminar rooms for college classes. The libraries were filled with nooks and crannies because research had shown that students used little niches more than open spaces in the old college libraries. Student rooms are brilliantly tucked into the irregular site on what are mostly efficient double-loaded corridors but seem unique because of the polygonal spaces at the ends and because the corridors bend to form interesting outdoor spaces. And a row of shops, which originally housed the Yale Co-op bookstore, shielded the residential compounds from traffic on Broadway.[31] The six-million-dollar project was a world away from the modest, functional dormitories Saarinen had designed for Antioch College a little more than a decade earlier. The distinction shows how much his range and ambition grew during his brief career.

The Morse and Stiles Colleges were published extensively. And whereas the thinking behind them was not far from that of Saarinen's most esteemed contemporaries, they were unusually controversial. In *Architectural Forum*, Walter McQuade called them "episodic architecture, seldom seen whole." He noted "the jagged, dynamic shadows thrown slanting down the walls by the angular buildings," which thus seem "almost visibly in motion. Lacking the texture of an expensive masonry wall, Saarinen depended upon these shadows for his detail, and it works," though "when the sun is not shining, everything dies a little." McQuade explained how difficult it had been to comply with modern building codes and still provide the separate entries for each group of rooms that were traditional at Yale, and that the firm had mocked up thirty full-size polygonal rooms and furnished them and therefore worked most of the peculiarities out of the space while preserving most of the individual flavor. "The new colleges are popular; many more than a full roster of students applied to transfer from older (and more spacious) quarters."[32]

British critic Reyner Banham, however, called the new colleges "disgusting" in the New Statesman. Demonstrating how theory swayed critical judgments, he claimed the buildings "exhibit the symptoms of a fairly advanced case of that mania for the picturesque (in the corny sense of the word) that has affected recent academic architecture on both sides of the Atlantic." He spoke of the "unbelievable tawdriness of the . . . random lumps of stone embedded in structural mass concrete. It is difficult to imagine a more obviously cheap and nasty way of trying to style up concrete to look like something romantic. Far worse . . . is the way in which the Gordon Craig–type scenic effects (equally suitable for Macbeth or The Desert Song) have been bought by providing interior spaces that fall below even medieval standards of student accommodation." He called the buildings a "gross dereliction of professional duty—to encourage an architect thus to play at being a 'pure' artist is to amputate the factor of use."[33]

When Saarinen died, Banham published "Fear of Eero's Mana," an article addressing the way Saarinen had been mistreated during his lifetime. "Injustice was certainly done; suspect any man who claims that his record on Saarinen is clean, or any man who insists too loudly that Saarinen was a really great architect. Both are already possessed by Eero's mana. . . . and I have to confess that my own record has some dirty patches. But I still stick to the general view of Saarinen that . . . he was never a really great architect, and I have some reservations on practically every building he did. But only some, and those are not enough to detract from the fact he was a darned good designer who left a stamp of stunning professional expertise on everything he did. Perhaps the detractors who now compete in praise were just jealous?"[34]

The most significant appraisal of Morse and Stiles colleges came from the esteemed critic and historian Henry-Russell Hitchcock in Zodiac: "Rudolph's decision at Wellesley in the Jewett Art Center to work towards an 'equivalent' of the nearby Gothic buildings did not come out very well. But an exception to the grim rule that you are damned if you do attempt to harmonize a new building in an academic group with its older neighbors and equally likely to be damned if you don't is the new work of Saarinen. . . at Yale."[35]

"That Eero was not averse to his own sort of romanticism, once the strong reaction against the outmoded romanticism of his father that led him toward Mies came to an end with his father's death, was already evident in his MIT Chapel of 1954–55, so strongly influenced in its curved walls and red klinker brickwork by the nearby Baker House of the Finnish Aalto. But a careful examination of the plans of the Yale colleges, as of the photographs, will indicate Eero's planning and handling of materials in the very comparable residential wings is far franker and more direct than Aalto's. Eero's apparently exiguous openings, dramatically arranged

as vertical breaks in the fortress-like walls, are actually larger than Aalto's, and his rooms, therefore rather better lighted."

Interestingly, when architect Steven Holl was designing the recent Simmons Hall dormitories at MIT, he said, "The two dormitories I had to compare myself to were Aalto's Baker House and Eero Saarinen's Morse and Stiles at Yale. Those are tough acts to follow."[36]

When the colleges were new, Hitchcock mentioned the "granite rubble in relatively large irregular rock-faced chunks piled up in the forms and grouted with a very liquid cement filler, a method of construction allowing the use of much relatively unskilled labor, which has proved . . . even more economical than was expected. . . . [And] a remarkably appealing surface finish has been readily achieved. . . . The student rooms . . . seem exemplary." He concluded, "The Yale College and the [Dulles] airport would seem to establish him as one of the great 'makers' in architecture of our day, nor need such works fear comparison with the major monuments of other periods."[37]

In 1963, the colleges received the sanction of the architectural profession in the United States. The American Institute of Architects singled out Morse and Stiles and the TWA Terminal (1958–62) for honors in its annual awards competition from the 411 submissions that year. Surprisingly, perhaps, Morse and Stiles won the First Honor, while TWA merely received an Award of Merit.[38] Today the airport is more widely acclaimed (though no longer as useful), perhaps because it seems to foreshadow the architecture of our own time. But Morse and Stiles were a remarkable achievement, both because they met a formidable program on a formidable site and because they were, like Saarinen's airport terminals, completely original. And they were courageous, a modern take on a beloved historic type with a budget one-third the size. After the Postmodern movement, the colleges seem less shocking than they did when they were new, but also less quaintly of their period than the airports. Saarinen managed to make them "of our time but also timeless."

Opposite: J. Irwin and Xenia Miller House, Columbus, Indiana,
1953–1957, living area with conversation pit.

The last place you are likely to find avant-garde architecture is on Main Street, USA. While it is unusual for a major university or corporation in this country to commission one pioneering building, it is almost unheard of in small-town Middle America. It is hard to imagine that Eero Saarinen would have been asked to design such archetypal structures as a small-town bank, a glass-walled house, and a suburban church had it not been for J. Irwin Miller.

Miller was a client like no other. He was passionately interested in architecture, art, and music. His family owned the bank, downtown real estate, and a major manufacturing company in Columbus, Indiana. He had been intrigued by architecture since he was a schoolboy, when he studied ancient history and sought out the classical columns and pediments on buildings in downtown Columbus. He was at Yale just before Saarinen enrolled there (and studied afterward at Oxford). But the two only met when Miller's mother, Nettie Sweeney Miller, who was chairwoman of the building committee, hired Eliel Saarinen to design the Tabernacle Church of Christ (1939–42), and Eero began going to Columbus with his father to work on it (see chapter 3).[1]

The friendship that developed between the two men led to Saarinen's chance to design buildings unlike any others in his body of work and, to some extent, in modern architecture. And it fostered a unique kind of patronage that made Columbus a very unusual place where the churches, schools, and other public buildings—institutions that touch the lives of everybody in the town—were designed by an impressive roster of architects.

That, of course, was the point. Miller built with a sense of commitment to his community that, rare at the time, is almost inconceivable now. But in the 1950s many families were firmly rooted. Most Americans lived in small cities and towns, and the future seemed bright. Columbus was growing fast. Despite the cold war, things seemed to be on the upswing.

Irwin Miller's great-grandfather Joseph Irwin had been born on a farm near Columbus. He moved into town at age twenty-four in 1848, worked in a store, saved his money, invested in real estate, and opened a dry-goods shop of his own, where he kept a safe that was so secure that customers began asking if they could keep their money in it. Before long, he was in the banking business. In 1881, he built a rather grand Victorian building on Washington Street (Columbus's main thoroughfare) with an arch-shaped broken pediment on top of a projecting cornice. When his son, William G. Irwin, took over, he merged the Irwin Trust with the Union Trust of Columbus, built an even grander Renaissance Revival

edifice down the street in 1925, and weathered the Depression by converting his holdings to cash before the stock-market crash.[2] William Irwin's sister Linnie, who was Irwin Miller's grandmother, married the Reverend Zachary T. Sweeney, minister of the Tabernacle Church of Christ.

William Irwin and Linnie Irwin Sweeney donated the land across the street from their house at Fifth and Franklin streets for the new church, and William became its principal patron, so it is not surprising that Linnie and Reverend Sweeney's daughter, Nettie Sweeney Miller, were involved in the planning. Designing and building the Tabernacle Church of Christ, which was one of the first and remains one of the finest modern churches in America, became a two-generation family affair.[3] All the Irwins, Sweeneys, Millers, and Saarinens were involved. Although the church (which was later renamed the First Christian Church), with its textured buff brick skin, delicate abstract decoration, and freestanding bell tower, is clearly the work of Eliel, Eero's influence seems likely in its pure rectangular blocks, subtle interior planning, and dramatic natural lighting. This church, more than any of the Saarinens' other American work, shows the influence of the Finnish architects Alvar Aalto and Erik Bryggmann, and, although Eliel went back to Finland every summer, it was Eero who had worked there in the mid-1930s.[4] The church is also notable for reinforcing the city block where it is located; the Sunday-school wings run along the street, creating a courtyard on a lower level.

The church was completed after the United States entered World War II. Irwin Miller joined the army and was stationed in Washington, DC. Eero Saarinen joined the Office of Strategic Services and the two saw a lot of each other during that time. After the war, Saarinen went back to Bloomfield Hills and practiced with his father, subsequently earning a substantial reputation for himself with the General Motors Technical Center and various college buildings. Miller returned to Columbus and went to work for the Cummins Engine Company, a manufacturer of diesel engines that had been invented by a family chauffeur, Clessie Cummins, and financed by his uncle William Irwin.

Within a few years, Irwin Miller became president of Cummins Engine, and when his father, Hugh Thomas Miller, died in 1947, he became president of the Irwin Union Trust Company as well.[5] Three years later, he hired Eero Saarinen to design a new transparent, glass-walled, one-story building for what was then called the Irwin Union Bank & Trust Company (1950–54) across Washington Street from the imposing classical bank his uncle had built. The building symbolized the bank's progressive approach, which included offering some of the first credit cards and earliest drive-through banking. Instead of a fortress guarding a vault, as

its predecessor had been, the new bank looked open and inviting. The old vault had been moved across the street and into the basement, where it would be accessible to customers in relative privacy. The new building was simply erected around it.

The shiny new bank occupied a busy corner downtown, but because it was lower than the buildings around it and surrounded by a tight row of sycamore trees, it looked almost like a green space. It was intended to provide a sort of park in the middle of the city, some breathing room. It took up only the front third of the site. The back was given over to a drive-through window (now there is a whole row of them) and a large parking lot, also surrounded and intersected by a grid of trees. The landscaping, designed by Saarinen's old friend and collaborator Dan Kiley, became the norm for surface parking lots in Columbus, which are surrounded by walls of plantings instead of the usual chain-link fences or chunky bollards, so seas of cars are hidden from view. (It took a few years for the bank to acquire the entire property. Initially, there was a small store at the back of the parking lot.)

From the perspective of the twenty-first century, when many small American towns are full of holes left by demolished stores that could not compete with suburban strip malls, it may seem strange to create an intentional gap in the cityscape. But in the early 1950s, these little downtowns were still thriving, and the problem seemed to be how to relieve the congestion caused by growing numbers of automobiles. The Irwin Union Bank proposed a creative solution to a common problem. And, although its walls were set back slightly from the other properties on Washington Street, at Saarinen's insistence, the trees maintained the street line of continuous shopfronts. Later, Miller hired Saarinen's friend Alexander Girard to make the old-fashioned stores up and down Washington Street appear quaint, with new color schemes and tasteful signage.

The trees shade the inside of the bank, along with four-foot-six-inch roof overhangs and bamboo drapes. When extra illumination is needed, supplemental lighting is provided by downlights in canisters on the perimeter and dramatic hanging lamps encased in a grid of nine domes, which also give the boxy pavilion some three-dimensional interest from inside and out. The motif is similar to that in the auditorium of the Kingswood School (1929–31), except that the bank features fewer, larger domes, with spaces between them. The thin-shell concrete vaults were engineered by Severud-Elstad-Kreuger, the firm that helped design the Saint Louis Gateway Arch and the Yale Hockey Rink. Bolt, Beranek & Newman, the acousticians responsible for the success of MIT's Kresge Auditorium, lined the insides of the domes with acoustic plaster to soften the sound in the space.

This page: Irwin Union Bank & Trust Company, aerial view with domes.

Opposite: Miller House, facade facing river.

The little glass pavilion looks very simple; however, like all the projects undertaken by the Saarinen office, it was the result of extensive research—once more coordinated by Wilhelm von Moltke—into every aspect of the way the space would be used. The ceiling is eleven feet, six inches high; thus the pavilion does not seem oppressive. Files are contained in a freestanding solid structure in the center, much as they would be at the Deere & Company offices, so that the rest of the floor remains uncluttered. Instead of in cages, the tellers work at inviting colorful counters with plastic hoods that can be removed as more windows are needed. A small private elevator and spiral staircase give tellers access to the cash vault below; pneumatic tubes connect the pavilion with the three-story office building next door, which has room for transactions requiring privacy. In the middle of the space, a light floating staircase, supported by steel rods like some of those at the General Motors Technical Center and the Milwaukee War Memorial, leads to the cloistered basement vault.

Despite all the carefully considered functional solutions, in architecture that aspires to art—and perhaps even in that which does not—there is always an element of serendipity. Here it is the grid of large domes pressing through the ceiling plane. Writing to his friend Astrid Sampe, with whom he had just spent a few days in southern Spain, Saarinen explained, "I fly from Dallas to Columbus, Indiana where before the war we built a church. Perhaps you remember it. The same family, only a younger generation, wants to build a bank. We now have what I think is a very good scheme. I don't think that it would be just the way it is unless you and I had been to Cordoba and seen the mosque. It is a wonderful opportunity to do something really good and different because the client is simply out of this world. It is going to be a bank without any pompousness, absolutely no intention to impress. All it is is a very low glass enclosed marketplace-like little building in the middle of the town. . . . It also has nine cupolas, just like San Marco. All this sounds a bit bad but it really isn't."[6]

Townspeople joked about the domes. They called the bank the "brassiere factory,"[7] but they loved the building, which was built for $690,000, or $22 per square foot. Although it was only a few feet from its predecessor, customers increased fourfold. This little jewel of a bank, like much in Columbus, has been perfectly preserved, complete with Saarinen's Number 71 chairs and other furnishings. It is a perfect period structure of the 1950s still in good working order.

The Miller House

Referring to Irwin Miller in his letter to Sampe, Saarinen wrote, "It is the same client for whom Sandro Girard and I are doing a house in Canada." The low-slung, flat-roofed house on a rocky promontory overlooking a lake in Ontario (1950–52) was later partially destroyed in a fire and rebuilt by Kevin Roche. It was cozy and unpretentious, with rough stone walls inside and out, as well as wood-paneled walls and picture windows framed in wood. Because, like Hvitträsk, it was designed to follow the contours of the land, it had hardly any straight lines. "It is a landscape that Eero understood because it is very much like Finland," Miller explained.[8] The Miller family had owned property there since the turn of the twentieth century, but the rocks had not been built on before. And when they were, it was without cutting. The house just grew up around the rocks.

The situation was completely different in Columbus, where Miller and his wife, Xenia Simons Miller, who had worked at Cummins Engine, asked Saarinen to design the Miller House (1953–57) for them soon after work began on the bank. Little existed that they wanted to preserve on the suburban site, which ran between a little river and a busy street into town. To avoid flooding, it made sense to place the house on the highest ground, close to the street, as far as possible from the river but facing it eight hundred feet away. The service entrance is off the main street, but guests enter from a side street through a grid of close-cropped horse chestnut trees. The landscape, by Dan Kiley, was firmly graded so that the property rises in steplike terraces and opens to gardens as geometric and architectural as the house itself. It is this grid of trees rather than the quietly luxurious house that makes the strongest impression.

Like the bank, the house is a one-story pavilion, divided into nine sections by the roof structure. But instead of separated solid domes, the house has bands of slightly projecting, translucent skylights running along the

154

edges and framing a thirty-by-forty-foot living space in the middle. The skylights are held in place by a welded grid of double steel channels, supported on sixteen cross-shaped steel columns, located at the intersections of the skylights[9]—a device conceived by Kevin Roche, who was so involved that his colleagues called it "Kevin's house." The columns, which have a white baked-enamel finish, stand free of the walls, so the light structural system is visible.

The house literally invites the outside in with a combination of glass walls, solid walls (blue-gray slate on the outside, white marble inside), and areas—such as the carport and loggias off the living and dining rooms—that open the house to the outdoors even further when glass partitions are pushed aside. Except for the ten-foot-tall, skylit central section of the house, the ceilings are considerably lower than those at the bank (eight feet six inches), and the roof overhangs are deep enough to protect a continuous white terrazzo terrace facing the garden). The terrace itself sits on a sort of podium filled with ivy and framed by rectangular slabs of cleft slate.

Inside, the eighty-by-one hundred-foot house is divided into four unequal zones—for parents, children, guests, and service—arranged in a pinwheel plan around the main shared living space. For guests there was only one small bedroom and bath, at least when the children were at home, while "service" took up two and a half quadrants with a maid's room, carport, kitchen, and casual dining area. The parents had a suite with bedroom, lounge, dressing rooms, and office. The five children each had a small bedroom and shared a cheery, functional playroom. The rest of the house was for living, lounging, dining, and quiet recreation. A fifty-foot-long, built-in storage unit—similar to the island of files at the bank but much narrower—frames the living and recreation rooms holding a rosewood television cabinet, bookshelves, musical instruments, and a small but fine and varied collection of art. A grand piano, along with a circular fireplace hung from the ceiling, are about the only objects in the central living space. (The fireplace was designed by photographer Balthazar Korab when he was working as an architect in Saarinen's office.) To avoid the "sea of legs" that so bothered Saarinen, most of the seating is tucked into a fifty-foot-square recessed "conversation

This page: Miller House, dining area.

Opposite: Miller House, terrace.

pit," an antecedent of the many "funky" conversation pits that were briefly in fashion during the late 1960s. This one was intended for reading, talking, and family musicals. Its marble sides were covered with sumptuous fabrics designed by Girard, who suggested changing the color scheme with the seasons—right before the same idea became the theme of Philip Johnson's now classic Four Seasons restaurant in the Seagram Building in New York City.

The house seems so simple, but getting it right was anything but easy. Irwin Miller said that Saarinen came up with almost a dozen schemes before they found the right one. Miller did not believe in telling an architect what to do—only what he wanted and needed, not what the final product should look like. Saarinen, he said, was amazingly patient, returning to the drawing boards with each rejection. The effort went on so long that the two relatively serious men became accustomed to joking around. Although Saarinen had a puckish sense of humor, only his closest friends and associates saw it. Miller was kindly but very reserved. He remembered one time when he and Xenia had returned from Europe with an El Lissitzky watercolor and laid it out on the

piano. Saarinen arrived and looked at it disapprovingly. "What's that?" he said with annoyance. "An El Lissitzky," Miller replied. Saarinen went back, with a bashful grin, and looked at it again: "An El Lissitzky? It's looking better every minute."

The house is distinguished by its careful proportions, exquisite materials, spaciousness, and subtle lighting. Striated glass diffusers modulate the skylights, which are supplemented by fluorescent tubes in the roof channels and generous light from the outside walls everywhere but in the bathrooms. White, sandblasted Georgian marble walls, travertine floors, and translucent silk curtains project a subtle glow. The built-in, eight-foot diameter white marble dining-room table, a version of Saarinen's Pedestal Table, has a lit fountain and pool in the middle. Lush colorful fabrics and folk objects installed by Girard add a light touch. And special closets with built-in drawers and shelving eliminate the need for most furniture, so the spaces can breathe.

The most dramatic aspect of the complex, though, is the geometric landscape by Dan Kiley that envelops the house, extending its regular rhythms and strict rectangular discipline into the gardens with low stone walls, tight hedges, neat grids of trees, and swaths of grass. Kiley was part of his team for the Saint Louis Arch, and landscaped the bank, but the Miller House was his masterpiece.

This page: North Christian Church, Columbus, Indiana, 1959–64.

Opposite: North Christian Church, plan.

Capitalizing on Saarinen's use of glass walls and skylights, which open the house to nature, Kiley extended the geometry of the house outward into the landscape. "I seized upon this transparency between interior and exterior space as a starting point," Kiley explained. "The house/landscape construct is more about a flow of articulated space than about reaching a static destination. One of the first moves was to pull the floor plane into the landscape. I worked closely with Saarinen's associate, Kevin Roche, to configure a nine-inch plinth that extends twenty-five feet out from the house. Along the east side a double row of white oak trees edges a central grass lawn bracketed between blocks of apple orchard. In the southwest corner of the grounds, a high evergreen hedge forms a swimming pool enclosure. Much like Eero's concept for the house, each area, or 'room,' has its own programme (orchard, children's lawn, recreation), yet all are bound together in a loose, dynamic order of spatial flow."[10] Some of the "rooms" created by allées terminate with

sculptures by Henry Moore or Jacques Lipschitz, but every space doubles back on the house itself.

The complete unity of building and landscape is, of course, something Eliel Saarinen advocated. But here unity is achieved with a completely modern, abstract, geometric composition that may be unique in the history of American domestic architecture and is equally unusual in the history of landscape design.

Model Church

The next building that Eero Saarinen and Dan Kiley designed for J. Irwin Miller was intended to remove man from the earthly natural world, so instead of being anchored to the ground by solid rectangles, its pointed angular form seems to hover and soar heavenward. In 1955, forty-three members of the First Christian Church decided to found a new Christian church affiliated with the Disciples of Christ. First they worshipped in one another's homes, then in an Episcopal church on Sunday evenings, and later in the Caldwell mansion. They hired their first full-time minister, Dr. James L. Stoner, in 1956, and two years later, with Irwin Miller's

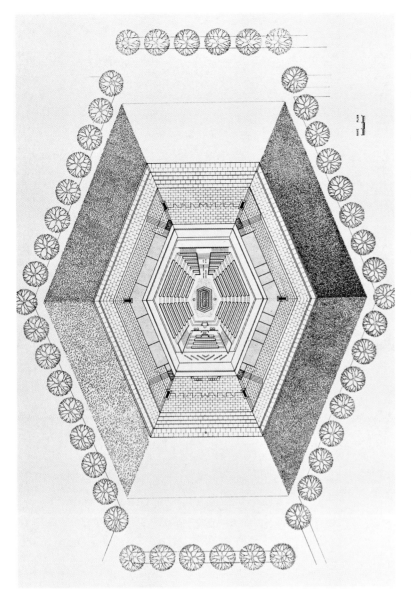

Church (1959–64). It did not generate much interest in the architectural press when it was being designed between 1959 and 1961, or when it was completed in 1964, after Saarinen had died. But in the decades afterward, modest (and sometimes very bad) copies of it sprang up across America, especially in the Midwest. The lack of journalistic interest may be one of the first signs of the "culture wars" that divided the United States during and after the Vietnam War, when privileged, highly educated Americans (including the architectural press and professoriate) lost interest in organized religion (and therefore in church architecture), while the middle classes embraced traditional values and religious practices. Though Eero Saarinen belonged to the former group, he was able to give meaningful form to the beliefs of the latter. And even though he knew what he wanted to do—or did not want to do—it became a struggle.

"We have to face first some of the problems of what has been happening in America today with the church and religion and architecture," he started out saying. "In the eleventh–twelfth centuries, there was the cathedral, and it was the significant thing. Today, there are Sunday school rooms and good-fellowship rooms and kitchens and gymnasiums and so forth. All these have tended to sprout into separate buildings and to get bigger and bigger and more and more important and the church itself has become an insignificant, almost forgotten little thing. So, in this church, I would like to put all that activity downstairs, maybe underground, hidden away, and put only the sanctuary above ground and make it the significant visual and architectural thing."[11]

He made the long, angular, symmetrical sanctuary and its 192-foot-tall spire a single intense, visible form reaching heavenward in one unified stroke. The Sunday-school and meeting rooms are in the hollowed-out basement, hidden by a berm and lit by windows from an ambulatory at the base of the church, so the hexagonal sanctuary above it almost appears to float. The six steel legs that hold the roof plates in place meet at the center to support the spire. Seen from the ground, the entire structure coalesces into a potent unified image.

Space for the underground auditorium and the classrooms that surround it was literally carved out of the earth in an elongated hexagon like that of the sanctuary above it. The sanctuary is elevated partly because it is on a flat site, so it can "stand proudly above the parked cars and the surrounding little ranch-type houses," Saarinen said. But that is not the only reason. Congregants enter at ground level and walk up to the sanctuary because, as he explained, "I don't think religion should be easy. I think you should have to work for it, and it should be a special thing. The architecture should express this. That is an absolutely marvelous experience at Borobudur and at Angkor Wat, when you keep climbing those steps and all the time are being subjected by the architecture to the awareness of special and spiritual qualities."[12]

help, purchased five and a half acres of land in a residential suburb and began to look for an architect.

Although Miller wanted Saarinen for the job, he felt it was important that the congregation make the selection. "I was on the building committee," Miller recalled. "We interviewed about six well-known architects. They all came with their slides [and talked about their work]. Eero just brought a notebook. He looked at us and said, 'What do you want? What do you want it to be? Don't tell me what you want it to look like, but what you want it to be like.'" Of course, it is easy to take that approach when you already have a reputation. They decided to hire him as soon as he left.

"Eero was both ambitious and humble. That's a very unusual combination," Miller said. "He didn't like the churches of the time. He wanted to make something that could serve as a model."

It certainly did. There may not be another building from the middle of the twentieth century that was copied as much as the North Christian

North Christian Church, interior.

When you enter the sanctuary of the North Christian Church, you become awestruck too, not because there are very many steps, but because of stark gray slate floors, dark mahogany pews, and the almost eerie natural light that enters through an oculus at the base of the spire in the center of the room. As at the MIT Chapel (1950–55), where light reflects up from the surrounding moat, and at the Concordia College Chapel (1953–58), where it seeps in from beneath the eaves, the light source is not immediately apparent and therefore appropriately mysterious. The sanctuary really is "the decompression chamber from the outside world" that the architect wanted it to be. Because communion is very important to the Disciples of Christ, a communion table is situated in the center of the space under the oculus. The members of the congregation sit around it, facing one another as a community. The sect practices "believer's baptism": When members are old enough to make

their own decision to join the church, they sanctify the ritual with immersion baptism. Space for that ritual is provided in a small, hexagonal reflecting pool at the end of the sanctuary in a separate room that can be used as a chapel when the pool is covered.

Although the North Christian Church was designed for an intensely religious community, the abstract architectural language works because it incorporates symbols, and its materials give the building a feeling of permanence and solidity. The six-sided structure represents the Star of David and the church's "roots in the Jewish faith out of which Christianity has emerged." The spire represents the reach toward God and heaven, as church towers, spires, and steeples have done for millennia. At the top is a five-foot-thirty-inch gold leaf cross, symbolizing Christ's sacrifice. In the Baptistery-Chapel, a sunburst design represents the Holy Trinity. The roof is slate. The supports that lead up to it and the fascia covering the joints are sheathed in lead-coated copper.

Irwin Miller, a founding member of the church, was not only active in Christian causes (he was, for example, the first lay member of the National Council of Churches); he also practiced what he believed in his civic life. To this day, the Cummins Engine Foundation, which he directed, pays the architectural fees of talented architects who design public buildings in Columbus—a unique kind of patronage that makes a significant difference with a relatively small investment and affects the entire community as well as the numerous visitors who come to see the famous buildings.

"We stumbled into it really," he once told the critic Carleton Knight III. "In the years after World War II, during which the city doubled in population, new schools became a necessity. The first two were prefab, hurriedly erected. They obviously were not going to last any time at all and were very bad places for young people to learn." So Miller told the school board that the foundation would pay the architectural fee for the next school if the board selected a designer from an independently created list of nationally prominent architects furnished by the foundation. "It wasn't a program," Miller said. "It related to a specific school building." Later on, the same arrangement was still available, Miller said, "provided you pick a different architect," and the program—eventually expanded to include any public building—was born.[13]

The famous list that architects hope to be on was developed at first by Eero Saarinen, Pietro Belluschi (then dean of architecture at MIT), and Douglas Haskell (editor of *Architectural Forum*). The current makeup is never made public.[14]

The program has made Columbus famous and its citizens proud, and the buildings have attracted tourists. But when Postmodernism was at its height and modern architecture was under siege from within the profession—a phenomenon that led to the eclipse of Eero Saarinen's reputation for some time—the town received some harsh criticism. In 1981, Ohio's Miami University department of architecture invited several distinguished critics, as it did every year, to join a group of graduate students at an architecturally distinctive location nearby where the students and critics divided into teams and were asked to sketch a design for a hypothetical building as a class project during a fall weekend. That year, it was to be a Museum of Architectural Archives for Columbus, Indiana. But when the critics gathered, instead of praising the program, they found the town's nineteenth-century main street more appealing than the famous modern buildings. Earlier, visitors would be disappointed to find that Columbus looked like a regular Indiana town, notwithstanding its churches by Eliel and Eero Saarinen, a library by I.M. Pei, schools by Harry Weese, John Carl Warnecke, John M. Johansen, Edward Larrabee Barnes, and Mitchell/Giurgola, and a dozen or so well-known buildings by Robert Venturi, Cesar Pelli, Hardy Holzman Pfieffer,

James Stewart Polshek, Skidmore, Owings, & Merrill, Caudill Rowlett Scott, and others. That year the reaction was very different. "It's quite a sad situation. The town looks as if it's infiltrated by strange objects that are like from the moon or something," Susie Kim exclaimed. Coy Howard concurred, "There is a conflict here between what this town is and really wants to be, and what the architects would like this town to be."[15]

In fact, most of the modern buildings in Columbus—many of the earliest by Saarinen's friends and former associates such as Kevin Roche, John Dinkeloo, Charles Bassett, Gunnar Birkerts, and Bruce Adams—are more sensitive to the surrounding context than much modern architecture of the period. And Alexander Girard's renovation of Washington Street was considerably ahead of its time in its appreciation of existing building fabric. But in the 1980s, the first generation of architects trained by the Modernists were in revolt, casting off the shackles of their education in order, in a very modern way, to begin again by doing the one thing that was considered taboo—embracing historic architecture. Unfortunately, in doing so, they rejected the modern work that was sensitive to the context, like Saarinen's, along with what was not. As a result of that revolt, Saarinen's story has taken a long time to be told.

Now there is a whole new group of buildings in Columbus by architects of that generation who never rejected Modernism in the first place, such as Richard Meier, Gwathmey Siegel, Peter Eisenman, Susana Torre, and Stanley Saitowitz, as well as by Postmodernists such as Hammond Beeby and Babka, Robert A.M. Stern, William Rawn, and Taft Architects, and architects who emerged after the Postmodern flagellation had ended, such as Thompson and Rose, and Deborah Berke. Architectural tourists are still coming. And most of the older buildings have held up very well, at least partly because they have been superbly maintained over the years. Columbus, Indiana, became a living museum of modern architecture and a testament to the dedication of J. Irwin Miller.

Opposite: United States Chancellery, London, England,
1955–60, facade detail.

It is one thing to place a modern building in a suburban landscape
and achieve success. It is quite another to insert one into a dense, traditional city center. Saarinen recognized this problem earlier and articulated it more clearly than most of his colleagues, and a high-profile
competition gave him the opportunity to try to solve it.

The 1955 invited competition for a new American embassy building in
London was the third federally sponsored competition in Saarinen's
lifetime, and he won it as he had the other two. The embassy competition—actually it was for a chancellery, an office building without an
ambassadorial residence—was significant because it was intended to
help create the American image abroad in one of the most visible places
in Europe. The United States Chancellery in London (1955–60) was
considered "the most important single project" in the State Department's
"current foreign building program,"[1] and it was an especially difficult
one, Saarinen realized, because the building needed to fit into historic
but changing Grosvenor Square.

"At one time the dominant characteristic of Grosvenor Square was low
row houses in a variety of styles and motifs, packed so closely next to
each other that they became a unified frame," he explained. "But the
Grosvenor Estate, which controls the square, has a new master plan,
whereby three sides of the square will form one large pseudo-Georgian
composition. These buildings, with a uniform cornice line, red brick walls,
Portland cement columns and balustrades will give the square a new
aspect." He added that "it is for the future square—not the one that
exists only in people's memories" that the new chancellery had to be
conceived and designed.[2]

Saarinen would not consider designing according to the Grosvenor
Estate plan, nor would he have been allowed to, according to the
brief prepared by the dean of Princeton's School of Architecture, Robert
McLaughlin, for the Architectural Advisory Committee of the State
Department's Office of Foreign Buildings Operations (FBO). The brief
required a design that "would engender good will through distinguished architectural quality." It explicitly "ruled out stylistic copies,"
asked for "the establishment of appropriate visual relationship to the
other three sides of Grosvenor Square," and stipulated that the building should "represent the United States at this time."[3] All eight of the
architects invited to apply—who were given four thousand dollars for
their efforts and required to visit the site—were Modernists.[4] And none
of them superbly solved the problem posed by the competition.

Saarinen's sedate and symmetrical scheme, though far from flawless,
"was unquestionably the most polished," according to Fello Atkinson,

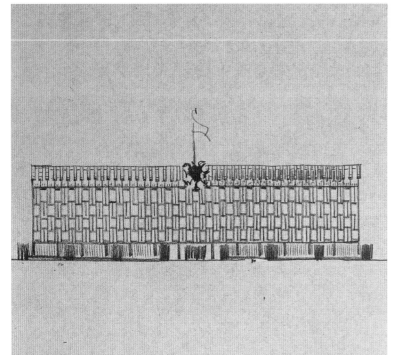

writing in Britain's *Architectural Review*.[5] The other entries tended to be boxier. The rectangularity was relieved in Edward Durell Stone's design by a dainty colonnade, glass facade, and roof loggia and in Yamasaki Leinweber's parallel blocks by lacy stone screens; but those projects seem more appropriate for a warm, sunny climate, as did Ernest Kump's big, long box, surrounded by an abstract, five-story colonnade with wrought-iron balconies. Hugh Stubbins's U-shaped rectangles on stilts formed an open court connected to nearby streets by a public arcade. José Luis Sert, Huson Jackson, and Joseph Zalewski's muscular brick block had chunky boxes that pushed and pulled through the facade defining interior spaces, even though it was intended to recall the rather delicate houses that once stood there.[6]

Architectural Record called the competition brief "a big order" and said, "the results seem not to have approached closely the difficult intangible goals. . . . No proposal appears to carry through any theme very completely." The author of the article, John Knox Shear, explained that most of the competitors had been accustomed to working in a subtractive idiom that "permits nothing in or on the building which is not directly a structural or similarly basic functional part," adding, "This lack is not peculiar to these buildings alone: the search for means of expression is architecture's biggest challenge in our time. And nowhere is the problem more apparent than in those buildings which must express our highest aspirations: our churches and our governmental buildings."[7]

Saarinen was better able to express those aspirations than most of his peers. But when the task was combined with the need to relate to a changing historic context and to meet other criteria, it was too much even for him. He tried to make the facade fit into its surroundings, provide a dignified image, and express the structure (as architectural theory at the time demanded). The walls carry the weight of the building and permit column-free interiors while they frame a pattern of interlocked operable and fixed windows scaled to those in the historic square. They are functional and structurally expressive, but more energetic than either a Georgian milieu or ambassadorial dignity requires. Saarinen tried to create a suitable image by using fine Portland stone and bronze, treating the facade as a modern version of a Greek temple—raised on a podium, with a peristyle at the base, and an "unemphatic central entrance, triglyph-like expression of beam ends, and entablature-like top story." This approach won the competition but created additional problems. As Atkinson (who was not alone) observed, "by setting the building back 40 feet, the continuity of Audley Street is lost" and the square, already too large, is exaggerated.[8]

As usual, Saarinen and his colleagues made numerous refinements to the design between the time he won the competition in 1956 and the completion of the building in 1960. (Glen Paulsen, for example, was in London for months. Bob Burley, Olav Hammarström, Spiro Daltas, and Edward Saad also helped significantly.) They also had to increase the size beyond the 150,000 square feet with offices for 750 people, as called for in the original competition program, to accommodate additional requests for space, so they added another lower floor and raised the overall height beyond the initial one hundred feet, without substantially altering the scale.

In the process, they developed what had been a sketchy interior scheme into something quite practical and beautifully detailed. They unified the auditorium, gallery, cafeteria, and other public spaces in the basement and gave them some character. They designed an entrance lobby with a lovely pool (now replaced by an unlovely bench); a fifteen thousand-square-foot consular section, where foreigners applying for visas could enter from one side street; an only slightly smaller information-library area for American citizens, who entered from the other side street; and an underground garage for twenty-five cars.

While enlarging the building, they created a sloping base that separates the building from the street, subtly providing additional security—a feature that was not required at the time but turned out to be valuable later when American embassies literally came under fire. The enlargement included a redesign of the structural system with a "diagrid" of criss-crossed beams that are visible inside and out and that allow the facade to overhang the column line, an element the Architectural Advisory Committee appreciated.[9]

Still, the facade was not substantially improved even after a thirty-five-foot-long gilded aluminum eagle by sculptor Theodore Roszak was positioned on the roof. The eagle, which replaced a seal with a picture of an eagle on it, added sculptural interest but turned out to be quite controversial. The building materials were intended to lend dignity, but the bronze was replaced by aluminum to save money, and the Portland stone failed to darken. Saarinen said he had chosen "the material generally used on official buildings in London which—if used with broken surfaces—gains with time a beautiful pattern and texture of whites and blacks."[10] But the stone never weathered because the British passed an antipollution law that cut down on soot and the Americans washed away the little grime that accumulated. The white stone and gold-anodized aluminum trim (which Saarinen insisted on calling "straw colored") made the building look gaudy. R. Furneaux Jordan, in the *London Observer*, likened it to "costume jewelry."[11]

British critics were very hard on the building despite the fact that local publications had enthusiastically endorsed the original scheme when it was first announced. The *London Times* had called it a welcome addition to the area and said it harmonized with existing facades, while the *Architects Journal* had praised its modernity and asserted that the design provided "a welcome example for future development in an area unduly wedded to neo-Georgian commonplaceness."[12]

When the embassy opened, however, it was a different story. British writers revealed a frustration with the new world order. Furneaux Jordan wrote, "The building fails between two stools—diplomatic delicacy and American status-seeking." In the *New Statesman*, Reyner Banham concurred, "Under the double impact of acceptance and affluence, modern architecture (in the U.S.) lost its dedicated muscularity and began to go Neo-Monumental in one direction, Ballet School in the other. Saarinen's chancery does both: monumental in bulk, frilly in detail." He also said, however, "The building abounds in details whose consistency and logic bespeak a standard of professional competence that few buildings in Britain can rival. Saarinen should have been commissioned to design a high quality office block and hang the brand image."[13]

"I think our main criticism is (and here I speak for the architects of my generation irrespective of nationality)," architect Peter Smithson wrote, "that the program sought such easy assimilation and we wanted it to be revolutionary. Revolutionary in a responsible way—which I suppose describes the role we would like to see America playing in order to fulfill its own dream. This would mean that the State Department would have to let some sort of speculation—as to the role of an embassy and the role of the building in the society it is placed in—be injected into the program writing."[14]

The State Department in 1961 was not much given to speculation, let alone revolution, and was more than a little disinclined to let architects dictate foreign policy. There had been a time, roughly from 1945 to 1952, when the State Department's Office of Foreign Buildings Operations operated with surprising independence under the leadership of Frederick A. Larkin and his chief architect, Leland N. King. The two had worked together since 1937 acquiring property for US State Department legations, which had been rented earlier and had usually been paid for by the ambassadors themselves. Legislation passed in 1946, however, allowed the FBO to use funds from war debts owed to the US government to pay for the acquisition of properties and to fund an ambitious building program to accommodate the country's new role on the world stage. Not only were new and larger embassy office buildings required, but so was housing for American personnel and quarters for consulates and the US Information Agency throughout the world.[15]

Between 1926 (when Congress first authorized the construction of foreign buildings) and 1946, the number of embassy office buildings owned

by the United States increased from six to 31 and residential units rose from 30 to 83. Between 1946 and 1951, the total climbed to 604 (114 office buildings, 55 embassy residences, 435 residential properties).[16] Operating with little oversight, no specific budget, or even a written program, King commissioned office buildings in Rio de Janeiro and Havana from Harrison & Abramovitz (who had just finished supervising the design of the United Nations Building in New York City), a tall office building in Madrid from Alan Jacobs and Garrigues & Middelhurst, and embassies in The Hague, Stockholm, Oslo, and Copenhagen from Ralph Rapson and his partner, John van der Meulen.[17] After Larkin retired in early 1952, King became FBO director and invited Gordon Bunshaft of Skidmore, Owings & Merrill (who had just completed Lever House) to design a series of consulates and "America Houses" to dispense "information" in Germany. And he asked Saarinen to design an addition to the American embassy in Helsinki.

Although there had been occasional criticism of the building program by members of Congress earlier, after President Eisenhower was elected in late 1952 and John Foster Dulles became secretary of state, the entire program suddenly came under fire both from within the State Department and from Congress. Serious functional problems in the glass-walled Rio and Havana office buildings came to light. The International Style buildings that had previously been heralded as suitable symbols of American modernity became associated with the feared "internationalism" of the United Nations. Waste and loose management were uncovered, and King was (rather unfairly) fired. Saarinen's embassy in Finland (the only project far enough along to be debatable but too far from completion to be safe) was canceled.[18] At least one congressman urged a return to traditional architecture. Consultants were brought in to evaluate the program, and one of them, a Princeton-trained engineer named Nelson A. Kenworthy, eventually became the new FBO director.

Although his tenure was brief, Kenworthy managed to preserve artistic freedom and architectural quality in the program. Charged with establishing a policy for architecture at the FBO, he negotiated the rough waters with consummate political skill, creating an Architectural Advisory Committee composed of three respected architects with different aesthetic learning—Ralph Walker, Henry Shepley, and Pietro Belluschi[19]— and Colonel Henry A. McBride, a former Foreign Service officer and assistant secretary of state who had been the administrator of the National Gallery of Art from 1939 to 1953. The committee, officially convened by Secretary Dulles in January 1954, drafted a guiding statement of philosophy (based on a policy statement that Kenworthy had already prepared) advocating an emphasis on "good will to other nations and efficiency of layout, not style" as well as the creation of a "well-balanced" advisory panel.[20] Belluschi added statements about the needs to consider "local conditions of climate and site, local customs, [and] the historical meanings of the particular environment, without being dictated by obsolete or sterile formulae or clichés, avoid being either bizarre or fashionable, yet not fear using new techniques or new methods," and said that the work would therefore "have a distinguishable American flavor."[21]

Clearly, the kind of provocation Peter Smithson had called for in his critique of the London embassy was not compatible with the political climate in America when it was being built. Attempts to save the FBO program led to the required contextualism in the London embassy competition brief. But a concern for the urban context was also in the air. Two years before that brief was prepared, in a session at the 1953 AIA convention on "The Changing Philosophy of Architecture," Paul Rudolph had said, "Architectural space is related to a room and to a city. The lessons from Rome indicate that it is possible to design a building which is complete in itself but also related to its neighbor." On the same panel, Harvard dean José Luis Sert said, "Architects have only lately become more conscious of cities related to their environment." The

166

dean of the architecture school at the University of California at Berkeley, William W. Wurster, said, "The greatest change of all is the acknowledgment of the total environment as compared to the care formerly lavished on a single structure without thought of the buildings which surround it," and "I think we should stress history more than we have." Eero Saarinen, who had always respected history and considered the next-larger scale, remarked, "In the Twenties there was an over-emphasis on the principle of functionalism. Have we gone overboard on too big windows, creating too many thermo-problems? Is the flat roof really the answer to all problems?"[22]

Forward-thinking architects were asking some of the same questions about modern architecture posed by those involved with the FBO program—without any political pressure to do so. All of these architects had been invited to design embassies—not because of their views, but because they were prominent. And they were considering answers to key questions almost twenty years before the Postmodern movement would ask those questions again with a vengeance.

The Oslo Embassy

Saarinen was commissioned to design the US Chancellery in Oslo, Norway (1955–59), the same year that the London embassy competition took place. As in the case of the IBM and Bell research laboratories commissioned to the office simultaneously, the thinking that went into one embassy affected the other. Although the Oslo office building was smaller and farther from the spotlight, it is regarded as more successful than the London chancellery, partly because more constraints were self-imposed. Saarinen realized that he had to relate the building to its site but that he could do it in a unique way. The site was peculiar—a triangle facing a main downtown street, the Drammensveien, across from the Royal Palace and the parklike gardens that surround it. It was an asymmetrical but prominent site, with greenery all along one side.

Unlike Ralph Rapson and John van der Meulen, who had devised an earlier scheme for the site (with a six-story box on pilotis in the middle of the triangle), Saarinen used the entire lot and created a triangular building with a four-story, diamond-shaped interior court. It has a fountain in the middle and a fifteen-foot-tall sculpture titled *Bong*, by the architect's old friend Harry Bertoia. "The climate of Oslo demanded that this court be enclosed and skylighted," Saarinen explained. "Moreover, since for many months the grey, cold weather demands a completely interior civilization, it seemed wise to give the court a feeling of warmth and enclosure. Hence, the warm beige Roman travertine floor, the teakwood walls, and the brick grille [perforated wall]. The diamond shape of the court is a natural result of the plan. It is a triangle with the two corners taken out for stairways, elevators, utilities."[23] The staircases are therefore intriguingly triangular, like those in Louis Kahn's Yale Art Gallery

(1951–53). Similar geometry is used for the folded planes of the atrium ceiling, which has skylights around its edges and small electric lights scattered throughout like stars.

Teak is also used for vents and benches as well as for window frames inside and out and for interior door frames, which have white jambs like those on the windows. Although the floor plan necessitates long, narrow rows of offices, aligned door frames between them encourage communication between occupants of adjacent spaces, and a band of ceiling lights, set to one side of the door frames, runs through the entire area and visually unites it further.

Since this embassy is in Scandinavia, where the transition from traditional architecture to modern had been smoother, Saarinen felt no compulsion to recall the shapes of nearby windows, so the window patterns reflect the office module. The facade treatment is regular, geometric, and abstract; the fenestration pattern and structural grid are unified smoothly. *Architectural Record* described the facade as "a three-dimensional screen that interestingly changes in aspect according to one's angle of view. From a distance it appears as a series of verticals; from nearby it becomes a pattern of horizontal and checkerboard traces, some mat, some glossy—some light, some dark."[24]

The facade treatment is one reason the Oslo embassy is more successful than the one in London; the material, which enhances that pattern, is another. Instead of the Portland stone, which was expensive but looks a bit like plain gray concrete, in Oslo Saarinen used new precast concrete, 90 percent of which was made of Norwegian emerald pearl granite, a lustrous dark green stone that gives the facade a dignified and slightly glistening appearance in its highly polished state.[25]

Saarinen had developed materials before, but in this case the material even had an impact on the local economy. "Precasting had not advanced as far in Norway as in the neighboring countries," he explained. "But a superb job was done here with help from experts from other Scandinavian countries and from Germany. A magnificent material was created and a new industry was started for Norway."[26]

The main entrance to the embassy is in the middle of the 190-foot-long Drammensveien facade across from the palace. Separate entrances for consular services and the USIA are at the ends. The building also succeeded in meeting the State Department's goal of pleasing the natives. *Architectural Forum* reported, "The elegant detailing and rich, quiet polish of the Oslo building seem quite at home with the spacious greenery of the Royal Palace park across the way. Nine out of ten Oslonians questioned by Forum say they like the new addition and some rank it among the city's major attractions."[27]

Sadly, because of its prominent site, the building is vulnerable to terrorists in the twenty-first century (there is not enough room to construct the required barriers), and it must be sold, though its physical character is protected by preservation covenants. And since it is essentially an office building, it should be able to serve other institutions.

The building—on which Cesar Pelli, David Powrie, and Gene Festa worked—won an Award of Merit from the American Institute of Architects in 1963, with praise for "its fine plan on a most difficult triangular site and an inventive departure from the normal curtain wall or screen."[28]

Not everyone was impressed, however. Congressional attacks—even on contextual modern architecture—persisted. Representative Wayne L. Hays, chairman of the House Subcommittee on State Department Organization and Foreign Operations, had threatened to withhold all funds from the Foreign Buildings Office of the State Department if the FBO's "pet architect," Saarinen, ever got another job. *Progressive Architecture* reported that despite Hays's dismissal of Saarinen's Oslo embassy, "the results proclaim the irresponsibility of the congressman's statements."[29] In fact, when Pietro Belluschi's term on the FBO Architectural Advisory Panel was up in June 1957, Saarinen was appointed to take his place along with two more conservative architects, Richard M. Bennett and Edgar L. Williams, who replaced Walker and Shepley.[30] But they, too, were infinitely more open-minded about modern architecture than most laymen. Clearly, despite the FBO's previous concessions to congressional criticism, the wide gap between the values of the architectural community and some of the country's leaders persisted at the end of the 1950s.

Page 170, from top: United States Chancellery, Oslo, Norway, 1955–59, facade facing park; presentation drawing of facade, c. 1955.

Page 171, from top: United States Chancellery, Oslo, model of entrance; United States Chancellery, London, drawing of facade in context.

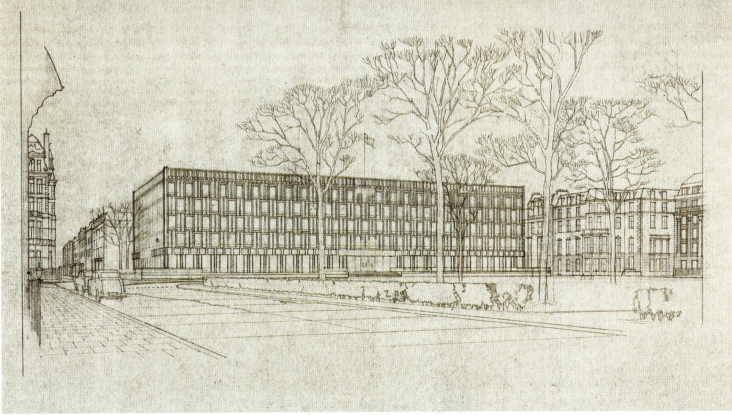

12. Big Ambitions in New York: The Vivian Beaumont Repertory Theater at Lincoln Center and the CBS Building

Opposite: Columbia Broadcasting System Headquarters, New York, New York, 1960–65.

Politics played a part—as did the gap between professional and popular taste—in what came to be called the Lincoln Center for the Performing Arts, where Saarinen designed the Vivian Beaumont Theater (1958–1965). But respect for the surrounding cityscape, so much a part of the embassy building program, was rarely a consideration on American soil in the 1950s. In American cities, bigger was seen as better, new was preferred to old, and faith in change and technology reigned supreme—at least until some of the hopes for Lincoln Center failed to materialize.

Lincoln Center was part of an urban-renewal plan that obliterated fifty-two acres of the urban fabric on the Upper West Side of Manhattan in New York City. By 1968, many American city centers had been destroyed more completely than the European ones that had been leveled by bombs during World War II. Much of downtown and midtown Manhattan remained unscathed, but in Harlem, Brooklyn, and the Bronx whole neighborhoods were demolished in an attempt to remove "blight," build roads, and provide adequate new housing for the poor.

At Lincoln Center, the goals were more convoluted. Robert Moses, the powerful chairman of Mayor Robert F. Wagner's Slum Clearance Committee, wanted to clear out what he called a "dismal and decayed" neighborhood just north of the site where he had recently built the Coliseum convention center on Columbus Circle.[1] The president of Fordham University wanted to build a midtown campus. Trustees of the Metropolitan Opera Company wanted to replace their 1883 house on Thirty-ninth Street, and the Philharmonic-Symphony Society had lost its lease at Carnegie Hall and hoped to build a better new hall. None of these institutions had the means to buy the kind of site it needed, but Moses—who was also New York City park commissioner, the city's construction coordinator, and a city-planning commissioner—had the power to seize property under the law of eminent domain. He also controlled the city's funds from Title I of the Federal Housing Act of 1949, which could be used for purposes other than housing, though the intention of that provision was to encourage merchants to serve new residential developments. However, things did not always happen according to the letter of the law in New York, where Moses called the shots.[2]

In the 1920s and 1930s Moses had built for New York the first and largest system of state parks in the nation. Then he created an astounding network of highways, bridges, and tunnels that linked the city and its suburbs (and produced vast amounts of money in tolls, which Moses controlled). Eventually, he built 148,000 apartments for more than half a million people, but by the 1950s he was coming under fire not only from people displaced by his projects but also from good-government groups opposed to his increasingly tyrannical methods.[3] It made sense

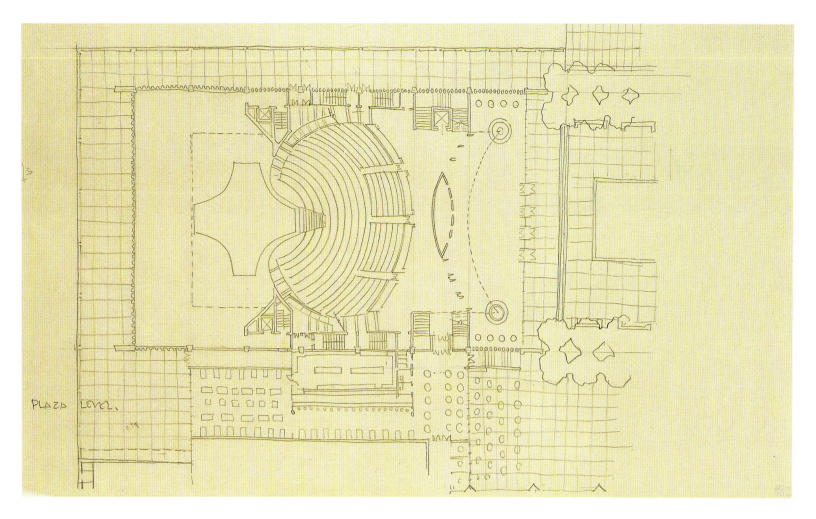

PLAZA LEVEL.

This page: Vivian Beaumont Repertory Theater, Lincoln Center for the Performing Arts, New York, New York, 1958–65, drawing of plan.

Opposite: Vivian Beaumont Repertory Theater, sketches.

for him to ally himself with a group of respected businessmen who were interested in building an art center that was likely to bring prestige to the city (and him), so he not only helped them assemble land; he helped them secure funding. In the end, the $165 million center received at least $40 million in public subsidies.[4] The money did not go to housing. The poor families who were driven from their homes had to find accommodations elsewhere. The 7,000 low-income apartments in the neighborhood were replaced with 4,400 units, 4,000 of which were for relatively high-income tenants.[5]

There were few logical reasons to locate the symphony and opera next to one another, but once the idea of a performing-arts center was suggested, it took on a life of its own. Soon it seemed self-evident that the whole would be greater than the sum of its parts and that the complex should contain a dance theater, a repertory theater, the Juilliard School, and a branch of the New York Public Library where the performing-arts collections would be housed along with a museum. The idea of building a group of performance spaces on the scale that the Lincoln Center planners envisioned was unprecedented, but the desire to create

new and visible facilities for the arts was typical of the time: Americans, having achieved economic, technological, military, and diplomatic dominance, desired cultural hegemony as well. In the following decades, other American cities would build their own, usually smaller versions of Lincoln Center.

Architect Wallace Harrison was the first to see the possibility of a performing-arts center. While he was having conversations with the opera trustees about a new house, Arthur Houghton from the symphony board asked him about the feasibility of building a new concert hall. The architect had recently designed a building on Fifth Avenue for Houghton's Corning Glass Company, and he had also led the team of architects who designed Rockefeller Center, designed the Rockefeller offices, helped the Rockefellers assemble the land for the United Nations Headquarters (with Robert Moses), and supervised the panel of architects who designed its buildings.

Because of these connections, Harrison's central role at Lincoln Center quickly became assured. It was cemented when the planners decided that they needed a Rockefeller to lead the committee and persuaded John D. Rockefeller III to do so. Ambitions for the center, which kept growing, were such that other prominent architects would have to be involved. The buildings, after all, were what people would see. Harrison, who already had the opera-house and symphony-hall jobs—though he

174

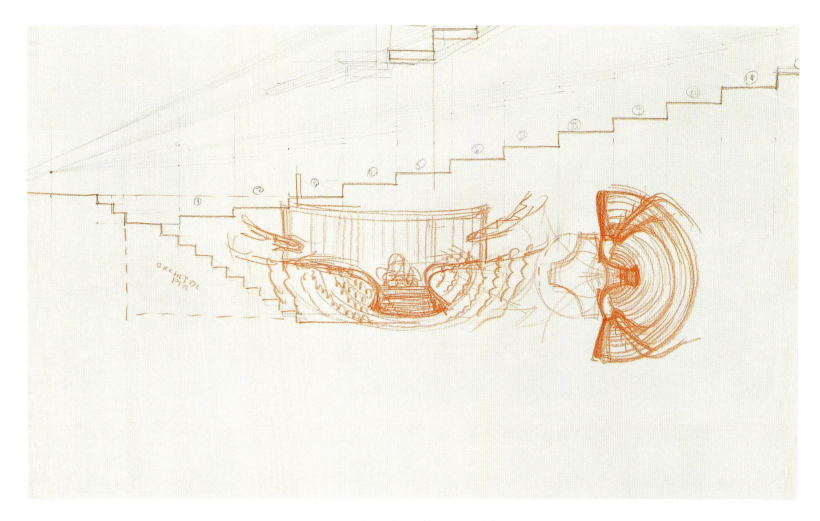

gave the latter to his partner, Max Abramovitz—was appointed coordinating architect. He put together a blue-ribbon international committee for the planning that included architects Alvar Aalto, Sven Markelius, Pietro Belluschi, Marcel Breuer, and Henry Shepley as well as acousticians Hope Bagenal, Richard Bolt, and Richard Newman.[6] When the plans began to take form and commissions were offered, younger American architects replaced the older Europeans. Philip Johnson was given the dance theater, Belluschi the Juilliard School; the Library-Museum, as it was named, went to Gordon Bunshaft of Skidmore, Owings & Merrill; and Eero Saarinen was asked to design the repertory theater.

Although he did not have an inside track to the organizing institutions the way Harrison, Abramovitz, and Johnson did, Saarinen's participation was crucial to the endeavor not only because he had more experience with auditorium design than any of the other architects but also because he was the most highly—and widely—respected midcareer architect in America. Although somewhat controversial, he was mainstream and avant-garde at the same time. His reputation lent extra prestige to an already prestige-driven enterprise.

Evidence that Saarinen could confer status simply by his involvement appears in an article that Philip Johnson wrote before the New York State Theater opened in 1964. Like Johnson's earlier article on his sources for the Glass House, "9 Actual Theatre Designs" attempted to buoy up

his own work by associating it with that of various masters. "There are, I propose, three categories among the nine designs," he wrote. "Four of the architects—Le Corbusier, Mies van der Rohe, Gropius and Stubbins—are straight, clear, international modern architects. Saarinen and myself refer in our halls to baroque prototypes. And the three others—Utzon, Aalto and Wright—one might call expressionist since their designs are arbitrary, emotional and personal."[7]

What Johnson actually built at Lincoln Center, generally regarded as more successful than Philharmonic Hall or the Metropolitan Opera House, bears very little resemblance to Saarinen's Vivian Beaumont Repertory Theater. Neither is obviously "baroque" in aesthetic, though by baroque Johnson meant a theater where members of the audience face each other. Johnson's New York State Theater is, like its neighbors, a modern version of a neoclassical building, with glitzy modernistic detailing that makes the gold-anodized aluminum on Saarinen's US Chancellery Building in London look absolutely refined. Quite unlike the respect for the urban fabric required in the London embassy competition, at Lincoln Center the context was considered something to be dispensed with as completely as possible. The neighborhood of late-nineteenth-century tenements and mixed-use buildings—home to twenty thousand mostly poor black and Puerto Rican people and hundreds of small businesses—was completely razed. Even a perfectly serviceable modern office building owned by the Kennedy family and leased to the Immigration Service

Vivian Beaumont Repertory Theater, Lincoln Center for the
Performing Arts, facade.

was demolished to make room for the stage house of the Metropolitan
Opera, which easily could have been located elsewhere on the site.[8]

The placement of the three main halls—Philharmonic Hall, the New York
State Theater, and the Opera House—was planned purely for grand
effect. Clad in travertine instead of the brick of nearby buildings and
set in open space like suburban mansions on a cul-de-sac (only at
right angles), they bear no resemblance to anything in the vicinity—or
elsewhere in New York City. The central plaza that connects the three
main halls is completely removed from the streetscape, the way American
college campuses often are. The plaza is set on a podium above the
street and separated from it by a drop-off driveway. The opera house
sits in the center, flanked by the New York State Theater and Philharmonic
Hall, which face a fountain and each other rather than the street. When
it was being built the press often compared the proposed Lincoln
Center plaza to the Piazza San Marco in Venice, yet it bears no resemblance to that asymmetrical square, which is actually a long rectangle,
open slightly at one end, and bordered by buildings that are deeply
embedded in the quirky street patterns of the city. The Lincoln Center
plaza is elevated as an entity unto itself, more like the Campidoglio in
Rome, though that is sensitively set into the hilly city, linking two levels
with a trapezoidal plaza. Lincoln Center plaza is an alien plopped in a

neighborhood that once had considerable grain. Over time, its presence
encouraged high-rise development all around, and now it appears less
disruptive than it did when it was new.

Critics reported that the ambition at Lincoln Center was to build "a
cultural fairyland,"[9] "a matchless showcase for the performing arts in
America,"[10] "one of the world's outstanding cultural centers" and "a
symbol of U.S. culture,"[11] "the most exciting vision as well as the largest
civic project ever undertaken anywhere on a private philanthropic
basis,"[12] "a new cultural vista,"[13] even "a miracle of democracy."[14] At
the groundbreaking ceremony, President Dwight Eisenhower said, "Here
will develop a mighty influence for peace and understanding throughout the world."[15]

With expectations like that, Lincoln Center was bound to disappoint. But
it turned out to disillusion people more than anyone imagined. There
were cost overruns and construction delays. The "perfect hall" that the
Philharmonic-Symphony Society had hoped to build had serious acoustical
problems. After numerous attempts to correct the deficiencies, the
interior was completely demolished and rebuilt in 1973, barely a decade
after it opened (and renamed Avery Fisher Hall). Music critics found
the musical programming old-fashioned and uninspired. The American
idea that bigger is better backfired, because in order to appeal to the
masses and fill all the halls, Lincoln Center had to offer concerts of

176

popular classical composers rather than the difficult and experimental fare that musicians and critics preferred. The assumptions that new would be better than old and that technology could compensate for tried-and-true practice—all so typical of the postwar years in the United States—led to a series of disasters at Lincoln Center that laid the seeds for the disillusion with Modernism and everything it represented in the late 1960s and 1970s. That disillusion eclipsed Saarinen's contribution to American architecture even though he was not guilty of the failings Modernism was thought to have, such as lack of expression. He even had his doubts about urban renewal: "We have these tremendous redevelopment projects, well financed, scientifically planned. They all look good on paper. Then you see them when they are up, and you wonder whether they are really better than what they replaced."[16]

Saarinen's Vivian Beaumont Theater was not a failure. Everything worked.[17] The *New York Times* architecture critic Ada Louise Huxtable called it "the sole moment" at Lincoln Center "that lifts the spirit of those to whom the twentieth century is a very exciting time to be alive and for whom the fleeting sensuality of lighting effects and matching travertine is not enough."[18] Saarinen's approach to the design was almost opposite that of Harrison, Abramovitz, and Johnson. In the first place, his client was not an established organization with its own ways of doing things. A repertory company had to be created for Lincoln Center, and when it was, the first producing director, Robert Whitehead (along with Harrison), chose Saarinen. When Whitehead brought in Elia Kazan as coproducing director, the two of them were able to work productively with the architect and well-known stage designer Jo Mielziner (who collaborated with Saarinen on the theater design) because they were all, as artists, on the same wavelength.

The Vivian Beaumont Theater was assigned a small site on the corner of West Sixty-fifth Street and Amsterdam Avenue next to the opera house, behind Philharmonic Hall, and almost invisible from the spacious central plaza. Gordon Bunshaft's Lincoln Center Library-Museum of the Performing Arts was offered a similarly cramped site in the same area, so the architects, who were friends, decided to combine the two programs in one building and collaborate on the design.[19] They had worked successfully together when Bunshaft's firm was designing the Air Force Academy and Saarinen was serving as a design consultant to the Air Force. The stolid, quietly dignified structure they produced at Lincoln Center bears little resemblance to the tall, glazed, colonnaded, travertine temples of culture that dominate the main square. The strong horizontal of the theater's heavy, overhanging roof forms a backdrop to a large rectangular pool that is the site of an imposing Henry Moore sculpture. The theater's glass facade and square concrete columns are almost hidden in shadow, and though there is travertine facing on the walls and overhang, the roof structure has an exposed aggregate finish, like the paving on the plaza in front of it originally did, instead of the more traditional travertine used on the main Lincoln Center plaza and its grand halls. (The concrete pavement was later covered with stone paving and is now a field of cracks, though renovations are planned.)

The composition resembles Saarinen's top-heavy designs for the University of Michigan School of Music (1952–56) and the University of Chicago Women's Dining Hall (1955–58), but here the proportions are graceful and masculine at the same time. The massive roof is both more refined and more rational here, for it also shelters the library and museum above and behind the theater, and surrounds the theater's vertical stage house. The concrete roof covers the lobby and the seating area in the theater and slices through the glass facade to shelter part of the plaza as well. The deep rectangular coffers of the ceiling contain lighting (both recessed incandescent downlights in cans and fluorescent uplights outlining the coffers) and are used throughout the library and museum as well as the theater, even in spaces that are more delicately scaled. Bunshaft's discrete, dark metal entrance pavilion, set neatly into a corner of the north plaza between the theater and the opera house, holds its own without upstaging its neighbors. (The plaza-level entrance leads to the lending library; there is another entrance at a lower level on the west side leading to the museum auditorium and exhibition galleries.) The bush-hammered concrete columns, which appear in both parts of the building, have triangular, bronze-finished capitals similar to those in Bunshaft's other works. The columns are connected by heavy steel pins to the exposed concrete soffit of the attic, which is framed with 20-foot-high Vierendeel trusses. These trusses, which support the stage house and the research library, span 153 feet between the columns and are cantilevered beyond them.[20] The New York Public Library's $7.5 million contribution helped defray the cost of the $17 million building, as did a gift of $3 million dollars from Vivian Beaumont Allen that covered the original projected cost of the theater.

Theatergoers enter the lobby from the plaza midway between the balcony and main floor levels, and then ascend or descend by broad double staircases on both sides of a curved wall. A second set of stairs leads to a small underground theater, later named the Mitzi E. Newhouse Theater. When the building opened, lockers lined the public spaces instead of a coat room, merging the theatrical experience with everyday life the way avant-garde theatrical productions did at the time.

Saarinen, working with Cesar Pelli and Jo Mielziner, created an unusually versatile main auditorium upstairs with steep, semicircular seating. It could be configured as a traditional proscenium theater, a deep thrust stage, or various other types of surround stages with different arrangements of audience seating. There were even hidden tunnels "to spew actors from the audience onto various fore-stages."[21] The adaptable design recalls Saarinen, Rapson, and James's winning entry to the 1938 National Theater Competition in Williamsburg, Virginia, which would have had three different configurations too. The Lincoln Center theater, however, also employed all the available technology to provide flexibility. The main theater seated 1,040 and the smaller "forum" theater on the lower level for rehearsals and the productions of small theater companies had 299 seats. Red carpeting and upholstery and gray satin stage curtains provided foils to the black-brown wood and metal surfaces used throughout the theater. Although Saarinen and Mielziner agreed about the kind of theater they wanted to create, their approaches were almost opposite, according to Hugh Hardy, who worked on it with them after college while he was deciding whether to become an architect or a set designer. (He became an architect and designed numerous theaters.) "Mielziner was so intuitive and vague, and Saarinen was so intellectual and thorough," Hardy said, imitating Saarnen's slow, deliberate speech patterns and showing with his hands the way Saarinen did, how he figured out every detail and its dimensions scientifically.[22]

"Of all the buildings at Lincoln Center, this newest is the most sober, simple, and serene . . . a somber gem set among flashier stones," *Progressive Architecture* observed when the theater opened, also noting that Eero Saarinen's "fundamental approach to problems is again evident in this theater."[23]

There was a lot less coverage in the press by the time the Vivian Beaumont Theater opened in October 1965 than there had been when the earlier Lincoln Center halls were completed, but there was less negative criticism, too. Olga Gueft, writing for *Interiors*, attributed the difference in success to the Saarinen-Bunshaft collaboration, while revealing the bias against old buildings typical of the time: "Much of the criticism leveled at each new architectural debutante at Lincoln Center has puzzled the unpretentious New Yorkers who have been taking naive delight in their first grimeless cultural center. After the sooty, cramped 57th Street corner of Carnegie Hall and the dank lobby of the Metropolitan Opera House, the airy porticoes, fountains, and diamond lights of Philharmonic Hall and The New York State Theater have been seized with glee by audiences unwilling or incapable of discerning what highbrow critics have called 'disastrous' acoustics and 'fashionably mediocre neoclassic' design. The respective architects, each a sitting duck, have stood without flinching under the showers of ripe verbal vegetables every real trooper can expect in the course of a public career. And yet even the targets—Max Abramovitz, Philip Johnson, and Wallace K. Harrison—have admitted that they could hardly resist the most overwhelming design temptation: the temptation to compete with each other rather than submerge their artistic egos in a presumably more desirable unity. Playing it cool with this limpid pool, the architects [of the Vivian Beaumont Repertory Theater and Library-Museum] have effortlessly outmaneuvered the fountain buildings out near the street. The element of surprise helps."[24]

The difference was really more than a matter of modesty and cooperation, though the architects did compromise at one point when Saarinen wanted three columns at the corners and Bunshaft wanted only one and both wanted to do the remunerative working drawings. They agreed to use single columns and have Saarinen's firm do the drawings since, as Bunshaft realized, Eero would make so many changes as the building progressed that there would be few profits.[25] The difference was attributable to subtlety, confidence, taste, and talent. The architects on the main plaza were good but not great designers, giving their clients— the trustees of the major cultural institutions—what they asked for: something grand, glittery, and conventionally pretty. Saarinen produced a more austere and modern building for challenging experimental theater that was in line with the critical and artistic taste of the time. When that taste changed and a more conservative approach came into vogue, the building was renovated to reflect it.[26] When tradition came back into fashion in artistic circles, old buildings like Carnegie Hall were considered valuable again. The failure of Bolt, Beranek & Newman's high-tech acoustics at Philharmonic Hall also made people appreciate the sound in Carnegie Hall.[27] Despite all the criticism of these acousticians (whom he had used at MIT's Kresge Auditorium), after Philharmonic Hall opened, Saarinen used them again at the Vivian Beaumont Theater, and the critics approved: "Acoustically, the theater is superb," Gueft wrote.[28] Saarinen also brought in structural and mechanical engineers he had worked with before (Ammann & Whitney and Syska & Hennessy). And he collaborated again with his old friend Dan Kiley, who designed the spare geometric plaza lined with rows of trees in front of the theater as well as, on the south side of the opera house, Damrosch Park with its band shell, outdoor seating, and grids of trees.

Saarinen did not live to attend the Vivian Beaumont Repertory Theater opening. The design work had been completed before he died, and his associate Maurice Allen saw it through construction. That cannot have been easy, as the management of the Lincoln Center Repertory Theater changed the year before the building was finished. But Saarinen was gratified to have worked with the other architects in what he described as a happily chaotic and contentious process.

Camaraderie

Working with other architects was Eero Saarinen's recreation. Even though he made all the major design decisions in his office, his associates remember being called in at all hours to help him develop ideas. Most of them assume it was their company he wanted as much as their contributions, though all say that he readily accepted ideas from everyone he worked with.[29]

Vivian Beaumont Repertory Theater, interior of main theater.

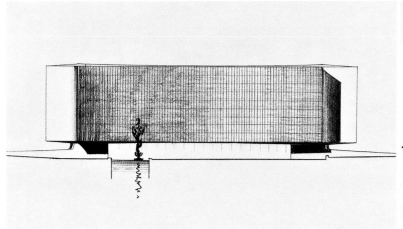
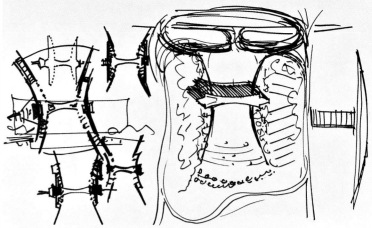

From left: World Health Organization competition scheme, 1960, facade; plan.

Gene Festa, who was the original project designer on the Vivian Beaumont Theater, recalls, "His working habits were probably more intense than any person I've ever heard of. He literally worked all the time. His office was based on that. It was not uncommon to put in ten- to twelve-hour days, six days a week. And sometimes Eero would have a thought on a Sunday morning and call you up and ask you if you'd come in and look at it, and you'd come in. It wasn't an organized thing, it was just the way he worked. He totally lived what he was doing. But there wasn't just work. Eero also liked to socialize and have fun and drinks and laughs. We had a lot of parties in the office, at the slightest excuse."[30] Festa went to work for Saarinen in 1954 after graduating from Columbia, where Saarinen's associate Glen Paulsen had seen his student work. Festa's wife, May, worked for Knoll, but both Festas went to work for Eero Saarinen and Associates when the firm moved to Connecticut and stayed to work for the successor firm, Kevin Roche John Dinkeloo and Associates.

Despite the workload, "there was very little turnover in the office except for the people who specifically came to do an internship for a year or something," Festa said. The practice grew from about twenty, when he arrived, to sixty in three years. It outgrew the simple wood-paneled building on Long Lake Road in Bloomfield Hills that Saarinen had designed in 1953. The large office was forced in 1957 to move into the old Wilson Cadillac dealership across the street on Woodward Avenue with its "Colonial" facade; four years later, they were ready to move again. Still, it "was almost an atelier. In other large offices, they regulated the amount of time spent on design, but in Eero's mind there was no point in going ahead until you had achieved the best possible solution to a problem."

Saarinen was in the process of moving to Connecticut during the summer of 1961 when he developed the brain tumor that took his life. Most of the firm's work at that time was on the East Coast (Lincoln Center, CBS, Morse and Stiles colleges at Yale, the IBM Research Center in Yorktown, Bell Labs, the TWA terminal, and Dulles Airport). Also, there was better air transportation from New York than from Detroit, and Aline's life and career had always been based in the New York area. Saarinen had bought a house for his family on one of the nicest streets in New Haven, Saint Ronan Terrace, and, to house his office, he acquired a mansion that looks like a castle overlooking a reservoir in nearby Hamden. After he died, his colleagues decided to go ahead with the move, and most of the associates uprooted their families to finish his work. Kevin Roche John Dinkeloo and Associates, which had a staff of ninety-four by 1963, still occupies the Hamden mansion and the modern addition behind it.

Saarinen's perfectionism and numerous commissions did not keep him from participating in professional activities. He was president of the Detroit Chapter of the American Institute of Architects and a member of the Michigan Society of Architects. He became a fellow of the AIA in 1952 at the age of forty-two, and won the Institute's Howard Myers Award for the article "Six Broad Currents of Modern Architecture," which he published in Architectural Forum in 1953.[31] He was elected a member of the National Academy of Design in 1954, became a fellow of the International Institute of Arts and Letters in 1958, and he was one of the few architect members of the Society of Architectural Historians. When Frank Lloyd Wright died, Saarinen was elected to "the architect's chair" at the American Academy of Arts and Letters in 1960.[32] (Later, when membership was expanded, Mies van der Rohe was also elected, then Gordon Bunshaft and Philip Johnson; today there are a number of architect members, including Saarinen's former associates Kevin Roche and Cesar Pelli.) Saarinen received honorary degrees from Yale, Dickinson College, and Wayne State University, and was the youngest person ever to receive the AIA Gold Medal when it was awarded posthumously in 1962.[33]

Saarinen spoke at AIA conventions, often acted as a critic at architecture schools, worked as a consultant on the UNESCO headquarters in Paris and for the Air Force Academy in Colorado Springs (designed by SOM), served as chairman of the Committee on Art and Architecture at Yale, and sat on numerous juries, including those for the Museum of Modern Art and Architectural Record's Hidden Talent Competition of 1949 (with Mies van der Rohe, Wallace Harrison, Harvard Dean Joseph Hudnut, and author Morris Ketchum), and the Sydney Opera House competition in 1957.

Saarinen's influential role in the controversial Australian competition has been the subject of speculation ever since. And although the building proved much more difficult to construct than expected, took many years to complete, and cost 60 million Australian dollars instead of 7.5 million, it became the symbol and pride of the city and one of the masterpieces of twentieth-century architecture. Antonio Román discusses the controversy thoroughly in Eero Saarinen: An Architecture of Multiplicity, pointing out that Jørn Utzon's winning design bears "strong affinities" to Saarinen's Kresge Auditorium and the preliminary designs for the TWA Terminal (1956–62), a project that in turn may have been influenced by the opera house. To what extent Saarinen dominated the jury is debatable, but his "vivid sketches, rendered quickly with chalk and charcoal, describe how Utzon's proposal would look in Sydney Harbor" in a way Utzon's own rough drawings do not.[34]

In 1960, Saarinen even took the time to enter the World Health Organization (WHO) competition for a nine-story office building in Geneva. His boldly sculptural but almost weightless, column-free office spaces with convex facades on both sides hover over the park-like setting, touching down only at the ends, where massive curved, triangular piers support them like the towers of a bridge. The dramatic scheme took second prize. The winner was a long, white rectangle on short, paired pilotis with prominent projecting sunscreens by native son Jean Tschumi, the father of the New York architect Bernard Tschumi.[35]

Saarinen's architectural activities were international, as was his office, which employed associates from Ireland (Kevin Roche), Argentina (Cesar Pelli), Latvia (Gunnar Birkerts), Canada (David Powrie), England (Peter Carter and Anthony Lumsden), and Hungary (Balthazar Korab). Festa notes, "Eero was really a global figure. That was when Americans in general had very little awareness of foreign cultures, which we now take so much for granted with jet travel." In an increasingly international world, Saarinen "was very tuned into the culture. Part of his genius was that he produced the right building at the right time. He knew instinctually what could be accepted."

That is one reason his work is important and why it is lucky for posterity that he designed at least one skyscraper, which, after all, is a particularly American building type and one very typical of the postwar period. The tower that he designed, not surprisngly, is unique.

Saarinen's Only Skyscraper: CBS

When Saarinen was designing the thirty-eight-story headquarters of the Columbia Broadcasting System in New York City (1960–65), the competitor in him went into high gear. He wanted to build the best modern skyscraper in the world, and in order to do that he had to surpass Mies van der Rohe's Seagram Building, which was only three blocks east on Park Avenue. Coincidentally, he had even influenced that building. As a young architect in 1954, Phyllis Bronfman Lambert was helping her father find the best possible person to design a building for his company (Joseph E. Seagram and Sons) headquarters, so she went to see Alfred Barr, the director of the Museum of Modern Art. He sent her to Philip Johnson, who had been the museum's curator of architecture, and Johnson sent her to Saarinen. "Eero was a great list maker," Lambert remembers, "and when I asked who the architect should be, he made three lists: Those Who Could but Shouldn't, Those Who Should but Couldn't, Those Who Should and Could. On the first list were the big firms like Skidmore, Owings & Merrill and Harrison & Abramovitz, which had the technical expertise but lacked genius. [SOM had just finished Lever House; Harrison had led the UN team.] On the second list were the younger people, who had the talent but were not yet experienced enough. One of them was Yamasaki. When it came to Those Who Should and Could, it was really just Mies and Le Corbusier, and at that time everybody was talking about Mies, especially Eero. He described everything he did in terms of how it was like Mies or not like Mies."[36]

After Lambert had gone to see various architects and their buildings, only two people came to make their own pitches to her. One was Saarinen, which she thought was fine. "He was a young guy, all bushy-tailed and enthusiastic." The other, though, was Walter Gropius. She thought that rather sad because he had once been considered one of the top architects in the world, now he was begging for a job. She chose Mies, and Philip Johnson managed to become involved and to design the interiors and the Four Seasons restaurant.[37]

The Seagram Building, with its exquisitely proportioned bronze and dark glass gridded facade, standing on pilotis behind an elevated plaza, turned out to be a masterpiece, the best modern skyscraper anywhere. That is what Saarinen hoped to equal—or outdo. But he knew he could compete only by taking a different tack, so in many ways CBS became the opposite of Seagram—stony granite instead of glass and steel, rooted in the ground on a sunken plaza instead of raised on stilts, almost maintaining the street line instead of set back, black instead of bronze toned (though the Seagram Building later darkened to near black), composed purely of uninterrupted vertical elements instead of a gridded frame. It is, in fact, too firmly implanted, and that is its greatest weakness. (It is also a foil to Saarinen's own glassy, curvaceous, suspended, and horizontal scheme for the WHO headquarters.) Unlike any other skyscraper in New York, CBS has triangular projecting piers that form a sculpturesque facade and meet the skyline with a jagged edge, the way the pleated facade at the University of Chicago Law School does, instead of a boxy-looking top. The piers, which are structural, make the tower appear to soar. They also contain space for air-conditioning and plumbing ducts, allow more light from different angles to enter the relatively small windows than conventional columns do, and provide better sight lines for views from the inside.[38]

Saarinen could at least try to beat Mies because at CBS he had another extraordinary client like Irwin Miller in Columbus, Indiana, and William Hewitt at Deere & Company. If you visit the CBS Building today, you will see a bronze plaque near the entrance commemorating CBS chairman William Paley, but it wasn't Paley who became Eero's accomplice at CBS. It was CBS president Frank Stanton, the company's conscience and intellectual, an independent-minded midwesterner like Miller and Hewitt. It was Stanton's idea to hire Saarinen. Paley, a social and glamorous businessman who had founded the company, fought Stanton every step of the way. The two men often played yin to one another's yang in the early days of the pioneering company. Stanton had grown up in Dayton, Ohio, married his high school sweetheart, earned a Ph.D. in the psychology of mass communications, and was hired by CBS because he had invented an electronic machine that measured audience reactions to programs. He rose quickly, became president less than ten years later (in 1946 at age thirty-seven), and held the job for more than twenty-five years.

While Paley concentrated on entertainment and advertising, Stanton was in charge of news, and he became a hero of journalistic history by establishing a "firewall" between news and entertainment, insisting that news need not pay for itself, and securing the same First Amendment rights for broadcast journalists that print journalists enjoyed. He aired the first presidential debates (between Richard Nixon and John F. Kennedy), stood behind Edward R. Murrow's criticism of Senator Joseph McCarthy's anticommunist hearings, and defied Congress by broadcasting The Selling of the Pentagon, a documentary about the US military's massive PR campaign. Like some of Saarinen's other clients, CBS was a major force in postwar America, at least partly because Stanton understood that free and unbiased broadcast news was essential to American democracy, and he knew how to support and enhance it. The achievements of his years at "the Tiffany Network" (so-called because of its high-quality programming) have never been equaled.

Stanton also took a serious interest in art and architecture—with exacting taste. He had even considered becoming an architect and had been accepted at Cornell University's architecture school, but he stayed in the Midwest, where his girlfriend was going to college and where he could more easily find work to pay his way through school, studying the liberal

Opposite: CBS Tower on the Avenue of the Americas.

arts. From the beginning, he knew he wanted Saarinen to design the CBS Building (largely because of the work he had done at the GM Technical Center), but it took some time to convince Paley, even though he was a patron of the arts who collected paintings and served on the board of the Museum of Modern Art.

"He bought the property and kept it idle for, I think, three years before we did a thing," Stanton recalls, "because I wouldn't give up on what I wanted and he wouldn't give up on what he wanted, and he didn't know what he wanted." Paley was "a friend of John Rockefeller, who had ties to Wally Harrison, and he knew Philip Johnson." Stanton knew Harrison, too, and was close to Gordon Bunshaft, but he wanted Saarinen for CBS, and eventually he prevailed. Another struggle took place again when it came time to select designers for the interiors and Stanton wanted Florence (Shu) Knoll Bassett, with whom he had worked before.[39]

"That was another bridge we had to cross," Stanton says. "Bill had a firm that had done work for him, I guess at [his house] Kiluna, out on Long Island, and he thought they ought to be given a crack at the interior work. Early on, in my own mind, there was only one way to go. John Dinkeloo was brokenhearted when we didn't have them do the interiors, but I made it clear from the beginning that I wanted to go a different way. I finally said to Bill, 'Why don't you get your architect to do three offices in the church?' (We owned a church down on the Lower East Side. God knows why somebody bought it. The idea was we would have a little television complex down there. It never worked. But we had the space.) During dinner one evening, we decided we would go down. I didn't want to be down there when the designer was there. It was the first he'd seen them (I hadn't seen them either), and he came out of there and he said, 'Gee, it's not very exciting, is it?' and I didn't have to follow it up. That was when I ensured that Shu did the building. I maintained that his office would be in his style, and everything else would be Knoll. And it was a handsome office [Paley's]. It would do well in London, but it wasn't Madison Avenue, and it sure as hell wasn't television."[40]

The fact that television was a young, not very well-established business encouraged Stanton to envision a bold modern tower, but also a substantial-looking one. He was actively involved in the design, which was done, as usual, with a lot of push and pull between client and architect. Saarinen and his colleagues experimented with various facade and base treatments (horizontal bands and vertical ones, emphatic corners, different types of columns, little slanted feet, an arch-shaped base) before they settled on what the architect described in a letter to his client as "the simplest conceivable rectangular free-standing sheer tower. The

From left: Mies van der Rohe, Seagram Building, Park Avenue and Fifty-second Street, New York, New York, 1954–58; CBS tower, model.

verticality of the tower is emphasized by the relief made by the triangular piers between the windows. These start at the pavement and soar up 491 feet." (Actually, they look as if they began underground and rose through the earth.) "Its beauty will be, I believe, that it will be the simplest skyscraper statement in New York."[41] Saarinen was right about that. It is the "proud and soaring thing" that Louis Sullivan had dreamed a skyscraper would one day be.

Stanton and Saarinen agreed that "it should look permanent," both because it was intended to house a new industry that created ephemeral products and because the other skyscrapers going up around it on Sixth Avenue were "flimsy looking," as Saarinen thought was the case with "too much modern architecture."[42] The street had been renamed the Avenue of the Americas to make it more attractive for redevelopment, and the area was gradually leveled, not for urban renewal, but by commercial speculation. A whole row of undistinguished aluminum and glass towers was being built, each with a plaza inspired by Seagram (and the zoning law it gave rise to, which allowed additional stories if a street-level plaza was built).[43] While a lone plaza, like

the one Mies excised on Park Avenue, could open up a city street to a little light and air, a whole row of them eroded the street, making it into something like a suburban strip filled with parking lots, only these were parking lots for pedestrians. Saarinen thought it was important "to place the building on its site so that we could have a plaza and still not destroy the street line. . . . It lets people sit in the sun and look at the sky," though he added, "A plaza allows a building to be seen."[44] There was no seating, though clearly the plaza is supposed to be a viewing area. It is several steps below the sidewalk. The tower is set back twenty-five feet, not only from the avenue but also from Fifty-second and Fifty-third streets, and located pretty much in the middle of its site. There are no stores at the base to enliven the street or compete with the tower's pristine beauty. Even the entrances are on the side streets, as is the only commercial space, a restaurant. The main purpose of CBS's plaza is to allow the tower to be seen on all four sides (and its inhabitants to look out on all sides).[45] Unlike those at Seagram, all four CBS facades are the same, so there is a consistency to the building. Because the columns project at 45-degree angles, the glass is barely visible. There is also less of it than in steel-and-glass skyscrapers, and because it is dark gray, its visual effect is subtle.

The CBS Building does not just look stony. It was the first New York skyscraper (and one of the only ones) to be built with a reinforced-concrete

CBS president Frank Stanton with model of CBS tower and neighboring buildings.

frame instead of a steel one. The plan of the almost-square, 135-by-160-foot tower is unusual too. Saarinen described it as "a rectangular donut. We put a ring of concrete columns around the perimeter and a concrete core containing services and vertical transportation in the center. It permitted clear office spaces [without columns in the way and eliminated] . . . wasteful public corridors. We made efficient use of the mechanical system by putting one mechanical floor at the bottom and another at the top with office floors between them."[46] The innovative structural system (similar to the one Minoru Yamasaki and Leslie Robertson later used at the much taller World Trade Center, only in steel instead of concrete) forms a sort of tube, supporting the building around the edges like a bearing wall and also in the central elevator and service core, so the space in between can be arranged any way the client chooses. Because of the five-foot-wide columns and five-foot-wide windows between them, CBS has a flexible five-foot planning module; and because the area between the core and the outer wall is only thirty-five feet deep in every direction, no work space is far from a window.

As with other Saarinen buildings, some critics thought the structural concept was not quite pure enough, because the columns were the same size and number at the top as at the bottom, where more support was required. One of those critics was engineer William J. LeMessurier, quoted in an *Architectural Record* cover story devoted almost entirely to structure and published when the CBS building opened. But Messurier admitted that the rigid wall structure would

improve bracing for wind and earthquakes. In the same article, the engineer who had designed the structure, Paul Weidlinger, was quoted as explaining, "While the over-all cross section of the columns remains constant, the effective cross section is gradually reduced towards the upper floors and the space gained is used to accommodate the down-feed duct system which increases in size [at the top]."[47] He also noted that the floor system was made of a lightweight concrete that weighs 25 percent less than standard concrete and that, placed on heavy and extremely rigid steel girders, the building had been erected over a subway tunnel that cuts across the site diagonally.

It is not surprising that Saarinen wanted the columns to be uniform from top to bottom because he always chose the simplest, cleanest concept when he could, even if it was not the most structurally efficient. Aesthetics counted for a great deal with him. Function did, too, and these were values not always championed in architectural theory. Function—or adherence to a client's needs—even trumped aesthetics sometimes. Saarinen and his associates would have preferred to make the tower a perfect square in plan.[48] Four of the five models they made of it had square floor plates. But since the site was deeper than it was wide, a slightly rectangular shape (which is not immediately apparent) allowed them to build more usable space within the new zoning envelope, which was still being developed. The architects even worked with the planning commissioners to be sure that the building would conform, so CBS ended up serving "as a demonstration model for the new zoning." The Saarinen office helped "develop realistic land coverage ratios to permit the plaza-surrounded sheer tower. As such, CBS set the shape and standard for New York building today," *New York Times* architecture critic Ada Louise Huxtable reported in 1966.[49]

But modern skyscrapers rarely measured up to expectations. Huxtable continued: "The first observation that one might make about the new CBS headquarters is that it is a building. It is not, like so much of today's large-scale construction, a handy package, a shiny wraparound envelope, a packing case, a box of cards, a trick with mirrors." And, she noted, it was built "for a figure estimated at not too far above the speculative norm of about $24 a square foot and well below the luxury building price of $40 and upward. And yet, the reaction to the building is extremely mixed. The dark dignity that appeals to architectural sophisticates puts off the public, which tends to reject it as funereal."[50] Once more, a gap in taste existed.

Saarinen did not live to oversee construction, but his unusually able associates, especially Harold Roth, came through here, as elsewhere. In Frank Stanton he had a client willing to go after black granite the way he went after First Amendment rights for his reporters: "One day Eero and I were having lunch, I guess, at the Four Seasons, and he was not recommending anything for the skin. I was pressing him for some idea. And I was wearing an old Harris tweed jacket. I don't know why I was wearing it on a weekday, but I was and I remember saying to Eero, 'I want something as rough as this and as dark as this.' And that's when he told me where I could go to see it, because I didn't want to take it without looking at it," Stanton recalls. "So my wife [Ruth] and I spent a weekend in Oslo [to see Saarinen's American Embassy] and were disappointed in the building, not the architecture, but the skin. I was convinced that we had to have a stone of some kind."

Every time Stanton attended a board meeting somewhere, he and Ruth would go to visit the nearest recommended quarry. He sent members of his staff to look at stone as well. The far-flung search entailed examining fifty varieties of granite and marble in Africa, Japan, Norway, Sweden, Germany, France, Spain, Portugal, Canada, and the United States. Meanwhile, Paley's wife, socialite Babe Paley, who was always on the best-dressed list (a much-talked-about distinction at the time), "knew that we were having trouble finding the skin. Bill came into my office one day and said, 'Babe's got the idea for the building.' And I said, 'What is it?' 'Pink granite.'" Finally, they found some black granite that Stanton liked in a family-run quarry in Quebec.

But that was just the beginning. Stanton (and Saarinen) wanted it rough, like the Harris tweed jacket, so "the surface was burned off under highly controlled conditions to create a uniform rough texture" in a "process called 'thermal stippling.'"[51] But, as Stanton later remarked, "it turned out to be as white as a shirt." More searches ensued. Eventually, they applied a process called "liquid honing," used to clean gun casings. It involved blasting a surface with water and minuscule glass beads under pressure. "Happily, this process not only cleaned the surface of the granite but darkened it as well."[52]

The black granite on its pleated facade, which is all you see from some angles, became the building's most distinguishing characteristic and the source of its nickname, Black Rock.

Stanton's attention to detail was similar to Saarinen's, but in the interiors it was not offset by the architect's sense of when to compromise, which was one of his great strengths. The building both gained and lost from Stanton's dogged pursuit of a vision. He let the Saarinen firm design the lobby, and Warren Plattner, an interior architect who had once been associated with the firm, designed the severely elegant Ground Floor restaurant. Florence (Shu) Knoll Bassett and the Knoll Planning Unit designed everything else, except Paley's office. "She developed the most fully articulated program of design control ever attempted by a corporation: employees worked in a stylish environment in which paintings, vases of flowers and pots of plants were virtually the only elements."

Personal possessions were not allowed, which was strange for a company with creative employees. (Similar restrictions were imposed at Deere & Company.) Still, Huxtable bemoaned "the failure to carry through its distinctive style and concept consistently into all of its major interior spaces."[53] Other critics, such as Patricia Conway, saw too much internal consistency.[54] Like the rest of the building, however, the interior design was otherwise very much celebrated in the press. The New Yorker even published a profile on Frank Stanton's desk.

The CBS Building did, as Huxtable suggested, set a standard, but it was not followed. Even a skyscraper as beautiful, dignified, elegant, and substantial as CBS could not compensate for the shortcomings of what was built all around it. Saarinen had foreseen the problem: "A tower should not be tied in with lower street buildings. . . . It should stand alone with air and light around it. A plaza is a very necessary thing in a city. But a plaza can be a dangerous thing. We have to remember the street line and we have to remember the space between is as important as the towers. These arrangements should be orderly and beautiful so the streets do not look like torn things and the towers like isolated teeth sticking up from a gaping mouth."[55]

The transformation of Sixth Avenue, unfortunately, was not under his creative control—or anybody else's. The market prevailed, and the new zoning code encouraged empty spaces beside the sidewalk. As in Grosvenor Square and at Lincoln Center, the context of the site was changing and taking the street line with it. When CBS acquired the site, there were four apartment buildings and a parking lot on it, as there were up and down the street only a few years before. Little more than a decade later, almost all the old mixed-use buildings with stores on the sidewalk were gone, and instead of horizontal rows of low-rise buildings for a tower to soar over, there was a parade of bland slab skyscrapers about the same height as CBS, each with a plaza cutting away from the sidewalk. On Park Avenue, the solid masonry buildings on both sides of the Seagram Building were replaced by bland, glassy, modern office towers with plazas of their own. A mile north of CBS, more traditional blocks had been replaced by the isolated plazas at Lincoln Center. The 1950s and 1960s were not kind to the streets of New York, and rising to replace the miles of urban fabric that were lost were only a few distinguished buildings. Eero Saarinen designed two of them.

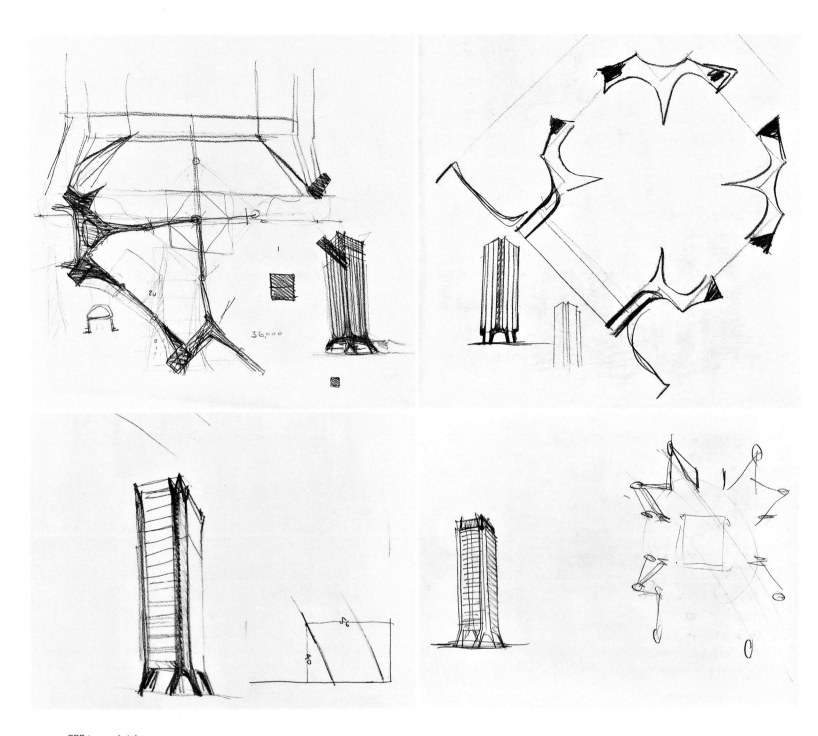

CBS tower sketches.

188

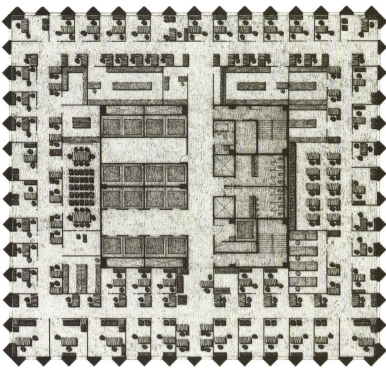

This page: CBS, views of interiors by Florence (Shu) Knoll Bassett and the Knoll Planning Unit; ground floor plan.

Opposite, from top: CBS, lobby interior by Eero Saarinen and Associates; reception area on upper floor by Florence (Shu) Knoll Bassett and the Knoll Planning Unit.

13. Symbolizing Modernity:
The Milwaukee War Memorial and the
Saint Louis Gateway Arch

Not all American cities experienced urban development pressure after World War II. Many grew at the edges while their downtowns deteriorated, deprived of middle-class residents and the taxes they paid. In some places, citizens organized to buoy up their cores. Sometimes they erected monuments intended to make their downtowns more attractive while they commemorated war dead or illustrious events in the city's history.

In Milwaukee, Wisconsin, they decided to create a "living memorial" to the soldiers lost in World War II, with facilities for veterans' organizations but also a much-needed concert hall and art gallery for the city. The "well-heeled citizens" who formed Metropolitan Milwaukee War Memorial, Inc. contacted Saarinen, Swanson, and Saarinen, who, just before the war, had built the Kleinhans Music Hall (1938–40) and won the competition for the Smithsonian Gallery of Art (1939). Both projects had been celebrated in the press.

In 1946, the first scheme for a Milwaukee War Memorial spread over six downtown blocks and recalled both of the earlier projects. Like the Kleinhans, it included auditoriums of three different sizes next to a reflecting pool. Like the Smithsonian scheme, its art gallery was composed of asymmetrically arranged long, low blocks with walls of glass or masonry. It incorporated meeting rooms for veterans groups and a long arcade where the names of all the war dead were to be carved, like the much later Vietnam Veterans Memorial in Washington, DC.[1]

The county had agreed to purchase a site, and the citizens' committee planned to raise the money to build the memorial by "popular subscription." But, as *Architectural Forum* reported, construction "would, fittingly enough, wait upon the termination of the housing shortage for the living veterans of World War II."[2] Debates about whether the memorial should be built and whether the public should help pay for it prolonged construction further.

By the time Milwaukeeans were ready to build in 1954, Robert Swanson had left the firm, Eliel Saarinen had died, and there were Korean War veterans to remember as well. The location and the program had changed, too, so Eero redesigned the Milwaukee War Memorial (1953–57) for a site overlooking Lake Michigan that he described as "a bridgehead extending beyond a forty-foot bluff."[3] Since only $2.7 million of the required $5 million had been raised, the concert hall was postponed (it was finally built in the 1960s near the City Hall and was designed by Saarinen's old friend from Cranbrook Harry Weese). The galleries for the newly formed Milwaukee Art Center (the result of a merger in 1957 between the Milwaukee Art Institute and the Layton Art Gallery) assumed more importance in the new scheme, though they

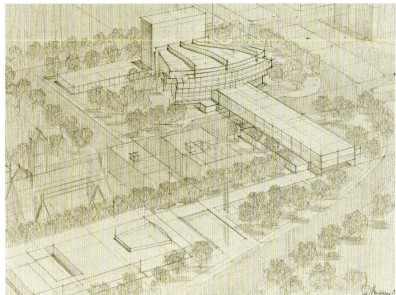

This page, from left: Saarinen, Swanson, and Saarinen, Milwaukee War Memorial project, 1946; Eero Saarinen and Associates, Milwaukee War Memorial, Milwaukee, Wisconsin, 1953–57.

Opposite, from top: Milwaukee War Memorial, courtyard; staircase.

provided only twenty-two thousand square feet of exhibition space. They were housed in an ashlar-clad "base which builds the mass up to the city level," where a bridge leads into a glass-walled lobby looking back on the downtown and leading out to a memorial court where the names of the war dead are inscribed in granite on the edges of a shallow pool. The court offers what the architect called "breathtaking views" of seemingly endless lake and sky, framed by massive wedge-shaped concrete piers that support the big, boxlike meeting halls and offices of the veterans' organizations on the third floor. These concrete-framed rooms with window walls are cantilevered outward almost thirty feet in three directions.[4]

The Milwaukee War Memorial (on which Gunnar Birkerts worked) is a functional building and a bold, inspiring, gravity-defying, cruciform monument. *Architectural Forum* described it rather hyperbolically: "Standing there, the court awakes a primeval sense of heroes up on a stage. And, fittingly, the outstretched wings, like Hamlet's four captains, bear a soldier to the stage."[5] The building does have more of a presence than its relatively small size would normally command, perhaps because, as Saarinen explained, "it differs from any vaulted or plastic form concrete, but it is a structure where every plane, whether vertical or horizontal, is a working part of the total structure. The building finishes are rough. It depends for monumentality and dignity on the clarity of its structure, on its 'guts' and its simplicity."[6] It is, however, not nearly as bold, inspiring, or sculpturesque as the Saint Louis Gateway Arch (1947–65). And because it housed the art center, there were later additions that encroached on its monumental form.

The first addition by Milwaukee architects Kahler, Slater & Fitzhugh Scott in 1976 tried to intrude as little as possible by creating a larger and lower base for the proud concrete cross. "We didn't seek to produce a monument but instead to create a quiet, unassuming, and low-keyed background for the soaring sculpture of the original Memorial Center and a neutral context that would not detract from the works of art to be displayed," David Kahler explained. They used the raw concrete that Saarinen had chosen to make his bold, masculine, structurally expressive statement as they provided an additional ninety thousand square feet of flexible exhibition space and sixty thousand square feet for other necessary facilities. Aware that Saarinen had said, "Looking back, I wish that the staircases" (which were hung with light steel cables like the ones at GM) "had been given the same qualities of 'guts' and boldness as the building itself," Kahler, Slater & Fitzhugh Scott created a massive concrete staircase. They are proud of the fact that "it is difficult to tell when you walk from the new structure into the original building, or back again."[7]

Still, the long new base, which extends northward along the lake, enlarging the memorial court and providing a setting for outdoor sculpture, necessarily undermines the sense that the building is perched there on the bluff like a giant eagle. The addition had to anchor it. After all, it contains a two hundred-by-two hundred-foot, three-story building. But it intrudes as little as possible, giving credence to the architects' statement that "our goal was to complement the original structure conceived by Eero Saarinen, not to compete with it."[8]

That was certainly not the idea twenty-five years later when the museum, having changed its name to the Milwaukee Art Museum in 1980, hired Santiago Calatrava to make a dramatic impression on the cityscape with an addition that is little more than a bridge, parking garage, and entryway. The enormous white metal and glass, seventy-five-million-dollar structure connects the museum directly with the center of the

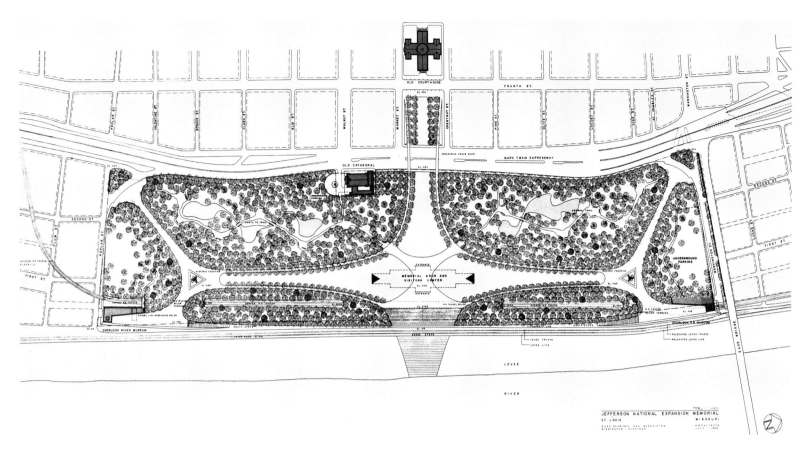

This page: Saint Louis Gateway Arch, plan.

Opposite: Saint Louis Gateway Arch, drawings from competition schemes.

through his work in the design of the PSFS skyscraper, in Philadelphia, in partnership with Bill Lescaze. 'So [Saarinen said] I decided to hire one of those people who had learned to do wonderful Beaux-Arts renderings. I was absolutely sure that our project would be the only one among the submissions to be presented that way. And I was sure that it would stop George absolutely cold!' A few weeks later, I happened to see George Howe," Blake recalled, "and asked him about it. 'That son of a bitch,' he said, beaming from ear to ear. 'He was absolutely right. I couldn't keep my eyes off those renderings. And then, of course, I realized that the design was simply the best one submitted.' That, needless to say, helped."[29]

Building the Saint Louis Arch

As impressive as the renderings are, they pale in comparison with the actual experience of the gargantuan stainless-steel-sheathed, concrete-framed structure that eventually rose on the banks of the Mississippi. But it had already taken Luther Smith and his colleagues a decade and a half to get to the proposal stage, and another sixteen years would pass before the arch was completed.

Long before it was finished, the arch was criticized for not deriving its form strictly from mathematical calculations. Saarinen never strove for that kind of purity.[30] He considered himself an artist. What a structure

looked like was always preeminent, but he worked with a gifted structural engineer from the very beginning. The engineer who helped him design the arch, Fred Severud (who also worked with him on the Yale Hockey Rink and with Matthew Nowicki on the Raleigh Livestock Judging Pavilion) was willing to—even challenged by—helping him do it. In building an object the size and weight of the Saint Louis Arch, there was not a lot of play, though there were choices to be made, as the engineer explained in an article that ran after the competition but long before construction began.

"During the preliminaries to the competition," Severud said, "Eero Saarinen told me he wanted a triangular ribbon floating in the air, of beauty and permanence," at a cost that would not render the scheme financially impossible. "The architects proposed a profile for the arch with suggested span and height. From this we worked out mathematically a curve which would place the pressure line as near the center of the arch as possible and at the same time give the architects an arch that was pleasing to the eye. We also made preliminary investigations to determine minimum sections for gravitational and aero-dynamic stability." After the architects won the competition, the engineers conducted a number of studies to gain a definitive idea of how much Saarinen's floating ribbon would cost. They hired a consultant to do wind-tunnel tests to see if the triangular sections had enough wind stability to prevent fluttering and what the load factors should be to resist wind from various angles. "The model proved the arch would be entirely satisfactory."[31]

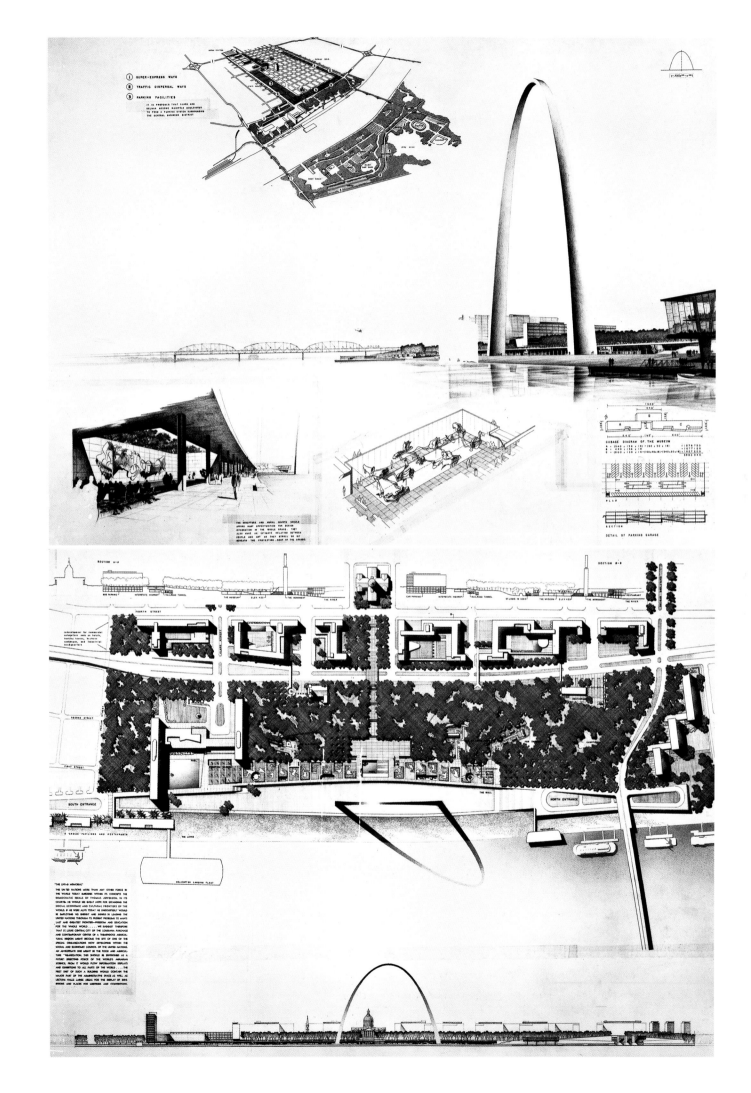

Severud explained why they decided to use a heavy-gauge stainless steel for the covering (a thinner, cheaper one would look "tinny" and might corrode) and why they decided to connect the plates tightly (to form a smooth skin and provide structural rigidity) and assemble plates with large head bolts (to minimize water penetration). The stainless-steel skin acts as reinforcement for the concrete inside it, which provides dead weight for wind bracing, along with the light structural-steel frame. This skeletal frame was used to erect the arch and was left in place while concrete was poured around it inside the skin, which replaced the usual formwork.[32]

After they won the competition, Saarinen and his associates had plenty of time to fine-tune the design, as construction did not begin until 1962, almost a year after he died. He worked on it "off and on from the time of the competition through the remainder of his career," continually refining and perfecting it as he did with all his work.[33] At one point the arch was moved closer to the river, then farther back toward the city.

Bruce Detmers, who joined Saarinen's firm in the early 1950s, later told the AIA Journal's Michael J. Crosbie about the trial and error involved in arriving at the final shape. "'It was a horrendous job to define the thing geometrically.' Model after model followed, ranging in size from a few inches to eight feet high. Saarinen studied their reflections in mirrors, photographed them, and viewed them from all angles." He found that they were either too flat on top, too pointed, or too heavy. "Saarinen knew that the shape of a pure catenary would make the arch very steep from ground level. A wider, weighted catenary form was desired." Crosbie explained that "Hannskarl Bandel, an engineer who worked for Severud, worked up half a dozen or so weighted catenary curve formulas and sent them over to Saarinen's office. There they were plotted, and models of each were built. Saarinen studied these models and finally selected one. Its shape was shallower than a pure catenary, and appeared less pointed when viewed from the ground. And geometrically, the catenary was true to its tapered legs. . . . 'If you hung it upside down, it would hang in this shape, because the legs become heavier toward the ground,'" Bandel told the writer.[34]

Crosbie described this back-and-forth, trial-and-error approach in an article that he wrote in 1983, at a time when Saarinen was not much in the news. It struck the journalist as strange that the curve is not a simple catenary but a weighted one, like a hanging chain with heavier links at the ends, because he thought, "a pure form . . . would seem more attractive to Saarinen." Crosbie puzzled over the architect's statement: "this arch is not a true parabola, as is often stated. Instead it is a catenary curve. . . in which the forces of thrust are continuously kept within the center of the legs of the arch."[35]

This is the way Saarinen always worked, with engineering in the service of aesthetics. Perhaps the almost parabolic shape made the arch seem as if it derived purely from engineering calculations. But the architect was creating a work of art (or architecture, or both), not a model for scientific illustration. Still, these departures from pure formula strike some critics, even today, as impure.[36]

He used the deviations because the arch looked better that way—more impressive, more powerful, awe-inspiring. The official purpose of the "Jefferson memorial" was to commemorate the third president of the United States and his role in the westward expansion, but that meaning is not obvious to the viewer—neither, of course, are the meanings of most classical monuments. (What does an obelisk have to do with George Washington or a classical colonnade with Abraham Lincoln?) Because it is an arch, it does suggest passage through Saint Louis to the Far West more than the other entries to the competition did, but what stuns the visitor is simply its presence.

Novelist and literary critic William Gass explained: "I place myself beneath the Gateway Arch to feel the sky freeze above a fall of stainless steel. A little leaflet tells me that the Louisiana Purchase was signed in the courthouse in front of me which its curve frames, that a little to the north there is the confluence of the Mississippi and Missouri, that nearby Lewis and Clark commenced their epical journey; that indeed, this shining hoop is 'the Gateway to the West' (what has Jefferson got to do with it? read on), and that a Dane with a strange name—a Swede? a Finn, fancy that—designed it; but I am the average guy and I am more interested in how it was built, in statistics, and in the strange little elevators which will jerk me to its apogee for a constrained, airplane-window view of the black odd tops of ugly buildings, of mud flats and weedy vacancies." Gass, who lived in Saint Louis, made these observations in an essay on the things man creates to defy mortality. The arch is the only Modernist monument he discussed, along with the Eiffel Tower, epic poems, great symphonies, and the skull shown in the corner of paintings of Saint Jerome. Of monuments in general, he wrote, "IT is what it increasingly stands for; it is the imposing symbol of itself."[37]

And indeed, when you visit the arch, you are absorbed by it. Jefferson certainly does not come to mind. The film they show and the books they sell cover mainly the arch itself and how it was made. It is presented as in a class with the Seven Wonders of the World, as perhaps the eighth or ninth. "Great monuments," Gass observed, "are curiously non-committal. Saarinen's graceful arch is actually a tribute to Platonic Forms, to the purity, beauty and nobility of Mathematics, of Mind."[38]

The arch also symbolizes modernity (because of its geometry), technology (because of its materials), and man's triumph over gravity (because of its height and lightness). The arch dwarfs the city. It is supernatural in scale. And it looks different from every point of view and in every light, as numerous photographers have shown. It can appear almost black, or blinding white; its profile changes.[39]

Gass describes the arch as "distinctly American . . . a perfect expression of our position. It aspires. It opens out. It looks west, but it has no face. Like the Golden Gate Bridge . . . it soars and spans. We look through it at the Courthouse, perhaps, but its meaning is modern . . . It is built of stainless steel, not of old stones." He also observes, "The monumental is always the focus of a fourfold struggle for domination between the person or occasion the monument presumably immortalizes (the signing of the Louisiana Purchase); the ideal embodied (the opening of the West); the architect (in which case it is called 'the Saarinen Arch'); and the actual pale pathway itself, whose presence, whose beauty, is such that the visitor is mesmerized (when it is simply 'The Arch')." It is "simple, direct, and grand enough to wrench a WOW! from a clod."[40]

It required huge teams of people to build the arch, including Bob Burley, Bruce Detmers, Byron Ireland, and John Owen from Eero's office, but it is reasonably associated with the architect because it is so unique. As in all of Saarinen's work, no matter how large and complex the project, it was he who made the decisions about the details and proportions and materials. The engineers told him what was possible, and he worked within their guidelines, but the decisions were ultimately his. And he did even more work himself on the arch than he did on any of his buildings.[41] "It was the thing that meant the most to him," Aline believed.[42]

Late in his life, the landscape architect Dan Kiley, who worked on the competition proposal and on the park around the arch, as well as on numerous other projects with Saarinen, said that it was difficult for him to concede so much control. Even though his collaborations with Saarinen constituted his earliest successes and some of his greatest achievements, he was often frustrated because the architect always had the last word. "My approach to design is to be slow, the opposite of Eero's. The design is waiting in all the jobs. The connections are waiting for you to open them up. Nature doesn't do everything in a hurry."[43] As a landscape architect, Kiley would let things develop gradually, but Saarinen wanted a total work of art—as soon as possible.

Considering the amount of control he exerted as well as the commitment he demanded, it is surprising that Saarinen retained so many unusually talented people in his office for so long. Many occasionally considered abandoning ship. His two closest associates, Kevin Roche and John Dinkeloo, who ended up taking over the firm after he died, actually did leave once. "At one point, in 1958, John and I decided to go into business

for ourselves; we were going to do product development. And Eero had a fit about it, so we came back," Roche explains.[44]

Saarinen had the ability not only to find gifted and ambitious architects but to retain them year after year, despite the demands of the job. One reason was that the office was like an atelier.[45] As huge as some of the projects were and as many as there were, the architects felt like artists toiling for a common cause.

Their continuing commitment was essential since construction of the arch did not even begin until after Saarinen died. Bills for appropriation were introduced to Congress in 1950, 1953, 1954, 1956, 1958, and 1961.[46] Funds were withheld during the Korean War and until the federal government balanced the budget afterward. One congressman argued that they ought to be used for a park but not for an arch.[47] Once a compromise was reached, another $3 million was needed to relocate the railroad tracks that ran across the site and build a tunnel for them. Finally, in August 1961, President Kennedy signed the final appropriations bill, and the money was available in 1962—$17.2 million in all ($24 million with the 1930s contribution). The city contributed $7.5 million, and the Terminal Railroad Association $500,000, and still more money was needed for the museum and visitors' center when the arch was finally dedicated in 1968 after $39,954,414 had been spent.

Despite all the citizens' efforts to secure the arch, in 1960, before building had even begun, the Saint Louis City Plan Commission and the mayor approved a developer's five-block-long scheme for a bland, 275-foot-tall high-rise apartment building next to the memorial park, over Saarinen's objections.[48] Although the commission consisted of different people than those in power when the project began, their action gave credence to the idea that the whole enterprise—for some, at least—was a real-estate deal.

Once construction started on 27 June 1962, however, the structure took on a new meaning to the citizenry. "Everything about the Arch—its steel skin, the special cranes that climbed the structure during construction, and the customized elevators that negotiate the catenary—is new and risky," Progressive Architecture later reported. "One of the spectacular moments in the documentary on the building of the Arch occurs when the two halves are joined 600 feet over the Mississippi. The sun on the southern half of the structure has caused it to expand more than has the northern half. Huge streams of water are sprayed on the southern half to cool it, and shrink it to fit. At the climactic moment, the two halves are joined. Nature is tamed."[49]

When it was topped out on 28 October 1965, the arch became, at 630 feet (40 feet taller than initially conceived), the tallest monument in

Saint Louis Gateway Arch, elevator to
viewing platform, drawing.

America—75 feet taller than the Washington Monument (and a whole lot wider), 305 feet taller than the Statue of Liberty, the height of a 62-story building, and infinitely more delicate. The wait for closure continued, however. The arch was not dedicated for three more years, until 5 May 1968, when the park around it was ready for visitors.

Today the arch still looks new, glowing, and sensational. The approach through Kiley's allées of mature trees creates an enforced period of anticipation as the visitor loses sight of the arch while entering the parking lot and emerges with it barely visible. Finally, in the middle of the park, it appears again. Here, the triangular shape of the legs is perceptible, and the color and tone of the skin change continually. Another double row of trees is visible on the other side, providing a sense of symmetry and the promise of meanderings beyond.

Visitors enter the museum under the arch from a sunken plaza between the legs, keeping the activity around the entrance from disturbing the view at ground level. The only mar in the experience, besides the chaos of shops and ticketing surrounding any tourist site, is the fact that visitors are crammed and cramped into little elevator cabins that ascend in a jerky motion. Somehow, it seems as if you should be conveyed straight up in bulletlike capsules or some other conveyance more in character with the aesthetics of the arch. The experience at the top is unexceptional. There are magnificent views, but they are no more spectacular than those offered by many low-flying airplanes, and the long, thin chamber fails to provide the sense of release that outdoor viewing platforms on skyscrapers like the Empire State Building do.

The arch, it seems, is best experienced from the ground. That is where it truly seems to soar. Because of its simple form, it also lives in memory and provides a perfect postcard view. It has become, unquestionably, a symbol of Saint Louis, which is something few cities have.

A Bittersweet Memory

When the arch was finally dedicated, the victory was bittersweet on a personal level. Both of Saarinen's wives attended. Afterward, Lily wrote to his sister Pipsan, "As for Saint Louis, the arch was superb. Somehow Aline had deleted the team of four helpers (me being the sculptor), and she told my daughter she thought it was 'very poor taste' for me to be going out there for the dedication. I had been sent two tickets, by Harris Armstrong and then I asked Perry Rathbone (head of the Boston Museum of Fine Arts) for four more and he immediately wired the Governor of Missouri to send them to me. When they arrived, it meant I could invite Susie and Kirk, Eric and his girl (to come from UCLA) and my 80-year-old mother to all meet there. It was well worth it despite a terrible storm."[50]

Lily and Eero's daughter Susie remembers with a distinct sense of irony that Aline had come with her sons from both marriages and that since Susie and her brother Eric got along with her, they spent the morning with their mother and the afternoon with Aline. The only problem was that Aline had gone to the top of the arch in the morning, and their mother went up in the afternoon, so they never got to see the view. Somehow, the mishap typifies the effect the divorce had on their lives. Both Susie and Eric experienced difficult years personally and professionally before they found their strides and were able to use their considerable talents, she as a landscape designer, artist, craftsman, and emissary for cultural interchange, he as a filmmaker of powerful, prize-winning commercials. In an especially charming and romantic ad that he made for the Finnish Railways that takes off from his grandfather's railway station in Helsinki, two doves take flight and then meet again, like the halves of his father's arch.

14. Taking Flight: The Trans World Airlines Terminal and the Athens and Dulles International Airports

Among Eero Saarinen's last commissions were three different kinds of airport projects that gave him a chance to use his talents—as a sculptor, planner, interior designer, manager, and architect at the height of his powers—to advance substantially the art of airport design.

The terminal he was commissioned to create for Trans World Airlines at Idlewild Airport (1956–62) is still one of the best-known and most beloved airport buildings in the world, even though it is (temporarily) out of service. The building did for TWA what the Saint Louis Arch, which was still a dream on paper at the time, would eventually do for Saint Louis—give it a powerful symbol. But it was one thing to create a memorable monument with no other purpose than commemoration and quite another to design a complicated new type of public building as a powerful expression of the activity it was built to house. Yet that is what Saarinen managed to do while making a workable terminal that was "all one thing," as he thought all buildings should be.

After World War II most European airlines were nationalized, but in the United States each was owned by a separate, competing private company. At the new Idlewild Airport in New York some of those companies occupied terminals of their own—not only TWA, but also American,

Eastern, Pan Am, and United. Other carriers shared terminals, and the enormous International Arrivals Building was used by the foreign airlines, so there was bound to be something of an architectural free-for-all, with each carrier trying to upstage the others, as countries do with their pavilions at a world's fair. This gargantuan "Terminal City" airport fifteen miles from midtown Manhattan covered 4,900 acres, equivalent to the area from the southern tip of Manhattan to Thirty-fourth Street. It was laid out between 1947 and 1954 like the residential subdivisions springing up around it on Long Island, with separate lots on cul-de-sacs. TWA's wedge-shaped site was right in the middle, on axis with the airport entrance, a position that is hard to appreciate today in light of the sprawling expansion of facilities at what is now called John F. Kennedy (JFK) International Airport.

Saarinen was the perfect choice for the TWA project because the airline's president, Ralph Dawson, wanted a building that captured "the spirit of flight."[1] Dawson envisioned for his company "a building in which the architecture itself expresses the drama and specialness and excitement of travel . . . not a static, enclosed place, but a place of movement and transition."[2] Working on a building like an air terminal that lacked an established form made it easy to innovate but difficult to get it right, because what was needed and how to make it work had yet to be devised.

This page: TWA Terminal.

Opposite: TWA Terminal, construction drawings.

Airports were relatively new when Saarinen received the TWA commission, and aviation was changing rapidly. In 1959, more people crossed the ocean by air than by sea for the first time. Early-twentieth-century airports had been little more than streamlined boxes with towers, though there were a few ambitious structures, mostly in Europe, such as Vilhelm Lauritzen's Kastrup Airport in Copenhagen (1936), which had glass walls, recessed concrete columns, and an undulating acoustical ceiling.[3] Yamasaki Leinweber & Associates' dramatic Terminal Building at the Lambert–Saint Louis Airport, which had a row of three tall, thin-shell concrete groin vaults, was just being completed and praised.[4] Saarinen would have known it because of his trips to Saint Louis and because of his friendship with Minoru Yamasaki. But although Lambert's soaring, light-filled spaces received a First Honor Award from the AIA in 1956, passengers had to walk long distances in grim, lower-level passageways, and the exterior supports for the vaults were concealed, so Saarinen considered it only a starting point.[5] Still, it exerted more influence on TWA than Skidmore, Owings & Merrill's International Arrivals and Wing Building at Idlewild of 1957, which was also considered a success at the

time. This lightweight steel-and-glass rectangle had aluminum-framed plate and spandrel glass walls, a big, wide parabolic arch on its facade, and an attached control tower. Perhaps because of customs inspections, it also separated incoming and outgoing passengers, a practice introduced at Dyssen and Arerhoff's Fuhlsbüttel Airport, Germany, in 1929 though not yet common in all hall-like terminals of the time but one that Saarinen would adopt at TWA.

There was plenty of work still to be done on airport design. As usual, Saarinen and his colleagues went about doing it enthusiastically. They "began looking for the form and the plan of the terminal in February 1956, by collecting data on planes and passengers, touring existing terminals with notebooks and stopwatches in hand, arranging plane positions on a plan of the tight wedge-shaped site [though the jet age was only beginning, TWA needed fourteen jet-sized docks] and conferring with planners from TWA and people at the Port of New York Authority who would operate Idlewild." They also studied activities that ranged from the way planes taxied to the gate to the manners in which passenger parking areas worked—everything that would affect the experience of travelers and the management of the terminal. In the end, they produced a terminal with a "smooth and luxurious switch from ground transportation to planes" that *Architectural Forum* called

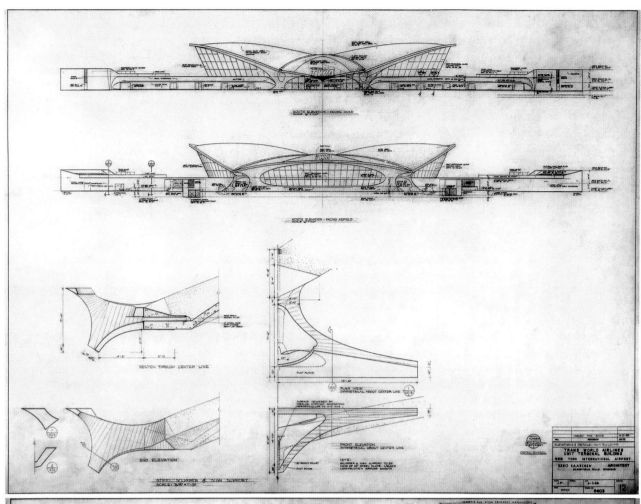

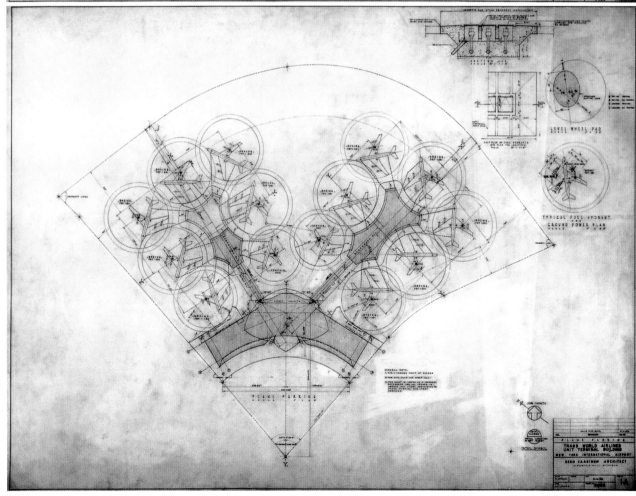

"the most telling evidence that the birdlike form is not mere caprice or design virtuosity."[6]

The terminal incorporated many new ideas that became standard practice. At check-in, passengers were separated from their baggage, which was taken to the planes on the ground level while the people took moving sidewalks to distant boarding rooms in "fingers." Those arriving retrieved luggage from moving carousels, another new idea. Incoming passengers arrived in one wing, outgoing passengers left through the other; and everyone gathered in the exuberant, vaulted, two-story lobby.

Getting to the point where everyone could move through the terminal smoothly was not easy. The architects made dozens and dozens of models at all scales.[7] Their first idea was to shelter departing passengers when they arrived at the terminal under a saddle-shaped concrete shell supported on four central columns. But the facade did not follow the curve of the entry road, the beams that would support the wide cantilevers were cumbersome, and Eero decided that the building looked "pigeon-toed."[8]

Kevin Roche recalls that while the architects were trying to find the right shape, "Eero was eating breakfast one morning and using the rind of his grapefruit to describe the terminal shell. He pushed down on its center to mimic the depression that he desired, and the grapefruit bulged. This was the seed for the bulges in the shell."[9]

Many wire-framed, rough cardboard models later, when a quadruple-mushroom shell was on the table for discussion, someone suggested breaking the long axis of the roof to follow the curve of the road, so Roche cut the thing in half with a saw, creating four adjacent shells that counterbalanced each other at the center. That approach solved two problems: it sheltered the main entrance and spread the rear supports to meet the tunnels to the boarding areas, which are located in the protruding fingers 125 feet away from the main terminal and connected by tubular, glass-ceilinged, covered bridges.[10] Each bridge contained moving sidewalks going in two directions with a stationary walkway between them. The design provided room for seven planes to dock around each boarding area and foreshadowed standard practice in the next generation of airports.

The architects—Kevin Roche, Cesar Pelli, Edward Saad, and Norman Pettula were all intimately involved—decided next to separate the vaults slightly to define the roof lines and added skylights in the slits. In this final scheme, there are three different sizes and configurations of bent, curved, diamond-shaped shells; the wings are identical rounded diamonds, but the narrow shell in the front is smaller than the wide one in the rear. Saarinen said he deliberately chose the shapes of these interacting vaults to emphasize an upward-soaring quality of line. They are supported by four curvilinear Y-shaped columns, 51 feet tall and 315 feet long, creating "a huge umbrella over all the passenger areas."[11]

The architects used models to design the interiors as well, starting with the entrance and gradually moving through the lobby to the waiting area. They only had to model half of the entire space of the building because it was symmetrical; a mirror on the edge of the model provided a picture of the whole space. "Gradually," Saarinen said, "we evolved a more flowing line for the bridge connecting the balconies, the stairways leading to them on each side, and the surfaces around the stairway."[12]

Designing the bulbous building was almost easier than the next stage of work. Since the early planning was done almost completely with models and every surface is curved, it was extraordinarily difficult to prepare construction drawings. Some initial drawings were made by photographing the model in order to translate its form into two dimensions. Saarinen's office spent 5,500 man-hours preparing what were essentially contour maps of the building's major parts, consulting with the engineers, Ammann & Whitney, at every stage.[13]

The contractors, Grove Shepherd Wilson & Kruge, who, luckily, were up to the superhuman effort required to build the terminal, had to take the 130 detailed drawings from Saarinen's office and develop even more elaborate plans showing every rib and connection for the formwork to shape the concrete. Creating these drawings required additional calculations, some of which were done by computer, though at the time there was no such thing as computer-aided architectural drawing. The carefully planned, four-step building process required steel-pipe scaffolding with the verticals placed exactly on a special grid. As many as 1,800 supports were made up of 5,000 tubular scaffold frames with special U-clamps to hold the ribs and beams, all calculated for the curvatures and laid on with 2,500 prefabricated wedges in twenty-seven different shapes. Some of the wood sheathing nailed atop these ribs was ordinary, but some boards had to be cut on a slant, others sliced on a curve and soaked to make them pliable enough to support the stronger curvatures. The computations for these calculations from the engineers and a computer company filled a whole book with figures down to one-eighth of an inch. And the formwork for the Y-shaped buttresses was even more complicated because of their convoluted shapes. Several hundred more drawings were needed to show the carpenters how to assemble these forms.[14]

The thin-shell, lightweight, umbrella-vault roof ranges in thickness from about seven inches at the edges to about forty inches where the wings meet the concrete buttresses, which are three feet thick and filled with enough carefully placed steel reinforcement to counter the roof's six-thousand-pound dead load.[15] Its cantilevers extend eighty feet.

The terminal was not easy to build, yet the work was done "by carpenters hired out of the hiring hall and possessed of no special skill. They were stirred to enthusiasm," Architectural Forum reported, "by the prospect of being able to see, for the first time perhaps, their own individual work in the completed building as it was uncovered—something that virtually never happens with formwork."[16] They managed to build it with an error of only one-sixteenth of an inch at the center plate. Like the architects in Saarinen's office, they rose to the challenge because they felt they were part of a grand adventure.

When the fifteen-million-dollar building opened in 1962, it was widely (though not universally) praised. Saarinen did not live to see it completed, but in April 1961, just before he got sick, he said, "TWA is beginning to look marvelous. If anything happened and they had to stop work right now and just leave it in this state, I think it would make a beautiful ruin, like the Baths of Caracalla."[17]

Happily, they did not have to stop. It is interesting that the architect compared it to a vaulted ancient ruin and not to a bird in flight, as most people did.[18] The fact that it resembled something that could fly was part of its popular appeal, but Saarinen knew that the likeness would also demean it in the minds of some critics. He maintained that "the fact that to some people it looked like a bird in flight was really coincidental. That was the last thing we thought about. Now, that doesn't mean that one doesn't have the right to see it that way, or to explain it to laymen in those terms, especially because laymen are usually more literally than visually inclined."[19] However, his own firm had issued a presentation brochure for the terminal with birds pictured on the cover, as architect Peter Papademetriou pointed out recently in Casabella.[20] Both Architectural Forum, which loved the terminal, and the British Architectural Review, which deplored it, called it a "concrete bird" when it was under construction.[21]

After it was completed, however, Architectural Review quoted Edgar Kaufmann Jr.'s rave review in Interiors, which recommended: "In order to understand this work, the first need is to forget the bird; whatever suggestions of lifted wings and grasping claws may have been aroused by the concrete structure alone, it no longer registers now that the essential window-walls have been added making the whole a strongly central composition." Review went on to follow Kaufmann's careful analysis, noting, "the full artistry of the space-modeling. And, this composition is based on the simple convenience of the passengers: the architect succeeded in transmuting the ordinary complex of travel facilities into a festival of orderly movement and exhilarating vistas." But the authors of the article, who had not seen the building at firsthand, added, "Many people would not agree with [Kaufmann] that the detailing is either vigorous or inevitable. . . . Returning voyagers from Idlewild have described the scale of the TWA interiors as mean, minute, toylike, sub-human or even 'a rat-maze.'"[22]

It is difficult to imagine anyone's seeing the festive, smooth-flowing, light-filled interiors of the TWA Terminal as "a rat-maze," but Architectural Review's assessment is typical of British reaction, generally, to Saarinen's work. His zestful, optimistic, expressionistic buildings may have captured the spirit of America at the time, but they often struck the British as self-indulgent. Oddly, in this review, the authors described Kaufmann's attempt to show historic precedents for the terminal as "meta-Scully, ultra-Yale," a curious charge in view of the fact that the Yale architectural historian Vincent Scully was one of Saarinen's most severe critics.

Scully, who wrote almost breathlessly about much of Philip Johnson's work, said Saarinen's Yale Hockey Rink (1956–59) "embodied a good deal that was wrong with American architecture in the mid-1950s: exhibitionism, structural pretension, self-defeating urbanistic arrogance." Comparing Saarinen unfavorably to his friend Kenzo Tange (who much admired Saarinen), Scully said, "The difference must be regarded as between a building thought through all the way and a PR package with a few calculated 'features' for everyone. Such can be seen in Saarinen's offerings at Kennedy and Dulles airports. The ingredients are always obvious, and they have remained the clients' delight: (a) one whammo shape, justified by (b) one whammo functional innovation, here tubes for the one and Afrika Korps troop carriers [the mobile lounges at Dulles] for the other, and by (c) one whammo structural exhibition which is always threatening, visually at least, to come apart at the seams; pseudo concrete choked with steel at Kennedy, finger-tip insecurity over marshmallow slab at Dulles with a motel drain stuck down the middle. Saarinen's buildings are the most popular packages of their time and a revealing image of it."[23]

Scully's acid assessments were atypical of their time in this country, but they were influential and probably constituted one of the reasons that Eero Saarinen's work stopped being discussed soon after he died—until recently.

The British reaction was another reason, often articulately phrased. Alan Colquhoun, writing in Architectural Design, objected to Saarinen's

TWA Terminal, aerial view with original
peripheral gates.

expressionism by pointing out that TWA "ignores the fact that the dynamic form of aircraft are arrived at from necessity, whereas to imitate them in a building is an act of caprice." He objected to what he saw as "Saarinen trying to breathe new life into the Beaux Arts theory of 'character' and attempting to discover in each programme its own essence," particularly because Colquhoun saw it as "an appeal to the value of advertising." Interiors that Americans found exciting, he found exhausting, and he could be very funny in making his point: "One imagines that the emotionally battered traveler wants nothing more than to attain the relative terra firma of the plane, where at least he can be sure that his Scotch will remain orthogonal to his own axis even if the plane is describing expressionist patterns in the sky."[24] He simply could not relate to Saarinen's very American can-do spirit; he much preferred Louis Kahn's more abstract and paradoxical approach to function, which Kahn called "function follows form." Its sober intensity better captured the spirit of the difficult postwar years in Britain, when the country was struggling to rebuild its cities and its economy and to adjust to its new diminished place in the world, while the United States was celebrating its newfound leadership and reveling in unprecedented prosperity. That was the mood that Saarinen's architecture, particularly TWA, captured, and most American critics applauded it.

The careful and enthusiastic critique of TWA that Kaufmann wrote in July 1962 for Interiors when the terminal opened was much more in

line with the typical American view. (Kaufmann was a writer and critic, and director of the Department of Industrial Design at the Museum of Modern Art; his parents had built Frank Lloyd Wright's Falling Water.) "Eero Saarinen's T.W.A. building at Idlewild is one of the few major works of American architecture in recent years that reaches its full stature as an interior," he wrote. "However memorable the outside shape, it is but a carapace for the channels of life within. . . . Space is defined by a full orchestration of curved forms, unfamiliar, but immediately comprehensible thanks to their bilateral correspondence around an open, unmistakable center. Light permeates this space from every direction. Space, form, and light merge into one effect. The low front wings . . . flow into the principal, four-lobed space, which is shielded from full view of those entering by the surprising sculpture of the information desk. There, centrally, the full artistry of the space-modeling is revealed in the broadly-flowing steps, in the wide, over-arching bridges and balconies, in the integral seating, in the promise of continuing adventures of space and form, all richly echoed and accented in a magisterial clarity of composition."

Kaufmann went on to ask: "How did Saarinen come to this full-scale achievement, one of the crisp peaks of modern architecture?" He noted the presence of "a client with vision and confidence"; the fact that the "noticeably costly and controversial" project remained alive through numerous changes in TWA administration because of the leading roles played by George Clay and Byron Rathbun; and an architect who was "not only a man of winning warmth, tact, and resilience, but a deft utilizer of the prestige which he had consolidated over a period of years."[25]

The Interiors review discussed earlier works that led up to TWA—the Aspen Music Tent (where "the enclosing form is anchored directly to the ground; daylight diffused through canvas, spread vibrantly and mutantly throughout the sheltered space"), the big hemisphere at the General Motors Technical Center (though here "the interior is one simple shape, closed to the sun, and rising from low vertical walls"), the MIT Auditorium (with its thin shell vault "where he [Saarinen] encountered the subtleties of arched edges"), the MIT Chapel ("whose concentrated expression lies within, and where elaborate, indirect backlighting is one of the chief devices"), and the Yale Hockey Rink (with its "intricately warped shell roof and elaboration of beams and beam-ends").[26] Other writers believe that Jørn Utzon's Sydney Opera House may also have been an influence, since Saarinen knew it well and had urged the jury to select it.

Still, "what remains an unexplained wonder is the rapidity and certainty with which his art matured. In part this extraordinary fulfillment must have been quickened by Saarinen's sophisticated understanding of the architecture of the past." Kaufmann mentioned a number of historic works that could have provided inspiration, from the "expressive changes in level deployed by the Egyptians at Deir el Bahari, circa 1400 B.C.," to Michelangelo's Laurentian Library steps in Florence, to the work of Antonio Gaudí in Barcelona and Erich Mendelsohn's Einstein Tower in Potsdam. "The ordinary air traveler today is heir to the great arts of Pharaohs, Dictators, Popes."

Kaufmann described the roof that covers one and a quarter acres as a "vast central space divided into two stories joined by a pair of curving staircases." He noted the floors and walls surfaced with tiny round white terrazzo tiles from Japan, the interior's superb acoustics, the influential twenty-foot-diameter baggage-claim carousels ten strides from curbside taxis and limousines, and the curved, inlaid, marble-topped information desk, calling these elements detailing that allows "unity to prevail throughout a multiplicity of materials and a bewildering variety of junctures between them."[27]

Progressive Architecture concurred: "Out of the floor of what must be the most original interior in decades, sculptural furniture elements seem to grow organically. No distinction exists in the architect's design between architecture, interior design, and decoration. Everything bears witness to Saarinen's desire to have each element belong to 'the same form world.'"[28] (Warren Plattner was very involved with the interiors.)

Although the furnishings were more integrally part of this building than they had been in Saarinen's earlier work—seating was even used to direct pedestrian circulation—they belong to his larger body of design work. The main lobby has a conversation pit like those at the Miller House (1953–57) and at the Noyes dormitory at Vassar College (1954–58). Some TWA couches derive from the Womb Chair, and the benches that grow out of the floor are similar to the Pedestal Tables and Chairs the Saarinen office was designing around 1956 for Knoll.

The terminal had been frequently published from the time the design was announced in 1957 and was even exhibited at the Museum of Modern Art two years later, but as it neared completion and opened, the barrage of articles in architecture magazines around the world and in American general-interest publications made it one of the first architectural media events. The terminal had its detractors—it was too radical and assertive for everyone to accept it immediately—but most reviewers found it praiseworthy. Progressive Architecture ran a brief debate, but the negative criticism was faint: "The restlessly obtrusive interiors obscure Saarinen's bold, poised space conception."[29] More typical was Architectural Forum's comment: "In the 4,900 acres of Idlewild, it is one of a great ring of competing structures, each inhabited by rival airlines seeking to woo travelers to their ticket counters with design. There can be little doubt about who won."[30] Still, it would be another forty years before

the full impact of the building was revealed when the Port Authority of New York and New Jersey tried to mothball it to make way for the kind of "progress" the TWA terminal so powerfully symbolized.

Athens International Airport

The airport Saarinen was asked to design for the city of Athens, Greece, in 1960 presented a challenge that was almost antithetical to the one he faced at Idlewild. Instead of a crowded carnival of a site, jam-packed with other terminals, he was given an "idyllic setting" at the foot of Mount Hymettus on land that slopes down to the Bay of Saronikos, where his building would be visible in the landscape, very much like an ancient temple.[31] Instead of a tour de force of expressly modern form and technology, all curves and squiggles in raw concrete, in Athens he created a proud structure with a dignified colonnade, up-to-date and bold in its massing but made of creamy white concrete mixed with Pentellic marble chips in a process similar to that used at the American embassy in Oslo. "The challenge," he said, was to create "a building that would belong proudly to the twentieth century, but would simultaneously respect and reflect the glorious tradition of Greek architecture."[32]

Although the design used post-and-lintel construction like a classical temple, these were some posts and some beams—huge, daring concrete things. With a dramatic counterthrust upward, the massive, cruciform columns cut through the slab they supported while their capitals curled around to pick up the hollow beams hung between them. On the field side, where the airplanes landed, the columns branched out to support cantilevers. The columns also contained ducts for the air-conditioning installed throughout the building.

Eero Saarinen and Associates was brought in by Ammann & Whitney, the engineers they were working with at Idlewild, who were extending the main runway at the old Hellenikon airport to prepare it for modern aviation. Improvements were long overdue. When President Dwight Eisenhower visited in 1959, Greek officials had had to tear down "a score of villas" to make room for his Boeing 707 to land.[33] The new runway and the $3.6 million Saarinen terminal were part of a $10 million expansion of the Athens airport that included taxiways, aprons, and navigation and communications equipment, largely financed with an $8.2 million loan from the United States.

Saarinen's Athens International Airport building (1960–69) stood alone at the eastern edge of the old airport, where it commanded the view. Deplaning passengers approached it along beautifully landscaped terraces instead of through tunnels from enclosed boarding rooms, considered unnecessary in the "virtually rainless climate."[34] What they saw was an enormous colonnade housing the four-story structure, with a kind of

This page: TWA Terminal, lobby and information desk.

Opposite: TWA Terminal, conversation pit in waiting area.

abstract entablature containing a restaurant and government offices cantilevered out over the top. That 10-foot-tall superstructure was 250 feet long and 120 feet deep, and it extended over the main terminal 22 feet in three directions (a little like the Milwaukee War Memorial, but with flatter proportions). The overhanging roof structure on the field side was intended to cast a huge shadow to help protect the oversize windows below from the afternoon sun.

The main body of the building was 240 feet wide, but 260 feet deep and 20 feet high on the third level, where the visitors' lounge overlooked the arrival and departure halls on the second floor and offered dramatic views out through huge plate-glass windows. On the second level, passengers left for and arrived from planes outside through the terraces between a pair of pools. Airline offices and services were on the lower, runway level. Visitors arriving from the city to the north entered on the third level and found a monumental stairway to the restaurant and bar on the top. The spatial experience depended on the interpenetration of volumes, as it did in Paul Rudolph's work, rather than on expressive organic shapes as it did at the TWA Terminal.[35]

When the building design was first announced during the summer of 1961, soon after the architect presented it to government officials, the New York Times reported, "Experts say it will be one of the most modern airports in Europe," and noted that it would accommodate air traffic through 1980.[36] It was to have twenty-eight positions for foreign airplanes and sixteen for domestic use, though it ended up serving only international flights. Work started in 1962, but a military junta diverted funds, and it wasn't completed for another seven years, by which time it was already outmoded.

However, Saarinen's associate Gene Festa, who worked on the airport, remembers that "it had fine materials," such as ivory marble from Rhodes, and that it "was open and airy, had nice spaces, a plaza above the main lobby, and a restaurant overlooking the sea." Festa had been involved with the Vivian Beaumont Repertory Theater at Lincoln Center (1958–65) when Kevin Roche selected him to go to Athens and work on the airport with Ammann & Whitney. "I left in March or April of 1961. We were talking about moving the office to Connecticut then. Before I left I had several sessions with Eero about what parts were important. And at some point during one of those meetings, Eero got a terrible headache, so severe that we had to stop. I think that was the beginning of his illness," Festa now realizes sadly.[37]

The airport with Saarinen's proud terminal ten miles south of the city was replaced in 2001 by the much bigger, new Eleftherios Venizelos International Airport twenty miles east in the hills near Spata. After a plan to convert the entire Hellenikon Airport to an Olympic Village reusing Saarinen's Athens International Airport fell through, the old domestic carrier airport buildings just west of it were turned into sports facilities for the 2004 Olympic Games.[38] Saarinen's terminal has been used for exhibitions.[39] Now the plan is to convert the entire area to a park, but the project has yet to be funded. One hopes that the Saarinen airport's dramatic interior spaces and restaurants with sweeping views will find a new life there.

Dulles International Airport

If the TWA Terminal emphasized the aesthetic aspect of architecture (imagery and symbolism) and the Athens International Airport was concerned primarily with context (the physical surroundings and historic traditions of the area), the design for Dulles International Airport (1958–63) was driven primarily by an interest in how an airport works. And whereas the TWA design, with all its curves, suggests movement, Dulles was actually made of movable parts.

Even though it was to be "the first commercial airport really planned from the start for the jet airplane," as Saarinen put it, the architects "were not asked to grapple with the problem of the jet-age terminal beyond the question of pure architecture." But, as usual, he believed attending to every aspect of function was part of his job, so together with the team of Ammann & Whitney engineers, airport consultant Charles Landrum, and Burns & McDonnell, mechanical engineers, "we decided to make a fundamental analysis of a large terminal for jet airplanes. We sent out teams with counters and stop-watches [again] to see what people really do at airports, how far they walk, their interchange problems. We studied baggage handling, economies, methods of operations."[40] They conducted time-and-motion studies of passengers getting on and off planes at National Airport in Washington, Willow Run in Detroit, O'Hare in Chicago, Love Field in Dallas, and Lambert Field in Saint Louis and researched how weather conditions and activity peaks affect apron occupancy and runway operations.[41]

As in Athens, Eero Saarinen and Associates had been brought in by the engineers Ammann & Whitney, but once the architects joined the team, Saarinen assumed the leading role. He said they found there were three critical areas: the time and distance involved in getting the passengers to the planes, the cost of taxiing jet airplanes, and the increasing need for greater flexibility in operations. The major idea that the architects and consultants devised—"mobile lounges," roomlike vehicles that could detach from the terminal and carry passengers directly to the planes half a mile away—solved all three problems. Something similar to a movable waiting room was being discussed in airport design circles at the time, and buses were already being used to take passengers to planes at international airports in Europe, but the way the architects conceived of the lounges—as integral parts of the building—was a radical

Athens International Airport at Hellenikon Airport, Athens,
Greece, 1960–69.

and a brilliant solution to a whole series of problems. It was not, however, exactly an architectural one. And because Saarinen wanted every project he did to be "all one thing," the mobile lounge idea dominated his thinking about the entire terminal. Every other decision flowed from it.

Certainly the lounges were not the team's sole concern. The enormous new Washington International Airport (it was later named after President Eisenhower's secretary of state, John Foster Dulles) that they were designing for the Federal Aviation Agency to serve jets coming to the nation's capital was intended to present an image that was powerful, dignified, and in keeping with Washington's classical architecture, but also one adventurous enough to suggest jet-age travel. The team (with Kevin Roche, Kent Cooper, David Jacob, Paul Kennon, Norman Pettula, and Warren Plattner) came up with an organic-looking colonnade covered with what *Architectural Forum* called "one of the biggest hammocks of concrete ever suspended in the sun."[42] The roof deck hangs between two rows of gigantic concrete pylons that slope outward to counteract the pull of the cables supporting the roof. Sloping, they form a natural marquee for arriving passengers and shade the huge expanses of glass

between the columns, the way the overhangs at the Athens airport do. The slope also provides a certain dynamism, enhanced by the piers' riblike shape, a curtain wall with rounded corners (like airplane windows) and a curved entablature that curls around at the ends. They are sixty-five feet high on the approach side and only forty feet high in the back, so the building is asymmetrical in profile, and the interior takes on a lively shape. Yet its sixteen white columns rising out of the flat Virginia landscape do suggest a classical colonnade, suitable for a government building, if a rather fluid, modern one. (The terminal was commissioned and owned by the federal government.[43]) But the approach is much more dramatic than the typical blocky Washington building located at the end of a long, straight axis.

When the land around it was undeveloped, passengers arriving from Washington by the special fourteen-mile-long road for airport use only would first see it from a gentle hill about two miles away, framed by the Blue Ridge Mountains in the distance. As they slipped into a shallow valley, they would lose sight of it, then pass a low hill and glimpse it on the left, then lose it again. Finally, when the road turned, before them on a long podium would be "two rows of bony concrete pillars, leaning outward against the load of an immense curved roof slung over them on suspension cables."[44]

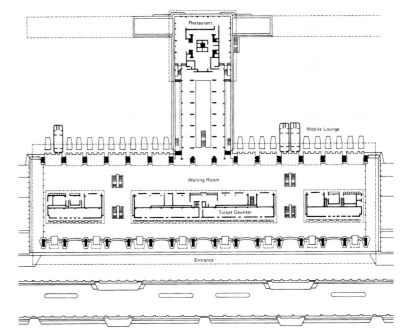

This page: Dulles International Airport, plan.

Opposite: Dulles International Airport, Chantilly, Virginia, 1958–63, column under construction.

"On a functional basis," Saarinen said, "we had carefully worked out approach ramps on three levels. Aesthetically, we realized we could make those into a base for the terminal."[45] Access for departing passengers' vehicles is located at the highest level (leading directly to the concourse for ticketing); deplaning passengers and buses use the middle level where the baggage claim is located; and the ground level leads to parking. This kind of division is commonplace today, but it was innovative when Dulles was designed.

The area around the new terminal was planned for both immediate and future use, when the concourse would be expanded on the ends but maintain the same depth. And the airport precinct was surrounded by "a cultivated forest of several million trees and saplings" (designed by Dan Kiley) "to insulate the still empty land around it from the screeching roar of silver sky birds," as *Architectural Forum* reported.[46]

The most overwhelming thing about Dulles is its size, though because of the mobile lounges, it was a third smaller than it would have been with boarding rooms in fingers, and the walking distances were a mere fraction of those at comparable airports. Even before it was substantially enlarged, Dulles, on a 9,800-acre site (15 square miles, exactly twice the size of Idlewild), was the largest airport in the United States. The terminal was 600 feet long and 150 feet deep, and the concourse was a single, gigantic room. (Another 300 feet were added on each end in 1996, doubling its length.) In the middle, strangely, there was "a huge sculptured drain pipe which could carry 12,500 gallons of roof water per minute down through several levels of the building into a pipeline emptying into a man-made lake nearby."[47] The columns are spaced 40 feet apart. Behind the terminal, a sleek, columnar control tower, capped with a massive stacked capital and crowned with an orb, rises to the height of a fourteen-story building. It is artfully connected to the terminal by a landscaped promenade with an observation platform and a restaurant that wraps around the tower, but a vertical element is somewhat foreign to the coherent colonnaded horizontal structure as a whole.[48] The building cost $175 million.

It was not exactly easy to build. Since the airport was federally funded, appropriations had to be approved by Congress, and estimated costs rose from $50 million in 1956, to $85 million in 1959, to $105 million in 1961, to the final figure, which did not even include hangars. Also, the first site the government had purchased—a thousand acres in Burke, Virginia, eight miles closer to Washington—became an impediment when nearby residents persuaded Senator Harry Byrd to block

further appropriations. Eventually, that site was sold, and the much less convenient but much bigger one in largely undeveloped Chantilly, Virginia, was acquired. The twenty-three-mile distance from the city made Dulles Airport less desirable to many passengers than the smaller, older National Airport (now Ronald Reagan National Airport)—and still does.[49]

The mobile lounge concept made Dulles less desirable to many carriers too. When the team first presented it in March 1958 to the predecessor of the FAA, the Civil Aeronautics Administration (CAA), the commissioners liked the idea. "First Charles Whitney talked about problems of traffic, access, drainage, paving, and structures," CAA project engineer Herbert H. Howell recalled. "Then Bob McDonnell talked about the extraordinary problems of handling power, communications, fueling, and sanitation. Finally Eero got up. 'You have heard Mr. Whitney talk about the "bones" of the airport,' he said. 'You have heard Mr. McDonnell talk about the "heart" of the airport. Let us now talk about the soul of the airport.'" Howell said, "He told us we should build a great entrance to the U.S., not just another airport, and that is what we wanted to hear."[50]

"Saarinen was not famous for telling people things because they wanted to hear them," as Walter McQuade has pointed out. "Unpretentious in person, he was, in his later forties, a man of no notable physical architecture—fairly heavyset, in a middle-aged way, thoughtful, methodical, pipe-puffing with spectacles he didn't like to wear. His speech pattern had been set in its intonations as well as in its trudging rhythm in his early Finnish boyhood, and he was not a wordy man ordinarily. But underneath he had fierce ambition that filled him with immense force."[51] And he did not give up easily.

After the CAA had approved the design, the team had to convince the airlines that it was desirable, for although the government was building

This page: Dulles International Airport, south elevation.

Opposite: Dulles International Airport, view from tarmac.

Pages 220–21: Dulles International Airport, concourse under construction.

the airport, it would eventually be paid off with fees paid by the carriers that used it. A meeting was scheduled in July 1958 to present the scheme to about fifty representatives of the airlines. None sent their presidents, but the people who came found the idea too radical, so the design team took the show on the road. Saarinen asked his old friends Charles and Ray Eames (who would later design some of the furniture for the terminal) to make an eight-minute film showing how the mobile lounges would work, and used it when the team made presentations to the airlines one by one. And one by one he won their support. Only three (Eastern, Northwest, and Delta) remained holdouts. Saarinen's solid research and powers of persuasion—his absolute commitment to improving the way airports worked—won the day.

At that time, one of the main challenges to airport design was (already) the amount of walking that passengers had to do through terminals with conventional boarding rooms in fingers (1,250 pedestrian feet in Los Angeles, for instance). The longest distance in Dulles would be 260 feet. Other considerations were the amount of space the new jets took up and the substantial costs of bringing them to a gate and servicing them. Mobile lounges eased all those concerns and made it possible to create a terminal with one enormous concourse for all departing passengers, and an equally large one below it for arrivals and baggage distribution. The great colonnaded departure concourse was covered with the great concave, cable-tensioned roof, slung between the colonnades in the front and back. Unlike the somewhat flexible roof of the Yale Hockey Rink, which stretches over a central arch, attaches to the walls on either side, and is stabilized with external guy wires, the Dulles roof hangs down like the deck of a suspension bridge on cables, stiffened by reinforced-concrete ribs that were poured around them.

Architectural Forum creatively compared the structure to that of a Bedouin tent but went on to explain that "Today's buildings and building codes demand starch in the canvas, and this is the reason for the stiffening ribs. For if the wind sweeping over the curved plane at Dulles developed sufficient lift to flap the roof, the motion could destroy the structure, to say nothing of the designers.

222

The pouring of the stiffeners is a combination of complex computations and sweat."[52]

Amazingly, the terminal was built without fixed scaffolding, a substantial cost savings. The stiffening ribs were poured with sandbags stacked to stress the cables at the proper curve. As each rib was completed, the crews had to heft the heavy sandbags over two stations that were being formed for pouring and put them into place at the third. At the end of the process, the immense edge beam had to be test-loaded with more sandbagging.[53] After the cables were strung, the workmen "laid precast concrete plaques on them to form the great sloping surface," McQuade wrote in *Fortune*. "Then the cables themselves were encased in forms hung from the roof deck, with reinforcing steel around them, and a towering hydraulic crane fed the concrete up to a moving aerial tramway for the pour."[54] At the end of the structure, a traveling scaffolding was used to install the ceiling.

Even more daring gymnastics were required to build the columns that support the roof, each of which required at least sixteen tons of steel reinforcing rods (the taller ones needed twenty tons). The rods were placed in steel cages on the ground and hoisted into place; then the

formwork was built around them. A workman had to remain in the cage until the last minute, churning the concrete with a gigantic vibrator to eliminate air pockets while it was setting.[55] The structure looks as heroic as the building process actually was. It even has excellent acoustics. What is most impressive is that it represents a fusion of architecture and engineering that, as the historian and critic Henry-Russell Hitchcock pointed out, beat "the engineers at their own games (needless to say with plenty of engineering advice) and yet achieved an architecture that no Nervi or Candela entirely on their own could rival."[56]

Continually rising costs and numerous construction delays, however, made the building process less than triumphant. There were frequent squabbles between the consultants and the staff of the FAA, which was sometimes absorbed with more pressing business—such as a series of airplane crashes that required an overhaul of the national air-traffic-control system. Finally, in January 1961 President Kennedy's appointment of Najeeb Halaby as head of the FAA saved the day. Halaby (better known today as the father of Lisa Halaby, who became Queen Noor of Jordan) was a Texas-born flyer and later a Pan Am president. He believed in the project and shepherded it through completion, even riding in the first test of a mobile lounge when it was shown to the

This page: Dulles International Airport, restaurant and control tower.

Page 224: Dulles International Airport, drop-off by entrance.

Page 225: Dulles International Airport, check-in area.

presidents of the airlines and convincing them that it would not only work, it would save money.

On the way to that point, the mobile lounges had encountered other obstacles. Chrysler won the contract to build them, and the architects were dissatisfied with the initial design. Costs rose. The sixty-foot-long and fifteen-foot-wide vehicles, which accommodated seventy-two seated passengers and twenty-six standees, ended up costing $232,737 each. They could move in either direction (toward a plane or toward the concourse) without turning around, and could be raised to fit various heights of aircraft entrances with sealed enclosures. They did not quite feel like boarding rooms, but they were much more roomlike than buses, and under optimal conditions they worked very well. When the airport was overcrowded and when airplanes grew to supersizes, however, they ceased to function so well because there was such a limited number of them and it took many mobile lounges to fill a jumbo jet. As an idea, complete with piped-in music and air conditioning, they were very

much of their time—and even predated the whimsical plug-in architecture of Archigram and other avant-garde architects of the later 1960s. Some of the Saarinen firm's sketches for mobile lounges have the same science-fiction spirit. One was intended "for some future era, when airplanes will presumably have been replaced by passenger rockets."[57]

Saarinen was a dreamer, but despite the brash American spirit of his imagery, he was a very Finnish one, with both feet planted firmly on the ground. The unconventional mobile lounges were actually built and used. But as planes continued to grow bigger and flights more numerous than the designers had imagined, the gimmick of the mobile lounges made Dulles less prophetic than it might have been. Still, Eero Saarinen was never afraid to try. If anything, he was too willing to experiment with new ideas before he had fully developed existing ones.

When he last saw Dulles Airport under construction on 21 June 1961, a few months before he died, he said, "I think this airport is the best thing I have done. I think it is going to be really good. Maybe it will even explain what I believe about architecture."[58]

It does, of course, because it represents an attempt to take architecture beyond buildings to a place where it could reorder society, not simply create a backdrop for life. That was the magnitude of Saarinen's ambition. And he died while that kind of optimism was still possible.

Less than a decade later, the pop-styled architects of Archigram and Superstudio—not to mention Rem Koolhaas in *Delirious New York*—began to add irony to their utopian visions. Modernism's great promise of humane progress was called into serious question by Vietnam, race riots, student revolts, and the nuclear weapons buildup that came out of World War II. In the face of continuing turmoil and inequity, the kind of earnest optimism that Saarinen's work so poignantly embodies was out of place and increasingly hard to appreciate.

The Airports Afterward

Although it was Dulles Airport that the architect himself considered the best thing he had done (and his successor Kevin Roche still thought so twenty years later when he told an interviewer, "it embodies really all of his interests more than any other building"),[59] it is the TWA Terminal at JFK that has lived in legend. Dulles received neither the enthusiastic reception nor the harsh criticism that TWA did, because Dulles is more conceptual than kinesthetic, despite the literal mobility of its lounges. Edgar Kaufmann Jr., who wrote one of the most positive and penetrating reviews of TWA, said, "Dulles, in fact, is not simple; that is its victory—to give serene form to a complex situation. And Dulles is far from perfect, either in detail or execution; but its sane, smiling grandeur absorbs flaws quite easily."[60] Most critics writing about Dulles addressed its programmatic innovations, scale, structure, and mobile lounges. It was celebrated and respected but not loved the way TWA was.

Despite the fact that several insensitive alterations were made to the building over the years, the only objections voiced in the architectural press came in 1988 from the critic Peter Blake, who called it one of the capital's few "first rate modern buildings" and said, "Dulles represents a giant step in airport planning, a giant step in long-span buildings, and a giant step in the area of urban buildings. No one, in this century, has designed so splendid an aerial Gateway, anywhere." Therefore, he wondered why its custodians at the Washington Metropolitan Airports Authority did not seem to appreciate it. He objected to the early purchase of "a cut-rate, so-called Planemate that looks like a poor, stripped-down version of the original Mobile Lounge—which, in fact, it is." He criticized the insensitive design of security checks, departure lounges that blocked access to departure gates, further disturbing the original unfettered access, the construction of several "unsightly Apron buildings" that "clearly violated Saarinen's design concept." He worried that new plans to build a large open parking lot to replace the sunken one created by Saarinen and Dan Kiley "would be comparable to building a supermarket on Washington's Mall."[61]

Blake's plea for the airport's preservation was a solitary one. Earlier that year, when Dulles received a 25-Year Award from the AIA, an article in *Architecture* mentioned, without apparent objection, that "to increase the waiting area, in the late 1970s the Washington office of Helmuth, Obata & Kassabaum pushed the boarding gates 50 feet toward the apron through a pair of low sheds appended to the south facade."[62]

The only response when Skidmore, Owings & Merrill added a new International Arrivals area in 1991 and doubled the length of the main terminal in 1996 (to 1,200 feet) was a very positive review in *Architectural Record* that concluded that the architects "clearly subordinated their esthetic design talents [and] let Mr. Saarinen call the tune."[63] (SOM also renovated the concourse in 2002 and is adding a People Mover Station as part of the current $160 million modernization.) Obviously, architect Marilyn Taylor and her colleagues at SOM recognized the subtle connection between the long, low terminal and tall control tower and the validity of Saarinen's long-range plan for Dulles, which proposed extensions at the ends. They did as he had suggested and replicated "the original scheme of draping concrete panels over catenary cables tensioned by the outward slanting piers." They even used the mobile lounges to keep the terminal operating while it was under construction. (The lounges are also still used to take passengers to boarding gates in flimsy new detached structures on the tarmac.) If there were objec-

tions to the ways they reglazed the building and accommodated other contemporary demands, they were not raised in the press.

The TWA Terminal, however, started to become a cause célèbre in the 1990s before it was even threatened, probably because a period of abrupt technological change and economic optimism, much like that of the 1950s, was emerging.[64]

When TWA was purchased in 2001 by AMR, the parent company of American Airlines, and the new owners announced they would be vacating the terminal, dozens of articles protested the move and a plan by the Port Authority to mothball it and build a new terminal around it. Because the TWA Terminal had Landmark status, the Authority could not simply tear it down. Originally, the Port Authority proposed to commission the architects who had restored New York's Grand Central Station, Beyer Blinder Belle, to renovate the TWA Terminal for later use as a convention center, restaurant, or some other unidentified function. Surrounding it would have been the curving arms of a new 1.5-million-square-foot terminal for United and JetBlue airlines designed by William Nicholas Bodouva, a former Port Authority architect who had recently designed other decent, workable but uninspired terminals for them. But there was no client and no funding for the conversion of TWA.

Critics were not impressed with the Port Authority plan. In *New York* magazine, Joseph Giovannini ranked it with "the crushing tower once proposed directly atop Grand Central—it leaves the landmark technically intact but degrades the context that gives it meaning." He went on to call the TWA Terminal "the most inspired of" New York City's "few Modernist masterpieces."[65]

At a Museum of Modern Art symposium, Yale architecture school dean, architect, and author Robert A.M. Stern called it "the Pennsylvania Station of the air age," referring to the demolition that had sparked the historic-preservation movement in New York.[66] Writing for *Architectural Record*, critic Suzanne Stephens called it "our Parthenon of early jet flight," noting that its "transcendent preflight experience is now threatened."[67] *Architecture* published a debate on the plan; articles appeared in the *New York Times*, the *New York Observer*, and other magazines and newspapers from the time the plan was announced.[68]

Architects, historians, and critics from all over the world sent letters in the terminal's defense, arguing that TWA was designed for transportation and should somehow be used for travel, not mothballed and hidden from view, where it was sure to be neglected.[69] Exhibitions and panel discussions were organized.[70] The Municipal Art Society in New York even commissioned Hal Hayes, an airport designer who had worked for SOM and HOK, to develop an alternative plan for the TWA Terminal

to demonstrate that the Port Authority's plan was not the only practical way to accomplish its goals. Hearings were jammed with people who cared about preserving the terminal, even when the meetings were held in almost impossible-to-find buildings on the periphery of the airport. The TWA Terminal was named one of the National Trust for Historic Preservation's eleven Most Endangered Historic Places in America in 2003. At this writing there is a new plan for Gensler to create a JetBlue terminal next to TWA and use the Saarinen terminal for ticketing, but just how has yet to be determined. The plan will surely be carefully scrutinized.

There are many reasons why the TWA Terminal has garnered so much support. The architecture of the past is always seen through the eyes of the present, and for almost a decade the most popular architect of the day has been Frank Gehry, whose wildly expressionistic, structurally acrobatic buildings make Saarinen's comparatively modest and measured ones seem prescient. Young avant-garde architects are experimenting with curved forms made possible by new computer technology. The Postmodern movement that had eclipsed Saarinen's reputation is over as a critical force, and the preservation establishment has come to embrace midcentury modern architecture, which is now officially historic (more than fifty years old). For all of these reasons, it is possible now to look at Eero Saarinen's work with fresh eyes.

This page: Dulles International Airport, facade.

Opposite, from top: Dulles International Airport, mobile lounge
connecting to airplane; mobile lounge, interior.

Eero Saarinen died, at age fifty one, while ten of his most important projects remained unfinished. Rumor maintains that the onset of his illness came suddenly and he was dead in a matter of days, but there were signs that something was wrong weeks, even months, in advance— severe headaches, exhaustion, occasional lapses of memory. Before his surgery, his wife Aline asked Eero's children to come out to Michigan so that he could tell them about it. But he couldn't bring himself to. Eric remembers going to the Field Club, as usual, but his father laid down to rest, which he had never done before. The illness never came up.[1]

News of the impending surgery, however, spread quickly because Aline contacted numerous friends beforehand. When Eero died the day after an attempt to remove a malignant brain tumor, there was first an outpouring of grief; then a brief critical evaluation; and then, too soon, oblivion.[2]

"Oh Christ, this is so bloody unfair!" the critic Peter Blake wrote to Aline as soon as he heard from her: "Look—if you need to talk to someone who won't talk back . . . If I can hold your hand, or if you would like me to write anything to Eero, or if you would like me to give you a very stiff drink," he offered helplessly. And like other writers, he immediately expressed regrets: "I had to go to Idlewild yesterday, and I take back everything I may have said against TWA, it's absolutely magnificent."[3]

In another of the hundreds of letters to Aline from famous architects, corporate leaders, ambassadors, college presidents, museum directors, critics, editors, and publishers the world over, the *New York Times* architecture critic Ada Louise Huxtable said that the article she had written after Eero died[4] "was one of the most difficult things I have ever done" and that a "number of heartfelt adjectives were deleted in the editing— for *Times* objectivity, I suppose. 'Brilliant' was one."[5]

Actually, Huxtable's story had been flattering, if not glowing, and she had ended by giving the architect a chance to explain his often-questioned lack of an identifiable style: "When this reviewer expressed concern about the pitfalls of free experimentation, he agreed that it presented great dangers, but said, 'there would be greater danger if we didn't try to explore at all.'"[6]

Huxtable also told Aline, "I know how lonely you must be—a shared professional and personal life is an extraordinary tie."

But Olgivanna Lloyd Wright, who had lost her husband Frank Lloyd Wright two years earlier, believed that only she really understood. "I am with you in your sorrow. Who can understand it better than I?"[7] her telegram said. A few weeks later, she invited Aline and her son Eames to come to Arizona and "stay with us for as long as you can."[8]

Matthew Nowicki's widow, Siasia, told Aline, almost too honestly, "I wish there was anything I could say; even time is of not much help." But she added, "Don't forget you made Eero very happy,"[9] a point many people made.

Unlike most architects, who felt the need to place Eero, Paul Rudolph simply offered a memory, "You and Eero were together looking for a place to eat in New Haven the last time I saw him. I thought at the time that you both looked so young, so well, so happy, and so in love. I am grateful that I have this incident to remember."[10]

Philip Johnson wrote, "I think mainly of you of course. Eero's place is secure. His work will live on in its greatness. You, our hearts go out to. And I think of us, his contemporaries. He was way out front, leading us toward the proper architecture of our day. We can only be sorry for ourselves now."[11] (Johnson had not always been quite so complimentary and had complained, only half jokingly, that Saarinen had all the best clients.)

"I suspect now that the loss of Eero for all of us and for his time is too great—and for this reason one is stunned into silence," the couple's friend Robert Osborn explained. "You know that . . . if Corbu departed tomorrow it would not be too serious, we would have one or two of his splendid buildings denied to us . . . but his idea we would have. I cannot delude myself that this is true of Eero. I feel seriously robbed by his death."[12]

He was not alone. Many of the people who wrote to Aline talked about the tragic loss of Eero's legacy—the continually challenging body of work that they had expected to see for some time.[13] Saarinen was "the most interesting of the second generation of modern American architects [and] the most eclectic of all architects, [so] he had everyone perpetually trying to figure out what he would do next," *Interiors* observed.[14]

"There was so much genuine love for Eero Saarinen and his quietly dogged, devotedly straightforward approach to life," Thomas Creighton noted in *Progressive Architecture*. "He was an innately good, a warmly loving, and modest great person . . . tremendously enthusiastic, and . . . utterly tireless." Saarinen's extraordinary energy and life force—an energy that reverberated in many of his buildings—made his early death all the more shocking. Creighton said he had been struck by Eero's "ability to work long hours and to relax when the time came with a good drink, a good meal, a good pipe, and good talk. But always he worked and he rested, to an end: always with a purpose."[15]

Eero's death touched many people on a personal level, but few realized at the time that it represented the end of an era. Edgar Kaufmann Jr.

wrote to the youngest one whom it affected most, his son Eames, "Your father was a wonderful man who made our world a better place."[16]

That, in a nutshell, was Eero's ambition. But he also hoped for a place in history.

The first assessment of his career as a whole came the year before he died, in *Architectural Forum*, where Lawrence Lessing called him "the most controversial and hardest to place" of the younger architects "of the first rank."[17] He saw Saarinen as important because of his "deep concern with industrial materials and processes [which] was once a vital part of the modern movement, weakened today by advocacy of a single set of materials and an overdependency on stock solutions."[18] Lessing pointed out that Saarinen's office differed from any other in two ways: "It is more oriented toward research" and it "does over 80 percent of design in the round on working scale models," a technique "carried over from the Renaissance" that is "particularly important for the development of new forms."[19] He described the four phases of Saarinen's design process as: definition of the "functional program" with considerable research, "expression of the program" in the concept, selection of appropriate "structure," and only then "design."[20]

Saarinen's emphasis on research and development was one of his main contributions to architecture. But it did not lead to the kind of "universal" solutions that many architects were looking for at the time—one way of building that would solve all architectural problems in all locations. In fact, it did just the opposite. Because of his exhaustive research, his belief that a building should be tailored to its site (what was called "concern for the context" in the Postmodern period) and designed to express its purpose, every building was different. Some critics saw this individualization merely as a matter of "branding."[21] Others (among them some of his competitors) saw it as evidence that he was, like many commercial architects, treating architecture merely as a service industry, though that was obviously not true. His were unusual, ambitious, challenging buildings. The variety in the work, the "style for the job" philosophy, as it was called, was really the result of the way he worked and the fact that he believed architectural form should derive from function in the broadest possible sense.

"When I approach an architectural problem," he once explained, "I try to think out the real significance of it. What is its essence and how can the total structure capture that essence? How can the whole building convey emotionally the purpose and meaning of the building? Conveying significant meaning is part of the inspirational purpose of architecture and, therefore, for me, it is a fundamental principle of our art."[22]

After he defined the essence of an architectural problem, he began the dogged research. Since he had clients who were the technical innovators of his period (General Motors, MIT, IBM, Bell Labs), he was able to use their resources to develop his firm's expertise at a time when there was great excitement about new technology in the society at large that was not much reflected in architecture (except superficially) and has not been again, until recently. Even today, there is more interest in computer technology for design than in materials and new building methods, though the growing interest in green design could help change that.

One reason technology was not explored more later is that many of the experiments of the modern movement proved disastrous. Flat roofs leaked. Glass paneling fell out. Concrete deteriorated. And these failures fueled the reaction to Modernism that occurred in the postmodern period. But another reason is that there were few, if any, architects who explored technical possibilities with Saarinen's zeal.

He was able to develop new materials, forms, and techniques because he had an unusually talented staff and knew how to make the most of its abilities. At management, he was a kind of genius. "Saarinen recognized that the sure way to get good employees was to get interesting jobs, and developed into a forceful client's man to do so,"[23] Walter McQuade pointed out in one of the most thoughtful attempts to sum up his contribution, written about six months after his death. Eero did not simply wait for architects to show up. He recruited them actively, and he treated them with genuine respect. One told McQuade, "He never, simply never, let you down."[24] While making substantial demands, he gave them room to grow. And though he was a man of few words, he had a wry sense of humor.

"When a young designer came into the Saarinen office looking for a job he was likely to be given a test: 'Draw a horse.' It wasn't the accuracy of the drawing he was judged by, but the zest with which he reached for the paper and pencil and went to work. (One applicant insisted he had never seen a horse. 'Then draw a woman with no clothes on,' was the rejoinder.)[25]

Saarinen joked with clients too, but he won them with ability. Elia Kazan, with whom he worked on the Lincoln Center Repertory Theater, told McQuade, "I've never seen a man absorb so much. [But] he was not totally absorbent; when a hurried member of a client's committee interrupted him in the middle of a design presentation, and asked him if he could talk a little faster, Saarinen listened to the question politely, puffing his pipe, then said calmly, 'No.' Puff, puff. 'But I can say less.'"[26]

Yale president Whitney Griswold explained, "Eero was always patient, with no desire to score back wittily against critical clients who went after him. There was no false pride. He had an unmatched ability in site planning, a feeling for history as a continuous steam, rather than as a series of unrelated episodes. He was both an artist and a scholar."[27] (This from a Yale president about a man who was ambidextrous, often wrote backward, and may have had dyslexia.)

Eero could meet each client on his own terms. He respected his clients and what they wanted to do (something that many architects with their own objectives fail to do) because, though he believed architecture should aspire to be art, he saw it as one grounded in use.

Saarinen had many of the most powerful, prominent, and prestigious clients in his time, not because of a marketing effort, but because of his track record, self-confidence, and willingness to take their desires seriously—to listen. Robert Venturi, who worked for Saarinen in his youth, pointed out that almost everyone in the office was designing, while today a firm of its size would have half its staff doing marketing of some kind.

His ability to work with people—clients and staff—was more than a talent. Eero Saarinen was a quiet leader, an unusually able manager, and a inspiring one. And the people who worked for him—many of the most gifted, productive, and influential architects of the next generation—constitute a significant legacy.[28] Their work and their former employees have greatly spread his influence further, but not in obvious ways.

Had Saarinen restricted himself to one identifiable style and had his heirs done the same, the way Mies van der Rohe and his followers did, it would be easy to see his influence. But because he made a particular effort to symbolize his clients' enterprises, his work represents the aspirations of an entire era in brick, glass, concrete, steel, and stone.

Maude Dorr realized this at the time. "The result of Saarinen's constant probing has been that he has left us a series of architectural portraits. Each one makes us aware of a particular aspect of our society and, taken as a whole, they are curiously representative of America at mid-century. Moreover, the search itself is characteristic of the times, and Saarinen, perhaps more than any other architect, exemplifies our repeated attempts to find ways of making life more comfortable and efficient, and our continual search for an expression of individual identity," she wrote, soon after he died, in *Industrial Design*.[29]

Because he believed that every building should be designed to suit its site, its purpose, its owner, and the people who would use it, the tenor of that time does not coalesce into a single image, the way it does in the work of Mies or even of Louis Kahn. However, its variety represents a time when there were significant achievements and changes in so many areas—technology, education, business, diplomacy—and there is something in his buildings that tells us a great deal about all of these fields. It may be because he was born in Finland and then came to America, because he reveled in history and also became so much a part of American society in his time that he could understand its culture from the inside and the outside and could therefore give form to the aspirations of the age in unique ways. His buildings provide a set of images of an era in material form.

He wrote very little. Most of what Eero Saarinen said was said to explain specific decisions he had made about particular buildings. He believed it was the work, not what you say about it, that counts. In the late twentieth century, that was not always true, at least not for the making of architects' reputations.

Aware of this possibility, Aline collected his statements, edited them, and published them in a handsome book with large black-and-white photographs of his major works the year after he died.[30] Also in 1962, the architecture critic of the *San Francisco Chronicle*, Allan Temko, published a small black-and-white monograph on Eero Saarinen in Braziller's "Makers of Contemporary Architecture" series. His intelligent, articulate, and critical discussion of the architect's life and work is a valuable, if brief, contemporary appraisal. In keeping with the criteria of the time, it places more emphasis on structural clarity, and less on imagery and context, than most studies would today—or would a decade later. Nevertheless, although it was written before many of Saarinen's buildings were completed, it remains an essential source since no longer, fuller monographs followed.[31] In fact, less than ten years after Eero died, though his and his father's buildings were winning AIA 25-Year Awards, there was virtually no mention of his work in print.

One reason is that magazines concentrate mainly on new buildings and there were no new buildings after the Saint Louis Gateway Arch was finally dedicated in 1968. Even book publishing tends to follow rising stars. Another reason is that Eero's widow, Aline, who had continued to champion his career, also developed a brain tumor and died in 1972 at fifty-eight. And once the Postmodern movement arrived, at around the same time, interest in postwar Modernism disappeared. Modern architecture was not just ignored then, it was ridiculed. And even though Eero Saarinen's work contained the symbolism, embodied the sensitive response to site, and reflected the respect for architectural history that the Postmodern movement called for, it was dismissed along with abstract, unresponsive, rootless buildings of the same period.

But Saarinen's amazing body of work is being rediscovered now. Clearly he has achieved a place in history, as he had hoped. The exact nature of that place is still being debated and will always be to some extent. All reputations fluctuate through time as they reflect the values of the present. That is one reason why interest in his work has resurfaced. Some of the most sought-after architects today—Frank Gehry, Zaha Hadid, Santiago Calatrava—exhibit similar expressionist tendencies and the most daring furniture from the 1950s, including Saarinen's, is more broadly popular than it has ever been. Even his commitment to research is echoed in the interests of some young architects today, so now, at least the groundwork is being laid so that people can see what the work has to teach.[32]

Eero Saarinen's unquestioned belief that architecture was the highest calling, that there were no easy answers, that every technological, social and critical resource should be brought to bear in its creation should be an inspiration—and a challenge—to architects everywhere.

"I think of architecture as the total of man's physical surroundings," he said, "from the largest city plan, including the streets we drive on and its telephone poles and signs, down to the building and house we work and live in and does not end until we consider the chairs we sit in and the ashtray we dump our pipe in."[33] He knew that the most important problems of his time—how to integrate new buildings into the city, how to design urban spaces, how to blend old and new—had not been solved. And they have yet to be. But there are important lessons to be learned from his humility and grit, dogged pursuit of carefully studied rational solutions, and ability to involve his colleagues and clients in the quest. No one has ever done that more effectively than Eero Saarinen. It is not, however, the scope of his concerns, which extended to whole corporate and college campuses, as much as his ability to take the practical requirements of a building program, with all its attendant traditions and aspirations, refine and redefine them with research, adopt them to take maximal advantage of the site, and transform them into meaningful, memorable architectural form that is his unique legacy.

Acknowledgments

I used to read acknowledgments impatiently thinking that the author was needlessly thanking everyone he or she had ever known. But during the last two-and-a-half years, I have had to request favors from so many friends and colleagues that I have come to realize that authors are more likely to underestimate their debts than overstate them. My husband Ted traveled throughout the United States and Europe with me to see all of Eero Saarinen's buildings and talk to his former clients and associates. He made interviews into lively three-way conversations and provided a badly needed second pair of eyes and ears.

I am grateful to the people who opened their homes, hearts, and offices to us: Gunnar and Sylvia Birkerts, Gene and May Festa, Dan and Ann Kiley, Balthazar and Monica Korab, Irwin and Xenia Miller, Kevin and Jane Roche, Frank Stanton, Robert Venturi and Denise Scott Brown, Public Affairs Officer Dennis Wolf of the American Embassy in London; Ambassador John Ong, Public Affairs Officer Erik Holm-Olsen, and Information Resource Director Petter Naess of the American Embassy in Oslo; Vicki L. Eller, Ken Golden, Brandy Kolb, and Craig S. Mack of Deere & Company; Ed Eckert of the Lucent Archives at Bell Laboratories; Timothy J. Dallman of the IBM Manufacturing Facility in Rochester, Minnesota; Jennifer Hall of IBM's Thomas J. Watson Research Center in Yorktown Heights, New York; Jo Patton of the General Motors Technical Center in Warren, Michigan; Kristen R. Carlson of Kleinhans Music Hall; and the owners of Case Study House Number 9, who wish to remain anonymous.

Many of Eero Saarinen's former colleagues (Don Albinson, Edmund Bacon, Jill Mitchell, Cesar Pelli, David Powrie, and Ralph Rapson) were unusually helpful as were architects who worked on his buildings later (David Kahler of Kahler, Slater & Fitzhugh Scott in Milwaukee, Gerald L. Strickland Jr., and Ted Lownie of Hamilton Houston Lownie Architects in Buffalo) and people who worked in the buildings (Rob Marx and Gregory Mosher). Veronica Wirseen wrote to me on behalf of her father, the late Olav Hammarström. Glen Paulsen and Henry Scripps Booth were very generous many years ago when I was a graduate student working on Eliel Saarinen's buildings at Cranbrook.

The custodians of the Saarinen legacy there and at other institutions made my work not only possible but often a delightful adventure. Cranbrook Archivist Mark Coir was a constant source of information for the early chapters and continued to offer information graciously and immediately throughout the entire project. His Cranbrook colleagues, Marcia Moir, Kathryn Kozora, Leslie Edwards, Jeff Welsh, and Gregory Wittkopp were also helpful. Dagmar Frinta was the most amazing guide any writer could hope to have, and became a friend. I am also grateful to Scott Sanders and Nina Myatt of Antioch College; Wendy Hurlock and Liza Kirwin of the Archives of American Art; Karen Adler Abramson of Brandeis University, who led me to Jaya Kader Zebede and William Lebovich, authors of important student papers who allowed me to use their findings; Bridget Carr of the Boston Symphony Orchestra archives (for Tanglewood); Dr. Robert Roethemeyer and Pam Nielsen of the Concordia Theological Seminary; Kristiina Nivari, Elina Standertskjöld, and Timo Tuomi of the Museum of Finnish Architecture; Lauren Cadmus of Knoll International; Dean William Mitchell, Mary Eleanor Murphy, Gary Van Zante, and Taryn Marie Zarrillo of the Massachusetts Institute of Technology; Bobbie Burk and Bennie Ruth Gilbert of Stephens College; Bill Hooper and Diane Francis of the Time, Inc. Archives; and Nicholas Adams, Ron Patkus, and Dean M. Rogers of Vassar College. Howard Shubert of the Centre Canadien d'Architecture led me to the indispensable David Powrie; the museum's founding director, Phyllis Brontman Lambert, shared important memories of Eero with me. Richard Szary and the ever-patient Danelle Moon of the Manuscript and Archives, Yale University Library were enormously helpful, as were Dean Robert A.M. Stern, Eeva-Liisa Pelkonen, and Rosamond Fletcher. Elise Kenney of the Yale Art Gallery went out of her way to help answer nagging questions.

Countless other people provided assistance in dozens of different ways: Cathy Chase of Kevin Roche John Dinkeloo and Associates; Connie Tingle of Irwin Sweeney Miller Foundation; Theo David, Dianne Ludman Frank, George Leventis, Reinhold Martin, Marna T. Nemon, Antonio Román, Karen Pipsan Swanson, Louis Wassenhoven, Alex Washburne, and Caroline Zaleski. My highschool classmate, Ambassador Joyce Leader, helped me find my way through the State Department. Kentaro Tsubaki translated the articles by Nobuo Hozumi, Kenzo Tange, and Tsukasa Yamashita in *Architecture + Urbanism*. Research assistants Radhika Desai, Elizabeth Donough, Kathryn Kozora, and Marya Messatesta were invaluable. One of the happiest outcomes of my research was that it led me back to Charles H. Sawyer, who gave me my first professional job as an assistant curator at the University of Michigan Museum of Art, when he was director there and then became my mentor. Eero's childhood friend and frequent collaborator, Florence (Shu) Knoll Bassett spoke freely and enthusiasti-

cally with me and saw to it that I stayed on the right track. Eero's children Eric and Susan Saarinen were welcoming and open with me. I am especially grateful to them.

So many friends provided help and encouragement at various stages. Nina Rappaport suggested that I take the book to Phaidon Press. The members of my writing group (Janet Abu-Lughod, Christine Boyer, Zeynep Celik, Geoffrey Fox, and Susana Torre) offered wisdom and commiseration. I only wish that there had been time to draw more on their vast combined knowledge. Gloria Anderson, Robert Benson, Bill Burk, Sara Caples, Helen Castle, Martha Dunkelman, Deborah Gans, Alexander Gorlin, Robert Ivy, Everardo Jefferson, Laurie Kerr, Diane Lewis, Audrey Matlock, Mameve Medwed, Anne Moore, Henry Stolzman, Howard Weinberg, and Claire Weisz offered continuous consolation and comic relief, as usual. Various architects provided insights and information, especially Mark Dubois, who even read the manuscript, as did my friend and colleague William Morgan. His wide-ranging knowledge, wisdom, and support were crucial. I am grateful for the patience and encouragement of Megan McFarland and Andrea Codrington, my editors at Phaidon Press, as well as for the photographic research that Julia Rydholm and Jesse Donaldson provided.

Most of all, I appreciate the understanding and good sense of my husband and children—Ted, Mary, and Janie Merkel—who make everything worth doing. It is to them that I dedicate this book.

Notes

A great deal of disagreement on the dates of buildings still exists within the critical literature on Eero Saarinen. Most authors have used the dates published in Aline Saarinen's book, Eero Saarinen on His Work, *in 1962, even though ten of the buildings were still unfinished when it went to press, so naturally many completion dates were off by a year or two. I found, however, that a number of beginning dates were erroneous, too, since the projects mentioned had been published in magazines before they were said to have begun. Since a number of research projects on Eero Saarinen are underway now, readers should assume that many of the dates published here will be subject to change. Errors in dating will, of course, be corrected in any future editions of this book.*

Introduction: A Man of His Time

[1] William A. Hewitt, the chairman of Deere & Company, made this statement in an address at the Convocation Dinner of the Fellows of the American Institute of Architects (AIA) in San Diego, California, on 6 June 1977.
[2] Eero Saarinen, in a lecture at Dickinson College, 1 December 1959. This statement is reprinted in *Eero Saarinen on His Work*, edited by Aline B. Saarinen (London and New York: Yale University Press, 1962), p. 5.
[3] Ibid., p. 14. This comes from a letter from Eero Saarinen to a friend.

1. Son of Eliel

[1] Interview with Eero Saarinen published in the *New York Times*, 29 January 1953, reprinted in *Eero Saarinen on His Work*, p. 14.
[2] Interview with Susan Saarinen, Eero's daughter, Wellfleet, Massachusetts, 28 September 2003.
[3] Ibid.
[4] Marika Hausen, Kirmo Mikkola, Anna-Lisa Amberg, Tytti Valto, *Eliel Saarinen Projects 1896–1923* (Cambridge: MIT Press, 1990), p. 10.
[5] Ibid.
[6] Albert Christ-Janer, *Eliel Saarinen, Finnish-American Architect and Educator* (Chicago and London: University of Chicago Press, 1948; reprint, 1984), pp. 5–6.
[7] Christ-Janer, p 7.
[8] Eliel Saarinen, *Search for Form, A Fundamental Approach to Art* (New York: Reinhold Publishing Corporation, 1948), p. xi.
[9] Gesellius, Lindgren, and Saarinen set up their office in 1896 and received their diplomas in 1897; see Christ-Janer, p. 135. Although the young architects formed the partnership in 1896, they did not register their partnership in the trade register until 1899, according to Hausen et al., p. 14.
[10] Christ-Janer, p. 8.
[11] Hausen et al, p. 19.
[12] Marika Hausen, "Gesellius—Lindgren—Saarinen at the Turn of the Century," *Arkkitehti Arkitekten*, 1967, p. 3, translated from the Finnish by the author. One definition of *sisu* is "the ability to walk through granite," as the art historian and critic William Morgan has observed.
[13] They also won the bronze and silver medals and were to be presented the medal

of the Legion of Honor, but the Russian government, which controlled Finland at the time, would not allow them to accept it. Christ-Janer, p. 11.

14 Hausen et al, pp. 48–50. The interiors of some rooms were completed or improved over a number of years.

15 Christ-Janer, p. 25. Lindgren had been artistic director of the Central School of Industrial Arts since 1902, so his decision to leave the firm for teaching was a gradual one. He opened an office in Helsinki when he left Hvitträsk and the firm.

16 Nils Erik Wickberg, *Finnish Architecture* (Helsinki: Otava, 1959), p. 80.

17 The published sources say that he was born at Kirkkonummi because that is the town where the birth was registered, but it is also the town where Hvitträsk is located. Susan Saarinen confirmed that he was born at home.

18 Christ-Janer, p. 18. Peter Behrens (1868–1940) was a successful and influential German architect for whom Walter Gropius, Mies van der Rohe, and Le Corbusier all once worked; Josef Maria Olbrich (1867–1908) was a prominent and progressive Austrian associated with the Secession movement.

19 The Finnish Parliament Houses in Helsinki were not built until 1931, and then to plans by Johan Sigfrid Sirén.

20 Hausen et al, p. 212.

21 Christ-Janer, p. 39.

22 Hausen et al, p. 210. The main avenue is now known as Munkkiniemen puistotie.

23 Christ-Janer, p. 55, says it was partly because he was unable—and perhaps disinclined—to supervise construction, quoting the head of the architectural department at the Institute of Technology in Helsinki, professor J.S. Sirén, who delivered an address at the opening of the Eliel Saarinen memorial exhibition in Helsinki in 1955.

24 The 281 entries were widely discussed in the magazines, exhibited at a dozen North American universities, and published in book form: *The International Competition for a New Administration Building for the Chicago Tribune, Containing All the Designs Submitted in Response to the Chicago Tribune's $100,000 Offer Commemorating Its Seventy-Fifth Anniversary, June 10, 1922* (Chicago: Tribune Company, 1923).

25 Sullivan's review, "The Chicago Tribune Competition," appeared in *Architectural Record*, February 1923, pp. 152–153.

26 Henry-Russell Hitchcock, *Architecture, Nineteenth and Twentieth Centuries* (Baltimore: Penguin Books, 1963), p. 361. Hitchcock cites *American Architect*, vol. 126, 1924, pp. 467–84.

27 Kenneth Reid, "Eliel Saarinen—Master of Design," *Pencil Points*, September 1936, p. 465.

28 Aline B. Louchheim, "Now Saarinen the Son," *New York Times Magazine*, 28 April 1953, p. 26.

29 Christ-Janer, p. 59.

30 Eliel Saarinen, "Project for Lake Front Development of the City of Chicago," *The American Architect and Architectural Review*, 5 December 1923, p. 487.

31 Manfredo Tafuri, Francesco Dal Co, *Modern Architecture* (New York: Harry N. Abrams, 1976), p. 226.

32 Drawings of the plan are in the collections of Suomen Rakennustaiteen Museo in Finland, and in the Cranbrook Academy of Art Museum. They are reproduced in Christ-Janer, pl. 73–78, pp. 62–65, and in Robert Judson Clark, David G. De Long, Martin Eidelberg, J. David Farmer, John Gerard, Neil Harris, Joan Marter, R. Craig Miller, Mary Riordan, Roy Slade, Davira S. Taragin, Christa C. Mayer Thurman, *Design in America, The Cranbrook Vision 1925–50* (New York: Harry N. Abrams in association with the Detroit Institute of Arts and the Metropolitan Museum of Art, 1983). pp. 50–52.

33 The Saarinens' neighbor Page A. Robinson published the plan as the lead article in *The American Architect and Architectural Review*, 5 December 1923, pp. 486–514. (The publication was later called *The American Architect and Building News*.)

34 Author's interview, in 1967, Bloomfield Hills, Michigan, with Booth's son, Henry Scripps Booth, who was a senior at the University of Michigan architecture school at the time Eliel Saarinen arrived.

35 Not only was Booth impressed by the reception that the Finnish architect was given, his own architect, Albert Kahn, recommended Eliel Saarinen for the plan.

2. Creating Cranbrook

1 Eliel Saarinen, "The Story of Cranbrook," an unpublished manuscript in the Saarinen Family Papers, Cranbrook Archives, Cranbrook Educational Community, Bloomfield Hills, Michigan.

2 The Finnish architect J.S. Sirén mentioned this in "A Discourse at the Opening at Eliel Saarinen's Memorial Exhibition in Helsinki, Finland, on June 1, 1955," an unpublished manuscript in the Cranbrook Academy of Arts Library, p. 11.

3 Robert Judson Clark, quoting Eliel Saarinen in the essay, "Cranbrook and the Search for Twentieth-Century Form," *Design in America*, pp. 29–30. Clark draws on various passages from Eliel Saarinen's book, *The Search for Form: A Fundamental Approach to Art* (New York: Reinhold, 1948), pp. 326–47.

4 "Younger Saarinen Follows in His Fathers Footsteps," by Russell Gore, a copy of a newspaper article in the Cranbrook Archives. The name, date, and page number of the newspaper are missing, but it is assumed to be the *Birmingham Eccentric* and the date must be some time in 1925, since Eero is said to be fifteen.

5 Like Morris, George Booth hoped to improve taste, which he believed had deteriorated as a result of the industrial revolution, and there was an element of religious moralizing in his mission. Booth had founded the Cranbrook Press in 1900, which was modeled on William Morris's Kelmscott Press, according to Davira S. Taragin, "The History of the Cranbrook Community," *Design in America*, p. 36. He also commissioned tapestries for Christ Church Cranbrook from William Morris's Merton Abbey looms, according to Cranbrook archivist Mark Coir.

6 Taragin, p. 36.

7 George Gough Booth was born in Toronto in 1864, so he was nine years older than Eliel Saarinen and considerably less privileged and sophisticated. He had an uncle who was an architect, for whom he worked briefly, before his family moved to Windsor, Ontario, near Detroit. Because of his marriage and success in business, however, he had financial resources that were almost unimaginable to the talented, cultivated Finn.

8 Albert Kahn (1869–1942), who was a Russian immigrant without formal architectural training, was the first American architect to design significant modern factories, such as a 1905 plant for the Packard Motor Company, a 1906 Pierce Arrow factory in Buffalo, Henry Ford's enormous River Rouge Plant of 1917–22, and, later, hundreds of factories in the USSR. He also designed a number of historicizing houses for members of the Detroit establishment, the General Motors Headquarters beyond downtown Detroit, and the elegant Renaissance Revival Clements Library at the University of Michigan.

9 Diana Balmori, "Cranbrook: the Sustainable Landscape," *Journal of the Society of Architectural Historians*, March 1994, p. 39.

10 Henry Scripps Booth was also involved with buildings on the Cranbrook campus (Brookside, like Christ Church, is across Lone Pine Road). The Brookside School was embellished with objects from the Wiener Werskstätte and the Arts Décoratifs et Industriels Modernes of 1925 in Paris, as well as with work by Cranbrook craftsmen.

11 George Booth had known the founder of the firm, Bertram Goodhue, for some time through the Arts and Crafts Movement and wanted him to design Christ Church, but the architect died suddenly before he could make his first visit in the spring of 1924, so the church was designed by an associate in the firm, Oscar H. Murray, according to Mark Coir, *George Gough Booth and the Planning of Cranbrook* (a manuscript in progress by the Cranbrook archivist based on materials in the Cranbrook Archives, to be published by Wayne State University Press, Detroit), chapter 5.

12 Coir, *George Gough Booth and the Planning of Cranbrook*, Chapter 5.

13 Ibid.

14 Swanson resigned from the partnership in 1946 because he always wanted to watch the budget and Eero always wanted to spend whatever it took to do the best possible job. And Eliel always sided with Eero.

15 Coir.

16 Cranbrook School for Boys (1926–30) was in use by 1927, but some dormitories and athletic facilities were not completed until 1930.

17 Maróti was the first of the European artists that Eliel Saarinen brought to Cranbrook. He worked there from 1927 to 1929. Balmori, p. 50.

18 The school was originally built to house three hundred boys, two-thirds of whom were boarders, but it almost doubled in size later.

19 The Cranbrook Architectural Office prepared preliminary and construction drawings as the Cranbrook campus was created over time. Mechanical and engineering drawings were done by outside firms but there was an in-house civil engineer, John Buckberrough, as Coir notes. There was also a landscape architect, C. De Forest Platt, who had graduated from Harvard University's landscaping program in 1924. He designed the planting schemes for the Architectural Office, other early Academy buildings, and Cranbrook School.

20 Henry P. Macomber, "The Michigan Home of Eliel Saarinen," *House Beautiful*, September 1933, p 136 (the article covers pages 133–36).

21 The table and chairs were made by the Company of Master Craftsmen from W. and J. Sloane in New York. According to R. Craig Miller, in an essay on "Interior Design and Furniture" in *Design in America*: "[T]wo versions of the table are known, both have octagonal bases and circular inlaid tops. One design featured a single pedestal; the executed version has a base made of four fluted panels," p. 95.

22 Brendan Gill, "Eliel Saarinen at Cranbrook: Restoring the Finnish Architect's 1930 residence in Michigan," *Architectural Digest*, April 1993, p. 42.

23 Henry Scripps Booth made preliminary drawings for Kingswood School in the winter of 1927–28. They had already been approved by the Cranbrook Foundation when George Booth decided to give the commission to Saarinen, according to Coir.

24 Cranbrook Road is another verdant residential street in Bloomfield Hills that runs perpendicular to Lone Pine Road to the northwest. The main entrance to the Cranbrook communities today is from Woodward Avenue, a main street leading to and from Detroit, just beyond the place were Cranbrook Road enters it.

25 Coir reports that a foreman, Dominick Vettraino, told him in an interview of 27 February 2002 that the architect asked the workers to save their urine and apply it to the copper surface to achieve a consistent patina.

26 "The Kingswood School for Girls, Cranbrook, Michigan," *Architectural Forum*, January 1932, p. 40. Most of the rugs and other fabrics at Kingswood have been replaced over the years, as often as possible to resemble original designs.

27 The Viipuri Library chairs were designed in 1931–33, according to Marian Page, *Furniture Designed by Architects* (New York: Whitney Library of Design, 1980), p. 194.

28 Mies's M Chair most closely resembles the auditorium chairs Eero designed for Kingswood. Eero's drawings for Kingswood School chairs even somewhat resemble Mies's drawings; see illustrations of his drawings in the Cranbrook Museum of Art in *Design in America*, p. 99.

29 Christ-Janer, pp. 75–78, and Coir, citing the Cranbrook Archives' Eero Saarinen files in the George Gough Booth papers (box 19, folder 31).

30 The building was designed between 1931 and 1933. Christ-Janer gives 1933 as the completion date, but David G. De Long's later scholarly essay, "Eliel Saarinen and the Cranbrook Tradition in Architecture and Urban Design," in *Design in America*, p. 65, specifies that it was not constructed until 1936–37. Since the science museum was not published until 1936 (and then in *Museum News*), and not in an architectural publication until 1938 (*Architectural Forum*), the later completion date seems more likely.

31 Coir explains that vibrations from passing traffic, the swaying of the tower, and heat from nearby chimneys created too much interference.

32 "Institute of Science Building, Cranbrook Academy, Bloomfield, Hills, Michigan," *Architectural Forum*, December 1938, p. 418. The critical standards of the time held that the more modern (plain, abstract, geometric) a project was, the better it was.

33 Christ-Janer, p. 137.

34 Taragin, p. 44. And emphasis was now placed on architectural design rather than craftsmanship.

35 Clark mentions these lecturers in "Cranbrook and the Search for Twentieth-Century Form," p. 44.

36 Le Corbusier even mentioned Cranbrook in his book *When the Cathedrals Were White: A Journey to the Country of Timid People* (New York: McGraw-Hill, 1947), pp. 172–73. As usual, he got some facts wrong, but his take on it is interesting nevertheless.

37 Christ-Janer, p. 102.

38 Walter Gropius, Mies van der Rohe, and Marcel Breuer all arrived in 1938. Gropius became chairman of the department of architecture at Harvard. Mies became head of the Armour Institute (later the Illinois Institute of Technology) in Chicago, where other former members of the Bauhaus set up a small, underfinanced "New Bauhaus" in exile. Breuer settled first in Boston, where he worked and taught with Gropius, and then in New York City to practice.

39 According to Henry Scripps Booth's history of 26 October 1939, in the Cranbrook Archives, Saarinen intended the peristyle to rise no higher than the adjoining roofs, but James Scripps Booth, a member of the Building Committee, urged him and the donor to enlarge it.

40 The decision to place it that way may have been Booth's, not Saarinen's, as a sketch dated February 1936 shows the Academy laid out along its present lines. See a letter from George Gough Booth to Henry Scripps Booth, 16 February 1936, folder 3, box 10, accession no. 1982-05, Henry Scripps Booth Papers, Cranbrook Archives, Cranbrook Educational Community, Bloomfield Hills.

41 The Orpheus Plaza was actually completed in 1938, before the Academy Museum and Library, according to Coir, who contends, on the basis of evidence in the Cranbrook Archives, that E. A. Eichstaedt designed the gardens that surround it, but Balmori attributes much of the work to Loja Saarinen (pp. 44–45). They agree that she assumed responsibility for the floral plantings around the Orpheus Fountain and Triton Pool for many years, but disagree about whether she was responsible for the rows of horse chestnuts around the latter. The idea of having a horticulture program at the Academy was also abandoned. All of this is ironic in view of the pivotal role landscape plays at Cranbrook.

42 Clark pointed out the resemblance to Hoffman's sketch in "Cranbrook and the Search for Twentieth-Century Form," p. 26.

3. Family Business

1 According to an obituary for Loja Saarinen by Margaret Russell, a former Cranbrook publicist who knew Loja well, "At any early age Loja Saarinen indicated a strong predilection for the arts and at the age of 23 she went to Paris to study sculpting under the master Injalbert. She had already revealed considerable talent in the Konstforeningen, an art school in Helsingfors."

2 Eero often said, "I am a child of my period," as he did, in a lecture at Dickinson College, 1 December 1958, excerpted in *Eero Saarinen on His Work*, p. 6.

3 "Younger Saarinen Follows in His Fathers Footsteps," by Russell Gore, a copy of a newspaper article in the Cranbrook Archives (see chapter 2, note 4).

4 *Bulletin of the Beaux Arts Institute of Design*, June 1932, cited by Peter Papademetriou, in "On Becoming a Modern Architect: Eero Saarinen's Early Work 1928–1948," *Oz, Journal of the University of Kansas*, vol. 8, 1987, p. 58.

5 *Bulletin of the Beaux Arts Institute of Design*, May 1933.

6 *Bulletin of the Beaux Arts Institute of Design*, August 1932.

7 A letter from Elina Standertskjöld, curator of the Archives at the Museum of Finnish Architecture, Helsinki, dated 20 August 2004. There were fifteen entries. Eero entered under his own name. The winners were published in *Arkkitehti*, no. 11, 1934; Eero's entry appears on page 168.

8 Hauser et al., p. 338. The drawings are dated 1931 and 1934.

9 Christ-Janer, p. xvi.

10 Interview with Florence Schust Knoll Bassett, 22 December 2002.

11 Letter from Eero Saarinen to Astrid Sampe of 2 May 1953, in the Cranbrook Archives.

12 Interview with Shu Bassett. She explained that she went to study architecture at the Architectural Association (AA) because "Aalto had just come back from the AA and had lunch with us. Eliel was saying that I needed to get into a regular architectural school, and Aalto suggested the AA." Then, when World War II started, the American ambassador sent all the American students home, so she ended up going to Columbia University, but only briefly because Joseph Hudnut, the dean who had introduced a modern curriculum, had left for Harvard and the school was in chaos when she arrived.

13 Interview with Ralph Rapson 2 February 2004. Rapson went on to work for Richard Neutra, teach with László Moholy-Nagy at the New Bauhaus in Chicago, and teach at MIT when William Wurster was dean. He remained close to Florence (Shu) Knoll Bassett and landed several jobs designing American embassies through her husband, Hans Knoll, who was supplying furniture to consulates and embassies abroad. For many years he directed the architecture program at the University of Minnesota and still lives in Minneapolis. Rapson is perhaps best known for his design of the Tyrone Guthrie Theater in Minneapolis.

14 Interview with Shu Bassett.

15 Edmund N. Bacon, *Design of Cities* (New York: Viking, 1967; reprint 1974).

16 Cathy Price, ed., *Saarinen Swanson Reunion Proceedings* (Bloomfield Hills, Michigan: Cranbrook Educational Community, 2001), p. 13.

17 Eliel Saarinen, *The City: Its Growth, Its Decay, Its Future* (New York: Rheinhold, 1943).

18 Ibid.

19 Eero Saarinen, "A Combined Living-Dining Room-Study Designed for The Architectural Forum," *Architectural Forum*, October 1937, pp. 303–05.

20 The Community House was the first project Eliel and Eero designed in their new partnership, Saarinen and Saarinen. *Pencil Points*, November 1942, pp. 44–-47. It was 160,00 cubic feet and cost about $80,000.

21 Peter Papademetriou, "Desperately Seeking Saarinen," *Architecture*, July 2000, p. 72.

22 James D. Kornwolf, *Modernism in America, 1937–1941*, catalog of an exhibition of four architectural competitions: Wheaton College, Goucher College, College of William and Mary, and the Smithsonian Institution, organized by the Joseph and Margaret Muscarelle Museum of Art, College of William and Mary, 1985, p. 32. Hamlin's review appeared in *Pencil Points*, September 1938, p. 552.

23 "Wheaton College Art Center," *Architectural Forum*, August 1938, pp. 148–49.

24 Kornwolf, p. 72. The jury was composed of the chairman of the Commission of Fine Arts in Washington, Gilmore A. Clarke, architect John Holabird, Yale architecture school dean Everett V. Meeks, the college president, and a professor.

25 Ibid., pp. 72–73. Third prize went to Frost and Frost for a symmetrical campus plan based on Jefferson's University of Virginia with Beaux-Arts buildings in the stylized manner of Paul Cret. Thompson, Holmes, and Converse won fourth prize with a neo-Georgian scheme.

26 Ibid., p. 133.

27 Lewis Mumford, "The Skyline," *New Yorker*, 11 March 1939; *Time*, 13 March 1939.

28 "First Prize-Winning Design: National Theater Competition," *Architectural Record*, April 1939, pp. 61–64. The jurors were professor (and later dean) Lawrence B. Anderson of MIT, Frank Lloyd Wright protégé Antonin Raymond, TVA engineer Roland Wank, the innovative New York set designer Lee Simonson, and William and Mary professor of fine arts Leslie Cheek, who was also a friend of Eero's from Yale.

29 Kornwolf, p. 129. The theatrical people included Maxwell Anderson, Katharine Cornell, Lynn Fontaine, Arthur Hopkins, Sidney Howard, Robert Edmund Jones, Alfred Lunt, Guthrie McClintic, Jo Mielziner, Lee Simonson, and Otis Skinner. Much later Eero would collaborate with Jo Mielziner on the Lincoln Center Theater.

30 *Time*, 13 June 1938; "Report of the Jury," *Architectural Forum*, August 1938, p. 143; "Wheaton College Art Center; Designs and Plans," *Architectural Forum*, August 1938, pp. 148–49; "Architectural Competition for a Festival Theatre and Fine Arts Building at the College of William and Mary, Williamsburg, Virginia," *Architectural Record*, November 1938, p. 33; Talbot Hamlin, "Competitions," *Pencil Points*, September 1938, p. 552; "Competition Announcements," *Pencil Points*, March 1939, p. 61; "Festival Theatre Competition Prize Winners Announced," *Architectural Record*, March 1939, p. 10; *Time*, March 1939, p. 41; Lewis Mumford, "The Skyline," *New Yorker*, March 11, 1939; "First Prize-Winning Design: National Theater Competition," *Architectural Record*, April 1939, pp. 61–64; Rosamund Gilder, "American National Theatre and Competition," *Theatre Arts Anthology*, September 1946, pp. 501–06.

31 "Proposed Pavilion Designed for Summer Symphonic Festivals," *Architectural Record*, January 1939, pp. 44–45.

32 *Kleinhans Music Hall*, a brochure published by the Kleinhans Music Hall, Buffalo, New York, July 1945, p. 39.

33 "Crow Island Revisited," *Architectural Forum*, October 1955, p. 130.

34 The others were the Jefferson Memorial Competition for the Gateway Arch in Saint Louis (1947–48) and one for the American Embassy in London (1955).

35 "The Smithsonian Gallery of Art Competition," *Architectural Forum*, July 1939, p. i.

36 Quoted in Allan Temko, *Eero Saarinen* (New York: George Braziller, 1962), p. 17.

37 "In This Issue," *Pencil Points*, August 1941, p. 496; an article by Lorimer Rich, "A Study in Contrasts," on pp. 497–516 of the same issue compares the design to John Russell Pope's National Gallery of Art, which sits across the Mall from the Smithsonian Art Gallery site. The article reports that conservative architects objected to the competition jury; many refused to enter, believing that only a modernist could be selected. In "The City That Might Have Been," in the *Washington Post*, 5 January 1991, Benjamin Forgey discussed the competition and credited its conception and outcome to "Edward C. Bruce, chief of the Treasury Department's fine arts section and the New Deal's most innovative arts bureaucrat" and wondered why President Franklin Delano Roosevelt did not defend the scheme.

38 One unfortunate consequence of the Smithsonian Art Gallery's remaining on paper is that Eero Saarinen never got to design a museum, though Eliel and Robert Swanson did design fine-art galleries for the Des Moines Art Center (1944–48), which later received additions by I.M. Pei and Richard Meier & Partners.

39 Richard Kimball was associate architect, Christ-Janer, p. 150; see also Papademetriou, "On Becoming a Modern Architect," p. 63. Papademetriou cites the Old Building Files, box 110: Wilkins Papers, annals of the Auditorium, Oberlin College Archive.

40 The 1.67-million-cubic-foot church was built for $750,000 and received national coverage in *Time*, 27 January 1941, pp. 39–40.

41 "Tabernacle Church of Christ, Eliel and Eero Saarinen, Architects; E.D. Pierre and George Wright Associate Architects," *Architectural Forum*, October 1942, p. 35. The article observed it was "almost unique in the annals of American church building in that it was designed by a distinguished firm of modern architects with the full cooperation of an intelligent building committee which had ample funds at its disposal." A.C. Wermuth of the Charles R. Wermuth Construction Company was general contractor.

42 Miller, who had long been interested in architecture but became a devotee after his association with Eero, established a foundation to improve the quality of public buildings in his hometown. The foundation pays the architectural fees of talented architects who are selected by a board of prominent architects. Eero was its first chairman. The program has made Columbus, Indiana, a virtual museum of distinguished modern architecture, though the buildings by well-known architects did not have much influence on private construction.

43 Christ Church Lutheran was published in *Architectural Forum*, July 1950, pp. 80–85; *L'Architecture d'aujourd'hui*, December 1950–January 1951, pp. 79–81; and the *AIA Journal*, May 1977, pp. 28–29.

44 "A Complete Church Plant in Three Versions, Projects for the First Baptist Church, Flint, Michigan," *Architectural Record*, June 1948, pp. 134–37.

45 "Designs for post-war living, announcing the winning designs in the architectural competition sponsored by California Arts and Architecture magazine, 1st prize Eero Saarinen and Oliver Lundquist PAC method prefabricated houses," *California Arts and Architecture*, August 1943, pp. 20, 28–31, 33, 43.

46 "War housing, Center Line, Michigan," *Architectural Forum*, May 1942, pp. 261–[348]; "FPHA dormitories to serve a midwestern bomber plant," *Architectural Record*, July 1942, p. 47; "Willow Run Town Center," *Architectural Forum*, March 1943. p. 38-41; "Defense Houses at Center Line, Michigan," *Architectural Forum*, October 1941, p. 229; "Dormitory Houses at Center Line, Michigan," *Architectural Forum*, October 1941, p. 229; "Dormitory plan in two versions: first and second Willow Lodge projects near Ypsilanti," *Architectural Record*, October 1943, pp. 54–60.

47 *Architectural Forum*, March 1943, pp. 37–41.

48 A copy of a booklet Eero prepared while at the Office of Strategic Services, titled *Army Personnel Control, Troop Basis and Accounting System*, and dated April 8-July 4, 1944, along with letters complementing him on the job he had done, are in the Eero Saarinen Papers in the Manuscripts and Archives, Yale University Library, folio VII, folder 3.

49 Eero Saarinen's appointment as department chief of the OSS was discussed in the exhibition, "Eero Saarinen: A Reputation for Innovation," curated by Mina Marafet and shown at the A+D Museum in Los Angeles from October 5, 2012 to January 3, 2013. The appointment, based on Mrarget's research, was discussed in an *LA Weekly* blog by Wendy Gilmartin on October 9, 2012.

50 The "Raseman" Booth mentioned was Richard P. Raseman who had been hired to help turn Cranbrook into a more typical art school. His name appears on the letterhead that Eliel Saarinen used to reply, where Eliel is listed as president and director, Department of Architecture and Design. Raseman's title was executive secretary.

51 Copies of these letters are in the George Gough Booth Archives, numbered GGB 19:33, in the Cranbrook Archives.

52 Papademetriou, "On Becoming a Modern Architect," p. 62.

53 "Detroit Will," *Interiors*, July 1949, pp. 17–18.

54 "$50 Million Civic Center is created by the Saarinens for Detroit," *Architectural Forum*, April 1949, pp. 12–13.

55 Ibid., The firm was Harley, Ellington and Day.

4. Breaking Away

1 Neil Levine, *The Architecture of Frank Lloyd Wright* (Princeton, New Jersey: Princeton University Press, 1996), p. 218.

2 Robert Judson Clark, "Cranbrook and the Search for Twentieth-Century Form," *Design in America*, p. 30. Feiss was at Cranbrook in 1932–33.

3 R. Craig Miller, "Interior Design and Furniture," *Design in America*, p. 109.

4 Ibid., p. 84.

5 "3 Chairs/3 Records of the Design Process," *Interiors*, April 1958, p. 118.

6 Eric Larrabee and Massimo Vignelli, *Knoll Design* (New York: Harry N. Abrams, 1981), p. 56.

7 The exhibition, titled "Exhibition of the Work of the Academy Staff," took place December 1–29, 1939, and was recorded in an unpaginated issue of *Academy News* in 1940.

8 Miller, p. 109.

9 Eliot F. Noyes, *Organic Design in Home Furnishings* (New York: Museum of Modern Art, 1941), p.13.

10 Temko, p. 18.

11 Antonio Román, *Eero Saarinen, An Architecture of Multiplicity* (New York: Princeton Architectural Press, 2003), p. 132.

12 Wallace Harrison was involved in the design of Rockefeller Center, the United Nations, and prefabricated housing for the United Nations.

13 Florence Schust Knoll Bassett, a typed, undated memoir in the Knoll Furniture Company Archives, p. 3, substantiated in an interview with the author, 27 December 2002. Subsequent quotations by Bassett in this chapter are taken from her memoir.

14 Eero even went with her to consult a lawyer about patents. "We did get patents, which is remarkable," recalls Florence Knoll Bassett, "and it's the only chair I know of that has a patent. Oddly enough, the patent was based on cutting a hole and a few other things." (The distinctive hole may have been the result of the cone molding process, and there also had been a hole in the seat of one of the chairs that Eames and Saarinen had designed together five years earlier for the Museum of Modern Art competition.)

15 Quoted in Larrabee and Vignelli, p. 56.

16 Ibid., p. 57.

17 Ibid.

18 Drawings for the Pedestal Chair are dated ca. 1955 in Miller, color plate 16, p. 120. Although Charles and Ray Kaiser Eames—who moved to the West Coast in 1941 and went on to design everything from town plans and graphics to exhibition installations and educational films—worked with Knoll's main competitor of the time, the Herman Miller Furniture Company, Knoll didn't have much other competition. Shu's Planning Unit offered interior design services unlike those available from any other manufacturer at the time. When she found that furnishings were needed that did not exist in the line, she designed them herself. Now many of her simple, geometric, well-detailed "background" pieces, like the furnishings she designed for Eero's lobbies at the General Motors Technical Center (1948–56), are classics in their own right.

19 Architects' statement in "Prize Winners in California Arts and Architecture's 'Designs for Postwar Living' competition," *Architectural Forum*, September 1943, p. 89. Note that in 1940 editor John Entenza had dropped "California" from the magazine's title, but *Architectural Forum* used it in its headline as that is how the magazine was commonly known.

20 The article in *Pencil Points*, August 1944, pp. 42–45, 48, attributes the projects to "Saarinen and Swanson Architects," but shows all three architects. The firm was usually known as Saarinen, Swanson, and Saarinen.

21 Ibid., p 44.

22 Ibid., pp. 43–44.

23 *Pencil Points*, June 1946, pp. 72–73.

24 The Eames and Saarinen houses, Case Study Houses Numbers 8 and 9, were initially published in *Arts & Architecture*, December 1945, pp. 43–51.

25 Esther McCoy, "Arts & Architecture Case Study Houses," *Blueprints for Modern Living: History and Legacy of the Case Study Houses* (Cambridge, Massachusetts: MIT Press, 1989), catalogue of a traveling exhibition, curated by Elizabeth A.T. Smith, originating at the Museum of Contemporary Art, Los Angeles, pp. 15-16. (Elizabeth Smith went on to publish an even larger monograph on the program: Elizabeth A.T. Smith and Peter Gössen, ed. *Case Study Houses, the Complete CSH Program 1945-1966* (New York: Taschen, 2001).

26 Peter Papademetriou, "Eames, Saarinen: A Magic Box," *Casabella*, December 1998–January 1999, p. 121, notes that "The original design, clearly ascribed to Eames and Saarinen, has been compared with a truss-form bridge house attached to a hillside, designed in 1934 by Mies van der Rohe, and exhibited in 1947 at an installation at the Museum of Modern Art which Eames is known to have seen."

27 De Long, p. 74.

28 See Larrabee and Vignelli, p. 57; and "Case Study Houses 8 and 9 by Charles Eames and Eero Saarinen," *Arts & Architecture*, July 1950, pp. 26–39, 43–46.

29 Papademetriou , p. 124.

30 Ibid., p. 127.

31 Boston Symphony Orchestra Archives, series 56, scrapbooks, v. 67, contain the article where Koussevitzky's statements about his desire to "recreate the art of opera" in a "laboratory" appeared: "Symphonic Music and Opera Open Tanglewood Theatre, Dr. Serge Koussevitzky, Conductor Addresses 1,110 Patrons hall Provoc Ideal for Musical and Speaking Programs," *Pittsfield Massachusetts Eagle*, 14 July 1941. Other information about the two halls, along with this final quotation, came from Herbert Kupferberg's *Tanglewood* (New York: McGraw-Hill, 1976), pp. 81–82, 174–74.

5. A Break and a Breakthrough

1 Anthony J. Yanik, "Workplace for a Civilized Society, The Architecture of the Technical Center," *GM Tech Center, Where Today Meets Tomorrow*, a booklet produced for the company by McVey Marketing & Advertising of Flint, Michigan, in 2002, p. 14.

2 US Air Force General O.P. Weyland and Navy Rear Admiral Frederic S. Withington spoke, too. The presence of these military figures seems strange today, but 1956 was the height of the Cold War, the memory of World War II was strong, and General Motors had had numerous military contracts during the war.

3 Reinhold Martin, *The Organizational Complex, Architecture, Media, and Corporate Space* (Cambridge, Massachusetts: MIT Press, 2003), p. 129.

4 Robert Swanson told Eliel Saarinen's biographer, Albert Christ-Janer, "The first contract for the GM design was . . . in our joint names, Saarinen and Swanson. I managed to persuade Eero, on the strength of this large contract to come back to Bloomfield Hills. . . . Eero returned, under the firm's name of Saarinen, Swanson, and Saarinen, the search for program solution went forward." Christ-Janer, pp. 116–17.

5 *Architectural Forum*, August 1945, pp. 7, 91; *Architectural Record*, September 1945, pp. 16, 98; *Pencil Points*, September 1945, p. 16; and *Architect and Engineer*, October 1945, p. 12.

6 *Eero Saarinen on His Work*, p. 32. Unless otherwise noted, subsequent quotations by Eero Saarinen in this chapter are taken from the same source.

7 Michael J. Crosbie, "GM Technical Center Receives AIA's 25-Year Award," *Architecture*, April 1985, p. 15.

8 Interview with Robert Venturi, Philadelphia, Pennsylvania, 27 May 2002. Subsequent quotations by Venturi in this chapter are taken from this interview. More than anyone, Venturi was responsible for the advent of the Postmodern movement in architecture, which ended up dampening interest in the kind of mid-century modern architecture that Eero Saarinen practiced and the GM Technical Center epitomized. But that was not exactly Venturi's intention when he wrote the book *Complexity and Contradiction in Architecture* (New York: Museum of Modern Art Papers on Architecture, 1966), which launched the movement.

9 Interview with Kevin Roche by Tsukasa Yamashita, "Eero Saarinen and His Works," *Architecture + Urbanism*, April 1984, p. 20.

10 Interview with Gunnar Birkerts, *Architecture + Urbanism*, April 1984, p. 223.

11 Architects who have worked for Eero Saarinen include: Bruce Adams, Don Albinson, Sanford Anderson, J. Henderson Barr, E. Charles Bassett, Gunnar Birkerts, Robert Burley, Peter Carter, Spiro Daltas, Claude De Forest, Niels Diffrient, John Dinkeloo, Gene Festa, Chuck Gathe, Olav Hammarstrom, Hugh Hardy, Nobuo Hozumi, Mark T. Jaroszewicz, Paul Kennon, Balthazar Korab, Joe Lacy, Anthony Lumsden, Jill Mitchell, Glen Paulsen, Cesar Pelli, Warren Platner, David Powrie, Kevin Roche, Harold Roth, Edward Saad, Pete Van Dyke, Robert Venturi, Lebbeus Woods, Tsukasa Yamashita, and Robert Ziegelman.

12 "Saarinen Architecture for Saarinen," *Architectural Forum*, May 1953, pp. 142–45.

13 Richard P. Scharchburg, "Charles F. Kettering . . . Inventive Genius of the Nation's Second Century," *GM Tech Center, Where Today Meets Tomorrow*, pp. 45–49.

14 Ibid.

15 Lynden A. Ruester, "Design Wizard Harley Earl," *GM Tech Center, Where Today Meets Tomorrow*, p. 20. Ruester notes that Eliot Noyes drove a Porsche and a Land Rover.

16 Ibid., p. 28.

17 John McAndrew, "First Look at the General Motors Technical Center," *Art in America*, April 1956, pp. 26–33.

18 "General Motors Technical Center," *Architectural Forum*, November 1951, p. 112.

19 "GM's Industrial Versailles," *Architectural Forum*, May 1956, p. 123.

6. GM Progeny

1 Nobu Hozumi, translated by Kentaro Tsubaki, "Learning from Eero Saarinen," *Architecture + Urbanism*, April 1984, p. 6. Subsequent quotations by Hozumi in this chapter are taken from this source.

2 The honorary degree was actually a master's.

3 Letter from Eero Saarinen to Astrid Sampe, 2 July 1949, Cranbrook Archives, Sampe Papers, first folder. Subsequent quotations from letters from Saarinen to Sampe are taken from correspondence in the Cranbrook Archives.

4 Betty Friedan in *The Feminine Mystique* (New York: Dell, 1963) made the same observations a full ten years later.

5 Louchheim, "Now Saarinen the Son," pp. 26–27, 44–45.

6 "Eero Saarinen Weds Critic Aline Louchheim," *Architectural Forum*, February 1954, p. 41. The announcement said that they were married "this month . . . in her Manhattan apartment." According to his children, he provided so generously for Lily and the children that he and Aline could not afford to build a house, so they renovated the Victorian he had lived in with his family. Lily moved to Brattle Street in Cambridge, Massachusetts, and later built a house in Wellfleet, on Cape Cod, with Olav Hammarström, a Finnish architect who had worked for Eero, on the same pond where Marcel Breuer and Ivan Chermayeff kept houses.

7 Louchheim, p. 26.

8 Ibid., p. 45.

9 Walter McQuade, "Eero Saarinen, A Complete Architect," *Architectural Forum*, April 1962, pp. 104—05. McQuade also reported that Aline had told him that, years before, when he was coming to New York to court her at fancy restaurants, she remembered, "At first I was amazed, then amused at Eero for carrying around a little list of the best vintages of wines in his pocket. While the waiter stood by, he would take his list out and thoughtfully check the restaurant's wine list with his own categorized notes. What impressed me was that, in contrast to most men I knew, he had the strength of a man who didn't have to pretend."

10 Interview with Susan Saarinen, 28 September 2003.

11 Interview with Jill Mitchell, by telephone, 16 January 2004.

12 An internal memorandum in the Time, Inc. Archives dated 14 December 1956 describes the company's series of building plans. They are also recounted in Robert T. Elson, *The World of TIME, INC., The Intimate History of a Publishing Enterprise, Volume Two: 1941–1960* (New York: Atheneum, 1973), pp. 331–33.

13 Time, Inc. internal memorandum.

14 Peter C. Papademetriou, "Eero Saarinen, Thin Skin, the IBM Production Facility in Rochester," *Casabella*, December 2002–January 2002, pp. 145–53, 178–79. Noyes worked as a consultant while he continued his private architectural and industrial design practice.

15 Papademetriou, ibid., cites technical articles that maintain that the thickness is actually 11/32 of an inch, but they are described as a more comprehensible 5/16 in *Progressive Architecture* ("Saarinen Uses Curtain Wall 5/16 Thick," June 1957, p. 57), *Architectural Forum* ("Factories Planned for People: In Rochester, Minnesota, IBM Joins the Community in Preserving the Rural Surroundings of a New Prestige Plant," October 1958, pp. 140–43), and *AIA Journal* (Clinton H. Cogwill, "Industrial Buildings, Part I," November 1960, pp. 93–95).

16 Temko, p. 36.

17 Ibid.

18 Papademetriou describes the construction system and its modular character in detail in *Casabella*. The bays of the structural grid in the manufacturing areas run 6 by 5; the administrative area bays run 9 by 3; and in the cafeteria they run 10 by 8.

19 John Peter, *The Oral History of Modern Architecture, Interviews with the Greatest American Architects of the Twentieth Century* (New York: Harry N. Abrams, 1994), p. 210.

20 Temko, pp. 36–37.

21 Martin, *The Organizational Complex*. Martin discusses in depth several of Saarinen's works, the IBM design program, and other mid-century buildings. He makes the point that IBM Rochester resembled the company's products.

22 According to a company brochure, groundbreaking took place on 31 July 1956, and the building was dedicated on 30 September 1958. In 1963, a million dollar addition of 100,000 square feet brought the total floor space to 685,000, and more space was added in 1969.

23 As a result, Saarinen was the unanimous choice of the people at Bell Labs according to H.J. Wallis, "The Holmdel Laboratories," in *Bell Laboratories Record*, October 1962, p. 317. Wallis explains that the selection committee also chose the site and determined the criteria for the new facilities.

24 *Eero Saarinen on His Work*, p. 70. The 24-foot deep laboratories and 12-foot deep offices can be reconfigured on a 6-foot module to produce clear floor spaces of 5,000 square feet. And each scientist is able to control the lighting and temperature in his work space.

25 "Research in the Round," *Architectural Forum*, p. 82.

26 *Eero Saarinen on His Work*, p. 72.

27 Jennifer Hall, company spokeswoman of IBM Watson Research Center, in conversation with the author, 12 July 2002.

28 *Eero Saarinen on His Work*, p. 72. Saarinen spells "storey" throughout, according to the practice of the 1950s. The author has changed the spelling to conform to contemporary practice and for consistency.

29 Ibid.

30 Ibid., p. 70.

31 Later, scientists there developed the first communication satellites, hardware for radar and data communications, electronic switching systems, pathways for telephone connections, and equipment for speakerphone and Touch-Tone dialing—all before the new building even opened.

32 The successor firm to Eero Saarinen and Associates, Kevin Roche, John Dinkeloo and Associates, was responsible for the additions here, as at the other corporate campuses. The five original stories above ground rest on an huge concrete podium over the auditorium and the underground shipping, maintenance, and mechanical facilities. The podium, which houses ducts for air-conditioning as well as out-of-sight shipping and receiving facilities, is supported by 90-foot prestressed reinforced concrete beams. There are also 83-foot-tall, 35-by-60-foot elevator towers in the corners, rising to the full height of the building and containing stairwells and restrooms.

33 Early articles noted the sheer quantity of material employed in the Bell structures: 50,000 cubic tons of reinforced concrete, 4,000 tons of reinforced steel, 100,000 square feet of glass, 5,000 3-by-6-foot panes, and 1,000 tons of black anodized aluminum to hold the panes in place. The interior spaces may seem confined today, when natural light and operable windows are in vogue again, but many laboratories require sealed spaces, and most scientists work at computers (some have two or three), so sunlight on their desks is not desirable. The informal meeting spaces and little conference rooms along the long corridors, however, are very much in vogue in the twenty-first century, because studies have shown that people do their best work when they can confer casually with colleagues.

34 Anthony Vidler, "Bell Laboratory," *Architectural Design*, August 1967, p. 355.

35 Walter McQuade, "The Telephone Company Dials the Moon," *Architectural Forum*, October 1962, pp. 88, 91.

36 Quoted in Wallis, p. 320.

37 Ibid.

38 Interview with David Powrie, 15 December 2003, by telephone between New York City and Madison, Connecticut. Subsequent quotations by Powrie in this chapter are taken from this interview.

39 William A. Hewitt, "Remarks for the Convocation Dinner for Fellows of the American Institute of Architects in San Diego, California, June 6, 1977," p. 3. Subsequent quotations by Hewitt in this chapter are taken from this source.

40 Walter McQuade, "John Deere's Sticks of Steel," *Architectural Forum*, July 1964, p. 77.

41 Ibid.

42 Eero Saarinen, *Challenge to an Architect*, a brochure prepared for the opening of the Deere & Company Administrative Center on June 5, 1964, with the architects' statements posthumously edited by Aline Saarinen.

43 John M. Jacobus Jr., "John Deere Office Building, Moline, Ill., USA," *Architectural Review*, May 1965, p. 366.

44 The complex had already been published in *Architectural Forum*, *Architectural Record*, and *Perspecta* (the Yale architecture school journal). *Forum* published

another flattering nine-page spread, *Record* ran three more articles (one seven pages long), *Interiors* covered it, and there were major articles in *L'Architettura*, *Deutsche Bauzeitung*, *Domus*, and *Architectural Review*.

45 "First Honor, Eero Saarinen & Associates' Deere & Co Administrative Center," *AIA Journal*, July 1965, pp. 31–32.

46 "Deere HQ Wins Saarinen Sixth 25-Year Award," *Progressive Architecture*, February 1993, p. 18.

47 Mildred and Edward Hall, *The Fourth Dimension in Architecture: The Impact of Building on Man's Behavior* (Santa Fe, New Mexico: Sunstone Press, 1975). The Halls' study typified a concern with proxemics (how people use space) at the time. In general, it showed that Deere & Company employees were very happy with their building and that they worked hard and efficiently in it.

48 By contrast, the 1979 addition to the west by the successor firm has a gigantic gambrel-roofed atrium that is popular with employees but, with its indoor landscaping, diagonal orientation, and shiny metallic trim, now appears dated.

49 Walter McQuade, "John Deere's Sticks of Steel," p. 84.

50 Ibid., p 77.

51 Jacobus, p. 365. All subsequent quotations by Jacobus in this chapter are taken from the *Architectural Review* article.

7. Campuses for the Modern World

1 Nobuo Hozumi, "Learning from Eero Saarinen," *Architecture + Urbanism*, April 1984: "[M]ale college graduates averaged around 60,000 in 1946. It increased to 170,000 in 1948, 260,000 in 1949 and reached 330,000 in 1950." In 1947, there were 2.5 million students enrolled in American universities according to Joseph Hudnut "On form in Universities," *Architectural Record*, December 1947, p. 91.

2 *Eero Saarinen on His Work*, p. 12.

3 His address books in the Manuscripts and Archives, Yale University Library (series VII, box 11, folder 95) show that he knew virtually everyone in the world of architecture and a significant number of people in the art world, publishing, politics, and corporate America.

4 Interview with Ralph Rapson, 2 February 2004.

5 Quoted on the Antioch College website, www.antioch-college.com.

6 "The Beginning of Something More," typed manuscript of a speech by Eero Saarinen, Architect, at the ceremony to lay the cornerstone of Hugh Taylor Birch Hall, Antioch College, June 9, 1946, Antioch College Archives.

7 "Typical Dormitory Rooms for One or Two at Antioch College; Saarinen, Saarinen and Associates," *Architectural Record*, December 1947, pp. 86–87; "Antioch College Dormitory for Women," *Progressive Architecture*, August 1949, pp. 49–53, 89; "Women's Dormitory, Antioch College, Yellow Springs, Ohio," in *Progressive Architecture* competition, *Progressive Architecture*, June 1949, p. 56.

8 "The Death of Eero Saarinen, Creator of Master Plan," a newspaper clipping from the *Record*, 20 October 1961, held in the Antioch Archives. Mercer, who was also an Antioch alumnus, ended his article by saying, "He once told us that every town of over 5,000 people in the United States could have been rebuilt completely with the money spent on the Second World War. He hated such tragedies of human waste.... He died before his work was done, before the end of his era. The question now is—can we complete it for him?"

9 Christ-Janer, pp. 121, 151. Eliel's design for the chapel was published in *Progressive Architecture*, June 1951, pp. 14-15; Eero's chapel, which was built, was published in *Progressive Architecture*, June 1958, pp. 132-137.

10 Christ-Janer, p. 115.

11 "A University Campus Plan Under Way for Drake University, Des Monies, Iowa," *Architectural Record*, December 1947, pp. 76, 81.

12 "Dormitories and Dining Hall," *Progressive Architecture*, April 1955, p. 18.

13 "Theological School and Chapel, Drake University," *Progressive Architecture*, February 1957, pp. 148-52.

14 Jaya Kader, "Eero Saarinen at Brandeis 1949–1952," a senior undergraduate thesis written at Brandeis University, May 1984, Brandeis Archives, p. 7.

15 William Lebovich, "The Forgotten Campus Plan of Eero Saarinen," an unpublished paper written at Brandeis University, April 1974, Brandeis Archives, pp. 2–3.

16 Kader, p. 16, cites a "Report on the First Six Master Plan Buildings and Equipment Projects" in the Brandeis Office of University Planning, as well as the "Final Report and Papers of the Office of University Planning: 1948–1952."

17 Kader, p. 17, quoting a letter from Eero Saarinen to President Sachar of 27 July 1949, in the Brandeis Office of University Planning.

18 *Eero Saarinen on His Work*, p. 12.

19 Letter from Mark Jaroszewicz to Cranbrook Archivist Mark Coir, 14 September 1995, Cranbrook Archives.

20 "An Obituary for Matthew Nowicki, 1910–1950," *Architectural Forum*, September 1950, p. 54.

21 Kader describes the first edition of the brochure on p. 19 and the second edition on p. 21. The article in *The American School and University—1951–1952* filled pp. 313–26.

22 Letter from Jaroszewicz to Coir.

23 Kader, p. 20, citing David Berkowitz, "A Plan for Tomorrow—Today," *Review Issue*, Official Publication of Brandeis University, 29 October 1950.

24 Kader, p. 65.

25 Kader, p. 55.

26 Kader, p. 84, citing a memorandum for Wilhelm von Moltke in the Brandeis Office of University Planning dated 21 February 1951, in which he reports on a trip to Philadelphia and Boston , 14–15 February 1951, p. 3.

27 Kader, p. 26, quoting von Moltke, whom she interviewed on 27 February 1984.

28 Kader, p. 86.

29 Ibid., citing an article in the *Justice*, 18 February 1953, p. 6.

30 *Brandeis Under Construction* (exhibition catalog) (Waltham, Massachusetts: Rose Art Museum, 1972), pp. 8–9. The exhibition, organized by the Poses Institute of Fine Arts, ran 13 May–1 October 1972 and was curated with the guidance of professor Gerald Bernstein, under Rose Museum of Art director Michael J. Wentworth. The catalog included an essay by Ann Lorenz based on interviews with Max Abramovitz, Archie Riskin, Chancellor Sachar, and Gerry Schiff of Harrison & Abramovitz.

31 University archivists and the authors generously made these unpublished works available to the author.

8. The Cutting Edge on Campus

1 According to the monthly calendar Saarinen kept at his office, he met with the people at MIT on 9 August 1951, though the projects were probably not designed until sometime the next year. He had an appointment at Brandeis on August 10. The calendars are in the collection of the Manuscripts and Archives, Yale University Library, Eero Saarinen Collection, series VII, box 11. Planning for the facilities at MIT, however, must have occurred even earlier, because it was dean William Wurster who recommended Saarinen and he left office in 1950. See Meredith Clausen, *Pietro Belluschi, Modern American Architect* (Cambridge, Massachusetts: MIT Press, 1994), p. 205. The official names of the buildings are the Kresge Auditorium and the Kresge Chapel, but the chapel is known as the MIT Chapel.

2 Joseph Hudnut, "On Form in Universities," *Architectural Record*, December 1947, p. 94.

3 Quoted in Clausen, p. 205.

4 Ibid., p. 96.

5 Some accounts say the hall seats 1,200 or 1,250 and 200 musicians, but the issue of MIT's *Technology Review* (June 1955) devoted to the buildings at the time of the dedication specifies 1,238 and 250 (p. 395).

6 "MIT Dedicates New Auditorium," *Architectural Forum*, July 1955, p. 128.

7 "Saarinen Challenges the Rectangle, Designs a Domed Auditorium and a Cylindrical Chapel for MIT's Laboratory Campus," *Architectural Forum*, January 1953, pp. 126-33. Though the drawings of the schemes he had done with Saarinen for Brandeis had been published in the University's brochures and in the article Eero Saarinen wrote, "Planning the Campus of Brandeis University," for *The American School and University—1951–52*, pp. 313-25, they were not discussed in relation to the buildings at MIT. However, a November 1956 article in *Architectural Record* used a building by each of them as the examples of buildings for Public Assembly and said, "The structural spectaculars of our time are the [Live] Stock Pavilion at Raleigh and the Kresge Auditorium on the campus of the Massachusetts Institute of Technology"; "One Hundred Years of Significant Building," *Architectural Record*, November 1956, pp. 197–200. The North Carolina Livestock Pavilion was constructed by architect William Henry Deitrick after Nowicki's death with the gifted engineer Fred Severud, of Severud, Elstad & Kruger, and the William Muirhead Construction Company between 1950 and 1952.

8 "Saarinen Challenges the Rectangle," pp. 126–27.

9 "Buildings in the Round," *Architectural Forum*, January 1956, p. 121.

10 "MIT Dedicates New Auditorium," pp. 128–29.

11 "Three Critics Discuss MIT's New Buildings," *Architectural Forum*, March 1956, p. 157. Subsequent quotations by the three critics are taken from this article.

12 "Challenge to the Rectangle; MIT Campus Center with Auditorium and Chapel," *Time*, June 29, 1953, p. 64; "Puddled Spire; Chapel for MIT," *Time*, 5 December 1955, p. 88; Paul Thiry, "Eglises modernes aux Etats-Unis"; "MIT Chapel, Cambridge, Massachusetts—Church of Christ the King, Seattle, Washington," *Construction moderne*, January 1957, pp. 30–35; "Projet pour l'Institut technique du Massachusetts (MIT)," *L'Architecture d'aujourd'hui*, December 1953, p. 48; "Auditorium du MIT, Cambridge," *L'Architecture d'aujourd'hui*, March 1956, pp. 50–53; "Chapelle universita-ire Cambridge, Mass (MIT)," *L'Architecture d'aujourd'hui*, April 1957, pp. 56–57; N. Keith Scott, "Eero Saarinen's New Auditorium for MIT," *RIBA Journal*, February 1955, pp. 168–69; "MIT dedicates New Auditorium," pp. 128–29; "Saarinen Dome a Year Later; MIT Auditorium," *Architectural Record*, May 1954, p. 2; Edward Augustus Weeks, "Opal on the Charles; MIT Auditorium," *Architectural Record*, July 1955, pp. 131–37; "Chapel: Interdenominational, MIT's Kresge Chapel," *Architectural Record*, January 1956, pp. 154–57; "One Hundred Years of Significant Buildings: Kresge Auditorium, Massachusetts Institute of Technology," *Architectural Record*, November 1956, pp. 197–200; "Long-span Concrete Dome on Three Pendentives, Auditorium, Cambridge, Massachusetts," *Progressive Architecture*, June 1954, pp. 120–25, 130–31; "New Chapel at MIT," *Progressive Architecture*, January 1956, pp. 65–67.

13 "The Opal on the Charles," pp. 131–37.

14 N. Keith Scott, "MIT Auditorium: An English View," *Architectural Record*, July 1955, pp. 138, 268.

15 The Julius Adams Stratton Student Union was built in 1963 and designed by Eduardo Catalano with Brannen & Shimamoto.

16 Letter to the author from Charles H. Sawyer, 28 January 2003. Sawyer, who was director of the Division of the Arts and dean of the School of Fine Arts at the time, writes: "We were faced with the problem of selecting an architect for a projected wing to the art gallery, as Philip Goodwin, who had been appointed by the previous administration, indicated that he could not continue to serve. George Howe, who had been appointed chairman of architecture [which was not yet a school in its own right] the previous year and I had the primary responsibility for selecting an architect and Eero was our first choice. He was very much involved at the time with the GM Tech Center and reluctantly concluded that he could not undertake this assignment within our time limit, which called for the completion of the building by the fall of 1953. He concurred in the choice of Louis Kahn as the architect."

17 "Proposed Physics Building for Yale University, Douglas Orr and Eero Saarinen & Associates, Architects," *Architectural Record*, September 1953, pp. 141–47.

18 Schweikher's building is one long rectangle instead of a composition of several blocks forming courts. The new science buildings, which include Philip Johnson's Kline Biology Tower and Kline Chemistry Laboratory (1963–65), occupy the same area Saarinen planned.

19 "At the University of Michigan, an Answer to Expansion: Don't Extend the Old Campus; Add Another One," *Architectural Forum*, June 1953, p. 119.

20 Ibid.

21 Aline Saarinen dated the project to 1954 in *Eero Saarinen on His Work,* and, in a speech he gave to the University of Michigan Regents, Saarinen himself specified 1955. But since the plan was published in *Architectural Forum* in June 1953, it must have begun earlier. He had also mentioned it in a letter to Astrid Sampe of 28–29 June 1952.

22 "U Plans Expansion Program, Regents Approve Five-Year Plan," *Michigan Daily, Construction Supplement*, spring 1955, p. 1.

23 "North Campus Area Shows Rapid Development," *Ann Arbor News*, 14 February 1967, section III, p. 27. Eventually, the Theater School became part of the School of Music, and the School of Architecture and Design moved to the North Campus, but by that time the tight-knit Saarinen plan had been abandoned, and each school was a separate entity, with ample parking, even though bus service was provided. The School of Architecture moved to the North Campus in the 1970s and was designed by the successor firm to Pipsan Saarinen and Robert Swanson.

24 "Proposed School of Music," *Architectural Record*, January 1956, p. 134.

25 In addition to *Eero Saarinen on His Work*, the following books omit mention of the School of Music: Allan Temko, *Eero Saarinen*; Rupert Spade and Yokio Futagawa, *Eero Saarinen*; and Antonio Román, *Eero Saarinen, An Architecture of Multiplicity*.

26 Undated typewritten copy of a lecture Eero Saarinen gave to the president and regents of the University of Michigan, with handwritten notes and additions in the margins, Manuscripts and Archives, Yale University Library, series VII, box 13.

27 Ibid.; see also Saarinen's "College Buildings."

28 According to Charles H. Sawyer, in his letter to the author, "Yale had become rather frozen in its Beaux Arts tradition and obviously needed some shaping up and new perspectives. To that end, we appointed an advisory committee of which Eero was one of the primary members." Yale hired artists like Josef Albers, who had taught at the Bauhaus, and tried to revise its curriculum by adopting some of the Bauhaus methods, which involved a common foundation program and cross-fertilization of the various arts, similar to that at Cranbrook under Eliel Saarinen. Sawyer's explanation is reiterated in an article in the *Yale University Art Gallery Bulletin* 2000, by Susan M. Matheson and Elise K. Kenney, "Prologue to Kahn: The Philip Goodwin Design," pp. 89–104. The article describes an earlier modern addition to the Yale Art Gallery, which was designed by Philip Goodwin, one of the architects (with Edward Durell Stone) of the 1939 Museum of Modern Art in New York. It shows the various schemes that Goodwin developed between 1941 and 1951, confirms the fact that Eero Saarinen was approached (on p. 98), and notes similarities between some of Goodwin's schemes and Louis Kahn's design.

29 Telephone interview with David Powrie, 27 September 2004.

30 At the exact moment the David S. Ingalls Hockey Rink was being designed, Otto Frei was writing his book on hung structures and conducting studies on mechanically stressed and pneumatically stressed membranes; Paul Rudolph and Ralph Twitchell were gaining attention for the little tension structure (a house, really) in Florida; Eduardo Catalano had used one on a small house in Raleigh near the Livestock Judging Pavilion; Bill Irwin in Melbourne was working on an Olympic Swimming Stadium and a Music Bowl with two different groups of architects; Luigi Nervi was building the Sports Palace in Rome. Hugh Stubbins would soon design a cross-cable saddle for the Congress Hall in Berlin (1957); and, in 1958, the year Ingalls was completed, Edward Durell Stone would use a wheel-over-the-pillbox for the United States Pavilion at the Brussels World's Fair. There was also interest in bold, curved concrete shell structures such as Le Corbusier's Notre Dame du Ronchamp, Felix Candela's Church of San Antonio de Las Huertas in Mexico City, and a restaurant in Long Beach, California, by Raymond and Rado. But none were quite as personally expressive as the hockey rink.

31 Fred N. Severud and Raniero G. Corbelletti, "Hung Roofs," *Progressive Architecture*, March 1956, pp. 99–107.

32 A typed speech dated January 1959, held in the Manuscripts and Archives, Yale University Library, oversize folio 13C, folder. The speech is reproduced in *Eero Saarinen on His Work*, p. 54.

33 Ibid.

34 A. Whitney Griswold, Letter to Yale provost Norman S. Buck, 30 July 1957, Manuscripts and Archives, Yale University Library, Griswold Papers, YR6 2A16, box 200, folder 1823.

35 A. Whitney Griswold, Letter to David S. Ingalls, 28 December 1956, Manuscripts and Archives, Yale University Library, Griswold Papers, YR6 2A16, box 36, folder 332.

36 Letter of 12 December 1956 to A. Whitney Griswold signed by Sumner McK. Crosby, George Heard Hamilton, Charles Seymour Jr., and Vincent Scully, Manuscripts and Archives, Yale University Library, Griswold Papers, YR6 2A16, box 36, folder 332. Hamilton was identified as "a professor and curator of the Abbey," the Yale Art Gallery's collection of drawings and other materials on Shakespearean themes, by Edwin Austin Abbey (1852–1911). Hamilton was the faculty's only specialist in nineteenth- and twentieth-century art, which explains the relevance of his comments on the hockey rink.

37 Typed speech in the Yale University Library, January 1959. In *Eero Saarinen on His Work*, p. 54, editor Aline Saarinen changed the passage to read, "one of the best buildings," presumably because she assumed that if he had lived to see more of his other buildings completed, the hockey rink would only be one among several "best buildings."

38 "Yale's Whale," *Sports Illustrated*, February 1958, pp. 52–53; Robin Boyd, "The Counter Revolution in Architecture," *Harper's Magazine*, September 1959, pp. 40–48; "Old Hands at Odd Shapes: Eero Saarinen, Kanao Sakamoto," *Life*, 14 March 1955, p. 82; Donald Vesley, "Yale Architecture and the Hockey Rink," *Criterion*, January 1959, pp. 15–18; Fred N. Severud, "Cable Suspended Roof for Yale Hockey Rink," *Civil Engineering*, September 1958, pp. 60–63; Fred N. Severud, "Arches and Catenaries Carry Rink Roof for Yale's Hockey Rink, New Haven," *Engineering News Record*, 10 April 1958, pp. 30–31, 33; "D.S. Ingalls, Université de Yale, E. Saarinen," *L'Architecture d'aujourd'hui*, September 1959, pp. 20–22; Robin Boyd, "Under Tension," *Architectural Review*, November 1963, pp. 324–34; Walter McQuade, "Yale's Viking Vessel: Saarinen's Hockey Rink," *Architectural Forum*, December 1958, pp. 106–11; "Hockey Rink at Yale," *Architectural Record*, August 1957, pp. 186–89; "Yale's Hockey Rink," *Architectural Record*, October 1958, pp. 151–158; "Recent Work of Eero Saarinen, with some Statements of Eero Saarinen," *Zodiac* 4, 1959, pp. 46–53; Peter C. Papademetriou, "Intentions in Tension, Eero Saarinen: David S. Ingalls Hockey Rink, Yale University, New Haven 1956–1959," *Casabella*, December 1999–January 2000, pp. 86–99, 170–71.

39 McQuade, "Yale's Viking Vessel; Saarinen's Hockey Rink."

40 Temko, pp. 44–46. The biggest problem, fifty years later, is that larger rinks are becoming standard, and the only way to enlarge the 200-by-85-foot rink in a 333 by 183-foot building is to eliminate seating. Today, more seating is desired, not less. But nobody wants to abandon the Ingalls rink.

9. College Campuses in Context

1 Concordia College brochure, 1958, Cranbrook Archives, Glen Paulsen Papers, accession number 1991-25.

2 Ibid.

3 Eero Saarinen, "College Buildings: Campus Planning, the Unique World of the University," *Architectural Record*, November 1960, p. 129.

4 Memorandum to Eero Saarinen from Glen Paulsen, 16 July 1953, Cranbrook Archives, Glen Paulsen Papers, box 1, folder 8.

5 Ibid.

6 Among Saarinen's characterizations of the committee were: "Edgar Buenger . . . because he is an architect and because he realizes the wisdom of good sites, he is interested, . . . H.J. Neeb is a secretary of the Missouri Synod board. . . . He is a very intelligent and far sighted person and in many ways the brain behind this senior college. . . ." Memorandum from Eero Saarinen to Dave Geery and Joe Lacy, 16 July 1953, Cranbrook Archives, Glen Paulsen Papers, box 1, folder 8.

7 "For a New College: An Old Village Silhouette," *Architectural Forum*, December 1954, pp. 128–35.

8 Eero Saarinen, "The Design Process: Concordia Senior College, Fort Wayne, Indiana," Cranbrook Archives, Glen Paulsen Papers, box 1, folder 8.

9 Letter from Eero Saarinen to Dr. Martin J. Neeb, 11 March 1955, Cranbrook Archives, Glen Paulsen Papers, box 1, folder 7.

10 The weavings were made by Cranbrook student Brigita Fuhrmann in the studio of Glen Kaufmann. The cast bronze shields of the Evangelists and Apostles were made by Richard Thomas, the former dean at Cranbrook. The communion ware was designed by the Swedish designer Sigvard Bernadotte for Georg Jensen. The art program is described in a booklet, *Art and Design at Concordia Senior College*, in the Concordia Theological Seminary Archives. The pride of the school is a huge Te Deum mosaic in the entrance to the library by Siegfried Reinhardt of Saint Louis. Also of particular note are the carved wood and polished metal symbols of the Old Testament prophets in the Classroom Buildings by Clark Fitz-Gerald.

11 The space was recently restored by the original project architect, Leonard Parker, who now practices in Minneapolis, according to Karen van Lengen and Lisa Reilly, *Vassar College, The Campus Guide* (New York: Princeton Architectural Press, 2004), pp. 89–92.

12 "The Situation Called for an Arc-like Plan," *Architectural Record*, September 1959, pp. 68–69.

13 "Court for Coeds," *Architectural Forum*, February 1961, p. 120.

14 Dan Graham made his observations during the discussion period following a lecture by the author at Columbia University on 10 March 2002.

15 The architectural historian William Morgan shared this anecdote with the author.

16 Saarinen, "College Buildings," p. 127.

17 Ibid.

18 "Law School Center, University of Chicago," *Architectural Record*, November 1960, p. 132. Saarinen described the entire complex an attempt to relate both to the neo-Gothic dormitories on one side and the unnamed style of the Bar Association Center.

19 "Two Sparkling Stones in Different Settings," *Architectural Forum*, August 1956, p. 113.

20 "Law School Center," p. 132.

21 *Eero Saarinen on His Work*, pp. 80-81.

22 Lawrence Lessing, "The Diversity of Eero Saarinen," *Architectural Forum*, July 1960, p. 95.

23 Peter Collins, "The Form-Givers," *Perspecta* 7, 1961, p. 92.

24 Colin Saint John Wilson, "Open and Closed," *Perspecta* 7, 1961, p. 97.

25 James Gowan, "Notes on American Architecture," *Perspecta* 7, 1961, p. 77. Gowan also wrote, "Question two: what precisely is the relation between this architecture and society's building codes? Since the nineteenth century, iron and steel construction has proved to be an appreciable fire risk, and the heady reply of devoted Miesians that these are no ordinary structures, but steel frames anticipating the arrival of a new fireproofing material, is an evasion of the problem until this magic solution exists." The "exposed" steel of the towers is merely a veneer; the real steel supports have been encased in concrete for fireproofing.

26 Sybil Moholy-Nagy, "The Future of the Past," *Perspecta* 7, 1961, p. 66.

27 Paul Rudolph, *Perspecta* 7, 1961, p. 51.

28 Philip Johnson, *Perspecta* 7, 1961, p. 3.

29 Louis Kahn, *Perspecta* 7, 1961, p. 16.

30 Eero Saarinen, *Perspecta* 7, 1961, pp. 30, 32.

31 The shops were insensitively renovated when they were leased to Barnes & Noble in the late 1990s, but they still function to make the area lively.

32 Walter McQuade, "The New Yale Colleges," *Architectural Forum*, December 1962, pp. 105–10.

33 Banham's article, which first appeared in the 13 July *New Statesman*, was reprinted in *Architectural Forum*, December 1962, p. 111, with a footnote from McQuade that read, "Mr. Banham! Really, Mr. Banham?" Banham also wrote, "It might appear better . . . to pass over Morse and Stiles as a late aberration of a good architect—most U.S. critics will probably do this anyhow, partly because no one is anxious to cross the formidable Saarinen widow. . . . Not only do the dormitories exemplify that creeping malady that causes an increasing number of returning Europeans to say, 'Yale is a very sick place,' the malady of gratuitous affluence irresponsibly exploited, but they exemplify something that could happen here."

34 Reyner Banham, "Fear of Eero's Mana," *Arts Magazine*, February 1962, pp. 70–73. Although this article actually appeared before the *Spectator* and *Architectural Forum* articles, it was probably written later; the others just took longer to appear in print. Banham also wrote, "I encountered any number of examples at first hand in the States a few weeks before his death, and reflected then that the Biblical injunction against stone-throwing by those not free from sin had come into conjunction with the proverbial ban on stone-throwing by those who (literally) live in glass houses." He admitted, "Saarinen's complete technical, design, and research-center for General Motors was the building that the hour required as surely as were Louis Kahn's equally misleading Richards Medical Research towers."

35 Henry-Russell Hitchcock, "American Architecture in the Early Sixties," *Zodiac* 10, 1962, p. 13. Hitchcock wrote, "The New Haven and Chantilly [Dulles Airport] projects are likely to be the finest, as they are among the last, of Eero's works, and they epitomize, in their apparently totally dissimilar modes, despite their essentially identical material, the vitality and variety of all his production and also, perhaps more significantly, the basic ambiguities of current architectural development."

36 Author's interview with Steven Holl, New York City, 8 October 2002.

37 Hitchcock, pp. 14–16.

38 "The 1963 AIA Honor Awards," *AIA Journal*, May 1963, pp. 27–41. The jurors were Robert J. Durham (chairman) William L. Caudhill, Mark Hampton, Ernest J. Kump, and Hugh A. Stubbins.

10. Building the Basics in a Small Midwestern Town

1 A rumor occasionally surfaces that J. Irwin Miller and Eero Saarinen were roommates at Yale, but Miller denied it in an interview with the author on 11 June 2002. He and Saarinen did not overlap at Yale. Miller graduated in the spring of 1931 and Saarinen arrived that fall.

2 "Now, a Pavilion in a Park: A Gift to the City, an Invitation to Bank," *Architectural Forum*, October 1955, p. 160.

3 A letter from J. Irwin Miller to the author, 5 January 2004, following up on some questions asked in an in-person interview in Columbus, Indiana, 11 June 2002.

4 David G. De Long, "Eliel Saarinen and the Cranbrook Tradition in Architecture and Design," *Design in America*, p. 68.

5 In 1953, Irwin Miller was elected chairman and turned the presidency of the bank over to S. Edgar Lauther.

6 Letter from Eero Saarinen to Astrid Sampe, 28–29 June 1952, with sketches, Cranbrook Archives, Sampe Papers.

7 "Now a Pavilion in a Park," p. 163.

8 Interview with J. Irwin Miller and Xenia Miller, Columbus, Indiana, 11 June 2002. Unless otherwise indicated, subsequent quotations by the Millers in this chapter are taken from this interview.

9 "A Contemporary Palladian Villa," *Architectural Forum*, September 1958, p. 127.

10 Dan Kiley, "Miller House," *Dan Kiley, The Complete Works of America's Master Landscape Architect* (Boston: Bulfinch Press, Little Brown and Company, 1999), pp. 21–23.

11 *Eero Saarinen on His Work*, p. 88.

12 Ibid.

13 J. Irwin Miller quoted in Carleton Knight III, "J. Irwin Miller: Patron, Client, but Always a Businessman," *Architecture*, June 1984, p. 63.

14 Ibid.

15 Quoted in Jayne Merkel, "Architectural Museum Design Charrette," *Progressive Architecture*, April 1981, pp. 68, 80.

11. Big Ambitions in Big Cities Abroad

1 John Knox Shear, "Competition for U.S. Chancellery Building, London; Eight Designs Submitted," *Architectural Record*, April 1956, p. 220a.

2 *Eero Saarinen on His Work*, p. 48.

3 Shear, pp. 220a–220f.

4 "New US Embassy for London," *Architectural Forum*, April 1956, p. 138. The architects were Anderson, Beckwith and Haible; Ernest J. Kump; Eero Saarinen; Jose Luis Sert with Huson Jackson and Joseph Zalewski; Edward Durell Stone; Hugh Stubbins; Wurster, Bernardi & Emmons; and Yamasaki, Leinweber & Associates. The jury was made up of Pietro Belluschi, Henry Shepley, and Ralph Walker of the FBO's advisory board, along with AIA president George Cummings, deputy undersecretary of state Loy Henderson, FBO director William P. Hughes, and assistant secretary (for Europe) Livingston Merchant.

5 Fello Atkinson, "U.S. Embassy Building, Grosvenor Square, London," *Architectural Review*, April 1961, p. 253.

6 The submissions were published both in *Architectural Forum* ("New US embassy for London, Saarinen wins government design competition among eight of country's leading architect," April 1956, pp. 138–45) and *Architectural Record* (John Knox Shear, "Competition for U.S. chancery building, London; eight designs submitted," April 1956. pp. 220a–220f.). Also, Jane C. Loeffler, *The Architecture of Diplomacy* (New York: Princeton Architectural Press, 1998). Loeffler, who interviewed some of the participants, says that the jury was not completely satisfied with any of the entries and that Stone placed second (p. 203).

7 Shear, p. 220

8 Atkinson, pp. 257–58. Atkinson attributed the first instance of this observation to James Cubitt, and the architectural correspondent of the London Times. In the *New Statesman*, Reyner Banham agreed that "Saarinen, by opening a sizable hole in each corner of the square lets any sense of enclosure drain away." Banham's statement was reprinted in "Controversial Building in London," *Architectural Forum*, March 1961, p. 84. The article contained republication of a selection of reviews by British critics on pp. 80–85.

9 Loeffler, p. 205.

10 *Eero Saarinen on His Work*, p. 48.

11 "Controversial Building in London," p. 84.

12 Loeffler, pp. 204–05.

13 Comments by Jordan and Banham are reprinted in Loeffler, pp. 204-05.

14 Comments by Smithson are reprinted in Loeffler, p. 81.

15 The building program is described in detail by Loeffler, pp. 200–201.

16 Ibid., p. 47.

17 Ibid., pp. 37–50. Rapson had been recommended by Hans Knoll, who was supplying furniture for the embassies.

18 Ibid., p. 122.

19 Ibid., p. 123. Walker was a partner in the New York commercial firm of Voorhees, Walker, Foley & Smith and had been president of the AIA from 1949 to 1951; Shepley was a partner in the Boston firm of Shepley Bulfinch Richardson and Abbott, which had designed many buildings at Harvard; Belluschi had designed one of the first modern office buildings in America, the Equitable Savings and Loan Building in Portland, Oregon, and was then dean at MIT.

20 Ibid., p. 115.

21 Ibid., p. 125.

22 Paul Rudolph, José Luis Sert, William Wurster, and Eero Saarinen quoted in "The Changing Philosophy of Architecture," *Architectural Record*, August 1954, pp. 180–82.

23 *Eero Saarinen on His Work*, p. 46.

24 "New U.S. Embassy in Oslo," *Architectural Record*, December 1959, p. 108.

25 The choice of materials was a happy accident after the black granite with bronze trim he originally imagined had proved too costly, according to Loeffler, p. 196.

26 *Eero Saarinen on His Work*, p. 46.

27 "Norway's Precast Palazzo," *Architectural Forum*, December 1959, pp. 130–33.

28 "Award of Merit, Eero Saarinen and Associates, Engh, Quam & Kiaer, Associate Architects," *AIA Journal*, April 1960, p. 85. The award also went to Engh, Quam & Kiaer, the associated architects responsible for supervising construction. Susan Tucker was responsible for interiors. The structural engineers were Bonde & Co., Gjert Aasheim were the mechanical engineers, and Sverre Bolkesjo did the electrical engineering. Nils Stiansen was general contractor.

29 "Exciting Embassy by Saarinen Opens Under Fire, Gracious Court Is Building's Heart," *Progressive Architecture*, November 1959, p. 90.

30 Richard M. Bennett was a partner in the Chicago firm of Loebl, Schlossman & Bennett who had graduated from Harvard's architecture school, been Edward Durell Stone's first employee, taught at Pratt and Vassar, and served as chairman of Yale's Department of Architecture in the mid-1940s. He had also won the Wheaton College Competition with Caleb Hornbostel in 1938 when Eero earned a fifth place on his own. Edgar I. Williams had graduated from and taught at MIT after spending three years at the American Academy in Rome. He had practiced in New York since 1920, served as consulting architect to the New York Public Library, and been president of the National Academy of Design, Architectural League of New York, and Municipal Art Society.

12. Big Ambitions in New York

1 The Mayor's Slum Clearance Committee was created by Mayor Wagner's predecessor, Mayor Michael O'Dwyer, at Robert Moses's suggestion, before the Urban Renewal program was even created. Moses had heard about the impending legislation from Yale classmate Senator Robert A. Taft and immediately talked Mayor O'Dwyer into creating a committee and making him chairman.

2 Robert A. Caro, *The Power Broker, Robert Moses and the Fall of New York* (New York: Vintage, 1974), p. 1013. It was Fordham president Father Laurence J. McGinley who made the request for a midtown Manhattan campus; Moses always tried to accommodate the Archdiocese of New York (and other powerful bodies).

3 Ibid., pp. 1–10.

4 "Lincoln Center," *Travel*, September 1962, p. 47. Other estimates place the figure at $50 million. It is difficult to determine the exact amount, as public funds came from a variety of sources. The state of New York gave $15 million for the New York State Theater as its contribution to the 1964 New York World's Fair. The city contributed $12 million. There were various hidden Title I contributions as well as the land itself.

5 Caro, p. 1014.

6 Edgar B. Young, *Lincoln Center, the Building of an Institution* (New York and London: New York University Press, 1980), pp. 79–80.

7 Philip Johnson, "9 Actual Theatre Designs," *Musical America*, January 1961, pp. 12–13, 160–61. Johnson's sister Theodate Johnson was the publisher of *Musical America* at the time. His earlier article was "House at New Canaan, Conn., Philip Johnson, Architect," *Architectural Review*, September 1960, pp. 152–59.

8 Caro, p. 1014. Moses purchased the building owned by the Kennedy family "for $2.5 million, a price so high that while the land under the buildings adjacent to the one owned by the Kennedys was worth $9.59 per square foot, the land under theirs became worth $62.88 per square foot."

9 Harold C. Schonberg, "Progress Report on the New Arts Center," *New York Times Magazine*, 25 May 1958, p. 38.

10 "Culture City," *Look*, 19 January 1960, pp. 40–42.

11 "Lincoln Square Developing Toward World Cultural Center," *New York Times*, 23 July 1956, p. 1, col. 1.

12 Alex Morris, "Colossus on Broadway," *Saturday Evening Post*, 19 July 1958, p. 28.

13 Howard Taubman, "A New Cultural Vista for the City," *New York Times Magazine*, 22 April 1956, p. 14.

14 "To Lift the Spirit," *Musical America*, 15 December 1957, p. 4.

15 "Addresses by Eisenhower and Moses," *New York Times*, 15 May 1959, p. 14, col. 2. Moses used the occasion to squelch protest. He said, "You cannot rebuild a city without moving people any more than you can make an omelet without breaking eggs."

16 Temko, pp. 26-7.

17 Young, p. 189. There were problems with the automated lighting system before opening night but they were resolved before the first performance.

18 Ada Louise Huxtable, *Will They Ever Finish Bruckner Boulevard?* (New York: Macmillan, 1970), p. 24. Huxtable's comments originally appeared in "Adding Up the Score: Lincoln Center," *New York Times*, 25 September 1966.

19 All the architects involved at Lincoln Center had agreed to revise the master plan, eliminating the park on the southwest corner to make more room for both the Library-Museum and the Repertory Theater, but they were not able to persuade Robert Moses to forgo the park, according to Carol Krinsky, *Gordon Bunshaft of Skidmore, Owings & Merrill* (Cambridge, Massachusetts, and London: MIT Press with the Architectural History Foundation of New York, 1988), p. 150.

20 "A Thrust Forward for the Theater," *Progressive Architecture*, November 1965, p. 191.

21 Olga Gueft, "Lincoln Center's Masterpiece: Or What Happens When Two Distinguished Firms Decide To Team Up," *Interiors*, December 1965, p. 84.

22 Conversation with Hugh Hardy, New York City, 16 December 2004.

23 "A Thrust Forward for the Theater," pp. 189, 191.

24 Gueft, pp. 84–85.

25 Krinsky, p. 152.

26 When theater in the round went out of style in the 1980s, the Vivian Beaumont Theatre was renovated by I.M. Pei & Partners with a traditional proscenium stage, according to Lincoln Kirstein, "Lincoln Shelter," a review of Edgar B. Young's *Lincoln Center, The Building of an Institution* in the *New York Review of Books*, 13 August 1981, p. 12, col. 3. At this writing, all the Lincoln Center buildings and the plaza itself are being redesigned to accommodate changing tastes by Diller + Scofidio.

27 One reason acoustical problems developed at Philharmonic Hall was that the architect was encouraged to add more seats than the acousticians had suggested because there were complaints about elitism in the press. Politics pushed technology a little too far.

28 Gueft, p. 85.

29 Kevin Roche mentioned this in an interview with the author on 17 March 2004; David Powrie said the same thing on 1 February 2004.

30 Interview with Gene Festa, New Haven, Connecticut, 5 February 2004. Subsequent quotations by Festa in this chapter are taken from this interview.

31 Eero Saarinen, "Six Broad Currents of Modern Architecture," *Architectural Forum*, July 1953, pp. 110–15.

32 *Architectural Record*, January 1960, p. 28. "Mr. Saarinen will occupy Chair No. 9, formerly held by Frank Lloyd Wright. Membership in the Academy is limited to 50 men and women, chosen for special distinction from the 250 members of the National Institute of Arts and Letters, its parent body." Today the two organizations are combined

into one and there are 250 equal members.

33 "Eero Saarinen Named to Receive 1962 A.I.A. Gold Medal," *Architectural Record*, February 1962, p. 10. "In the 55-year history of the Medal, it is the fist time it has ever gone both to a father and his son. Youngest Winner? It is also probably the first time the Gold Medal as been awarded to so young a man: earlier records are not clear on this point, but it is certainly at least 30 years since the Medal has gone to an architect under 60."

34 Román, pp. 186–91. Antonio Román draws on Philip Drew, *Sydney Opera House* (London: Phaidon Press, 1995), pp. 6–7 and Sigfried Giedion, "Jorn Utzon and the Third Generation: A New Chapter of Space, Time and Architecture," *Zodiac* 14, 1965, pp. 36–47.

35 Temko discusses and illustrates Saarinen's scheme in *Eero Saarinen*, plates 123, 124A, 124B, p. 119. The jurors in the competition were Sven Markelius, Gio Ponti, Sir Howard Robertson, and Pierre Vago, WHO officials and the head of the Geneva Department of Public Works.

36 Interview with Phyllis Lambert, New York City, 25 September 2003. Subsequent quotations by Lambert in this chapter are taken from this interview.

37 For some time, the building was attributed to Mies van der Rohe and Philip Johnson, ostensibly because Johnson had served as architect of record since Mies was not licensed in New York. But drawings of the building show that another architect, Ely Jacques Kahn, was architect of record, so quite how Johnson came to get so much credit is not clear.

38 Román, p. 177.

39 Florence Schust Knoll had married Harry Hood Bassett in 1958 and was known as Shu Knoll Bassett or Shu Bassett by 1965.

40 Interview with Frank Stanton, Boston, Massachusetts, 13 April 2003. Unless otherwise indicated, subsequent quotations by Stanton in this chapter are taken from this interview. Paley's very traditional office was designed by Jansen, decorators from Paris with mahogany furniture, French Empire antiques, and luxurious dark green fabrics and wallpapers, according to Robert A.M. Stern, Thomas Mellins, and David Fishman, *New York 1960* (New York: Monacelli Press, 1995), pp. 409–10.

41 *Eero Saarinen on His Work*, p. 16.

42 Ibid.

43 When the Seagram Building was built, the owners were charged taxes on the entire site, though they had built only on part of it. Anger over what seemed an injustice led to changes in the 1961 zoning code, which reversed the tax ruling and had the effect of encouraging the construction of plazas by offering additional height for building them. That ruling led to too many plazas, each undermining the other's reason for being. Saarinen and his colleagues worked with members of the City Planning Commission while the law was being prepared so that CBS would conform and be able to make maximal use of its site.

44 *Eero Saarinen on His Work*, p. 16.

45 Ibid.

46 Ibid.

47 "Saarinen's Skyscraper," *Architectural Record*, July 1965, p. 118.

48 Román, p. 176.

49 Ada Louise Huxtable, "Eero Saarinen's Somber Tower," *New York Times*, 13 March 1966, Section II, p. 27. Reprinted in Huxtable, *Will They Ever Finish Bruckner Boulevard?*, pp. 98–102. New York City planning commissioner James Felt was particularly involved in the negotiations with the Saarinen firm. The floor area ratio (FAR) agreed upon for the area allowed a 715,440-square-foot tower on the 696-square-foot site.

50 Huxtable, "Eero Saarinen's Humble Tower."

51 Frank Stanton, memorandum to all CBS employees, 15 April 1964.

52 Ibid.

53 Stern et al., p. 409. CBS designer Lou Dorfman made some contributions, and Carson, Lundin & Shaw were the official interior architects.

54 Patricia Conway, "Design at CBS," *Industrial Design*, February 1966, p. 54. Conway was particularly critical of the strict rectangularity and micromanagement of every design detail.

55 *Eero Saarinen on His Work*, p. 16.

13. Symbolizing Modernity

1 "Milwaukee's Proposed Memorial Center," *Architectural Record*, November 1947, p. 75.

2 "Saarinen Memorial, Milwaukee Plans a Spacious Center for Community Use," *Architectural Forum*, December 1946, p. 12.

3 *Eero Saarinen on His Work*, p. 40.

4 Temko, p. 44. Temko explains, "The compressive strength of concrete is brought strongly into play by the egg-crate form of the upper structure. The very considerable cantilever—29 1/2 feet—was facilitated by an ingenious system of reinforcement devised by the engineers Ammann & Whitney, in which steel rods at the top of the building take major tensile forces, counterbalancing the wings. To be sure, spaces of the same size could have been enclosed more directly and lightly in steel, or a three-dimensional grid of prestressed concrete, but the subjective expression of almost pugnaciously poised mass, the visible triumph over obstacles, might have been lost"

5 "Milwaukee's Living Memorial," *Architectural Forum*, December 1957, p. 91.

6 *Eero Saarinen on His Work*, p. 40.

7 "Milwaukee Art Center, A Big and Bold—but Modest—Addition to a Modern Monument," *Architectural Record*, July 1976, pp. 87, 90.

8 Ibid., p. 87.

9 "Art Houses, New Museums in Milwaukee and Saint Louis," *New Yorker*, 5 November 2001, p. 98.

10 "Museum with a View," *Time*, 4 November 1957, p. 82.

11 Sigfried Giedion, *Space Time and Architecture* (Cambridge, Massachusetts: Harvard University Press, 1967), pp. 200–01.

12 At least the buildings were photographed and documented before they were destroyed, and some of the building fabric was preserved for reconstruction, though it ended up being used for land fill.

13 Merrill D. Peterson, in *The Jefferson Image in the American Mind* (New York: Oxford University Press, 1960), contends that real estate development was the primary reason for creating a monument and notes that mayor Bernard Dickman, who was in office when the citizens committee to create it was formed in 1933, was the former head of the real estate exchange. See also Hélène Lipstadt, "Form-making between Money and Memory: The Competition for the Jefferson National Expansion Memorial, 1934 –1951," a paper in the Cranbrook Archives, Cranbrook Educational Community, Bloomfield Hills, Michigan. Architectural historian Lipstadt takes a similar position to Peterson's, though she also recognizes the city's attempt to promote modern monuments as opposed to representational ones and to defeat the idea of utilitarian "living memorials."

14 Actually, the memorial was also to commemorate James Monroe and Robert Livingston, aides to Jefferson "who negotiated the Purchase of $15 million, and for the explorers Lewis and Clark, and for the frontiersmen and pioneers who went West," according to James Deakin, "Completed Arch Will Fulfill 30-Year Effort," *St. Louis Post Dispatch*, 16 February 1964.

15 "Jefferson Memorial Competition Winners," *Architectural Record*, April 1948, p. 93. The project was not universally popular, however. Suits were filed in state and federal courts to block it, though the motivation seems to have been politics rather than preservation. And the idea of tying the funding to Emergency Relief appears to have been more political than real. A substantial percentage of the Saint Louis workforce was already unemployed, and few found work in the demolition effort, nor were they likely to.

16 "Jefferson National Expansion Memorial Competition Winners Announced," *Progressive Architecture*, March 1948, p. 18.

17 Lipstadt notes that competitions were also associated with the same democratic values attributed to Jefferson at the time as well as specifically associated with him, because he had himself entered the competition for the President's White House of 1792.

18 "Jefferson National Expansion Memorial Competition," *Architectural Forum*, March 1948, p. 14.

19 Ibid.

20 Among the other finalists were University of Illinois student architects Gordon A. Phillips and William Eng with student painter George N. Foster, who won the $20,000 second prize (as well as $10,000 for reaching the finals). Third prize went to New York architects William N. Breger, Caleb Hornbostel, and George S. Lewis with landscape architects Donald L. Kline and Chris Tunnard, sculptor Ralph J. Menconi, and painters Alan Gould and Andre Schwob. Saint Louis architect Harris Armstrong, who entered on his own, was another finalist, as was the team made up of Cleveland architect T. Marshall Rainey and Cincinnati planners Robert A. Deshon and John B. Sheblessy, landscape architect John F. Kirkpatrick, painter Robert S. Robinson, and sculptor Julian F. Bechtold.

21 Temko, p. 19.

22 M.G. Mercer, "Win First Prize in Jefferson Memorial Competition: Views and Plans, Eero Saarinen & Associates," *Progressive Architecture*, May 1948, p. 58.

23 "Jefferson Memorial Competition Winners," p. 92.

24 "Jefferson National Expansion Memorial Competition," p. 14. Each of the five finalists received $10,000 after the first round; after the second, the winners were awarded another $40,000, those who won second place received $20,000 more; third place yielded another $10,000, and each of the runners-up was awarded $2,500.

25 "Jefferson National Expansion Memorial Competition Winners Announced," p. 18.

26 Ibid, p. 17.

27 "Saint Louis Selects Modern Design," *Art News*, March 1948, pp. 53–54.

28 Mercer, "Win First Prize in Jefferson Memorial Competition," p. 58.

29 Peter Blake, "Monument to the Dream," *Interior Design*, January 1991, p. 138.

30 The brilliant Italian structural engineer Pier Luigi Nervi certainly took that position, and Temko argues that the arch does conform to mathematical principles. He describes the arch as "a stroke of rational structural functionalism: a catenary arch which geometrically was as predictable as a circle. The steel plate shell of the G.M. dome and the concrete shell of the M.I.T. auditorium are governed by the same geometric purism, and thus absolutely subject to the laws of what Nervi calls 'Building Science.'" See Temko, p. 42.

31 Fred N. Severud, "Structural Study: Jefferson Memorial Arch, Eero Saarinen and Associates Architects," *Architectural Record*, July 1957, pp. 151–53.

32 Ibid.

33 Michael J. Crosbie, "Is It a Catenary?" *AIA Journal*, June 1983, p. 78. See also "Revised Scheme, Revived Hope for Saarinen's Saint Louis Arch," *Architectural Record*, November 1957, p. 11.

34 Crosbie, p. 79.

35 Ibid, p. 78.

36 Lipstadt sees the departure from pure geometry as an attempt to conceal the true meaning of the arch, which she describes as "the opportunity to 'improve one's lot,'" suggesting that the main thing that the Louisiana Purchase offered settlers was economic opportunity, not freedom. "In the fifties," she writes, "Saarinen went on to conceal the Jeffersonian source of his design by associating it with the mathematical and formal purity of the catenary arch. The purity is illusory and the explanation deceptive (if not deceitful), since he knowingly had his engineers calculate an impure, weighted catenary." See Lipstadt, "Form-making between Money and Memory," p. 10.

37 William H. Gass, "Monumentality/Mentality," *Oppositions* 24, fall 1982, p. 138.

38 Ibid.

39 It can "appear and disappear in the landscape," as Hélène Lipstadt observed in "Learning from St. Louis, The Arch, the Canon, and Bourdieu," *Harvard Design Review*, summer 2001, pp. 5–6.

40 Gass, pp. 142, 143, 141.

41 Letter to the author from Cesar Pelli in response to questions, 20 October 2004.

42 Sally Bixby Defty, "Mrs. Saarinen on Scene for Arch Topping," *St. Louis Post Dispatch*, 6 May 1968. A copy of the article is held in the Cranbrook Archives, Goldman Collection.

43 Interview with Dan and Ann Kiley, Charlotte, Vermont, 23 July 2002.

44 Interview with Kevin Roche, Hamden, Connecticut, 17 March 2004.

45 Interview with Gene Festa, New Haven, Connecticut, 5 February 2004.

46 "Saarinen's St. Louis Arch Project Finally Approved," *Architectural Forum*, May 1958, pp. 16–18.

47 "St. Louis Park Funds Voted, but None for Saarinen Arch," *Architectural Forum*, September 1956, p. 9.

48 "St Louis Ready to Approve Project beside Saarinen's Arch, His Views Unrecorded," *Architectural Forum*, June 1960, pp. 5–6; "Saarinen Feels Building Near St. Louis National Arch Should Not Exceed 200 Feet—but City Rejects Idea," *Architectural Forum*, July 1960, p. 7.

49 Michael McCoy, "Attitudes Toward Technology; Between Nature and Culture," *Progressive Architecture*, April 1991, p. 106.

50 Letter from Lily Swann Saarinen to Pipsan Saarinen Swanson, 3 June 1968, Cranbrook Archives.

14. Taking Flight

1 Alastair Gordon, *Naked Airport: a Cultural History of the World's Most Revolutionary Structure* (New York: Metropolitan Books, Henry Holt, 2004), p. 154.

2 *Eero Saarinen on His Work*, p. 60.

3 *Naked Airport:*, pp. 80–81.

4 Buford L. Pickens, the dean of the School of Architecture at Washington University in Saint Louis, praised it in "Terminal Building, Lambert-Saint Louis Airport, Proud Architecture and the Spirit of St. Louis," *Architectural Record*, April 1956, pp. 195–202. It is often attributed to the successor firm of Hellmuth, Yamasaki & Leinweber, Architects, but Yamasaki was the chief designer.

5 G.E. Kidder-Smith objects to the Lambert-Saint Louis passageways and hidden supports in *The Architecture of the United States, The Plains States and the Far West*, vol. 3 (New York: Anchor Books/Doubleday; Museum of Modern Art, 1981), p. 438.

6 "TWA's Graceful New Terminal," *Architectural Forum*, January 1958, p. 79. Today the Port Authority is called the Port Authority of New York and New Jersey. It still operates the airport and is actively involved in design.

7 The models ranged from 1:5,000 to 1:1 for some details, though the most important were at 3/4-inch scale, according to Peter C. Papademetriou, "The Calculation and the Invention of the Form, Flight of Fantasy," *Casabella*, December 2001, p. 183. The photograph on the book jacket of *Eero Saarinen on His Work* shows him surrounded by these models.

8 "TWA's Graceful New Terminal," p. 81.

9 Kevin Roche quoted in Hart Laubkeman, "Form Swallows Function," *Progressive Architecture*, May 1992, p. 108.

10 Ibid.

11 *Eero Saarinen on His Work*, p. 60. Papademetriou explains that there are two support points for each vault, and a center plate joins all four vaults.

12 "TWA's Graceful New Terminal," p. 83.

13 "Shaping a two-acre sculpture," *Architectural Forum*, August 1960, p. 119. "Saarinen's TWA Flight Center," *Architectural Record*, July 1962, p. 129 notes: The team for the TWA Terminal consisted of structural engineers Ammann & Whitney with Boyd Anderson deeply involved, mechanical engineers Jaros, Baum & Bolles, lighting consultant Stanley McCandless, acoustical consultants Bolt, Beranek and Newman, contractor Grove, Shepherd, Wilson & Kluge with Kenneth P. Morris field project manager, built-in seating from the Lehigh Furniture Corporation, food service design by Raymond Loewy/William Smith, and the architecture and engineering departments of the Port of New York Authority.

14 Ibid., pp. 119–20, 122.

15 Ibid., p. 122.

16 Ibid., pp. 120–22.

17 *Eero Saarinen on His Work*, p. 60. Saarinen made the statement after his last visit to the site on 17 April 1961, when only the concrete vaults had been completed.

18 Robin Boyd, "The Counter Revolution in Architecture," *Harper's Magazine*, September 1959, pp. 40–48. Boyd discussed the way it raised "the fundamental question of architectural expression" in an article aimed at an educated mass (as opposed to professional) audience.

19 *Eero Saarinen on His Work*, p. 60. This statement was made on June 19, 1959 in an interview done for *Horizon* magazine.

20 Papademetriou, p. 182.

21 "The Concrete Bird Stands Free," *Architectural Forum*, December 1960, pp. 114–15; "Concrete Bird: Progress at Idlewild," *Architectural Review*, February 1961, p. 7.

22 "Forget the Bird: TWA Appraised," *Architectural Review*, November 1962, pp. 306–07. The quotations by Kaufmann are taken from Edgar Kauffman Jr., "Inside Eero Saarinen's TWA Building," *Interiors*, July 1962, p. 86.

23 Vincent Scully, *American Architecture and Urbanism* (New York: Henry Holt and Company, 1969; reprint 1988), p. 198.

24 Alan Colquhoun, "TWA Terminal Building, Idlewild, New York," *Architectural Design*, October 1962, p. 465.

25 Kaufmann, "Inside Eero Saarinen's TWA Building," pp. 86–87.

26 Ibid., pp. 87, 89.

27 Ibid., pp. 89, 91–92.

28 "Architecture of Interiors: TWA Terminal, New York International Airport, New York," *Progressive Architecture*, October 1962, pp. 158–65.

29 "TWA Spreads its Wings," *Progressive Architecture*, July 1962, p. 68.

30 "I Want to Catch the Excitement of the Trip," *Architectural Forum*, July 1962, p. 72.

31 Saarinen was quoted as calling it an "idyllic setting" in "Athens Airport Being Expanded, $10,000 Will be Spent to Meet Needs of Jet Age," *New York Times*, 6 August 1961, section V, p. 11, col. 4.

32 "Saarinen's Athens Airport, a Classic Pavilion," *Progressive Architecture*, August 1962, p. 51.

33 "Athens Airport Being Expanded," *New York Times*.

34 "Saarinen's Athens Air Terminal," *Architectural Record*, August 1962, p. 112.

35 The New York architect and planner Alex Washburne, who visited Greece every summer as a boy, shared this perception with the author on 26 October 2004.

36 "Airport Terminal Started in Athens," *New York Times*, 31 May 1962, p. 55, col. 1.

37 Interview with Gene Festa, New Haven, Connecticut, 5 February 2004.

38 Telephone interview with George Leventis of Langan Engineering in New York City who prepared the plan with professor Loudovikos Wasenhoven of the National Technical University of Athens, 28 October 2004. Professor Wasenhoven and his students then conducted additional studies.

39 Telephone interview with New York architect Theo David, 27 October 2004.

40 *Eero Saarinen on His Work*, p. 92.

41 "A New Airport for Jets," *Architectural Forum*, March 1960, p. 179.

42 "Saarinen's Terminal Building at the Dulles International Airport," *Architectural Forum*, September 1961, p. 111.

43 Although the Federal Aviation Agency (FAA) became the client, the commission was initially awarded to Ammann & Whitney by its predecessor, the Civil Aeronautics Administration (CAA). The original team consisted of Ammann & Whitney Engineers of New York, Eero Saarinen and Associates Architects of Bloomfield Hills, Michigan, Burns & McDonnell engineers of Kansas City, and planner Ellery Husted of Washington. Landrum & Brown of Cincinnati joined the team later, according to Walter McQuade,

"The Birth of an Airport," *Fortune*, March 1962, p. 96. The project manager was Kent Cooper of Eero Saarinen and Associates, Ellery Husted was associated architect, mechanical engineers were Burns and McDonnell, traffic and economic forecasts for airports by Charles Landrum of Landrum and Brown, lighting consultant Richard Kelly, landscape consultant Dan Kiley, contractor Corbette Construction Company, finishes by Humphrey & Harding. The FAA was the owner (now the Washington Metropolitan Airports Authority owns the airport). The enclosed area is 362,422 square feet, costing $16 million (according to US Congressional appropriations). The frame is reinforced concrete bush hammered with roof of precast concrete panels suspended on tension wires; the wall is glass in aluminum framing. These figures were published in "Portico to the Jet Age," *Architectural Forum*, July 1963, p. 82.

44 McQuade, p. 96.

45 *Eero Saarinen on His Work*, p. 96.

46 "Portico to the Jet Age," p. 72.

47 Ibid., p. 80.

48 Ibid., p. 79.

49 The airport is located 23 miles from Washington according to Frederick Gutheim, "D.C. Airport To Be Jet-Age Prototype," *Progressive Architecture*, May 1959, p. 109. However, the *AIA Journal* said it was 27 miles away ("Washington's New Jet Age International Airport," *AIA Journal*, March 1960, p. 33). In an earlier article *Architectural Forum* said it was 17 miles away ("Saarinen Designs Lounge-Bus for Chantilly Airport," *Architectural Forum*, May 1959, p. 9). It is so enormous (15 square miles) that it depends on whether you count the distance from the beginning, middle, or end of the property. Ronald Reagan National Airport has been enlarged and redesigned by former Saarinen associate Cesar Pelli in a manner, intended to reflect the Federal Style architecture of Washington, DC, that recalls nineteenth-century exhibition halls.

50 Herbert H. Howell quoted in McQuade, p. 96.

51 McQuade, p. 96.

52 "Saarinen's Terminal Building at the Dulles International Airport," p. 111.

53 Ibid.

54 McQuade, p. 95.

55 Ibid.

56 Henry-Russell Hitchcock, "American Architecture in the Early Sixties," *Zodiac* 10, 1962, p. 16.

57 "Portico to the Jet Age," p. 82.

58 *Eero Saarinen on His Work*, p. 96.

59 Interview with Kevin Roche by Tsukasa Yamashita in "Eero Saarinen," *Architecture + Urbanism*, April 1984, p. 20.

60 Edgar Kaufmann Jr., "Our Two Largest Airports: Critique," *Progressive Architecture*, August 1963, p. 94.

61 Peter Blake, "Save Dulles Airport!" *Interior Design*, October 1988, pp. 300–01.

62 "Eero Saarinen's Dulles Airport Wins AIA 25-Year Award," *Architecture*, May 1988, p. 43.

63 Allen Freeman, "SOM's Addition to Dulles International Airport Respects Eero Saarinen's Modern Masterpiece," *Architectural Record*, March 1997, pp. 62–67. "Ampliamento dell'aeroporto Dulles (1985–2004), *Casabella*, December 2001–January 2002, p. 36, appeared along with several other articles on Saarinen's airports, but it was very brief, only published in Italian, and mainly listed SOM's airport projects. A story on a design inspired by Dulles: "Copy Cat," *Architecture*, June 1998, p. 67, reported that Gensler's design for the new terminal at San Diego International Airport resembles Eero Saarinen's Dulles Airport. However, the resemblance is superficial.

64 "Landmarks: TWA Terminal, JFK," *Progressive Architecture*, May 1992, pp. 96–107; "TWA Trans World Airlines Flight Center/Kennedy Airport," *MAMA: Magasin för Modern Arkitektur* (Sweden), May 1992; Ahmed Sarbutu, "Expression und funktion: der TWA Terminal von Eero Saarinen in New York," *Archithese*, September–October 2002, pp. 32–35. The British architect Nigel Coates, discussing a new terminal at Heathrow in the *Independent* ("Coming to an Airport Near You," 17 August 2003), said, "In contrast to the extraordinary TWA Terminal at JFK, Eero Saarinen's archetypal but utterly untypical building, links the ground to the air and makes an effective link between the identity of New York and all its destinations. This building continues to celebrate the glamour of flying despite all the current pressure to sell and serve the passengers up to the hilt."

65 Joseph Giovannini, "Clipped Wings," *New York*, 10 September 2001, p. 172.

66 "Architects and Preservationists Rally for Saarinen's TWA Terminal," a report of a panel discussion at the Museum of Modern Art with Philip Johnson, Peter Samton, Robert A. M. Stern, and Agnes Gund, published in *Architectural Record*, September 2001, p. 13.

67 "TWA's Fight for Flight: What Preserves a Landmark Most?" *Architectural Record*, November 2001, pp. 63–66.

68 "Will This Bird Fly? Mark Lamster and Joseph Giovannini Debate the Port Authority's

Proposed Restoration of Eero Saarinen's Famed TWA Terminal," *Architecture*, December 2001, pp. 100, 104; "TWA Terminal Placed on National Trust's Endangered List," *Architectural Record*, July 2003, p. 36; Herbert Muschamp, "Architecture Hands Off the Baton to Preservation," *New York Times*, 4 April 2001; David W. Dunlap, "Unusual Planning Dual Over Kennedy Terminal," *New York Times*, 28 November 2002; Corey Gilgannon, "J.F.K. Project Would Reopen Famed Terminal," *New York Times*, 19 October 2003; Greg Sargent, "Airport Grab: Jet Blue Cramps TWA Jewel," *New York Observer*, 25 August 2003.

69 In an effort organized by preservationist Caroline Zaleski, testimonials came from architects Frederic Borel, Mario Botta, Henri Ciriani, Henri Gaudin, Richard Gluckman, Franck Hammoutene, Steven Holl, Philip Johnson, Masayuki Kurokawa, Greg Lynn, Jean Nouvel, Cesar Pelli, Dominique Perrault, Kevin Roche, Fred Schwartz, Francis Soler, Jean-Michel Wilmotte; professors Stanford Anderson, Carol Krinsky, Hélène Lipstadt, Peter Papademetriou; editor Karen Stein; curator and author Mildred Friedman, curator Paola Antonelli, representatives of the Art Center College of Design in Pasadena, California, various DOCOMOMO chapters, the Design Museum in London, the Mies van der Rohe Foundation in Barcelona, the Museum of Finnish Architecture, the Museum of Modern Art in New York, the University of Ljubljana in Slovenia, US/ICOMOS, and numerous other institutions internationally.

70 The Municipal Arts Society organized an exhibition of photographs of the TWA Terminal, and in October 2004 curator Rachel K. Ward organized an exhibition in the concourse, Terminal 5, with nineteen prominent artists from around the world participating. The building played a role in the 2002 Steven Spielberg movie *Catch Me If Can*. The Trans World Flight Center was the only terminal of its era included in an exhibition of "World Airports" at the German Architecture Museum in Frankfurt am Main, 29 June through 22 September 2002.

Postscript

1 Interview with Eric Saarinen, Venice, California, May 12, 2003.

2 The surgery, it turned out, was hopeless from the start. Aline requested the autopsy findings from Eero's doctor, Edgar A. Kahn, and was told in a letter of 11 September 1961, in the Manuscripts and Archives, Yale University Library (series IV, boxes 7 and 8: Letters of Condolence, folders 80-81): "There was a tumor well forward which infiltrated into both of the frontal lobes by way of what we call the corpus callosum. There was spread of the tumor far back into the left frontal lobe and this we had not even reached. It was the most malignant type of the tumors of the cerebral hemisphere. After seeing the post mortem examination, which meant a lot to us, I was doubly grateful that the end came so fast.

3 Letter from Peter Blake to Aline Saarinen, from Water Mill, Long Island, 1 September 1961.

4 Ada Louise Huxtable, "Eero Saarinen, 1919–1961," *New York Times*, 10 September 1961, II, p. 26.

5 Letter from Ada Louise Huxtable to Aline Saarinen, from New York City, 19 September 1961. The *Times* also ran a short story after his brain surgery on August 31 and a long obituary when he died the next day. "Saarinen Has Brain Surgery," *New York Times*, 1 September 1961, p. 8, col. 3; "Eero Saarinen, Architect, 51, is Dead," *New York Times*, 2 September 1961, p. 15, col. 1 (no author's name is included). Subheads continued, "Versatile Designer Created Terminal for T.W.A. Here and Embassies of U.S., Disciple of His Father, Received Many Awards—Worked With Mielziner on Lincoln Center Theatre." The article listed his buildings and projects, honors and awards, and concluded: "Perhaps as accurate a summation as any of the work of the architect was written in 1953 by the woman who became his second wife a year later." She wrote that his contribution was "in giving form or visual order to the industrial civilization to which he belongs, designing imaginatively and soundly within the new esthetics which the machine demands and allows. His buildings, which interlock form, honest functional solutions and structural clarity, become an expression of our way of life."

6 Huxtable, "Eero Saarinen, 1919–1961," p. 26, column 4.

7 Western Union Telegram from Olgivanna Lloyd Wright in Taliesin, in Spring Green, Wisconsin, 7 September, 4:03 p.m.

8 Letter from Olgivanna Lloyd Wright at Taliesin West, 26 September 1961.

9 Letter from Siasia Nowicki, Villanova, Pennsylvania, 4 September 1961.

10 Letter from Paul Rudolph from an airplane, 3 September 1961.

11 Letter from Philip Johnson, New York City, 8 September 1961.

12 Letter from Robert Osborn, no address, 21 September 1961, signed, "B."

13 She preserved the letters and donated them to the Manuscripts and Archives, Yale University Library.

14 Olga Gueft, "Eero Saarinen, 1910-1961," *Interiors*, November 1961, p.128.

15 Thomas H. Creighton, "A memorial service for Eero Saarinen," *Progressive*

Architecture, October 1961, p. 238.

16 Letter from Edgar Kaufmann, Jr., New York City, 4 September 1961. It was accompanied by a letter to Aline.

17 Lessing, "The Diversity of Eero Saarinen," p. 94.

18 Ibid., p. 95

19 Ibid., p. 96

20 Ibid.

21 "Obituary: Eero Saarinen," *Architectural Review*, November 1961, p. 301; Reyner Banham, "The Fear of Eero's Mana," *Arts Magazine*, February 1962, p. 73.

22 Statement from a lecture delivered at Dickinson College, December 1, 1959, reprinted in *Eero Saarinen on His Work*, p. 6.

23 Walter McQuade, "Eero Saarinen, A Complete Architect," *Architectural Forum*, April 1962, p. 104 (the article runs from pp. 103–127).

24 Ibid.

25 Ibid.

26 Ibid.

27 Ibid.

28 Nancy Lickerman Halik wrote an article on this legacy at a time when Eero Saarinen's name was not much in the news: "The Eero Saarinen Spawn," *Inland Architect*, May 1981, pp. 14–45. She identifies those she mentions as follows: Edward Charles Bassett (Skidmore, Owings, and Merrill, San Francisco); Bruce Adams (Bruce Adams and Associates, New Haven, Connecticut); J. Henderson Barr (the well known delineator and architect, now retired); Gunnar Birkerts (Gunnar Birkerts and Associates, Birmingham, Michigan), John Buenz (Solomon, Cordwell & Buenz, Chicago, Illinois); Robert Burley (Robert Burley Associates, Waitsfield, Vermont); Kevin Roche and John Dinkeloo (Kevin Roche, John Dinkeloo and Associates, Hamden, Connecticut); Balthazar Korab (Balthazar Korab, Ltd. Architectural Photographers, Troy, Michigan); Paul Kennon (Caudill, Rowlett, and Scott, Houston, Texas); Joe Lacy (retired partner of Eero Saarinen and Associates); Anthony Lumsden (Daniel, Mann, Johnson and Mendenhall, Los Angeles, California); Leonard Parker (Leonard S. Parker Associates, Minneapolis, Minnesota), Glen Paulsen (retired partner, Terapota, McMann and Paulsen, now TMP, Detroit, Michigan); Cesar Pelli (Cesar Pelli and Associates, New Haven, Connecticut); Warren Plattner (Warren Plattner and Associates, New Haven, Connecticut); and Robert Venturi (Venturi, Rauch, and Scott Brown, Philadelphia, Pennsylvania). Others included Gale Abels, Maurice Allen, Raymond Bean, Tom Bosworth, Gary Brown, Kent Cooper, Spiro Daltos, Claude DeForest, Alan Dehar, Bruce Detmers, Niels Different, Manuel Dumlao, Gene Festa, May Festa, Jack Goldman, Olav Hammarström, Hugh Hardy, Dave Hoedemaker, Nobuo Hozumi, Byron Ireland, David Jacob, Mark T. Jaroszewicz, Roger Johnson, Jill Mitchell, Anthony Moody, Peter Morton, Matthew Nowicki, John Owen, Norm Perttula, David Powrie, Harold Roth, Paul Rudolph (briefly), Edward Saad, Sig Schreiber, Doris Smith, Hamilton Pike Smith, Jimmy Smith, Peter van Dijk, Wilhelm von Moltke, John Ward, Merle Westlake, Robert Zielgelman, Lewis Zurlo and probably numerous others we have not identified. And there were many more people, such as James Addis, Bruce Albinson, Florence (Shu) Knoll Bassett, Gordon Bunshaft, Charles and Ray Eames, Ulrich Franzen, David Kahler, Dan Kiley, George Moon, Ralph Rapson, James Smith, Abba Tor, Minoru Yamasaki, who worked with Saarinen as members of other firms on various projects.

29 Maude Dorr, "Portraits in Architecture: a review of the most recent buildings of the late Eero Saarinen," *Industrial Design*, May 1963, p. 63.

30 *Eero Saarinen on His Work*.

31 Temko. There was a small, largely photographic book six years later: Rupert Spade and Yokio Futagawa, *Eero Saarinen*, and in the 1980s, an issue of *Architecture + Urbanism* devoted to Eero Saarinen: "Eero Saarinen," *Architecture + Urbanism*, April 1984, A+U Publishing Company, Tokyo) and an issue of the Yale architecture journal, Carol Burns and Robert Taylor co-editors, "Coming of Age: Eero Saarinen and Modern American Architecture," *Perspecta* 21 (Cambridge, Massachusetts: MIT Press, 1985).

32 The Museum of Finnish Architecture in Helsinki is organizing a major exhibition "Eero Saarinen, Realizing American Utopia," which will open in 2006, accompanied by a comprehensive illustrated catalogue. Researchers at Yale University are studying drawings and documents from the successor firm, Kevin Roche John Dinkeloo and Associates, which have been donated to the University archives, and a scholarly symposium is planned. A documentary film is being produced, as is a three-dimensional interactive installation and a dedicated website for the exchange of information. Also, there was a book two years ago that grew out of a Ph.D. dissertation in architectural theory illustrated with black-and-white period photographs: Antonio Román, *Eero Saarinen, An Architecture of Multiplicity* (New York: Princeton Architectural Press, 2003).

33 Another statement from a lecture delivered at Dickinson College, December 1, 1959, reprinted in *Eero Saarinen on His Work*, p. 5.

Buildings, Projects, and Furniture

Hvitträsk
Kirkkonummi, Finland, 1901–03
Gesellius, Lindgren, and Saarinen; remodeling of north wing after 1922 fire, 1929-37, Eero Saarinen

Cranbrook School
Bloomfield Hills, Michigan, 1925–30
Eliel Saarinen with Loja, Pipsan, and Eero Saarinen and Cranbrook Architecture Office; Eero designed the school seal, the crane insert for dining room chairs, sculptural tile reliefs for south lobby fireplace, sculptural stone caricatures for exterior walls of Page Hall, bronze decorations for iron gates, and columns for baldachini

Cranbrook Academy of Art, Art Museum, and Library
Bloomfield Hills, Michigan, 1926–42
Eliel Saarinen with the Cranbrook Architecture Office

Saarinen House
Bloomfield Hills, Michigan, 1928–30
Eliel Saarinen with Loja, Pipsan, and Eero Saarinen, who designed the master bedroom

Kingswood School
Bloomfield Hills, Michigan, 1929–31
Eliel Saarinen with Loja, Pipsan, and Eero Saarinen and the Cranbrook Architecture Office; Eero designed the auditorium and dining-hall chairs, and collaborated on stained-glass windows and light fixtures

Student projects at Yale University, 1931–34

Cranbrook Institute of Science
Bloomfield Hills, 1931–37
Eliel Saarinen with the Cranbrook Architecture Office

Helsinki Post Office and Telegraph competition scheme
Helsinki, Finland, 1934
Eero Saarinen, unbuilt

Swedish Theater addition
Helsinki, Finland, 1935–36
Eero Saarinen with Jarl Ecklund and Eliel Saarinen

The Forum (mixed-use commercial) project
Helsinki, Finland, 1935–37
Eero Saarinen

Aiko competition
Helsinki, Finland, 1936
Eero Saarinen

Flint Institute of Research and Planning
Cultural Center project
Flint, Michigan, 1936–37
Eero Saarinen under Edmund Bacon

"A Combined Living-Dining Room-Study, Designed for The Architectural Forum" project, 1937
Eero Saarinen

Community House
Fenton, Michigan, 1937–38
Saarinen and Saarinen

Spencer House
Huntington Woods, Michigan, 1937–38
Eero Saarinen

Koebel House
Grosse Point Farms, Michigan, 1937–40
Saarinen Swanson and Saarinen; Eliel and Eero Saarinen were involved in initial design but Robert Swanson saw it to completion and Pipsan Swanson designed interiors

General Motors Futurama Building, 1939 World's Fair
New York, New York, 1938
Norman Bel Geddes and Albert Kahn with Eero Saarinen, Caleb Hornbostel, Worthen Paxton, et al.

Goucher College campus plan and library competition scheme (placed second)
Towson, Maryland, 1938
Eliel and Eero Saarinen with Ralph Rapson and other Cranbrook students

Nikander Hall, Finlandia University (formerly Suomi College)
Lampeteer, Michigan, c. 1938
Saarinen and Saarinen [not in Yale catalogue]

Tanglewood "Shed" (now Koussevitzky Shed)
for the Berkshire Music Festival
Lenox, Massachusetts, 1938
Saarinen and Saarinen

Wheaton College Art Center competition scheme (placed fifth)
Norton, Massachusetts, 1938
Eero Saarinen

American National Theater at College of William and Mary competition scheme (placed first)
Williamsburg, Virginia, 1938–39
Eero Saarinen, Ralph Rapson, and Frederic James, unbuilt

Kleinhans Music Hall
Buffalo, New York, 1938–40
Saarinen and Saarinen with Kidd & Kidd

Crow Island School
Winnetka, Illinois, 1938–40
Saarinen and Saarinen with Perkins, Wheeler & Will

Exhibition installation for student work at Cranbrook Academy of Art
Bloomfield Hills, Michigan, 1939
Eero Saarinen and Charles Eames

Smithsonian Art Gallery competition scheme (placed first)
Washington, DC, 1939
Saarinen, Swanson, and Saarinen, unbuilt

Tabernacle Church of Christ (now First Christian Church)
Columbus, Indiana, 1939–42
Saarinen and Saarinen with E.D. Pierre and George Wright Associate Architects

"Organic Design in Home Furnishings" for the Museum of Modern Art exhibition
New York, New York, 1940
Eero Saarinen, Charles Eames, et al.

"Demountable Space" Community House project for US Gypsum Company, 1940
Eero Saarinen

Hall Auditorium, Theater and Inn competition project
Oberlin College, Oberlin, Ohio, 1941
Saarinen and Saarinen, unbuilt

Opera Shed (Theater-Concert Hall) and Chamber Music Shed for the Berkshire Music Center
Lenox, Massachusetts, 1941
Saarinen and Saarinen

Samuel Bell House project
New Hope, Pennsylvania, c. 1941
Saarinen and Saarinen, unbuilt

A.C. Wermuth Residence
Fort Wayne, Indiana, 1941–42
Saarinen and Saarinen

Center Line Defense Housing (later Kramer Homes)
Center Line, Michigan, 1941–42
Saarinen, Swanson, and Saarinen; altered incrementally from the 1960s onward

American Museum of Natural History alteration project
New York, New York, 1942
Eliel and Eero Saarinen, unbuilt

Unfolding House project, 1942
Eero Saarinen, unbuilt

Willow Run War Workers Housing and Town Center Plan
Ypsilanti, Michigan, 1942–43
Saarinen, Swanson, and Saarinen, town center unbuilt, Willow Lodge demolished

Grasshopper Chair, 1943
Eero Saarinen with Florence (Shu) Schust Knoll

PAC System for Arts & Architecture's Designs for Postwar Living Housing Competition, 1943
Eero Saarinen and Oliver Lundquist, unbuilt

Detroit Civic Center project
Detroit, Michigan, 1943-51
Saarinen, Swanson and Saarinen, unbuilt

Army Troop Control brochure for Office of Strategic Services
Washington, DC, 1944
Eero Saarinen

War Room for the White House design, 1944
Eero Saarinen

Legislative Palace competition scheme
Quito, Ecuador, 1944
Eero Saarinen (Eliel Saarinen also submitted a scheme)

Serving Suzy Restaurant and Gift Shop projects, 1944
Saarinen, Swanson, and Saarinen, unbuilt

Lincoln Heights Housing for National Capital Housing Authority
Washington, DC, c. 1944
Saarinen, Swanson, and Saarinen

Antioch College campus plan
Yellow Springs, Ohio, 1944-45
Eero Saarinen with Saarinen, Swanson, and Saarinen and Max B. Mercer

Hugh Taylor Birch Hall dormitory, Antioch College
Yellow Springs, Ohio, 1944–47
Saarinen, Swanson, and Saarinen

Des Moines Art Center
Des Moines, Iowa, 1944–48
Eliel Saarinen with Saarinen and Swanson

Chicago City Plan
Chicago, Illinois, 1945
Eliel Saarinen, unbuilt

General Motors Technical Center project
Warren, Michigan, 1945–46
Saarinen, Swanson, and Saarinen, unbuilt

"Integrated Building: Planning Kitchen, Bathroom and
Storage Space" exhibition, Museum of Modern Art
New York, New York, 1945
Eero Saarinen

Drake University Campus Expansion Plan
Des Moines, Iowa, 1945–47
Saarinen and Saarinen

Fort Wayne Art School and Museum project
Fort Wayne, Indiana, 1945–47
Eliel Saarinen, unbuilt

Stephens College Campus Plan
Columbia, Missouri, 1945–47
Saarinen and Saarinen

Case Study House Number 8 (Eames House)
Pacific Palisades, California, 1945–48
Designed by Eero Saarinen and Charles Eames;
built differently by Charles and Ray Eames

Case Study House Number 9 (Entenza House)
Pacific Palisades, California, 1945–49
Eero Saarinen and Charles Eames

Drake University Pharmacy Building
Des Moines, Iowa, 1945–50
Saarinen and Saarinen

Birmingham High School (later Seaholm School)
Birmingham, Michigan, 1945–52
Saarinen, Swanson and Saarinen
(built by Swanson Associates)

Drake University Dormitories and Dining Hall
Des Moines, Iowa, 1945–55
Eero Saarinen and Associates

Knoll International Chairs Models 71, 72 and 75
1945–59
partially realized, Eero Saarinen

Christ Church project
Cincinnati, Ohio, 1946
Saarinen and Saarinen, built in altered form by David
Briggs Maxwell, 1957

Milwaukee War Memorial project
Milwaukee, Wisconsin, 1946
Saarinen, Swanson, and Saarinen
Washtenaw County Master Plan (home of Ann Arbor)
Washtenaw County, Michigan, 1946, unbuilt

Stephens College Campus Plan
Columbia, Missouri, 1946–50
Saarinen and Saarinen

Stephens College Chapel project
Columbia, Missouri, 1946–50
Saarinen and Saarinen

Womb Chair for Knoll International, 1946–48
Eero Saarinen

Detroit Riverfront Plan project
Detroit, Michigan, 1946–49
Saarinen and Saarinen

Bloomfield Hills General Development Plan
Bloomfield Hills, Michigan, 1947, unbuilt

Louisiana State University Plan
Baton Rouge, Louisiana, 1947
Saarinen Swanson and Saarinen,
built in modified form

Jefferson Memorial Competition scheme (placed first)
Saint Louis, Missouri, 1947–48
Eero Saarinen with J. Henderson Barr, Alexander
Girard, Dan Kiley, and Lily Swann Saarinen
(Eliel Saarinen also submitted a scheme)

Saint Louis Gateway Arch (Jefferson National
Expansion Memorial)
Saint Louis, Missouri, 1947–65, dedicated
1968Eero Saarinen and Associates with Dan Kiley

Christ Church Lutheran
Minneapolis, Minnesota, 1947–49;
alterations 1956, 1959; addition 1962
Saarinen and Saarinen; alterations by
Eero Saarinen and Associates

General Motors Technical Center
Warren, Michigan, 1948–56
Eero Saarinen and Associates with Smith,
Hinchman & Grylls, Architect-Engineers

Eero Saarinen House renovation
Vaughn Road, Bloomfield Hills, Michigan, 1947–59
Eero Saarinen

Houston Estate project
Cathedral Hills, Pennsylvania, 1948
Saarinen, Swanson and Saarinen, unbuilt

Los Angeles Auditorium and Opera House project
Los Angeles, California, 1948
Henry Dreyfuss, Gordon B. Kaumann, William
Rice Pereira, Eero Saarinen, William Wurster and
Wallace K. Harrison, unbuilt

UAW CIO Cooperative
Flint, Michigan, 1948
Eero Saarinen, demolished

General Motors Technical Center
Warren, Michigan, 1948–56
Eero Saarinen and Associates with Smith,
Hinchman & Grylls, Architect-Engineers

Music Tent for Goethe Bicentennial Convocation
and Music Festival
Aspen, Colorado, 1949; demolished 1963
Saarinen and Saarinen

Brandeis University Ridgewood Quadrangle dormitories
Waltham, Massachusetts, 1949–50
Eero Saarinen and Associates

Brandeis University Campus Plan
Waltham, Massachusetts, 1949–52
Eero Saarinen and Associates with Matthew Nowicki

Brandeis University Hamilton Quadrangle
dormitories, dining, and social buildings (later Shapiro
Hall and Sherman Student center)
Waltham, Massachusetts, 1949–52
Eero Saarinen and Associates

Yale University Master Plan
New Haven, Connecticut, 1949–53
Eero Saarinen and Associates

Yale University Physics Building project
New Haven, Connecticut, 1949–53
Eero Saarinen and Associates with Douglas Orr

Loja Saarinen House (Eero Saarinen Guest House)
Bloomfield Hills, Michigan, 1950
Eero Saarinen

Number 71 Armchair, c. 1950, Eero Saarinen

Number 72 Side Chair, c. 1950, Eero Saarinen

Miller Cottage (Miller House)
Lake Muskoka, Ontario, Canada, 1950–52
Eero Saarinen and Associates

Irwin Union Bank & Trust Company
Columbus, Indiana, 1950–54
Eero Saarinen and Associates

Kresge Auditorium at the Massachusetts
Institute of Technology (MIT)
Cambridge, Massachusetts, 1950–55
Eero Saarinen and Associates with Anderson & Beckwith

Kresge Chapel at MIT
Cambridge, Massachusetts, 1950–55
Eero Saarinen and Associates with Anderson & Beckwith

Student Center at MIT project
Cambridge, Massachusetts, 1953
Eero Saarinen and Associates, unbuilt

University of Michigan North Campus
Development Plan
Ann Arbor, Michigan, 1951–56
Eero Saarinen and Associates

University of Michigan Engineering Lab Group project
1951, 1956, unbuilt

American Embassy Addition project
Helsinki, Finland, 1952–53
Eero Saarinen and Associates, unbuilt

Chicago Tribune Sixth Annual Better Rooms
Competition project, 1952
Eero Saarinen and Associates, unbuilt

Time, Inc. Headquarters project
Rye, New York, 1952
Eero Saarinen and Associates, unbuilt

Drake University Theological School and Chapel
Des Moines, Iowa, 1952–56
Eero Saarinen and Associates

University of Michigan School of Music
Ann Arbor, Michigan, 1952–56
Eero Saarinen and Associates with the
university's Supervising Architect's Office

Milwaukee War Memorial (now Milwaukee
Art Museum)
Milwaukee, Wisconsin, 1952–57
Eero Saarinen and Associates

Eero Saarinen and Associates Office
Long Lake Road, Bloomfield Hills, Michigan, 1953
Eero Saarinen and Associates

UNESCO Competition project
Paris, France, 1953
Eero Saarinen, built to a design by Marcel Breuer,
Pier Liugi Nervi and Bernard Zehrfuss with Eero
Saarinen as design consultant

University of Michigan Continuation Center project,
1953
Eero Saarinen and Associates, unbuilt

University of Michigan Cooley Memorial project, 1953
Eero Saarinen and Associates, unbuilt

University of Michigan Dexter House
Development project, 1953
Eero Saarinen and Associates, unbuilt

University of Michigan Fletch Park Extension project,
1953
Eero Saarinen and Associates, unbuilt

Stephens College Chapel
Columbia, Missouri, 1953–56
Eero Saarinen and Associates

Irwin and Xenia Miller House
Columbus, Indiana, 1953–57
Eero Saarinen and Associates

Concordia Senior College (now
Concordia Theological Seminary)
Fort Wayne, Indiana, 1953–58
Eero Saarinen and Associates

Callahan House project
Birmingham, Alabama, 1954
Eero Saarinen and Associates, unbuilt

Time, Inc. Headquarters project
Pennsylvania, 1954
Eero Saarinen and Associates with Paul Rudolph

University of Michigan Aeronautical Engineering
Building project, 1954
Eero Saarinen and Associates, unbuilt

University of Michigan Central Service Stack
Building project, 1954
Eero Saarinen and Associates, unbuilt

University of Michigan Highway project, 1954
Eero Saarinen and Associates, unbuilt

University of Michigan Phoenix Building project, 1954
Eero Saarinen and Associates, unbuilt

University of Michigan Printing Building project, 1954
Eero Saarinen and Associates, unbuilt

University of Michigan Undergraduate Library project,
1954
Eero Saarinen and Associates, unbuilt

Pedestal Chairs for Knoll International, c. 1954–57
Eero Saarinen and Associates

Pedestal Tables for Knoll International, c. 1954–57
Eero Saarinen and Associates

Emma Hartman Noyes House (Dormitory),
Vassar College
Poughkeepsie, New York, 1954–58
Eero Saarinen and Associates

General Motors House of Tomorrow project
Warren, Michigan, 1954
Eero Saarinen and Associates, unbuilt

Greenwich Station project
Greenwich, Connecticut, 1955
Eero Saarinen and Associates, unbuilt

University of Michigan Children's Hospital project,
1955
Eero Saarinen and Associates, unbuilt

University of Chicago Development Planning Project
Chicago, Illinois, 1955
Eero Saarinen and Associates

University of Chicago Women's Dormitory and
Dining Hall
Chicago, Illinois, 1955–58
Eero Saarinen and Associates

United States Chancellery Building
Oslo, Norway, 1955–59
Eero Saarinen and Associates with Engh,
Quam & Kiaer

United States Chancellery Building
London, England, 1955–60
Eero Saarinen and Associates with Yorke,
Rosenberg, and Mardall

University of Chicago Law School
Chicago, Illinois, 1955–60
Eero Saarinen and Associates

International Business Machines Manufacturing
and Training Facility
Rochester, Minnesota, 1956–58
Eero Saarinen and Associates, continually expanded

David S. Ingalls Hockey Rink, Yale University
New Haven, Connecticut, 1956–58
Eero Saarinen and Associates

International Business Machines
Thomas J. Watson Research Center
Yorktown, New York, 1956–61
Eero Saarinen and Associates

Trans World Airlines Terminal, New York International
(Idlewild) Airport (now John F. Kennedy Airport)
New York, New York, 1956–62
Eero Saarinen and Associates

Drake University Women's Residence Dormitory
Number 4 and Jewitt Union Addition
Des Moines, Iowa, 1957

Hill Hall Women's (now co-ed) Residence Hall,
University of Pennsylvania
Philadelphia, Pennsylvania, 1957–60
Eero Saarinen and Associates

International Business Machines Thomas J. Watson
Research Center
Yorktown, New York, 1957–61
Eero Saarinen and Associates

Bell Telephone Corporation Laboratories
Holmdel, New Jersey, 1957–62
Eero Saarinen and Associates

Deere & Company Administrative Center
Moline, Illinois, 1957–63
Eero Saarinen and Associates

Samuel F. B. Morse and Ezra Stiles Colleges (New
Colleges), Yale University
New Haven, Connecticut, 1958–62
Eero Saarinen and Associates

Dulles International Airport
Chantilly, Virginia, 1958–63
Eero Saarinen and Associates with Ammann & Whitney,
Architect-Engineers, and Ellery Husted Associate Arch-
itect, expanded by Skidmore, Owings & Merrill 1996

Vivian Beaumont Repertory Theater Lincoln Center
for the Performing Arts
New York, New York, 1958–65
Eero Saarinen and Associates with Jo Mielziner;
Skidmore, Owings & Merrill designed the
Library-Museum of the Performing Arts in the
same building

North Christian Church
Columbus, Indiana, 1959–64
Eero Saarinen and Associates

World Health Organization competition scheme
(placed second)
Geneva, Switzerland, 1960
Eero Saarinen and Associates

Hamden Office of Eero Saarinen and Associates
Hamden, Connecticut, 1960–61
Eero Saarinen and Associates

Saarinen House Renovation, New Haven, Connecticut,
1960-61, Eero Saarinen

Columbia Broadcasting System Headquarters
New York, New York, 1960–65
Eero Saarinen and Associates

Athens International Airport
Athens, Greece, 1960–69
Eero Saarinen and Associates with
Ammann & Whitney, Architect-Engineers

Bibliography

BOOKS

Christ-Janer, Albert, *Eliel Saarinen, Finnish-American Architect and Educator*. Chicago and London: University of Chicago Press, 1948; revised edition with a foreword by Alvar Aalto, 1984.

Hall, Edward and Margaret, *The Fourth Dimension in Architecture: The Impact of Building on Man's Behavior*. Santa Fe, New Mexico: Sunstone Press, 1975.

Hausen, Marika, Kirmo Mikkola, Anna-Lisa Amberg, and Tytti Valto, *Eliel Saarinen Projects 1896–1923*. Cambridge, Massachusetts: MIT Press, 1990.

Kiley, Dan and Jane Amidon, *Dan Kiley: The Complete Works of America's Master Landscape Architect*. Boston, New York, London: Bulfinch Press, Little Brown and Company, 1999.

Larrabee, Eric and Massimo Vignelli, *Knoll Design*. New York: Harry N. Abrams, 1981.

Loeffler, Jane C., *The Architecture of Diplomacy*. New York: Princeton Architectural Press, 1998.

Martin, Reinhold, *The Organizational Complex: Architecture, Media, and Corporate Space*. Cambridge, Massachusetts: MIT Press, 2003.

Parvey, Constance, *Crossroads for a New Civilization: Notes on Eero Saarinen*. New Haven: Yale University Press, 1965.

Pinnell, Patrick L., *The Campus Guide: Yale University*. New York: Princeton Architectural Press, 1999.

Peter, John, *The Oral History of Modern Architecture, Interviews with the Greatest Architects of the Twentieth Century*. New York: Harry N. Abrams, 1994.

Román, Antonio, *Eero Saarinen, An Architecture of Multiplicity*. New York: Princeton Architectural Press, 2003.

Saarinen, Aline B., ed., *Eero Saarinen on His Work*. London and New Haven: Yale University Press, 1962.

Saarinen, Eliel, *The City: Its Growth, Its Decay, Its Future*. New York: Rheinhold, 1943.
Nakamura, Toshio, Nobuo Hozumi, and Tsukasa Yamashita, "Eero Saarinen," *Architecture + Urbanism*. Tokyo: A+U Publishing Company, 1984.

Spade, Rupert and Yokio Futagawa, *Eero Saarinen*. New York: Simon and Schuster, Library of Contemporary Architects, 1968.

Stoller, Ezra and Mark Lamster, *The TWA Terminal*. New York: Princeton Architectural Press, 1999.

Taideteoksena, Kofi, *Hvitträsk, The Home as a Work of Art*. Helsinki: Otava Publishing Company, 2000.

Temko, Allan, *Eero Saarinen*. New York: George Braziller, "Makers of Contemporary Architecture" series, 1962.

Young, Edgar B., *Lincoln Center, the Building of an Institution*. New York and London: New York University Press, 1980.

EXHIBITION CATALOGUES

Clark, Robert Judson, David G. De Long, Martin Eidelberg, J. David Farmer, John Gerard, Neil Harris, Joan Marter, R. Craig Miller, Mary Riordan, Roy Slade, Davira S. Taragin, and Christa C. Mayer Thurman, *Design in America, The Cranbrook Vision 1925–50*. New York: Harry N. Abrams in association with the Detroit Institute of Arts and the Metropolitan Museum of Art, 1983.

Drexler, Arthur, *Architecture And Imagery—Four New Buildings* [The National Opera House in Sydney, Australia, by Jorn Utzon; Notre Dame de Royan in France by Guillaume Gillet; First Presbyterian Church in Stanford, California, by Harrison & Abramovitz; the TWA Terminal at Kennedy Airport, New York, by Eero Saarinen]. New York: Museum of Modern Art, 1959.

Kornwolf, James D., ed., *Modernism in America, 1937–1941* [a catalog and exhibition of four architectural competitions: Wheaton College, Goucher College, College of William and Mary, Smithsonian Institution]. Williamsburg, Virginia: Joseph and Margaret Muscarelle Museum of Art, College of William and Mary, 1985.

Lorenz, Ann, *Brandeis Under Construction* [an exhibition at Brandeis University Rose Art Museum. 13 May–1 October 1972, organized by the Poses Institute of Fine Arts, curated with the guidance of professor Gerald Bernstein, under Rose Museum of Art director Michael J. Wentworth; Ann Lorenz's essay is based on interviews with Max Abramovitz, Archie Riskin, Chancellor Sachar, and Gerry Schiff of Harrison & Abramovitz

Noyes, Eliot F., *Organic Design in Home Furnishings*. New York: Museum of Modern Art, 1941.

Kleinhans Music Hall, a brochure published by the Kleinhans Music Hall, Buffalo, New York, July 1945

Price, Cathy, ed., *Saarinen Swanson Reunion Proceedings*. Bloomfield Hills, Michigan: Cranbrook Educational Community, 2001.

PERIODICALS

The following list has been selected from the hundreds of articles in magazines and journals that were used to illuminate the text and are cited in the notes. These publications are of a general nature and were particularly influential.

Banham, Reyner, "Fear of Eero's Mana," *Arts Magazine*, February 1962, pp. 70–73

Caplan, R., "Medium" [on Saarinen, Eero, 1910–1961], *Industrial Design*, January 1963, pp. 85–6

Carter, Peter, "Eero Saarinen, 1910–61," *Architectural Design*, December 1961, p. 537

Dean, Andrea O., "Eero Saarinen in Perspective," *AIA Journal*, November 1981, pp. 36–51

Halik, Nancy I., "The Eero Saarinen Spawn," *Inland Architect*, May 1981, pp. 14–45

Lessing, Lawrence, "The Diversity of Eero Saarinen," *Architectural Forum*, July 1960, pp. 94–103

Louchheim, Aline B., "Now Saarinen the Son," *New York Times Magazine*, 28 April 1953, pp. 26–27, 44–45

McQuade, Walter, "Eero Saarinen, A Complete Architect," *Architectural Forum*, April 1962, pp. 102–19.

Moholy-Nagy, Sibyl, "The Future of the Past: Cantus Firmus of Eero Saarinen," *Perspecta* 7, 1961, pp. 65–76.

Papademetriou, Peter, "Coming of Age: Eero Saarinen and Modern American Architecture," in Carol Burns and Robert Taylor (coeditors), *Perspecta* 21. Cambridge, Massachusetts: MIT Press, 1985, pp. 116–43.
Papademetriou, Peter C., "On Becoming a Modern Architect: Eero Saarinen's Early Work 1928–1948," *Oz, Journal of the University of Kansas*, May 1987

Saarinen, Eero, "Campus Planning: The Unique World of the University," *Architectural Record*, November 1960, pp. 123–30

Saarinen, Eero, *Foundation for Learning—Planning the Campus of Brandeis University*, November 1949, pp. 313–26

Saarinen, Eero, "Our Epoch of Architecture, text of a speech," *AIA Journal*, December 1952, pp. 243–47

Saarinen, Eero, "Six Broad Currents of Modern Architecture," *Architectural Forum*, July 1953, pp. 110–15.

Saarinen, Eero, "What Is Architecture?" *Perspecta* 7, 1961, pp. 29–42.

Saarinen, Eero, Jose Luis Sert, and William Wurster, "Changing Philosophy of Architecture," *Architectural Record*, August 1954, pp. 180–83

"Maturing Modern" [cover story on Eero Saarinen], *Time*, 2 July 1956, pp. 50–57.

Index

A

Aalto, Alvar, 28, 31, 36, 37, 49, 56, 75, 113, 175
Abramovitz, Max, 109, 175, 177, 178
Académie de la Grande Chaumière, 35
Adams, Bruce, 114, 161
AIA. *See* American Institute of Architects
Albinson, Don, 56
Alexander, W.B., 105
Allen, Maurice, 178
American Gas Association, 21
American Institute of Architects (AIA), 99, 166, 169, 180
American National Theater and Academy, 45
Ammann & Whitney, 209, 213, 216
Anderson, Beckwith & Haible, 115
Anderson, Lawrence B., 113, 115
Antioch College (Yellow Springs, Ohio), 72, 104–6, 133
Architects Collaborative, 50
Architectural Design, 92, 210
Architectural Forum, 40, 45, 46, 48, 49, 76, 80, 99, 108, 115, 118, 121, 123, 134, 138, 161, 168, 191, 192, 195, 206, 208, 210, 213, 217, 219, 222, 231
Architectural Record, 80, 106, 119, 123, 138, 164, 168, 195
Architectural Review, 164, 210
Architecture and Building News, 80
L'Architecture d'aujourd'hui, 80
L'Architettura, 117, 118
Art in America, 80
Art News, 196
Arts & Architecture, 59, 63
Aspen Music Tent, 66, 67, 109, 212
Asplund, Gunnar, 36
Athens International Airport, 213, 216, 217
Atkinson, Fello, 163, 164

B

Bacon, Edmund N., 42
Bagenal, Hope, 175
Baldwin, Benjamin, 37
Banham, Reyner, 165
Barnes, Edward Larrabee, 161
Barr, Alfred, 45, 181
Barr, J. Henderson, 66, 107, 195
Bassett, Charles, 75, 161
Bassett, Florence. *See* Knoll Bassett, Florence (Shu)
Bauhaus, 56, 57
Beckwith, Herbert L., 113, 115
Behrendt, Walter Curt, 45
Bel Geddes, Norman, 46, 70, 103
Bell Telephone Laboratories (Holmdel, New York), 6, 46, 85, 89, 91–93, 94, 95, 106, 136, 180
Belluschi, Pietro, 113, 161, 166, 175
Bennett, Richard M., 45, 169
Berke, Deborah, 161
Berkowitz, David, 106, 109
Bernardi, Theodore, 63
Bernstein, Aline. *See* Saarinen, Aline
Bertoia, Harry, 37, 55, 56, 73, 168
Beyer Blinder Belle, 227
Billings, Henry, 196
Birkerts, Gunnar, 75, 161, 181, 192
Blake, Peter, 196, 198, 227, 230
Bodouva, William Nicholas, 227
Bolt, Beranek & Newman, 115, 153
Bolt, Richard, 115, 175
Booth, Ellen, 22–23, 25
Booth, George, 21, 22–24, 25, 50–52, 69
Booth, Henry Scripps, 23
Bosworth, Welles, 113
Brandeis University (Waltham, Massachusetts), 104, 106–11, 114, 133, 134

Breuer, Caleb, 45
Breuer, Marcel, 28, 45, 56, 175
Broms, Selma (mother), 12
Brooks-Borg Architects, 105
Brown, Bill, 113
Buck, Norman, 125
Bunshaft, Gordon, 45, 166, 175, 177, 178, 180
Burley, Bob, 165, 201
Burns & McDonnell, 216
Burrowes, Marcus, 22

C

Calatrava, Santiago, 192, 194, 233
Calder, Alexander, 35, 73
Carter, Peter, 181
Case Study House program (Pacific Palisades, California), 63, 64, 65, 66–67
Cavin, Brooks, 62
CBS. *See* Columbia Broadcasting System Building
Christ-Janer, Albert, 31
Civil Aeronautics Administration (CAA), 219
Clarke, Gilmore D., 196
Clay, George, 212
Cobbs, Henry I., 140, 141
Coir, Mark, 52
College of William and Mary, 45, 103, 104
Colquhoun, Alan, 210, 212
Columbia Broadcasting System (CBS) Building (New York), 6, 172, 181–86
"Combined Living-Dining Room-Study, Designed for The Architectural Forum, A", 40, 43
Community House, 43
Compton, Karl Taylor, 113
Concordia College Chapel, 160
Concordia Senior College (Fort Wayne, Indiana), 133–38
Concordia Theological Seminary. *See* Concordia Senior College
Conway, Patricia, 186
Cooper, Kent, 217
Corbusier, Le, 31, 32, 56, 113, 117
Corfield, H.J., 22
Cor-Ten Steel, 7, 95, 96, 100
Cranbrook Educational Community (Bloomfield Hills, Michigan)
    about, 21–33
    Cranbrook Academy of Art, 24–25, 31–37
    Cranbrook Institute of Science, 28–31
    Cranbrook School, 23–24
Creighton, Thomas, 231
Crosbie, Michael J., 200
Crosby, Sumner McK., 125
Crow Island School, 46
Cummins Engine Foundation, 8, 161

D

Daltas, Spiro, 165
David S. Ingalls Hockey Rink, Yale University (New Haven, Connecticut), 83 123–31, 126, 127, 128–29, 130, 133, 153, 198, 210, 212, 222
Dawson, Ralph, 205
Dawson, Sasaki, 110
Deere & Company (Moline, Illinois), 6, 8, 46, 85, 95–101, 136, 154, 182, 186
Defense Housing for Kramer Homes (Center Line, Michigan), 40, 49, 86
DeMars, Vernon, 110, 113
Demountable Space, 56
Designs for Postwar Living competition, 59
Detmers, Bruce, 200, 201
Detroit Civic Center, 85
Detroit Museum of Art, 22
Detroit Riverfront plan, 15, 53
Detroit School of Design, 22
Diffrient, Niels, 56, 59
Dinkeloo, John, 75, 86, 95, 96, 161, 182, 201
Disciples of Christ, 158, 160
Dorr, Maude, 232

Drake University, 72, 85, 102, 104, 105, 107, 133
Dreyfuss, Henry, 95
Dulles International Airport (Chantilly, Virginia), 62, 180, 216–26
Dyssen and Arerhoff, 206

E

Eames, Charles, 37, 42, 46, 48, 52, 54, 55, 56, 59, 60, 62, 63, 67, 86, 107, 196, 222
Eames, Ray, 37, 56, 62, 63, 222
Eames House, 63
Earl, Harley, 69, 79
Eklund, Jarl, 36–37
Eero Saarinen and Associates Office, 76, 79, 80
Ehrman, Marli, 56
Eisenman, Peter, 161
Ellwood, Craig, 63
Embassies. *See* United States Chancellery
Emma Hartman Noyes House, Vassar College (Poughkeepsie, New York), 138
Entenza, John, 63, 66
Ethyl Corporation, 69

F

Feiss, Carl, 55
Ferriss, Hugh, 70
Festa, Gene, 169, 180, 216
Festival Theater for the College of William and Mary, 42, 43
Fiberglass furniture, 57
Finlandia University (Hancock, Michigan), 43
Finnish National Museum, 13
First Baptist Church (Flint, Michigan), 49
Fletcher, Norman, 50
Flint Institute of Research and Planning, 42
Foreign Buildings Operation (FBO), State Department, 165–68, 169
France, Anatole, 13
Franz, Joseph, 46
Frosterus, Sigurd, 13
Fry, Lynn W., 121
Fuller, Buckminster, 56

G

Gass, William, 200–201
Geery, Dave, 134
Gehry, Frank, 87, 228, 233
General Motors Technical Center (Warren, Michigan), 6, 68, 69–75, 76, 77, 78, 80, 81, 82, 83, 85, 106, 113, 115, 118, 136, 153, 154, 212
Gesellius, Herman, 12, 13, 14
Gesellius, Loja, 13, 14, 23, 24, 55
Giacometti, Alberto, 35
Giedion, Sigfried, 118, 194
Giovannini, Joseph, 227
Girard, Alexander, 97, 153, 161, 195
Glydén, Mathilda (Eliel's first wife), 13, 14
Goldberger, Paul, 194
Goldstein, Israel, 106
Goodman, Percival, 45, 196
Goodwin, Philip L., 45
Goodyear, A. Conger, 45
Gorki, Maxim, 11
Grasshopper Chair, 57
Green, Robert A., 45
Griswold, A. Whitney, 123, 125, 232
Gropius, Walter, 35, 45, 48, 50, 181, 196
Grove Shepherd Wilson & Kruge, 209
Gueft, Olga, 178

H

Hadid, Zaha, 233
Halaby, Najeeb, 223
Hamilton, George Heard, 125
Hamlin, Talbot, 43

Hammarström, Olav, 75, 165
Hammond, Beeby and Babka, 161
Hardy, Holzman, Pfeiffer, 161
Hare, Herbert, 195
Harkness, John, 50
Harmon, Henry Gadd, 105
Harrison, Wallace, 57, 107, 109, 174–75, 177, 178
Harrison & Abramovitz, 86, 109, 110, 166, 181
Hartwell, Frances W., 45
Haskelite Corporation, 56
Haskell, Douglas, 161
Hayes, Hal, 227
Hays, Wayne L., 169
Heifetz, Jascha, 46
Helsinki Polytechnical Institute, 12
Helsinki Post Office, 43
Helsinki Railroad Station, 13, 15
Hewitt, William A., 8, 95, 182
Heywood-Wakefield Company, 56
Hitchcock, Henry-Russell, 223
Hoffmann, Josef, 32
Holabird, John H., 48
Houghton, Arthur, 174
Howard, Coy, 161
Howe, George, 45, 48, 195, 196
Howell, Herbert H., 219
Hozumi, Nobu, 83
Hudnut, Joseph, 45, 48
Hugh Taylor Birch Hall, Antioch College, 104
Huxtable, Ada Louise, 177, 186, 230

I

IBM (International Business Machines), 6, 136
IBM Manufacturing and Administrative Center (Rochester), 8, 83, 85, 86, 87, 88, 90
Thomas J. Watson Research Center (Yorktown, New York), 8, 46, 85, 86, 89–90, 92, 106, 180
Imperial Alexander University, 12
Ingalls, Louise, 125, 126
"Integrated Building: Planning Kitchen, Bathroom And Storage Space" exhibition, 62
Interiors, 178, 212, 231
International Business Machines. *See* IBM
Ireland, Byron, 201
Irwin Miller House (Columbus, Indiana), 83, 154–58, 213
Irwin Union Bank & Trust Company (Columbus, Indiana), 153–54

J

Jackson, Huson, 62, 164
Jacob, David, 217
Jacobus, John, 100–101
James, Frederic, 43, 45, 103, 178
Jaroszewicz, Mark T., 107–8
Jefferson National Expansion Memorial Association, 194–95
Jensen, Georg, 138
Johansen, John M., 161
John F. Kennedy (JFK) Airport. *See* Trans World Airlines Terminal (TWA)
Johnson, Philip, 43, 175, 177, 178, 180, 181, 210
Jones, Susan, 63
Jordan, R. Furneaux, 165

K

Kahler, Slater & Fitzhugh Scott, 192
Kahn, Albert, 22, 69, 70, 72
Kahn, Ely Jacques, 31
Kahn, Louis I., 6, 106, 168, 196, 212, 232
Kaufmann, Edgar, Jr., 210, 212–13, 226, 231
Kayer, Jada, 111
Kazan, Elia, 177
Kennedy, Robert, 113
Kennon, Paul, 75, 217
Kenworthy, Nelson A., 166

Kettering, Charles, 69, 79
Kevin Roche John Dinkeloo and Associates, 180. *See* also Roche, Kevin
Kidd & Kidd, 46
Kiley, Dan, 50, 53, 104, 138, 153, 154, 155, 157–58, 178, 195, 201, 203, 227
Killian, James R., Jr., 113
Kim, Susie, 161
Kimball, Fiske, 195
King, Leland N., 165
Kingswood School for Girls, 25, 26, 35, 153
Klauder, Charles, 140
Kleinhans Music Hall, 191
Knight, Carleton, III, 161
Knoll, Hans, 57, 59
Knoll Bassett, Florence (Shu), 37, 42, 55, 57, 59, 77, 80, 186
Knoll International design program, 55
Knoll, 182, 186, 213
Koch, Carl, 113, 134, 196
Koenig, Pierre, 63
Koolhaas, Rem, 226
Korab, Balthazar, 83, 155, 181
Koussevitzky, Serge, 46, 67
Koussevitzky Shed. *See* Tanglewood "Shed"
Kramer Homes. *See* Defense Housing for Kramer Homes
Kresge Auditorium and Chapel. *See* Massachusetts Institute of Technology Kresge
Auditorium; Massachusetts Institute of Technology Kresge Chapel
Kump, Ernest, 164

L

La Beaume, Louis, 195
Lacy, Joseph, 85, 106, 134
Lambert, Phyllis Bronfman, 181
Landrum, Charles, 216
Langhans, Karl G., 32
Larkin, Frederick A., 165
Lauritzen, Vilhelm, 206
Lebovich, William, 111
Lescaze, William, 45
Lessing, Lawrence, 231
Life magazine, 80
Lincoln Center, 173–78
Lincoln Heights Housing Center, 50
Lindgren, Armas, 12, 13
Lipschitz, Jacques, 158
Lipton, Seymour, 90
Louchheim, Aline B., 196
Lumsden, Anthony J., 75, 91, 124, 181
Lundquist, Oliver, 50, 59
Lustig, Alvin, 63
Lyndon, Maynard, 45

M

Macomber, Henry, 24
Mahler, Gustav, 11, 46
Markelius, Sven, 175
Maróti, Geza, 11, 23
Matter, Herbert, 63
McAndrew, John, 45
McBride, Henry A., 166
McCandless, Stanley, 45
McLaughlin, Donald, 50
McLaughlin, Robert, 163
McNamara, Robert, 95
McQuade, Walter, 85, 92, 99–100, 126, 219, 223, 232
Meier, Richard, 161
Meier-Graefe, Julius, 11
Mendelsohn, Erich, 36
Mercer, Max, 104–5
Mielziner, Jo, 177, 178
Mies van der Rohe, Ludwig, 28, 36, 45, 70, 72–73, 87, 105, 110, 180, 181, 182, 184, 232

Miller, J. Irwin, 8, 49, 123, 151–61, 182
Miller, Nettie Irwin Sweeney, 49
Miller, Xenia Simons, 154, 157
Miller House. *See* Irwin Miller House
Milles, Carl, 11, 25, 31, 36, 37
Milwaukee War Memorial (Milwaukee, Wisconsin), 140, 154, 191–94, 216
MIT. *See* Massachusetts Institute of Technology
Mitchell/Giurgola, 161
Moltke, Wilhelm von, 109, 154
MoMA. *See* Museum of Modern Art
Montuori, Eugenio, 117
Moore, Henry, 158
Morse and Stiles Colleges, 7, 133, 142–49
Moses, Robert, 173
Mumford, Lewis, 31
Museum of Modern Art, 45, 56, 60, 62, 138, 181, 212, 213, 227

N

Nagel, Charles, Jr., 195
National Theater. *See* College of William and Mary
Nelson, George, 45, 62
Nervi, Pier Luigi, 117
Neutra, Richard, 45, 63, 195
Newman, Richard, 175
New Yorker, 186, 194
New York Times, 83, 177, 196, 216, 227
Niemeyer, Oscar, 123
Nikander Hall, 43
Noguchi, Isamu, 196
North Christian Church (Columbus, Indiana), 158–61
Nowicki, Matthew, 107–8, 110, 111, 124, 198, 231
Noyes, Eliot, 80, 86
Noyes dormitory (Vassar College), 138, 213

O

Oberlin College, 48, 49
Office of Strategic Services (OSS), 50
Opera House (Theater Concert) at Tanglewood (Lenox, Massachusetts), 66, 67
"Organic Design in Home Furnishings" exhibition, 56, 60, 86
Orr, Douglas, 120
Osborn, Robert, 231
Owen, John, 201

P

PAC (Pre-Assembled Component) system, 59, 62
Paley, William, 182, 186
Papademetriou, Peter, 210
Paulsen, Glen, 133, 134, 165, 180
Pedestal Chairs, 58, 59, 213
Pedestal Table, 157, 213
Pei, I.M., 161
Pelli, Cesar, 75, 161, 169, 177, 180, 181, 209
Perkins, G. Holmes, 45, 196
Perkins, Wheeler & Will, 46
Perry, Shaw and Hepburn, 113
Pettula, Norman, 209, 217
Pevsner, Antoine, 73
Pittsburgh Plate Glass, 62
Plattner, Warren, 186, 213, 217
Polshek, James Stewart, 161
Powrie, David, 95, 96, 123, 169, 181
Progressive Architecture, 106, 169, 178, 196, 201, 213, 231

Q

Quito, Ecuador, palace, 52

R

Rapson, Ralph, 37, 43, 46, 63, 103, 113, 166, 168, 178, 196
Raseman, Rachel DeWolfe, 37
Rathbun, Byron, 212

Rawn, William, 161
Reidy, Eduardo Alfonso, 123
Richards, J.M., 118
Richardson, Henry Hobson, 12, 110
Richmond and Goldberg, 109
Ridgewood Quadrangle. *See* Brandeis University
Riskin, Archie, 109
Roche, Kevin, 75, 79, 85, 154, 161, 180, 181, 201, 209, 216, 217, 226
Rogers, James Gamble, 123
Román, Antonio, 181
Root, John Wellborn, 45
Roszak, Theodore, 114, 165
Roth, Harold, 185
Rudolph, Paul, 166, 216, 231
Rutan & Coolidge, 140

S

Saad, Edward, 165, 209
Saarinen, Aline (second wife), 85, 121, 203, 230, 233
Saarinen, Eero
education of, 35–53
introduction to, 6–11
legacy of, 230–33
office procedure, 75–81, 83–84
Saarinen, Eliel (father), 11–53, 59, 63, 72, 73, 151, 191, 196
Cranbrook Educational Community, 21–33, 50–53
influence on son, 11–35, 55–56, 59, 63, 72, 73
Saarinen, Eric (son), 84, 85
Saarinen, Eva-Lisa "Pipsan" (sister), 13, 23, 24, 25, 28, 37
Saarinen, Juho (grandfather), 11–12, 14
Saarinen, Lily (first wife), 53, 84–85, 195, 203
Saarinen, Susan (daughter), 12, 84, 85
Sachar, Abram, 106, 109
Saint Louis Gateway Arch (Saint Louis, Missouri), 6, 53, 56, 107, 108, 153, 157, 190, 192, 194–203, 233
Saitowitz, Stanley, 161
Sampe, Astrid, 83, 85, 154
Sasaki, Walker & Associates, 90, 93, 96
School of Architecture, Yale University, 35
Schust, Florence. *See* Knoll Bassett, Florence (Shu)
Schweiker, Paul, 120
Scott, Caudill Rowlett, 161
Scott, Keith N., 119
Scully, Vincent, 125, 210
Seaver, Esther, 45
Sert, José Luis, 164, 166
Serving Suzy Restaurant (Pittsburgh, Pennsylvania), 62
Severud, Fred, 198, 200
Severud-Elstad-Kreuger, 153
Seymour, Charles, Jr., 125
Shear, John Knox, 164
Shepley, Henry, 110, 140, 166, 175
Sibelius, Jean, 11, 46
Siegel, Gwathmey, 161
Simonds, O.C., 22
Skidmore Owings & Merrill (SOM), 85, 161, 166, 175, 181, 196, 206, 227
Sloan, Albert P., Jr., 69, 79
Smith, Eberle, 45
Smith, Hinchman & Grylls, 75
Smith, Luther Ely, 194–95
Smithson, Peter, 165
Smithsonian Art Gallery, 47, 49, 70, 103, 191
Smithsonian Institution on the Washington Mall, 46
SOM. *See* Skidmore, Owings & Merrill
Soriano, Raphael, 63
Space Time and Architecture, 194
Stanton, Frank, 182, 184, 185
Steichen, Edward, 138
Stephens, Suzanne, 227
Stephens College (Columbia, Missouri), 72, 104, 107

Stern, Robert A.M., 161, 227
Stone, Edward Durell, 45, 164, 196
Stoner, James L., 158
Stowell, Kenneth, 46
Strengell, Gustaf, 13
Stubbins, Hugh, Jr., 45, 110, 164, 196
Styling Dome, 73, 81
Swann, Lily, 37, 42
Swanson, J. Robert F., 23, 47, 49, 52, 62, 70, 72, 103, 191
Sydney Opera House competition, 181

T

Tabernacle Church of Christ, 48, 49
Taft Architects, 161
Tanglewood Opera House, 109
Tanglewood "Shed" for the Berkshire Music Festival, 43, 67, 109
Tango, Kenzo, 210
Taylor, Marilyn, 227
Temko, Allan, 87, 130, 195, 233
Terragni, Giuseppe, 36
Thomas J. Watson Research Center (Yorktown, New York), 8, 46, 85, 86, 89–90, 92, 106, 180
Thompson, Benjamin, 110
Thompson and Rose, 161
Time magazine, 85, 194
Torre, Susana, 161
"total design" concept, 13
Trans World Airlines (TWA) Terminal (New York, New York), 8, 83, 180, 204, 205–13, 214–15, 226–28
Tulip Chairs. *See* Pedestal Chairs
TWA. *See* Trans World Airlines (TWA) Terminal

U

Unfolding House, 56, 63
United States Chancellery
London, England, 83, 162, 163–68, 175
Oslo, Norway, 83, 168–71, 186
United States Gypsum Company, 56
University of Chicago (Chicago)
Law School, 6, 7, 140, 141–42, 177
Women's dorms, 140–41
University of Michigan School of Music (Ann Arbor, Michigan), 123, 125, 140, 177
University of Pennsylvania, 138, 139, 140
Utzon, Jørn, 181, 212

V

van der Meulen, John, 166, 168
Vassar College (Poughkeepsie, New York), 138–40
Venturi, Robert, 75, 161
Veterans Memorial Building, 62
Vidler, Anthony, 92
Vivian Beaumont Repertory Theater, Lincoln Center (New York, New York), 173–78
Von Trapp, Josef, 46

W

Walker, Ralph, 166
Walker, Rodney, 63
Wank, Roland, 45, 195
Warnecke, John Carl, 161
Washington International Airport. *See* Dulles International Airport
Watson, Thomas J., Jr. *See* Thomas J. Watson Research Center
Weeks, Edward, 119
Weese, Harry, 37, 161, 191, 196
Weese, John, 196
Wermuth, Charles R., 23
Wermuth, A.C., 136
Wheaton College, 43
Whitehead, Robert, 177
Williams, Edgar L., 169
Willow Run, Michigan, worker dormitories, 49

Womb Chair, 57, 61, 213
Wood, Grant, 97
Women's dorms, 138–42
World Health Organization (WHO) competition, 180, 181
Wright, Frank Lloyd, 31, 32, 212
Wright, Henry, 62
Wurster, William, 63, 113, 168, 195, 196

Y

Yale University, 35–36, 120–31, 180
Yamasaki, Minoru, 75, 164, 181, 196, 206
Yamasaki Leinweber, 164

Z

Zalewski, Joseph, 164
Zevi, Bruno, 117

Photo Credits

Numbers indicate page number; t=top, b=bottom, l=left, c=center, r=right.

Reproduced from *A + U, Architecture + Urbanism*, April 1984 Extra Edition (Tokyo: A + U Publishing, 1984), 91 r, 96 b, 120, 145 l, 194, 219
© Peter Aaron/Esto, 130 b
© Wayne Andrews/Esto, 108 tr, 140, 142
© Antioch Archives, Antioch College, 104
Reproduced from *Architectural Forum* 67, 1937, 40 t and c
Reproduced from *Architectural Forum*, October 1941, 40 b
© Archives of American Art/Smithsonian Institution, 38–39
© Avery Architectural and Fine Arts Library, Columbia University, 36
© Axel Bahnsen, 105
Courtesy Florence Knoll Bassett, 188 b, 189 br and c (photo by Gene Cook)
© Stephanie Berger, 176
Courtesy Boston Symphony Orchestra Archives, 43 t, 66 tl
Courtesy CBS Photo Archive, 172, 183, 184 r, 185, 189 tl
© Chicago Historical Society, 184 l
© Cranbrook Archives, 7, 9 t (photo by Claude De Forest), 12 l and c, 14 bl, 16 bl (photo by Richard G. Askew), 18 r (photo by Atelier Apollo), 20, 22 b, 22 c (photo by Ransier-Anderson Photography) and b, 24 (photos by Harvey Croze), 25 (photo by Peter A. Nyholm), 26 t, 26 b (photo by Max Hebrecht), 27 t (photo by Betty Truxell), 27 b (photo by Habrecht), 30 t (photo by George W. Hance), 30 b, 31–32 (photos by Askew), 33 t (photo by Janet Burke), 33 b (photo by Croze), 34, 41 tr (photo by Askew), 42 (photo by Askew), 43 b (photo by Askew), 47 (photos by Askew), 50 t and b, 51, 54 (photo by Askew), 56, 63 (photo by Richard Shirk), 66 bl, 70 c, 79 (photo by De Forest), 80, 81 l, 96 t, 110 t and c, 110 b (photo by Shirk), 111, 116 b (photo by Shirk), 127, 132, 135 b, 136 tr and tl, 159, 164 t, 170 b, 171 b, 192 l (Glen Paulsen Papers)
© Robert Damora, 44 tr and tl, cr and cl
© Eames Office, 65
Reproduced from *Eero Saarinen* by Allan Temko (New York: George Braziller, 1962), 87 r, 114 l, 118, 122–123
Reproduced from *Eero Saarinen, an Architecture of Multiplicity* by Antonio Román (New York: Princeton Architectural Press, 2003), 207
Reproduced from *Eero Saarinen on His Work* by Aline Saarinen (London and New Haven: Yale University Press, 1962), 72
© Roland Halbe, 112, 117, 119
Courtesy IBM Corporate Archives, 92, 93 b
Courtesy Knoll, 57–61, 189 tr
© Balthazar Korab Ltd., opposite title page, 9 b, 29, 41 tl, 48, 50 c, 74 br and bl, 87 l, 88–90, 91 l, 93 t, 97–98, 102, 107 t, 114 r, 115, 125, 128–129, 131, 135 t, 136 br and bl, 137, 141, 143–144, 145 r, 146–147, 150, 152, 154–155, 157–158, 160, 162, 164 c and b, 171 t, 193 t, 197, 206, 208 b, 211, 218, 220–226, 228–229
Reproduced from *Modern Architecture Since 1900* by William J.R. Curtis (London: Phaidon Press, 1996), 70b
© Museum of Finnish Architecture, 10, 12 r, 14 t and br, 16 r (photo by E. Sundström), and tl, 17 r (photo by Mäkela) and l, 18 tl and b, 19, 22 t, 41 br and bl
Reproduced from *Pencil Points*, 25 August 1944. Courtesy Bay Brown, 62
Reproduced from *Progressive Architecture*, April 1955. Courtesy Bay Brown, 107 b, 108 l and br
Courtesy Perkins & Will, 44 br and bl
© J. Paul Getty Trust. Used with permission, Julius Shulman Photography Archive, Research Library of the Getty Research Institute, 64, 67
© Ezra Stoller/Esto, front and back jacket, 68, 73, 74 t, 76–78, 81 r, 82, 94, 99, 100 t and c, 116 t, 156, 179, 192 r, 193 b, 204, 208 t, 212, 214–215
© Special Collections, Vassar College, 139 t (photo by Ben Schnall) and b (photo by John Lane Studios)
© Manuscripts & Archives, Yale University Library, 66 r, 70 t, 71, 121, 126, 130 t, 166–167, 174–175, 180, 187, 188 t, 190, 196, 198–199, 202, 217

Phaidon Press Limited
Regent's Wharf
All Saints Street
London N1 9PA

Phaidon Press Inc.
65 Bleecker Street
New York, NY 10012

www.phaidon.com

First published 2005
Reprinted 2006
Reprinted in paperback 2014
© 2005 Phaidon Press Limited

ISBN-13: 978 0 7148 6592 8

A CIP catalogue record for this book is available from
the British Library.

Designed by Jenny 8 Del Corte Hirschfeld + Mischa Leiner/
CoDe. Communication and Design
Printed in Hong Kong

Made in the USA
Las Vegas, NV
29 July 2023

75395635R00070